Empirical Legal Analysis

This innovative volume explores empirical legal issues around the world. While legal studies have traditionally been work on and of letters and with a normative bent, in recent years quantitative methods have gained traction by offering a brand new perspective for understanding law. That is, legal scholars have started to crunch numbers, not letters, to tease out the effects of law on the regulated industries, citizens, or judges in reality.

In this edited book, authors from leading institutions in the US, Europe, and Asia investigate legal issues in South Africa, Argentina, the US, Israel, Taiwan, and other countries. Using original data in a variety of statistical tools (from the most basic chi-square analysis to sophisticated two-stage least square regression models), contributors to this book look into the judicial behaviours in Taiwan and Israel, the determinants of constitutional judicial systems in 100 countries, and the effect of appellate court decisions on media competition. In addition, this book breaks new ground in informing important policy debates. Specifically, how long should we incarcerate criminals? Should the medical malpractice liability system be reformed? Do police reduce crime? Why is South Africa's democratic transition viable?

With solid data as evidence, this volume sheds new light on these issues from a road more and more frequently taken—what is known as "empirical legal studies/analysis." This book should be useful to students, practitioners, and professors of law, economics, and public policy in many countries who seek to understand their legal system from a different, and arguably more scientific, perspective.

Yun-chien Chang is an Associate Research Professor at Institutum Iurisprudentiae, Academia Sinica, Taiwan, and serves as the Deputy Director of its Empirical Legal Studies Center. He was a visiting professor at the Faculty of Law, Hebrew University of Jerusalem in Fall 2011. His academic interests focus on economic, empirical, and comparative analysis of property law and land-use law. Professor Chang's articles have appeared in *Journal of Legal Studies*, *Journal of Legal Analysis*, *Journal of Law, Economics, and Organization*, *Journal of Empirical Legal Studies*, *The University of Chicago Law Review*, and *Notre Dame Law Review*, among others. His book, *Private Property and Takings Compensation: Theoretical Framework and Empirical Analysis*, was published by Edward Elgar in 2013. Professor Chang received his JSD and LLM degree from New York University School of Law.

The Economics of Legal Relationships
Sponsored by Michigan State University College of Law

Series Editors:
Nicholas Mercuro
Michigan State University College of Law
Michael D. Kaplowitz
Michigan State University

1 **Compensation for Regulatory Takings**
Thomas J. Miceli and Kathleen Segerson

2 **Dispute Resolution**
Bridging the settlement gap
Edited by David A. Anderson

3 **The Law and Economics of Development**
Edited by Edgardo Buscaglia, William Ratliff and Robert Cooter

4 **Fundamental Interrelationships Between Government and Property**
Edited by Nicholas Mercuro and Warren J. Samuels

5 **Property Rights, Economics, and the Environment**
Edited by Michael Kaplowitz

6 **Law and Economics in Civil Law Countries**
Edited by Thierry Kirat and Bruno Deffains

7 **The End of Natural Monopoly**
Deregulation and competition in the electric power industry
Edited by Peter Z. Grossman and Daniel H. Cole

8 **Just Exchange**
A theory of contract
F. H. Buckley

9 **Network Access, Regulation and Antitrust**
Edited by Diana L. Moss

10 **Property Rights Dynamics**
A law and economics perspective
Edited by Donatella Porrini and Giovanni Ramello

11 **The Firm as an Entity**
Implications for economics, accounting and the law
Edited by Yuri Biondi, Arnaldo Canziani and Thierry Kirat

12 **The Legal–Economic Nexus**
Warren J. Samuels

13 **Economics, Law and Individual Rights**
Edited by Hugo M. Mialon and Paul H. Rubin

14 **Alternative Institutional Structures**
Evolution and impact
Edited by Sandra S. Batie and Nicholas Mercuro

15 **Patent Policy**
Effects in a national and international framework
Pia Weiss

16 **The Applied Law and Economics of Public Procurement**
Edited by Gustavo Piga and Steen Treumer

17 **Economics and Regulation in China**
Edited by Michael Faure and Guangdong Xu

18 **Law, Bubbles and Financial Regulation**
Erik F. Gerding

19 **Empirical Legal Analysis**
Assessing the performance of legal institutions
Edited by Yun-chien Chang

*The first three volumes listed above are published by and available from Elsevier

Empirical Legal Analysis

Assessing the performance of legal institutions

Edited by Yun-chien Chang

Routledge
Taylor & Francis Group
LONDON AND NEW YORK

中央研究院
法律學研究所
Institutum Iurisprudentiae
Academia Sinica

First published 2014
by Routledge
2 Park Square, Milton Park, Abingdon, Oxon OX14 4RN

and by Routledge
711 Third Avenue, New York, NY 10017

Routledge is an imprint of the Taylor & Francis Group, an informa business

British Library Cataloguing in Publication Data
A catalogue record for this book is available from the British Library

Library of Congress Cataloging in Publication Data
Empirical legal analysis: assessing the performance of legal institutions / [edited by] Yun-chien Chang.
pages cm. – (The economics of legal relationships; 19)
Includes bibliographical references and index.
1. Law–Philosophy. 2. Law–Methodology. 3. Juristic acts.
I. Chang, Yun-chien.
K235.E47 2013
340'.1–dc23
2013021009

ISBN: 978-0-415-71444-0 (hbk)
ISBN: 978-1-315-86359-7 (ebk)

Typeset in Times New Roman
by Sunrise Setting Ltd, Paignton, UK

Contents

South America

Asia

Israel

Global

Figures

Tables

Contributors

David S. Abrams is Professor of Law, Economics and Public Policy at the University of Pennsylvania Law School and the Wharton School.

Alberto G. Araiza is an Associate at Morrison & Foerster LLP.

Jennifer Arlen is Norma Z. Paige Professor of Law at the New York University School of Law.

Yun-chien Chang is Associate Research Professor and Deputy Director at the Center for Empirical Legal Studies, Institutum Iurisprudentiae, Academia Sinica.

Daniel L. Chen is Chair of Law and Economics at ETH Zurich.

John J. Donohue is C. Wendell and Edith M. Carlsmith Professor of Law at Stanford Law School.

Yoav Dotan is Edwin A. Goodman Professor of Law at the Faculty of Law, Hebrew University of Jerusalem.

Theodore Eisenberg is Henry Allen Mark Professor of Law and Adjunct Professor of Statistical Sciences at Cornell Law School.

Talia Fisher is Professor of Law and the Director of the Taubenschlag Institute of Criminal Law at the Tel Aviv University Buchmann Faculty of Law.

Jerg Gutmann is Research Associate at the Institute of Law & Economics, University of Hamburg.

Bernd Hayo is Professor at the School of Business and Economics, Philipps-University Marburg.

Daniel E. Ho is Professor of Law at Stanford Law School.

Robert P. Inman is Richard K. Mellon Professor of Finance and Economics at the Wharton School, University of Pennsylvania.

Patrick Leahy is Research Fellow at Stanford Law School.

Issi Rosen-Zvi is Professor of Law at Tel Aviv University Buchmann Faculty of Law.

Daniel L. Rubinfeld is Professor of Law at New York University Law School and Robert L. Bridges Professor of Law and Professor of Economics Emeritus at U.C. Berkeley.

Stefan Voigt is Director at the Institute of Law & Economics, University of Hamburg.

Susan Yeh is Assistant Professor of Law at the George Mason University School of Law.

Foreword

“Empirical legal studies” has been regarded as the most forward-looking and rapidly developing approach to the study of the law in recent years. Despite its importance, the unusual demand of continuous effort and interdisciplinary knowledge required to undertake this approach have discouraged many legal scholars from engaging in this field. This is precisely why the Institutum Iurisprudentiae, Academia Sinica (IIAS), has designated empirical legal studies as one of its six core research fields and is committed to fostering its development in Taiwan.

As a member of Academia Sinica, the most prestigious research institution in Taiwan, the Institutum Iurisprudentiae has vowed to undertake research in fields that are fundamental for the cultivation and consolidation of legal culture in any given society, but in which ordinary law schools lack either sufficient resources or strong incentives to study. Based upon this criterion, the IIAS selected the six core research fields. Since its inauguration on July 1, 2004, the IIAS has hosted a good number of domestic as well as international conferences on our other five research fields—constitutional structure and human rights, administrative regulations and judicial remedies, law, science and technology, jurisprudence and social change, legal development in Taiwan, China, Hong Kong, and Macau—as tangible reflections of our initial accomplishments in those areas. To add the final piece of the entire picture, the First International Conference on Empirical Studies of Judicial Systems was held on June 21 and 22, 2008, and the Second International Conference on Empirical Studies of Judicial Systems was held on June 24 and 25, 2011.

We were honored to have many distinguished empirical legal scholars from around the world attend this second conference. Two eminent professors in empirical studies, Daniel Rubinfeld (Professor of Law, New York University Law School; Robert L. Bridges Professor of Law and Professor of Economics Emeritus, U.C. Berkeley) and Jennifer Arlen (Norma Z. Paige Professor of Law, New York University School of Law) delivered keynote speeches. In addition, eleven papers covering a wide range of issues concerning judicial systems were presented by six foreign scholars and five domestic researchers. These papers effectively demonstrated methods of conducting empirical legal research. More than 200 people from a variety of different fields participated in this conference, making it the greatest event in empirical legal studies in Taiwan—and, we dare to say, in East Asia.

After revision of the conference papers, submission for consideration for publication, and a peer review process, eight articles in English were accepted and collected in this book. Another book chapter, on the judicial behaviors in Taiwan, penned by the editor Yun-chien Chang, was added to book, lest East Asia be omitted in this globally oriented volume. This chapter is based on his prior work in Chinese that has undergone peer review processes in *Academia Sinica Law Journal*, a leading law journal in Taiwan. The publication of this book, we sincerely hope, marks another milestone in the development of empirical legal studies in Taiwan and elsewhere.

The task of organizing such a splendid international event in Taiwan and publishing this book required long and strenuous effort. My highest gratitude and sincerest congratulations go to the organizer of the conference and editor of this book, Professor Dr. Yun-chien Chang. We also owe special thanks to the project assistant Yi-sin Chen; our in-house editing assistants Hsin-I Yeh and Yen Chen; Chih-Lin Lee of New Sharing Publishing; and our student editors Jung Chen, Kai-Chih Chang, Chia Ju Chang, Ying Tien Chen, Man-Ting Chien, Han-Shin Lin, Cheng-Yeh Yang, and Da-Wei Yang. Finally, Yong Ling Lam, the commissioning editor at Routledge, and her colleagues were extremely capable and helpful. It is our pleasure to collaborate with Routledge in publishing this book.

Tzu-Yi Lin
Director & Distinguished Research Professor
Institutum Iurisprudentiae, Academia Sinica
May 2013

Introduction

Yun-chien Chang

The theme of this book is empirical assessment of the performance of legal institutions. While quantitative methods have been used in social sciences for decades, they did not arrive in legal studies until around the beginning of this millennium. Nonetheless, empirical methods attained prominence in legal academia in one decade. The Society for Empirical Legal Studies (www.lawschool.cornell.edu/sels/) organizes an annual conference with presenters from all corners of the world. Many law faculties, from the US to Europe to Asia, including my home institution at Academia Sinica (www.iias.sinica.edu.tw/en), have established research centers for empirical legal studies (www.els.iias.sinica.edu.tw). Despite the outpouring of empirical scholarship, practitioners of quantitative legal analysis find that there are not many monographs that weave together empirical works. Granted, leading scholars, such as Lee Epstein, Richard Posner, William Landes, Cass Sunstein, Tom Ginsburg, Ian Ayres, have published empirics-centered books; and I have very recently published a book on takings compensation from an empirical perspective. Still, the number of published empirical books is not a good indication of the influence of the quantitative approach in law. And a majority of the existing books focus on judicial behaviors in the US. That is, only one branch, only one country.

This edited volume, with nine original book chapters by scholars around the world, has a different approach. This book aims to demonstrate to legal practitioners, policymakers, and scholars who are still not familiar with the power of the empirical approach in law, how it is useful in analyzing a variety of legal issues, not just judicial behaviors. Indeed, local legal institutions (such as the federal constitutional structure in South Africa) and global phenomena (such as the proposals to reform the medical malpractice liability system in many countries) alike can be studied with a quantitative approach. In addition, this volume also shows that empirical legal methods are not a US-centric approach. The jurisdictions covered here are diverse—from Argentina to Israel, from South Africa to Taiwan. North and South America, Africa, East Asia, and the Middle East are all represented in the book. Indeed, the chapter by Jerg Gutmann, Bernd Hayo, and Stefan Voigt studies the judicial review systems in 100 countries over 55 years. Readily available data may be hard to come by outside the US, but empirical lawyers are proud of creating the data they need. The chapter contributed by Yoav

Dotan demonstrates how patience and hard work (coding 10 percent of 20 years of files in court archives) can produce new and useful data to analyze important legal issues—in Dotan's case, judicial activism in the highest court of Israel.

This book is unified by its diversity. Apart from the jurisdictions studied, the legal institutions examined in the book also vary. Several chapters look into different levels of judicial systems. Two chapters study the highest court of Israel. Daniel Chen, Susan Yeh, and Alberto Araiza's contribution examines the influence of the courts of appeal in the US. My chapter focuses on the court of first instance in Taiwan. Gutmann, Hayo, and Voigt's chapter involves the constitutional courts of many jurisdictions. John Donohue, Dan Ho, and Patrick Leahy's and David Abrams's contributions touch on the police and other law enforcement agencies. Jennifer Arlen's work examines private institutions such as managed care organizations and hospitals. Dan Rubinfeld's mathematical model illuminates how South African politicians play the "hostage game."

Traditional jurisprudence has challenged empirical legal scholars with normative questions. The essence of empirical legal analysis is to use social scientific methodology to tackle *positive* issues. Traditional lawyers, however, care mostly about *normative* issues—what should be done. The transition from "is" to "ought to" (or, in German, "sein" to "sollen") is of course a serious and difficult issue. In this volume, several contributors demonstrate the usefulness of empirical scholarship in shaping legal policies and dealing with normative questions. David Abrams, drawing on his own empirical works and those of others, explores how long criminals should be incarcerated, concluding that the optimal length of sentences depends on the cost of crime. Jennifer Arlen, backed by recent empirical evidence, challenges the classic model that relies on the analogy of accidents to analyze malpractice liability, and criticizes the reform proposals based on contractual liability. Arlen contends for a new medical malpractice theory that justifies the oft-criticized medical liability system, which she deems vital to the effective operation of health care market. Perhaps few empirical works can match the real-world relevance and significance of Robert Inman and Dan Rubinfeld's study on the democratic transition and federal structure of South Africa. As one of a series of works on South Africa's constitutional structure, their chapter asks a very basic question: given the fact that elites/whites are the minority and non-whites are the majority, why is the democratic transition there viable? Their insights are that the fruits of improved resource allocation and higher growth have been shared by all parties. Moreover, the elite's endowed human capital, the concentration of whites in one province, and the federal constitutional structure, taken together, contribute to the stable transition.

A myth outside the empirical legal study circle is that only the fanciest quantitative methods can produce reliable and/or publishable results. This unfortunate misunderstanding may have prevented many legal scholars from conducting empirical studies. As this book emphatically shows, while there is nothing inherently wrong about state-of-the-art econometric methodologies, the soul of an empirical legal study is a legally relevant factual question that has been unduly ignored or explicitly presumed. To take examples from the book chapters in this volume:

The chapter by Ted Eisenberg, Talia Fisher, and Issi Rosen-Zvi uses descriptive statistics and Fisher's exact tests to tease out, among other things, the profound effects of the case selection mechanism in Israel's high court. One of the co-authors, Ted Eisenberg, is revered as the "grandfather" of empirical legal studies, and yet his works often employ the most basic and intuitive tools (like a two-way scatter plot) to dissect complicated legal issues.

The chapter on the determinants of constitutionally safeguarded judicial review, authored by three economists, employs chi-square tests and correlation coefficients (both of which could be learned by any lawyer in a five-day workshop, I suppose). Their "plain vanilla" tools reveal that, for example, the geographical location of a country is significantly related to its implementation of judicial review in its constitution.

My chapter uses college-level logistic regression models and several carefully crafted figures to demonstrate the major determinants in judicial decisions to remove or preserve boundary-encroaching buildings.

Those who would like a taste of sophisticated econometric models should read Chen, Yeh, and Araiza's careful study on the effect of federal appellate court rulings in the US on competition in the media market and the variety of programming. These authors use differences-in-differences analysis and two-stage least squares regression models to sort out the otherwise elusive real-world effects of judicial decisions.

Finally, Donohue, Ho, and Leahy offer a cautionary tale for empirical scholars. They reexamine a natural experiment conducted by other empiricists. The moral of their study is that, contrary to myth, fancy approaches are *not* always reliable. Empirical lawyers should be careful when designing their empirical strategy and interpreting the results. In addition, more detailed data and institutional knowledge, while both difficult to acquire, are often necessary to tell a credible story. It is often said that a picture is worth a thousand words. A thousand could be the median, mean, mode of a picture's expressiveness. As an empirical scholar, I am keenly aware of the variances in the expressiveness of figures. In my assessment, the seven figures in Donohue, Ho, and Leahy's chapter are worth at least one million words (standard errors available upon request). Anyone who wonders how to visualize their empirical results should study the layout of their graphs, which are simple, clear, powerful, and often innovative.

1 Why was the democratic transition in South Africa viable?

Robert P. Inman and Daniel L. Rubinfeld

Introduction

On October 11, 1996, the National Parliament of the new Republic of South Africa unanimously approved a new democratic constitution. The constitution emerged from over six years of negotiations between South Africa's once ruling white elite represented by the National Party (NP) led by F. W. de Klerk and the long oppressed Black and Asian majorities represented by the African National Congress (ANC) led by Nelson Mandela.

In prior work we explained how the South African Constitution and the institutions of federalism (through the creation of nine provinces with allocative powers) provided self-enforcing protections for the economic interests of the white elite that had ruled during the apartheid era.[1] In South Africa, redistributive taxation is decided by the majority-controlled central government, but provinces, including the elite-run Western Cape, are assigned fiscal responsibility for the provision of at least some redistributive services–K-12 education, basic healthcare, and welfare transfers. Federal governance then creates a "hostage" game between a majority-controlled central government and the elite-run Western Cape that provides important redistributive services to majority residents. (As we will explain in detail, the Western Cape is able to ensure that it receives suitable allocations from the center because it has the implicit threat to distribute funds away from its majority residents—the "hostages.") We observed that the fiscal allocations from 1996 to the beginning of the current regime of Jacob Zuma were sustainable as a long-run policy equilibrium.

In this chapter we turn back history and ask a more basic question. Was the deal between de Klerk and Mandela in the long-term joint interests of the white minority as well as the non-white majority and, if so, why? To answer these questions, we evaluate the long-run economic performance of South Africa's federal democracy. We show that compared to the alternative of remaining in apartheid, the lifetime economic gains have been sizeable for all South Africans. We then compare the federal outcomes to what might occur were the federal equilibrium to collapse and South Africa to become a de facto unitary democracy (a serious possibility in the era of post-Mandela politics). Even in this case, unitary governance strongly dominates apartheid for both the majority and minority residents. The long-run economic performance of federal governance is modestly better than its unitary alternative, but either form of democracy appears sufficient, ex post, to economically justify leaving apartheid for whites as well as non-whites.

Federalism and the democratic transition: an overview

When South Africa undertook its transition to democracy, it required a constitution that was approved by both the elite white minority and the poor non-white majority. The constitution could have been either a *unitary* centralized democracy with a single, majority-elected central government setting all policies, denoted as **U**, or a *federal* decentralized democracy where policy responsibilities were shared between the national government and constitutionally created provinces, denoted as **F**. In the case of a federal democracy, the constitution would specify provincial boundaries and assign policy responsibilities between central and provincial governments. If minimal taxing powers were given to the provinces, then the constitution would also specify intergovernmental transfers from the central government to the provinces. South Africa opted for a federal system, with constitutionally specified *provincial boundaries* described by the share μ of majority residents originally living within the elite-controlled Western Cape. We view the case where $\mu = 0$ as equivalent to unitary governance, where a majority-run government taxes a fully separated elite to provide redistributive services and transfers to the majority.[2]

In our model, there is an initial constitutional state in which the form of government is chosen and an annual policy stage in which specific allocative decisions are made. In the policy stage, provincial *service assignments* are specified by $\lambda > 0$, reflecting the relative value or utility that a typical majority resident places on the redistributive services q assigned by the constitution to be provided by the provinces. In the case of unitary governance, all redistributive services are provided by the central government using elite tax revenues. We assume that the center is able to monitor the provision of redistributive services when it is in their interest to do so.

The value of any particular constitution will be the discounted present value of all future utilities that follow from the choice of the parameters μ and λ, and the constitutional form, denoted as κ. For majority (non-white) residents:

$$V_M(\mu, \lambda) = \Sigma\delta^t \times \omega_t(\mu, \lambda),$$

while for elite residents:

$$V_E(\mu, \lambda) = \Sigma\delta^t \times y_t(\mu, \lambda),$$

where ω is the utility of the majority worker, y is the utility of the typical member of the white elite, δ is the discount factor bounded as $0 < \delta \leq 1$ specified as $\delta = 1/(1 + r)$, where r equals the majority's and elite's rate of time preference (which may be different). For negotiations at the constitutional stage, the set of feasible democratic constitutions will be those for which both $V_M(\mu, \lambda)$ and $V_E(\mu, \lambda)$ are greater than or equal to the autocratic alternative in which the apartheid system is maintained (designated as A). Formally,

$$V_M(F) = V_M(\mu > 0, \lambda > 0) \geq V_M(A)$$

and

$$V_E(F) = V_E(\mu > 0, \lambda > 0) \geq V_E(A),$$

under federalism ($\mu > 0$) and:

$$V_M(U) = V_M(\mu = 0, \lambda > 0) \geq V_M(A)$$

and

$$V_E(U) = V_E(\mu = 0, \lambda > 0) \geq V_E(A),$$

under unitary governance ($\mu = 0$). Majority and elite welfares under autocracy (A) are exogenous.

A federal constitution specifying provincial borders ($\mu > 0$) and assignment ($\lambda > 0$) constraints will be *sufficient* for the peaceful transition to democracy if both the majority and the elite prefer either federal or unitary democracies to autocracy, but between the democratic constitutions federalism is mutually preferred to unitary governance: $V_M(F) > V_M(U) > V_M(A)$ *and* $V_E(F) > V_E(U) > V_E(A)$. The federal constitution becomes *necessary and sufficient* for the transition when both parties prefer a federal democracy, but the elite prefers autocracy to a unitary democracy: $V_M(F) > V_M(U) > V_M(A)$ *and* $V_E(F) > V_E(A) > V_E(U)$. Other rank-ordering of federal, unitary, and autocratic constitutions are possible, but it will be these rankings where federalism facilitates the transition to democracy.[3]

Whether a peaceful democratic transition occurs depends crucially on exactly how constitutional rules determine annual policy outcomes. In our previous work, we evaluated these policy outcomes. In this chapter, we estimate $V_M(\bullet)$ and $V_E(\bullet)$ and evaluate the constitution's ability to facilitate the democratic transition.

South Africa's economy—from transition to the present

We begin this section by describing the annual policy game played by the elite minority and the poor majority—a non-cooperative game in which the majority chooses between a unitary or federal system and the elite minority chooses whether or not to capture substantial revenues in the Western Cape. This allows us to specify the social welfare-maximizing outcome—a federal system with minimal shirking by the elite. We first describe the budgetary constraints and cost considerations that limit the available alternatives. This allows us to determine the annual utility that each group will achieve in pursuing each of its strategic alternatives.

Budget choices: The majority-controlled central government chooses an aggregate redistributive tax per elite resident (τ) whose proceeds are allocated to the provincial governments as a redistributive grant (g) to provide services for majority residents. The central government also sets national standards for the constitutionally assigned, provincially provided redistributive service inputs (q), which are provided at a cost $s(q)$.

The requirements for service inputs can be determined either by a constitutional requirement to provide a "fair" or "adequate" service level to all citizens, by presidential preferences, or by majority citizen preferences. Standards for the provincially assigned redistributive services that come from a constitutional court or an agenda-setting president, we call the *exogenous* q-regime. Standards set by majority rule politics, we call the *endogenous* q^*-regime; in this case q^* is set by the central government so as to maximize the welfare of the median majority resident. Our analysis will specify the feasibility and sustainability of democratic federalism under both the exogenous non-majoritarian q-regime and the endogenous majoritarian q^*-regime.

After satisfying the required service standard, provinces are free to allocate the remainder of their redistributive grant to services of their own choosing. All fiscal policies are decided subject to an aggregate redistributive budget constraint that requires that spending on redistributive services and transfers be financed by centrally raised and administered redistributive taxation.

The taxpaying elite is free to leave the country or to adopt tax avoidance strategies as the redistributive tax rate increases. Tax avoidance is the primary means by which the elite reduces its tax payments. There is a revenue hill for redistributive taxation. Revenues initially increase as the tax rate per elite resident rises, reach maximum at τ_U, and then decline. Majority dominated unitary governments always select the maximum rate. Given the revenue potential of national redistributive taxation, it will be important to see if democratic federalism will support an equilibrium redistributive tax rate, denoted τ_F, that is less than τ_U.

Provision of redistributive services: The primary inputs in the provision of redistributive services are public employees: teachers, doctors, nurses, social workers, and public administrators. Because all public employees are paid a common civil service wage, more productive public employees will be less expensive when providing any required service input bundle. We assume that elite public employees are well trained and therefore have cost advantage over majority, less well-trained public employees. It is this "inherited" productive advantage of elite public employees working in the Western Cape that will prove crucial to the elite's ability to check redistributive taxation. The majority needs the elite and therefore has an incentive to retain the elite's participation in the provision of redistributive public services.

If the unitary regime is chosen, the well-trained elite teachers, nurses, doctors, and civil servants are expected to reduce their effort or exit the public sector for comparable employment in the private economy. This assumption is important. It is the elite's cost advantage that protects the attractiveness to the majority of the federal form of governance, and it is only within federal governance that the elite has any ability to hurt the majority if they adopt too high a redistributive tax rate.

Fiscal effort: While the central government can monitor the inputs allocated by the provinces to redistributive services, it cannot monitor the level of redistributive transfers meant for the poor. These extra or "free" redistributive revenues (r) can be "captured" by the elite in the Western Cape for services consumed by the elite residents. The share that is captured ($0 \leq \varphi \leq 1$) measures a lack of redistributive effort by the province. The majority-run central government and the majority provinces would like minimal provincial shirking with $\varphi = 0$. We assume that majority-run provinces allocate all free redistributive revenues to their poor constituents. However, in elite-controlled provinces there is shirking.

We assume there is lower value of fiscal effort φ_{L}, perhaps very small, that the Western Cape can always allocate to elite residents, but there is an upper limit φ_{H} as well. The upper limit is set by the fact that majority residents in the Western Cape can leave the province. Given the cost of exit, the upper limit is set to equalize the welfare of a typical poor resident in the Western Cape with shirking and a majority-run province without shirking. If the majority does leave, the Western Cape will receive no redistributive transfers from the central government, have no redistributive responsibilities, and have no ability to affect the national redistributive tax rate.

Choosing a level of capture above the lower bound is not costless. When services to lower-income residents are noticeably reduced, poor residents within the Western Cape impose a "protest" penalty (ρ) on each elite resident. These costs come as the consequence of spontaneous marches or riots or from formally organized strikes. The costs of such protests may discourage redistributive shirking via high capture.

Economic welfare: Economic welfare of elite residents will equal their pre-tax income, Y, minus redistributive tax payments (τ) plus any resources "captured back" through reduced fiscal effort ($\varphi \bullet r$) in the Western Cape:

$$y(\tau, \varphi_{\mathrm{L}}) = Y - \tau + \varphi_{\mathrm{L}} \bullet r_{\mathrm{e}}(\tau; q),$$

under federalism with low capture;

$$y(\tau, \varphi_{\mathrm{H}}) = Y - \tau + \varphi_{\mathrm{H}} \bullet r_{\mathrm{e}}(\tau; q) - \rho,$$

under federalism with high capture, less a protest penalty; and:

$$y(\mathrm{U}) = Y - \tau_{\mathrm{U}},$$

under unitary governance. All elite residents are assumed to live in the Western Cape. The elite leadership wishes to maximize $y(\bullet)$.

The economic welfare of a typical majority resident will be the sum of private-sector income, W, the utility value of redistributive services, denoted $\upsilon(q)$, and any "free" redistributive revenues not captured by the provincial government, $(1 - \varphi) \bullet r$. For a majority resident living in the Western Cape with capture φ ($= \varphi_L$ or φ_H):

$$\omega_e(\tau, \varphi) = W + \upsilon(q) + (1 - \varphi) \bullet r_e(\tau; q),$$

while for the majority resident living in a majority province:

$$\omega_m(\tau, \varphi) = W + \upsilon(q) + r_m(\tau; q).$$

Because the provision of public services in the Western Cape is more efficient, $r_e(\tau; q) > r_m(\tau; q)$. In equilibrium this advantage must be sufficient to just compensate poor residents of the Western Cape for elite capture. In a federal equilibrium, a fraction (μ) of the majority residents will live in the Western Cape and $(1 - \mu)$ of the residents will live in majority-run provinces. We assume the majority leadership wishes to maximize the welfare of the average majority resident defined as:

$$\omega(\tau, \varphi) = \mu \bullet \omega_e(\tau, \varphi) + (1 - \mu) \bullet \omega_m(\tau, \varphi),$$

under federalism, and:

$$\omega(U) = W + \upsilon(q) + r(\tau_U; q)$$

under unitary governance.

Our goal is to find a sustainable constitution that implements *democratic federalism*. A federal constitution with elite-run provinces is not by itself sufficient to ensure that provinces have influence. The majority-run central government can always set a maximal redistributive tax rate, τ_U, while still using provinces to provide redistributive services. Or, stronger still, the central government can choose maximal redistribution and use a central bureaucracy to provide redistributive services. Here, provinces are irrelevant to the policy outcomes, in effect de facto *unitary democracy*. Only under *democratic federalism* are elite policy preferences respected.

Credible elite punishments: Two conditions, which we define more precisely in the next section, must hold for high capture to be a credible elite punishment in those instances when the majority leadership selects maximal redistributive taxation, τ_U. The first condition is the *assignment constraint.* It requires that constitutionally assigned redistributive public services be attractive enough that the majority-controlled central government still prefers to use a provincial system, even if the elite adopts high capture in the Western Cape. If the assignment constraint did not hold, then when the Western Cape adopted high capture, the majority-controlled central government could simply move to de facto unitary governance, supply redistributive services centrally, and deny the elite any access to high capture of free redistributive transfers. The annual level of redistribution services required by the central government will be decided by either the exogenous non-majoritarian (q-regime) or the endogenous majoritarian (q^*-regime) politics.

The second condition is the *border constraint*. This constraint sets a lower and upper bound on the number of majority residents who live in the Western Cape. If too few majority residents are in the Western Cape, then the elite's threat to adopt high capture is ineffective. But if there are too many majority residents in the Western Cape, high capture ceases to be a credible elite punishment.

When the assignment and border constraints are met, high capture becomes a credible elite punishment. The federal Constitution specifies these constraints. If they are met, then the resulting fiscal policy game becomes a "hostage" game.[4] The majority controls the central government's tax rate and thus holds the elite's income "hostage." Through the assignment and border constraints, the elite controls redistributive services to a significant share of the majority population and thus holds the welfare of the average majority resident "hostage." In our earlier paper (Inman and Rubinfeld 2012), we have shown the conditions under which this hostage game results in a less than fully redistributive fiscal equilibrium. But, was the move to this equilibrium in the economic interest of the white elite? We pursue that question in the next section.

Will South Africa's new federal democracy continue to be sustainable?

There is little doubt that South Africa's transition from autocracy to democracy would not have occurred had the majority ANC and the two major minority parties, the elite NP and the tribally based Zulu Inkatha Freedom Party (IFP), not been willing to accept a federal fiscal constitution with at least one politically protected province for each minority party, and with each province promised significant, but not fully autonomous, fiscal powers.[5] It was only after this agreement was reached in mid-April of 1994 (the Interim Constitution), could democratic elections could go forward. By all measures, the elections were a success. Ninety percent of the population voted in a peaceful and honest election, with Nelson Mandela elected president. The NP emerged as the leading opposition party with 21 percent of the national vote. Finally, as expected, the NP and IFP each won political control over their own province, Western Cape and KwaZulu-Natal respectively.

While the Interim Constitution created independent provinces and the ground rules for presidential and parliamentary elections, it left the fiscal details of the new federal system largely unspecified. The Final Constitution, approved in 1996, filled the gap by specifying the assignment responsibilities of the central and provincial governments, the allowable provincial taxes, and the role for intergovernmental transfers.

The status of democratic federalism in South Africa

Three facts have been evident in South Africa since the time of transition:

1 provincial governments have been given a significant role in the provision of redistributive services, funded entirely by grants from the central government;
2 the elite Western Cape receives approximately 20 percent less in redistributive services grants; and
3 basic service grants available for capture by the elite are significant.

The question now arises: Is the structure of redistributive public finance consistent with sustainable federal governance? For democratic federalism to be a viable long-run constitution it must first satisfy the border and assignment constraints specified for the q-regime, or, for the later budgets after financial year (FY) 2006/07, the q^*-regime. Will this regime continue to be sustainable in the future? In the remainder of this section we offer a brief version of our perspective.[6]

Crucial to the successful transition was that at least one important province—the Western Cape—be politically controlled by the elite. The borders of the Western Cape were explicitly drawn to ensure elite political control over provincial politics and a sufficiently large share of majority residents as "hostages" so that elite high capture would be a credible punishment if the poor majority chose maximal taxation at the national level. We estimated the resulting share of the majority voting-age population residing in the Western Cape to be $\mu = 0.184$. For our specification of the South African political economy, this value of μ satisfies the required border constraints for both the exogenous q- and endogenous q^*-regimes; the two alternative views can be seen in Figures 1.1 and 1.2.[7]

The Mandela presidency was arguably an exogenous q-regime. During Mandela's tenure, the level of redistributive services was approved by the ANC-controlled legislature. To fund the recommended level of redistributive services required substantial redistributive grants. These requirements are very close to actual redistributive funding for the budget years of the Mandela presidency (FY 1995/96 to FY 2000/01). Given $\mu = 0.184$, the exogenous q- of 0.53 falls within the set of feasible assignments for a q-regime as shown in the shaded area ABC in Figure 1.1. The Mandela presidency could sustain democratic federalism.

Matters became less certain under the leadership of Mandela's successor, Thabo Mbeki. The Mbeki budgets' levels of redistributive services were very near the Mandela/Financial and Fiscal Commission (FFC) recommendations until FY 2005/06, at which time redistributive spending began a strong upward trend toward today's values of $q = 0.85$. This break in required redistributive services suggests a possible break in underlying political regimes as well, away from a strong president setting required redistributive services exogenously and toward a president increasingly responsive to the preferences of the majority-controlled ANC. Concurrent political events culminating in the ouster of President Mbeki in favor of the populist candidate Jacob Zuma, first as head of the ANC (December

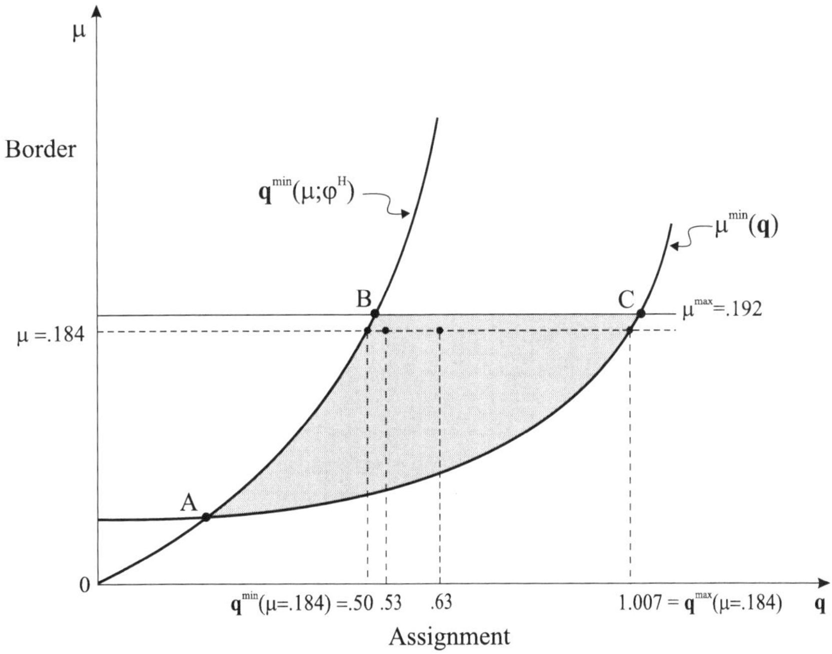

Figure 1.1 Feasible federalism for the *q*-regime

Notes:

Mandela Assignment $q = .53$

Mbeki Assignment (FY 05/06) $q = .63$

Coordinates for points:

A: $\mu = .050$; $q = .20$

B: $\mu = .192$; $q = .51$

C: $\mu = .192$; $q = 1.02$

2007) and then as President (September 2008), strongly suggest such a regime change. If so, South Africa's federal policies must meet the requirements for a q^*-regime. Our analysis for the Mbeki budget in FY 2008/09 is consistent with a democratic federalism equilibrium. We estimate that for this budget $q^*_H = 0.88$. For this budget, democratic federalism remains feasible.

The last budget that we were able to analyze is FY 2009/10, the first official budget from the new presidency of Jacob Zuma. The FY 2009/10 budget implies $q^*_H = 0.95$, just within the upper bound for redistributive services to support an equilibrium within the federal system. This is an 8 percent increase over the last Mbeki budget and a nearly 35 percent increase over what might reasonably be seen as the last presidentially decided budget of FY 2005/06. A slight increase in the majority's demands for redistributive services will push $q^*_H > 0.98$. This level of demand for redistributive services moves equilibrium fiscal policies outside the feasible set for democratic federalism in Figure 1.2 (area $A^*B^*C^*$), undermines the ability of the elite to impose a credible high capture penalty, and leaves the door open to maximum redistribution. In this case, democratic federalism is no longer a feasible check on redistributive taxation.

The sustainability of South Africa's federal contract

Even if democratic federalism is *feasible*, it might not be *sustainable*. For sustainability, the parties to the constitution must be sufficiently farsighted that they check their short-term inclinations to exploit the other party. Farsighted players will have values of their discount factor (δ) near 1; shortsighted players nearer 0. The true values of the discount factors for majority and elite residents are not known. The real current rate of interest for South African treasury bonds is about 7 percent; assuming the elite chooses to save at that rate, then $\delta_e = 0.93$. For those discount factors, democratic federalism can be sustainable for both the exogenous q- and endogenous q^*-regimes.

The question now remains: Anticipating that the Mandela budgets would be short-lived and the federal fiscal contract may be pushed to its redistributive maximum,

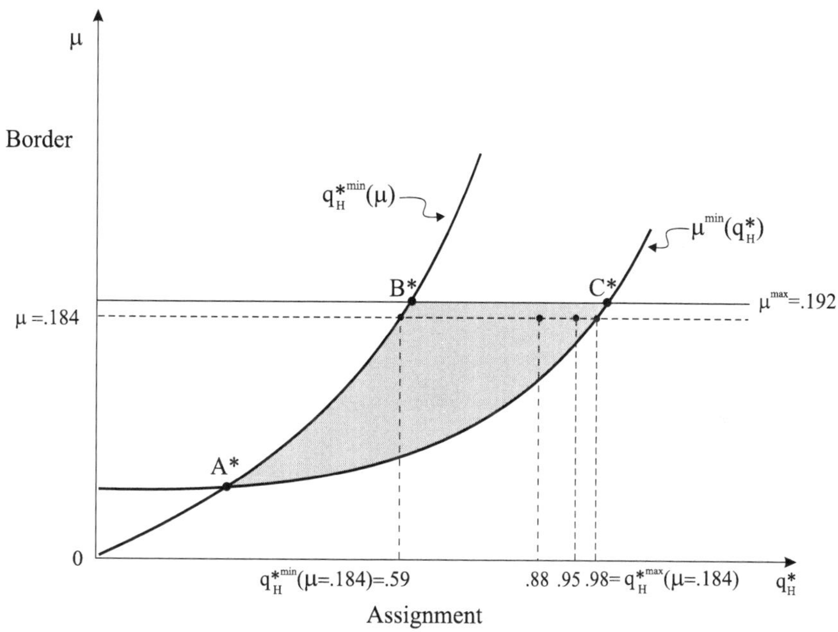

Figure 1.2 Feasible federalism for the q^*-regime

Notes:

Mbeki Assignment (FY 08/09) $q_H^* = .88$

Zuma Assignment (FY 09/10) $q_H^* = .95$

Coordinates for points:

A^*: $\mu = .055$; $q_H^* = .25$

B^*: $\mu = .192$; $q_H^* = .61$

C^*: $\mu = .192$; $q_H^* = .99$

did the elite make the right decision in agreeing to a peaceful democratic transition? The next section explains that they did.

The economic value of the democratic transition

The value of the democratic transition for South Africa's majority and elite residents equals the difference between the present value of economic welfare under democracy and that under apartheid. Under unitary governance this equals $\Delta V_M(U) = V_M(U) - V_M(A)$ for majority residents and $\Delta V_E(U) = V_E(U) - V_E(A)$ for elite residents. Under federal governance, $\Delta V_M(F) = V_M(F) - V_M(A)$ and $\Delta V_E(F) = V_E(F) - V_E(A)$ apply. A peaceful transition occurs when $\Delta V_M(U) > 0$ and $\Delta V_E(U) > 0$ or $\Delta V_M(F) > 0$ and $\Delta V_E(F) > 0$ hold. Using the results of the policy game to estimate annual utilities, we compute the ΔV's for the constitution game and evaluate the transition choice. The underlying data that were used to specify the parameters of the model are given in Table 1.1. With the continuation of apartheid, the typical majority resident is assumed to receive their market wage $W = 9{,}700$R per year. These wages were adjusted each year by our estimates, given in Table 1.2, for South Africa's rate of growth of income under the apartheid regime. Also under apartheid, the average majority resident is assumed to receive redistributive services through homeland governments of $q = 0.16$.[8] The elite resident under apartheid is assumed to receive their market wage of $Y = 86{,}000$R per year, also adjusted each year by the apartheid regime's rate of growth. Netted from elite incomes are

Table 1.1 Political economy of South Africa

Demographics and incomes
$N_0 = 9.6$ million elite $M = 25$ million majority $Y = 86{,}000$ (Real 2000) Rand/elite adult $W = 9{,}700$ (Real 2000) Rand/majority adult
Redistributive service costs
$S = 80{,}000$ (Real 2000) Rand/public employee (average uniform salary) $s_e(q) = (S/a_e) \cdot q = (80{,}000/17) \cdot q = 4{,}706 \cdot q$ (Real 2000) Rand/majority adult $s_m(q) = (S/a_m) \cdot q = (80{,}000/14) \cdot q = 5{,}714 \cdot q$ (Real 2000) Rand/majority adult $s_u(q) = (S/a_u) \cdot q = (80{,}000/7) \cdot q = 11{,}428 \cdot q$ (Real 2000) Rand/majority adult $s_U(q) = m \cdot s_m(q) + (1 - m) \cdot su(q) = 6{,}714 \cdot q$ (Real 2000) Rand/majority adult
Discount factor and redistributive preferences
$\delta = 0.97$ $\lambda \cdot \upsilon(q) = \lambda \cdot \ln(q)$, where $\lambda \geq 4123$
Special interest payments
$Z = 600$ Million (Real 2000) Rand

the annual real costs of homeland payments for local redistributional services plus expenditures for military, police, and prisons. Together, we estimate these annual tax costs of apartheid as 6,250R per elite adult resident.[9] Under democracy, the typical majority resident receives their initial market wage of 9,700R per year now adjusted by our estimates of income growth under democracy. Under democracy, the majority resident receives a significant increase in redistributive services, initially to $q = 0.53$ under Mandela and then to $q = 0.77$ in the last year of the Mbeki presidency. If South Africa remains a federal government, then we hold $q = 0.77$ as the limit of redistributive services consistent with democratic federalism. If, however, the federal contract collapses and South Africa becomes a de facto unitary democracy, then we set $q = q^*_U\ (\lambda = 4123) = 0.61$ as required for the majority choice of redistributive services.

The elite resident under democracy receives their initial wage of 86,000R per year, again adjusted annually by income growth under democracy. Expenditures for military, police, and prisons are still required under democracy. We estimate the annual tax costs per elite resident of these services at 8,145R.[10] Democracy's most significant fiscal consequence for elite welfare, however, is the large increase in redistributive taxation. If South Africa remains a federal government, the elite's annual tax costs for redistribution, net of any savings from provincial capture, are estimated as 29,242R per elite resident.[11] Under unitary democracy, the elite's annual tax costs for redistribution will be 32,000R per elite resident; there is no capture. Total annual tax burdens per elite resident will be 37,387R under a federal democracy and 40,145R under unitary democracy. Democracy will need to provide a significant growth dividend above apartheid for the elite to favor a transition to democracy.

Table 1.2 estimates this growth dividend by comparing the rates of growth of income in South Africa under apartheid (1950–93) to growth during the first fourteen years (1994–2007) of the new democracy. The apartheid years can be divided into three regimes. The early years, 1950–75, were largely peaceful and allowed South Africa's full participation in the world economy. That changed in 1976 with the Soweto massacre of innocent school children protesting the requirement they be taught in Afrikaans. The international community responded with a series of increasingly constraining trade sanctions lasting until 1993. We represent this regime by the indicator variable SANC = 1 for 1976–93 (0 otherwise). The third regime began in 1985 with the formation of the activist union federation known as The Congress of South African Trade Unions or COSATU. We represent this regime by the indicator variable COSATU = 1 for 1985–97 (0 otherwise). The post-apartheid years are represented by the indicator variable DEM = 1 for 1994–2007 (0 otherwise).

Table 1.2, column 1, provides estimates of the effects of each regime on South Africa's real rate of growth. Our estimates, based on data running through 2007, show an average rate of growth for the 25 peaceful years of apartheid of just over 2 percent per annum (SANC = COSATU = DEM = 0). For the nine years of sanctions only, the growth rate fell substantially; we estimate it to be just over 1 percent per annum. Importantly, from 1985 to 1993, when both sanctions and strong unions

Table 1.2 Economic growth under apartheid: 1950–2007

Independent variables	*GROWTH RATE* (1)	*GROWTH RATE* (2)	*OPEN* (3)	*INV* (4)
Constant	2.09 (0.36)*	–3.37 (1.74)*	60.14 (0.67)*	12.49 (0.37)*
OPEN	—	0.11 (0.03)*	—	—
INV	—	–0.099 (0.11)	—	—
SANC	–1.03 (0.65)	—	–14.16 (1.22)*	0.81 (0.68)
COSATU	–1.76 (0.74)*	—	–7.41 (1.39)*	–4.21 (0.78)*
DEM	2.33* (0.95)	—	1.81 (1.77)	2.19 (0.99)*
R^2(Adj)	0.24	0.16	0.84	0.37

Source: GROWTH RATE, OPEN, and INV are from the Penn World Tables, 6.3 and correspond to the PWT variables GRGDPCH, OPENK, and KI, respectively. OPEN is the ratio of (Exports + Imports)/GDP measured in percent and INV is ratio Gross Investment/GDP also measured as a percent.

Notes:

1 Dependent variable: annual real rate of growth of GDP per capita. Independent variables: OPEN (exports plus imports as a percentage of GDP), INV (gross investment as a share of GDP), DEM (1 for the years 1994–2007; 0 otherwise), SANC (1 for the years 1976–1993; 0 otherwise), and COSATU (1 for the years 1985–1993; 0 otherwise).

* Significant at the 5 percent level; standard errors within parentheses.

were in force, the annual growth of the apartheid economy became negative. Democracy restored a large positive rate of growth as trade sanctions were lifted (SANC = 0) and COSATU adhered to ANC economic policies (COSATU = 0).

Table 1.2, columns 2 and 3, illustrate the paths through which each regime impacted growth. Country growth depends fundamentally upon trade openness (OPEN = (Exports + Imports)/GDP)).[12] Sanctions and strong unions had their primary effect through restricted trade (column 3) during apartheid. Democracy's positive impact on growth has been through improved trade openness (column 3); at least as of 2000, there was no significant improvement in the rate of domestic investment under democracy (column 4).[13] In confirming the success of the transition to democracy, we have conservatively estimated the economy to be growing at an average annual (nominal) rate of 2.5 percent.[14]

We have used the data in Table 1.2 to compute the long-run economic benefits for majority and elite residents from the transition from apartheid to either a federal or unitary democracy. Annual utility for majority residents under apartheid equals $\omega_t(A) = W_t + \lambda \times v(q_t = 0.16)$, $\omega_t(F; \varphi^L)$ under democratic federalism, and $\omega_t(U)$ under unitary democracy. In each case we specify $\lambda \times v(q_t) = 4123 \times \ln(q_t)$ as the utility value of redistributive services to majority residents. Annual utility for elite residents equals $y_t(A) = Y_t - 6{,}250$ under apartheid, $y_t(F; \varphi^L)$ under democratic federalism, and $y_t(U)$ under unitary democracy. Utilities are discounted at a real rate of interest of 0.03 ($\delta = 0.97$) over a horizon of 70 years, beginning from 1994, the date of the transition decision.

For majority residents, both federal and unitary democracies are unambiguously preferred to apartheid, even from this strictly economic perspective. Majority residents gain from improved economic growth and receive a larger redistributive transfer. Federal governance is preferred, though only slightly. The lifetime welfare gain for a young majority resident is approximately 270,000R (US$39,000) by moving to a federal democracy and 275,000R (US$40,000) by moving to a unitary democracy.

Importantly, elite residents also benefit economically from the transition to democracy. Though redistributive taxation is significantly higher under both federal and unitary democracies, the growth dividend from abandoning apartheid is more than compensating. Elite residents prefer federal democracy because it controls maximal transfers and allows capture in the Western Cape of spending not required for redistributive services. More importantly, the gain for an elite resident of moving to a federal or unitary democracy has been very substantial. Elite residents with even a very modest real rate of time preference would have preferred democracy to apartheid.

For both the majority and elite residents of South Africa, moving from apartheid to democracy made good economic sense, primarily undoing the dysfunctional private economy created by the repressive apartheid regime. Both outside sanctions and inside economic pressures from organized labor imposed large penalties on the private economy. While the institutions of democratic federalism as implemented in South Africa add to the gains of the transition, we see with 20:20 hindsight that they may not have been necessary to the original democratic agreement. (Unitary democracy appears nearly as beneficial.) Still, from our analysis in the third and fourth sections of this chapter, federalism did provide the basis for a credible promise by the majority not to fully exploit the economic wealth of the minority. It was only with this credible promise in hand that negotiations could move forward to the election of Nelson Mandela as the President of the new South Africa.

Concluding remarks

South Africa's transition from autocracy to democracy stands as one of the significant political events of the last century. The transition was peacefully negotiated, the democratic bargain is holding, and the majority and elite residents of South Africa have, on average, shared in the significant economic dividend arising from the new democracy. Our model and its application to the South African transition also suggest three general lessons for what might be required to facilitate the move from autocracy to democracy in other settings.

First, if all parties in autocracy have the ability to veto the new democratic regime, then the democratic transition must provide additional economic resources sufficient to ensure that all parties can be made better off by the transition. (In other words, the democratic transition must be Kaldor–Hicks optimal.) There must be either a "peace dividend" from reduced outlays for military or police expenditures or a "growth dividend" from improved resource allocations and higher growth. It is the growth dividend that has proven so valuable for South Africans.

Second, all parties capable of blocking the democratic agreement must share in the benefits that the agreement creates, and each party's gains must be credibly protected against subsequent exploitation by the other agreeing parties. Providing these credible protections is the responsibility for democracy's new institutions. Giving minorities control over the military is certainly one option. Alternatively, one can use democratic institutions to create "hostage" games where each party to the new constitution can use a non-exploitable asset to penalize the other parties if they deviate from the agreed to division of the democratic dividend. In South Africa, these institutions were created by the federal constitution that utilized and protected the elite's human capital advantage in providing education, healthcare, and welfare administration. The Western Cape "controls" the provision of important public services to the majority; the majority central government "controls" elite after-tax incomes.

If the democratic transition was successful in South Africa, why did it fail in neighboring Zimbabwe? While the answers are many, one important difference is that the minority Rhodesians were never more than 5 percent of the population, and they were never concentrated in any particular province.

Third, since the benefits of democracy may be delayed, some or all of the negotiating parties may need to be sufficiently patient—that is, δ must be sufficiently high—to ensure that long-run gains from the transition exceed short-run costs. Older elites, or those with plans to retire to Switzerland, may not find the gains from a peaceful transition to democracy sufficiently attractive. In such cases, armed conflict may be the only option for the oppressed majority. Fortunately, South Africa's ruling elite took the long view.

Finally, these general lessons help to place our work in the wider debate as to the relative contributions of institutions or endowments to long-run economic growth. The South Africa experience provides a clear example of where institutional design–federalism–facilitated the democratic transition and it was the democratic transition that allowed subsequent country growth. At the same time, it was the elite's substantial endowment of human capital that gave reason and content to the institutions that allowed the democratic transition. In our analysis of South Africa, both institutions and endowments matter.

Notes

1 Robert P. Inman & Daniel L. Rubinfeld, *Federal Institutions and the Democratic Transition: Learning from South Africa*, 28 J.L. Econ. & Org. 783–817 (2012).

2 Alternatively, when $\mu = 0$, the elite could be given control over redistributive taxation, in which case the constitution codifies elite secession. Early in the negotiations the NP proposed such a constitution, but it was quickly rejected by the ANC; *see* Patty Waldmeir, Anatomy of a Miracle: The End of Apartheid and the Birth of the New South Africa (1997).

3 μ and λ can assume a variety of values. *Unitary democracy* occurs in this full information environment when there is no Pareto advantage to federalism for the majority and the elite prefers at least unitary governance to autocracy: $V_M(U) > V_M(F) > V_M(A)$ and $V_E(F) > V_E(U) > V_E(A)$. Since approval by both the elite and the majority are needed for the transition to democracy, *no transition* occurs when autocracy remains the elite's preferred option: $V_E(A) > V_E(F) > V_E(U)$.

4 *See, e.g.*, Oliver Williamson, *Credible Commitments: Using Hostages to Support Exchange*, 73 Am. Econ. Rev. 519 (1983).

5 Waldmeir, *supra* note 2, at ch. 13.

6 The results are described in detail in Robert P. Inman & Daniel L. Rubinfeld, *Understanding the Democratic Transition in South Africa*, 15 J.L. Econ. & Org. 1–23 (2012).

7 Figures 1.1 and 1.2 follow from our specification of the South African political economy. The upper bound on the majority that can be assigned to the Western Cape, denoted μ^{max} is $\mu^{max} = N(\tau_U)/M = 0.192$, where $N(\tau_U)$ is the maximum elite population paying taxes even when the majority chooses the full redistributive tax rate.

8 During the last years of apartheid, homeland budgets averaged about 1,052 Rand for each of the 25 million majority adult residents (Development Bank of South Africa, *Annual Reports*). We assume these services were provided by majority providers at a cost of 6,714 Rand per unit or q = 1052R/6714R = 0.16.

9 Average annual expenditures for military, police, and Justice Department services over the period 1977–93 totaled 33.7 billion (2000) Rand per year; South African Department of Information, Perskor, South Africa. Average annual homeland expenditures were 26.3 billion (2000) Rand per year; Development Bank of South Africa, Annual Report. Total expenditures are therefore 60 billion Rand, which when allocated over the 9.6 million elite adults, averages to 6,250 Rand per elite adult resident.

10 Total spending for military, police, and prisons has averaged 39.1 billion (2000) Rand per year since the end of apartheid. Under redistributive taxation, the elite population is estimated to be 4.8 million adults. Thus, the annual tax burden per elite resident for security spending will be 8,145 Rand (= 39,100 million Rand/4.8 million elite adults).

11 In the federal equilibrium, there will be approximately 5.1 million adult elite residents and 25 million adult majority residents. Taxes paid to the central government by each elite resident support g_F will be (25/5.1) × (6098) = 29,892. Elite capture at the rate of φ^L = 0.20 equals $0.20 \times [g_F - s_e(q)][M_e/N(\tau_F)] = 0.20[6098 - 2494] \times (4.6/5.1) = 650$ Rand/elite resident. The net tax burden will therefore be 29,892 – 650 = 29,242 Rand.

12 The effect of investment was not statistically significant; we attribute the small negative coefficient as most likely due to the substantial lag between investment and economic growth.

13 For anecdotal evidence on the importance of trade sanctions, *see* Waldmeir, *supra* note 2, at 23, 56; Geoffrey Hufbauer, Jeffrey Schott & Kimberly Elliot, Economic Sanctions Reconsidered: History and Current Policy 221–48 (2d ed. 1990).

14 Source: South African Reserve Bank, *available at* www.reservebank.co.za, Time Series KBP6244J.

References

Hufbauer, Geoffrey, Jeffrey Schott, and Kimberly Elliot. 1990. *Economic Sanctions Reconsidered: History and Current Policy*. 2d ed. Washington, DC: Institute for International Economics.

Inman, Robert P., and Daniel L. Rubinfeld. 2012. Federal Institutions and the Democratic Transition: Learning from South Africa. *The Journal of Law, Economics, and Organizations* 28: 783–817.

Inman, Robert P., and Daniel L. Rubinfeld. 2013. Understanding the Democratic Transition in South Africa. *American Law and Economics Review* 15: 1–23.
Waldmeir, Patty. 1997. *Anatomy of a Miracle: The End of Apartheid and the Birth of the New South Africa*. New York, NY: W.W. Norton & Company.
Williamson, Oliver. 1983. Credible Commitments: Using Hostages to Support Exchange. *The American Economic Review* 73: 519–540.

2 Reality check

How malpractice facts changed malpractice liability theory

Jennifer Arlen[1]

Introduction

States impose malpractice liability for medical negligence in order to induce medical providers to invest adequately in patient safety. The central challenge is how to structure liability to induce physicians and medical institutions to invest optimally in patient safety.

Scholars specializing in the economic analysis of law have long been at the forefront of efforts to analyze and reform medical malpractice liability. Initial efforts relied on the classic model of accidents. This produced a narrow and skeptical view of the role of malpractice liability and lent support to numerous efforts to curtail liability. Empirical legal studies has transformed the economic analysis of medical malpractice liability by altering our understanding of the central problems facing health care markets, and, in turn, has spurred theorists to develop a new model of malpractice liability. This new model, combined with the results of empirical analysis, has altered our understanding of the purposes of malpractice liability and reveals that many politically popular efforts to reform malpractice liability harm the people who are their purported intended beneficiaries, namely the patients and medical providers.

The traditional economic analysis of malpractice liability relies on the classic model of accidents. In this model, one party (here physicians) undertakes an activity that may injure another party (here patients). The injurer can reduce the risk of injury by investing in "care" (here treatment). Society wants potential injurers to make all cost-effective investments in care, and thus wants the injurer to select the level of care that maximizes social welfare. Liability is needed because injurers select the level of care that maximizes their own welfare. They thus take too little care when they bear the cost of care, but do not bear the cost of medical negligence. When properly designed, liability can remedy this problem by forcing injurers to pay for any injuries resulting from their failure to take optimal care.[2]

Scholars embracing this framework are, naturally, skeptical of malpractice liability. In this framework, liability is needed when physicians bear the cost of treatment, but is not needed when providers care about patients and do not bear the costs of "care"—as when patients are insured and medical providers can actually profit by providing higher quality treatment (care). Thus, in the case of patients with fee-for-service insurance, it would seem that the state need not intervene except in the case of incompetent ("bad apple") physicians. Moreover, when malpractice is caused entirely by incompetent physicians, liability may not be needed if the state can adequately address the incompetent physician problem through licensing and regulation.[3]

Beyond this, the classic model promotes a skeptical view of malpractice liability because it implies that a well-functioning system will not generate successful malpractice cases in equilibrium. In the classic model, competent physicians should never be found negligent if the tort system functions properly because they are assumed to know when they are providing optimal care and providers facing optimal malpractice liability will never select negligent care if courts correctly apply the standard of care and impose the correct level of damages.[4] Yet, competent physicians are regularly held liable for medical malpractice. This discrepancy would appear to suggest that malpractice is not functioning effectively and that most malpractice claims may be frivolous, brought by plaintiffs hoping to obtain large awards from pro-plaintiff, error-prone juries.[5]

Scholars adopting the traditional framework have naturally tended to embrace a skeptical view of the optimal scope of malpractice liability. In response, they have pushed for reforms designed to restrict the scope of malpractice liability, focusing on proposals designed to indirectly limit malpractice liability by allowing medical providers to offer patients contracts that restrict or eliminate patients' right to sue providers for medical negligence.[6] Similarly, state legislatures have embraced the idea that frivolous litigation and pro-plaintiff juries are the leading problems plaguing malpractice liability.[7] In response, state after state has adopted reforms to curtail damages or to otherwise restrict suits.[8]

Empirical analysis has turned most of this conventional wisdom on its head. In so doing, it has demonstrated that many reforms favored by politicians and traditional scholars make patients and providers worse off.

Empirical analysis of medical error shows that the core premises underlying the traditional approach to malpractice liability are incorrect. Specifically, empirical analysis reveals that the traditional model of accidents does not capture the root causes of most medical error. The traditional model assumes that negligence results when an individual injurer knowingly decides to take suboptimal care.[9] As applied to medicine, this framework assumes that medical negligence results from a decision by a medical provider to knowingly select a suboptimal treatment. Such a doctor is reasonably viewed as a "bad apple." By contrast, empirical analysis reveals that patients regularly are injured by medical errors and that most medical errors are caused by otherwise competent medical providers. Moreover, medical errors generally are accidental, in the sense that the provider did not knowingly select an erroneous treatment.[10] They occur because the physician accidentally misdiagnosed the patient, selected the wrong treatment, or provided the treatment incorrectly, often believing that he was providing appropriate care.[11] These accidental errors nevertheless warrant intervention because they are not inevitable. Instead they often result from doctors' (and medical institutions') failure to invest adequately in "expertise" (or "preventative interventions")—defined as investments by the physician or medical institution in the provider's capacity to correctly diagnose the patient, identify the correct treatment, and provide treatment without accidental preventable error.[12] These preventative interventions include investment by physicians and medical care institutions (hospitals) in medical expertise, procedures, supervision, and healthcare technology. This suggests that in order to optimally protect patients, malpractice liability must be designed to induce optimal investment by providers and medical institutions in expertise and various preventative interventions (including supervision, error detection/prevention systems—such as check lists—and healthcare technology).[13] Accordingly, in order to determine the proper scope of liability, we need a model of malpractice liability that recognizes that medical providers can err accidentally and can reduce the probability of error through investments in expertise and other forms of prevention.

Responding to empirical analysis, scholars have developed a model of medical negligence that explicitly recognizes that medical providers can affect patient welfare through decisions about how much to invest in expertise (and other forms of prevention), as well as through decisions about whether to try to provide the optimal treatment.[14] The latter decision determines whether the provider knowingly provides suboptimal care. The former investment determines the likelihood that the provider will err accidentally.[15]

Analysis of medical care markets employing this model reveals that optimal malpractice liability serves multiple goals: operating to regulate both investments in expertise and treatment choice. When patients are insured and medical providers are compassionate—in that they want to provide the right treatment—then providers will not deliberately provide suboptimal care, just as in the classic model. Nevertheless, unlike in the classic model, malpractice liability is still needed. Malpractice liability is needed—even if all physicians would happily provide the optimal treatment if they are able to correctly diagnose the patient and identify the optimal treatment—to ensure that physicians and institutions invest adequately in the expertise needed to enable them to determine and provide optimal treatment. Absent liability, physicians will not invest as much in expertise as patients want them to because physicians bear the full cost of expertise but do not obtain the full benefit.[16] This result holds even when doctors are other-regarding and care about patients' welfare—assuming, as is reasonable, that patients injured by medical error suffer more than their physicians (and thus have a higher willingness to pay to avoid error).[17] This analysis also shows that medical care is more sensitive to the magnitude of expected damage awards than is implied by the classic model of torts.[18]

Empirical analysis not only has transformed malpractice liability scholarship by inducing a revision in the model of negligence, it also has dramatically altered the debate about optimal malpractice liability reform. Scholars embracing the traditional analysis tend to assume that there is too much malpractice liability, and thus promote reforms designed to reduce the scope and magnitude of liability. Empirical analysis undermines the core premises of this reform effort in two ways. First, the empirically grounded model reveals that regular malpractice litigation does not signal that the malpractice liability system is broken.[19] Even in a well-functioning tort system, competent medical providers will provide negligent care accidentally because doctors cannot eliminate the risk of error by investing optimally in expertise.[20] Thus, evidence that competent physicians are found liable does not mean that malpractice liability is functioning suboptimally.[21] This undermines a core theoretical motivation for efforts to restrict malpractice liability.[22]

Second, empirical analysis has provided evidence that directly undermines a central premise of many liability-constraining reform proposals: that many settled malpractice cases are frivolous, with liability falling randomly on negligent and non-negligent providers. Empirical analysis reveals, to the contrary, that patients face a substantial risk of being injured by genuine medical error. Moreover, the vast majority of malpractice settlements involve patients whose injuries were caused by actual, genuine provider error.[23] While not all cases are resolved correctly, the evidence does not support the view that most errors in imposing liability favor patients. Instead, more than half of the erroneously decided cases resulted in negligent providers escaping liability; evidence suggests jury errors are particularly likely to favor providers.[24] These results undermine the premise that there is too much malpractice liability. Indeed, empirical analysis reveals that the core problems plaguing the malpractice system include under-claiming by patients injured by medical negligence and restricted liability for the parties with the most indirect and direct ability to affect medical error—hospitals and managed care organizations (MCOs).[25]

Beyond this, the empirically grounded analysis of malpractice liability reveals that states should reject proposals to allow medical providers to contract over liability with their patients.[26] The empirically grounded model reveals that even informed patients who value liability would be worse off under contractual liability than under well-designed malpractice liability because, among other reasons, malpractice liability provides a collective good. This undermines the claim that informed contracting would produce optimal decisions about when to impose liability because individual contracting over collective goods is plagued by coordination and free-rider problems, and thus generally does not result in the efficient provision of collective goods.[27]

Finally, empirical analysis, in concert with the empirically grounded model of medical negligence, reveals that rather than curtailing liability, malpractice liability reforms should be designed to expand liability to ensure that medical institutions bear liability for medical errors resulting from either their own decisions or those of the medical providers with whom they contract. Empirical analysis reveals that medical institutions disproportionately affect the probability of medical error through their control over the systems, healthcare technology, and personnel.[28] Some institutions, such as MCOs, even exert direct authority over treatment.[29] Empirical analysis also reveals that medical institutions face too little incentive to implement optimal systems, technology, and other practices.[30] Thus, states genuinely interested in patient welfare should focus on how best to use liability to provide optimal incentives to hospitals and MCOs, instead of embracing empirically questionable efforts to reduce malpractice liability.

This chapter proceeds as follows. The next section, Traditional view of medical malpractice and it limitations, describes the traditional view that there is too much malpractice liability. It begins by presenting the classic model of accidents and its implications. The following section, Challenge posed by empirical analysis for the traditional view, presents the empirical challenge to the classic model of malpractice and its implications, as well as a model of malpractice liability that incorporates insights from empirical analysis. The section after that, Reassessing classic reform proposals, utilizes a combination of empirical analysis and the empirically grounded model of malpractice liability to reexamine traditional malpractice reform proposals intended to directly or indirectly curtail malpractice liability. The section uses insights from the empirically grounded model to reveal why one popular reform, contractual liability, would reduce many patients' welfare. The section thereafter, entitled The empirically grounded case for organizational liability, combines empirical evidence and theoretical analysis to show that the best way to reform malpractice liability is not to restrict it; rather, states should expand the scope of liability to include the medical institutions that directly influence the quality of care that patients receive.

Traditional view of medical malpractice and its limitations

This section describes the traditional economic approach to malpractice liability and explains how this analysis, combined with a set of presumptions regarding the operation of the tort system, provides support for reforms designed to restrict malpractice liability.

Prior to empirical analysis of medical error, many people assumed that medical error was not a serious problem and was caused primarily by a small percentage of incompetent physicians—proverbial "bad apples."[31] This "bad apple" view of medical error implies that most doctors can be relied upon to provide error-free medical care when treatment costs are borne by others. This would appear to suggest that malpractice liability is not needed to provide competent physicians adequate incentives to invest in patient safety.

This conclusion is consistent with the implications of the classic economic model of accidents as applied to situations where most patients purchase fee-for-service health insurance, as was the case during the height of the tort reform movement of the late 1980s. Classic economic analysis models negligent accidents as involving encounters between an "injurer" and a "victim." The injurer is assumed to undertake an activity that creates a risk of harm to the victim; the probability of harm depends on the injurer's level of care. Social welfare is maximized when the injurer invests in the level of care that minimizes the sum of care plus expected accident costs. Injurers will not invest in optimal care if they bear the costs of care but do not bear the costs of accidents. Tort liability can redress this problem by ensuring that injurers bear the expected cost of any failure to invest in optimal care.[32] Yet tort liability is not needed if the injurer either does not bear the cost of care or otherwise bears expected accident costs. In standard analysis that views "treatment" as care, tort liability may not be needed to regulate medical care provided by competent physicians when patients are primarily insured by fee-for-service health insurers. First, reputation and physician compassion arguably ensure that physicians bear some cost of harms caused by medical error. Moreover, physicians treating insured patients often have no reason to avoid expenditures on costly treatments because the cost of care is borne by the fee-for-service health insurer, not the physician.[33]

This analysis predicts that, even when there is no liability and patients are not informed, physicians treating insured patients will not underinvest in care.[34] Thus, this analysis suggests that, even absent tort liability, patients face little risk of receiving suboptimal treatment if treated by competent physicians. This economic framework provided support for the view that the numerous malpractice suits filed were the result of excessive claiming—a conclusion that supported reform proposals designed to limit malpractice liability.[35]

Classic model of accidents and its implications

The traditional analysis of malpractice liability relies on the classic model of accidents. In the classic model of accidents one party (here physicians) undertakes activities that may injure another party (here patients). The potential injurer can reduce the risk of injury by investing in "care." In this framework, the goal is to induce injurers to take the level of care (treatment choice) that maximizes social welfare. Thus, care should minimize the joint cost of care and expected accident costs. Injurers will take optimal care if they keep investing in care up to the point where the cost of the additional care just equals the social benefit of the resulting reduction in expected accident costs.[36]

Tort liability may be needed to induce optimal care because potential injurers select the level of care that maximizes their own expected welfare, not that of society. In the classic model, this implies that absent either liability or market forces that internalize accident costs, each injurer selects minimal care because he bears the cost of care and does not bear expected accident costs. The state can use negligence liability to induce optimal care. In a well-functioning tort system, injurers who are held liable for accidents resulting from a failure to take optimal care minimize their expected costs by taking optimal care. Accordingly, informed injurers subject to optimal negligence liability should always take due care, so long as due care equals optimal care, liability is accurately imposed,[37] and expected damages are optimal.[38]

The classic model expresses these ideas more formally using the following framework, which we apply here to medical care. In the classic model, each doctor provides a valuable service (medical care) to patients. Treatment confers a benefit, b, if it is the correct treatment and is done properly. Yet treatment also may injure the patient, causing a harm of H. The doctor can reduce the probability of harming the patient, given by $p(x)$, by investing in care, x, at a cost of $t(x)$, which we can think of as the cost of providing treatment. In this model, a high level of care results in a small risk of medical error; low-cost care produces a higher risk of harm.[39]

Social welfare is maximized when the doctor invests in the level of care that minimizes the total social costs of care and expected accidents: $t(x) + p(x)H$.[40] This level of care is also the level that maximizes the welfare of patients who expect to bear the full cost of both medical error and care, either directly or through insurance premiums. The goal of tort law is to ensure that physicians want to invest in the optimal level of care. In the classic framework, malpractice liability is needed when physicians do not have optimal incentives to invest in care because they bear the full cost of care but do not obtain the full benefit of providing higher quality treatment.

Physicians do not bear treatment costs

In this model, malpractice liability is not needed to induce doctors to avoid low-cost suboptimal treatments when they do not bear the cost of care, as arguably is the case when patients are insured by a fee-for-service health insurer that pays for all treatment costs. Thus, if we stay within the classic model—in which negligence involves a knowing decision to select suboptimal care—it would seem that negligence liability is not needed since physicians have no reason to avoid high-quality treatments even if they are costly. The incentive to avoid suboptimal treatment is enhanced to the extent that individual providers feel compassion for their patients, and thus suffer some cost when they injure a patient.[41] In this situation, physicians have incentives to avoid providing inexpensive negligent care.[42]

Thus, the classic model of accidents predicts that doctors treating patients covered by fee-for-service insurance generally will not provide insufficient, negligent treatment—even absent liability.[43]

Evidence of the high cost of care in the US would appear to support the idea that most patients do not face a serious risk of receiving insufficient treatment because expenditures on care, $t(x)$, are high. Thus, this framework suggests that the problem of medical negligence (in the sense of insufficient care) should be limited to doctors who treat uninsured patients—and even then should not be extreme unless the doctor is a "bad apple" who does not care about patient welfare (or has a deficiency that renders him unable to take due care). States could control this problem through more careful regulation of the quality of care provided to the uninsured and by identifying "bad apples" and forbidding them to practice medicine.

Physicians bear the costs of higher quality treatment

Physicians do not select optimal treatment if they bear the costs of providing higher quality treatment instead of low-quality treatment, as is particularly likely to be the case with certain forms of health insurance. In this case, the classic model predicts that, absent liability, physicians will select suboptimal treatment because they bear the cost of care but do not obtain the full benefit of the increase in expected patient welfare resulting from higher quality treatment.

It might seem that market forces could ensure that physicians obtain the full benefit of providing due care instead of negligent care. Yet this is not the case. Reputational penalties do not ensure that physicians internalize the cost of negligence because patients cannot observe the providers' investments in care at the moment they contract for care. Nor do patients have good information on the expected outcomes of their individual provider. Thus, each patient's willingness to pay to receive care from a particular provider does not depend on a provider's actual or expected investment in care.[44] Consequently, providers who invest optimally in care cannot increase their prices accordingly. In turn, those who underinvest do not bear the full consequences of their neglect. Accordingly, the classic model predicts that if patients cannot observe provider quality, then medical providers will not take care absent tort liability. Moreover, they will deliver substandard care knowingly, not accidentally.[45]

In this framework, negligence liability can eliminate the risk of medical error if courts set the standard of care at the optimal level and hold physicians liable for the full cost of any neglect.[46] The fact that optimal care minimizes the joint cost of care and expected accident costs implies that each physician subject to malpractice liability minimizes his expected costs when he provides optimal care and avoids the risk of liability.[47] In this model, therefore, optimal liability eliminates doctors' incentives to select a low-cost, suboptimal treatment. Indeed, in this model, when "care" is defined as treatment choice, a well-designed negligence rule eliminates the risk of medical negligence.[48]

Several characteristics of the classic model and the equilibrium it produces are worth noting. First, under the classic model, injurers (doctors) are never negligent by accident: all negligence involves doctors who intentionally provide suboptimal care. Thus, doctors have little to fear from tort liability—even if damages are high—so long as the tort system is accurate: doctors can simply avoid all risk of negligence liability, and all risk of damages, by deciding to provide optimal care.[49] Moreover, if the standard of care is set too high, doctors can avoid liability by conforming to the standard of (customary) care, passing the costs on to patients or insurers. Thus, as long as the standard of care is predictable, doctors can generally avoid liability for medical negligence.[50]

Second, under the classic model, there should be no medical negligence in equilibrium if courts impose optimal negligence liability, with due care set equal to optimal care and optimal damages. As previously noted, the classic model assumes that providers know the costs and benefits of care.[51] Accordingly, malpractice liability should deter all medical negligence if courts set and apply the standard of care correctly and impose the correct level of damages.[52] Thus, physicians will only provide negligent care if either they are unable to live up to the standard of the care (i.e. incompetent), or if they face too little expected liability for negligence.[53] In turn, this framework suggests that competent physicians should not face legitimate suits for medical malpractice if courts set the standard of care correctly (or at least not too high) and physicians bear sufficient expected liability for medical error.

Conclusion

Accordingly, the classic model of accidents appears to imply that malpractice liability should either serve a relatively limited role or should not be experienced in practice. The traditional model implies that malpractice liability is not needed if insurers, not physicians, bear treatment costs. This is especially the case if physicians care about their patients. Beyond this, even when liability is needed to induce care, if the standard of care is clear and based on custom, and damages are optimal, the model predicts that malpractice liability should generate little litigation in practice. Informed physicians should avoid any risk of liability by selecting the optimal treatment. This suggests that we should not see any genuine instances of medical negligence under an effective regime unless a physician is incompetent and unable to live up to the standard of the profession. This prediction supports the view that medical error is caused by "bad apple" physicians and that competent physicians should not be subject to malpractice litigation if the system is well designed.

Implications of the classic model for malpractice reform

The classic model of accidents has implications for malpractice liability reform, especially when viewed in concert with the fact that doctors are regularly found liable for malpractice. The conclusion of the model that good doctors have no reason to select suboptimal treatment when patients are insured leads naturally to the conclusion that if we see a large number of malpractice lawsuits claiming suboptimal treatment by otherwise competent physicians, it is likely that these suits are not the result of genuine medical negligence. It is more likely that these are frivolous lawsuits, filed by patients hoping to win the malpractice lottery and obtain an enormous damage award from a pro-plaintiff jury. These frivolous suits would not occur were malpractice imposed optimally. But in fact malpractice liability is not imposed optimally: indeed, it is often imposed on negligent and non-negligent providers.[54] As a result, patients (and their lawyers) often can expect a positive payoff if they file frivolous suits. These frivolous suits are a problem for physicians and patients, as frivolous suits impose a burden on all physicians, who pass the costs on to patients in the form of higher healthcare costs. In this view, malpractice liability does not provide its promised deterrence benefits, but instead imposes a net cost on providers and many patients.[55]

Scholars and policymakers operating within this framework have embraced proposals to reform malpractice liability by directly or indirectly reducing the scope or magnitude of liability. Politicians tend to favor reforms that would directly reduce patients' incentives to sue by reducing expected damages.[56] These reforms include caps on noneconomic damages and wrongful death damages, collateral sources rule reform (which eliminates patients' ability to recover compensatory damages for expenses—such as healthcare costs—covered by their own insurers), and joint and several liability reform.

By contrast, leading economic analyses of law scholars tend to favor a different approach to reducing the threat of liability: changing the law to permit medical providers to contract with patients over the scope of malpractice liability. This reform would permit medical providers or health insurers to require patients to sign exculpatory clauses waiving their right to sue for medical negligence as a condition for seeing certain providers.[57] According to proponents, as long as patients are informed about the expected costs and benefits of liability, and contracting is voluntary, any patient who would have benefited from tort liability imposed by fiat will insist on imposing liability if given the right to contract over it. The only patients who will waive liability are those who are better off without it. Accordingly, proponents assert that contractual liability can only benefit patients by enabling those patients who do not benefit from liability to contract out of it, without reducing the expected benefit of liability to those who value state-imposed malpractice liability. Proponents argue that this reform will enhance the welfare of patients who do not obtain a net benefit from malpractice liability without hurting patients who do benefit from malpractice liability.[58] Thus, proponents of this reform contend that contractual liability should be attractive to supporters and opponents of malpractice liability alike.

Challenge posed by empirical analysis for the traditional view

Empirical scholarship has provided a wealth of evidence on the causes of medical error and the operation of the medical malpractice liability system. As this section shows, this scholarship provides evidence about the causes and frequency of medical error that are inconsistent with the structure of, and equilibrium produced by, the classic economic model of accidents. Empirical scholarship reveals that patients face a significant risk of being injured by medical error; the problem is not limited to a few "bad apple" doctors. Moreover, medical error generally does not result from the type of negligence captured by the classic model of accidents: a knowing decision to provide suboptimal care (to select less than due care, $x < x^*$). Instead, most medical error results from insufficient investment in expertise and other preventative measures by physicians and medical institutions—which is defined as a physician's investment in the information needed to properly diagnose the patient and select treatment and the systems needed to deliver error-free care and medical institutions investment in supervision, healthcare technology, and administrative systems.

Recognition of the critical role played by expertise and preventative measures reveals that we cannot rely on the classic economic model of accidents to evaluate optimal medical malpractice liability because the technology and timing of care—and causes of error—are materially different from the factors explored by the traditional framework. This section discusses an alternative model of malpractice, highlighting the role of expertise that was developed in response to empirical analysis on the causes of medical error. This model shows that malpractice liability is vital to the effective functioning of the medical care system, regulating the quality of care provided by competent and incompetent (or ill-meaning) physicians alike.[59]

As shown in the next section, the results of this empirically grounded model present a challenge to the view that the best way to reform malpractice liability is to reduce it. Specifically, analysis of this model reveals reasons why we should reject the overall goal of reforms designed to dramatically curtail malpractice liability, as well as the specific exhortation that legislatures and courts substitute liability created or limited by contract for standard malpractice liability.

Evidence on causes of medical error

Empirical analyses reveal that, contrary to the classic model, medical error is not a problem limited to "bad apple" physicians. Instead, patients seeking medical treatment face a serious risk that they will be severely injured or killed, instead of saved, by the medical treatment they receive.[60] Studies suggest that 4 to 18 percent of patients seeking care in hospitals are injured by the medical care they receive, with many patients suffering serious injury.[61] In addition, patients seeking care outside of hospitals are also regularly injured by medical error in that they do not receive the proper (medically recommended) treatment for their conditions. Studies also show that approximately 45 percent of patients with chronic diseases do not receive the care that is recommended for their conditions.[62] Twenty percent of patients receive care that is contraindicated by the medical literature.[63]

These medical errors cause enormous suffering to both patients and their loved ones ("nonpecuniary losses"). They also impose substantial monetary losses on the system, in the form of lost man-hours and increased medical costs associated with the treatments needed to remedy avoidable medical error. Studies place the direct monetary cost of preventable medical error at approximately $17–29 billion per year.[64] Adverse events in hospitals alone impose costs of $2,013 per patient admission (in 2005 dollars); injuries to hospital patients resulting from medical negligence increase costs by about $1,246 per patient admission.[65] Moreover, recent evidence confirms that medical error remains a serious problem. A recent study of hospitalized Medicare patients found that one in seven experienced one or more adverse events.[66]

Beyond this, the causes and nature of medical error are not consistent with the core structure of the classic economic model of accidents. The classic economic model of accidents assumes that injurers (here doctors) know the costs and benefits of care and select the level of care, given by x, that minimizes $c(x) + p(x)D$, where $c(x)$ is the cost of care, $p(x)$ is the probability of an accident (given care), and D, the level of damages (which is set equal to harm when x is less than due care and equals zero when care at least equals due care).[67] In this framework, doctors who provide negligent treatment decide to do so by underinvesting in care; they are not accidentally negligent. This model does not produce an equilibrium with regular negligence when expenditures on care are too high. Yet, in contrast with the traditional model of accidents, empirical evidence shows that negligence is not limited to incompetent physicians[68] and, moreover, usually does not result from an informed decision to select suboptimal treatment. Instead, most medical errors are caused by technically competent providers who err accidentally, often as a result of failures of systems and healthcare technology under the control of medical institutions.[69]

The fact that error is accidental is important to efforts to regulate medical care quality because evidence reveals that most of this accidental error is also preventable. Specifically, a recent study of settled medical malpractice claims found that almost half of all the errors were caused, at least in part, by inadequate physician knowledge or technical competence.[70] Providers could have prevented many of these errors by investing more in expertise—knowledge, training, supervision, or the use of adequate healthcare technology or administrative systems.[71] Thus, we see that medical error is not primarily the result of a knowing decision to deliver suboptimal care, but rather generally results from providers' failure to invest adequately in the capacity to provide good-quality care (i.e. their expertise).[72]

Empirical analysis thus reveals that we must revise our economic model of medical malpractice liability in order to design liability rules that optimally deter accidental, but preventable, negligence by individual providers by inducing them to invest in their *capacity* to select and provide optimal care. To do so, it is important to employ a model that incorporates the fact that medical error can be, and regularly is, accidental, in that it is caused by competent, well-meaning physicians who want to provide good-quality care and do not know they are erring. The model also should incorporate the fact that providers can reduce the risk of error both through deliberate decisions made when they are informed and through ex ante and ex post investment in their capacity to provide care: specifically, in expertise, technology, and systems (hereinafter "expertise") needed to give providers sufficient information and quality control to correctly diagnose the patient, select the right treatment, and deliver error-free care.[73]

Revising the economic model of malpractice liability

Scholars of theoretical law and economics responded to the challenge posed by empirical analysis by developing a new model of malpractice liability. This model incorporates the central insights of empirical analysis, that doctors often err accidentally as a result of inadequate knowledge of the patients' condition or the proper treatment, and that this error is preventable through investments in expertise that are largely unobservable, and can occur ex ante or ex post. The model also reflects the empirical reality that most patients have their healthcare costs covered by insurance, thus enabling doctors to increase their level of care—in the sense of treatment—without much (if any) private cost. Finally, the model incorporates the observation that many, if not most, doctors derive positive benefits from good patient outcomes and are unhappy when they kill or injure a patient. This part lays out a simple version of this model and presents its core results. It then shows that malpractice liability serves an important function even when doctors want to (and can costlessly) provide optimal treatment. Indeed, this model helps us understand why malpractice liability is needed even when medical error is accidental: liability for accidental error helps induce investments in expertise (including healthcare technology, systems, and supervision) that reduces the risk of error. This model also reveals that, although a well-functioning malpractice system could dramatically reduce physician negligence, some amount of physician negligence would still occur even if courts do not err. Thus, regular malpractice settlements are not enough, in and of themselves, to suggest that either the malpractice system is broken or that doctors are venal or incompetent.

Economic model of accidental medical error

This part describes an empirically grounded model of malpractice liability based on Arlen and MacLeod.[74] In this model, an insured patient seeks treatment from a medical provider, and relies on the provider for proper diagnosis, treatment selection, and treatment provision. The patient does not have sufficient expertise to oversee the care provided and does not know the quality of care that the provider has selected in the past.

The physician can provide any one of a number of treatments that differ in their net expected benefit for the patient. The expected benefit of a treatment to the patient is given by, b_t, where t is an index of treatment options and b is the ex ante expected benefit of treatment (taking into account the risks of treatment). For purposes of this chapter, it is assumed that b_t is the net benefit of treatment net of treatment costs, which are assumed to be borne by the patient (ex ante or ex post through insurance premiums).[75]

It is assumed that the physician genuinely cares about patients' welfare, benefiting directly from good patient outcomes and feeling loss when patients fare badly. We express physician compassion by assuming that the expected benefit to a physician of treatment is αb_t, where $\alpha < 1$. Thus, it is assumed that the benefit to the physician of treatment is proportionate to the net expected benefit of treatment to the patient. Physicians thus prefer good outcomes to bad outcomes, even when liability is not imposed, but do not bear the full social cost of bad outcomes. Accordingly, for purposes of this chapter, the joint welfare of patients and providers is given by $(1 + \alpha)b_t$. Joint welfare thus is maximized when the provider selects the treatment that maximizes the expected net benefit of treatment to patients.[76] We also restrict our analysis to the situation where the provider can either select a treatment that cures the patient, yielding expected benefit, b^*, or can provide erroneous care that seriously injures the patient, producing an expected outcome of b_0, where $b_0 < b^*$. Patients would be willing to pay $b^* - b_0$ not to receive erroneous treatment. The direct benefit to providers of delivering appropriate care is given by $\alpha(b^* - b_0) < b^* - b_0$.

Observe that physicians who are fully informed about the expected benefit of treatment, b_t, select the treatment that maximizes αb_t, which implies that they always select the treatment that maximizes the net benefit of treatment to society, and also the treatment that maximizes the net benefit of treatment to the patient. Thus, informed physicians always select the optimal treatment (b^*) when they are correctly informed about the expected benefit of each treatment. This structure enables us to examine whether malpractice liability is needed when physicians want to provide optimal care and never knowingly deliver suboptimal care.[77]

Although in this model physicians want to provide optimal care, they do not always have the ability to do so. In particular, it is assumed that physicians provide erroneous care, accidentally and unknowingly, when they do not have sufficient expertise to properly diagnose the patient or select the right treatment. For simplicity, it is assumed that this error results in the patient suffering an expected injury, $b^* - b_0$, relative to expected outcomes if the physician selected the correct treatment. Consistent with empirical evidence, we assume physicians can prevent many of these accidental errors by investing in expertise. We capture this formally by assuming that the physician can invest in expertise at a cost, $C(e)$; these investments determine the probability, e, that the physician has sufficient information to correctly diagnose the patient and determine the correct treatment. Thus, e is the probability that the physician who wants to deliver optimal care can actually do so. Consistent with the evidence, it is assumed that patients cannot observe either the amount the physician invests in expertise or the probability he provides erroneous care.

This framework enables us to consider informed decisions to provide optimal or suboptimal treatment, as well as the genuinely accidental provision of negligent care. Thus, this framework differs from the classic model of accidents in which injurers always know when they are negligent.[78]

Optimal vs. private incentives to invest in expertise

We now consider the level of expertise that maximizes the joint welfare of patients and providers and compare this with the level of expertise that the physician will select absent malpractice liability.

Assuming that informed providers select the patients' preferred treatment, and that uninformed providers provide erroneous care, we see that joint welfare is maximized when providers invest in the level of expertise that maximizes the expected benefit to patients and providers of medical care minus the cost of expertise:

$$(1 + \alpha)[eb^* + (1 - e)b_0] - C(e) \tag{2.1}$$

This implies that the parties' joint welfare is maximized when the provider selects the level of expertise at which the marginal benefit of expertise—which is the benefit to the patient and the provider of the patient receiving optimal instead of erroneous care—equals the marginal cost of expertise to the provider:[79]

$$(1 + \alpha)(b^* - b_0) = C'(e) \tag{2.2}$$

We now consider the physician's expertise when he is not held liable for medical error, assuming as before that he selects the patients' preferred treatment when informed and selects an erroneous treatment when he is not. Given the assumptions of the model, the physician's expected welfare is given by:

$$\alpha[eb^* + (1 - e)b_0] - C(e)$$

The physician thus will select the level of expertise where:

$$\alpha(b^* - b_0) = C'(e) \tag{2.3}$$

Comparing Equation (2.3) to Equation (2.2) we see that, absent liability, physicians underinvest in expertise because they bear the full cost of expertise, but do not internalize the full social benefit of expertise. Specifically, physicians do not internalize the full benefit to the patient of receiving optimal rather than suboptimal treatment, even when they are compassionate. They thus are not willing to pay as much as the patient is to reduce the risk of medical error. Accordingly, we see that even when physicians are compassionate and want to provide patients with the best quality care, they nevertheless will deliver care of lower than optimal expected quality because physicians' risk of error will be higher than is optimal.[80]

How malpractice liability regulates expertise

States can use negligence liability to optimally regulate both treatment choice and expertise. Moreover, negligence liability can be designed to ensure that medical providers select optimal expertise even when courts base the decision of whether to impose liability solely on whether the physician provided the optimal treatment, and not on the physician's underlying level of expertise.[81]

We can show this formally by considering a physician's expected welfare when he selects optimal care when informed, but faces a risk of liability for accidental error when he is uninformed. In this case, his expected welfare is given by:

$$\alpha e b^* + (1 - e)(\alpha b_0 - D) - C(e)$$

This implies the physician selects the level of expertise at which:

$$\alpha(b^* - b_0) + D = C'(e) \tag{2.4}$$

A comparison of Equations (2.4) and (2.2) reveals that the physician will select the optimal level of expertise (that satisfies Equation (2.1)) if damages are set equal to $b^* - b_0$. Thus, the physician invests optimally in expertise if damages require him to bear the full *expected* cost to the patient of receiving erroneous care instead of optimal care.[82]

Observe that in this framework, malpractice liability serves a valuable role in regulating medical quality even when physicians never knowingly provide negligent care, even absent liability. This is because physicians who want to provide optimal care nevertheless face a probability that they will err unknowingly. This risk of liability for accidental errors occurs with probability, $(1 - e)$. Physicians can reduce the threat of liability by investing in expertise. Thus, even when physicians are well meaning, malpractice liability potentially serves a valuable function by providing physicians with needed additional incentives to invest in expertise.[83]

Observe further that negligence liability is able to induce optimal investment in expertise even when the state cannot observe expertise. Negligence liability based on physicians' failure to provide optimal treatment can be used to induce both optimal treatment choice and optimal physician investment in expertise because physician liability for accidental errors operates as a form of strict liability for accidental errors, ensuring that physicians bear the full cost of their uninformed treatment decisions. States can use the zone of strict liability residing inside the negligence rule to regulate expertise optimally, so long as damages are set correctly. Specifically, providers erring accidentally must face expected liability costs equal to the net benefit of expertise—as given by the expected ex ante benefit to the patient of receiving optimal care instead of erroneous care.[84]

Nevertheless, even when tort liability and damage rules are set optimally, the resulting equilibrium does not eliminate the risk of patients receiving erroneous care, as long as optimal expertise is associated with a positive risk of error: i.e. $e^* < 1$. This contrasts with the classic model of accidents in which injurers are never negligent in equilibrium in a perfect world.[85] It is consistent with the evidence that most errors are accidental and with our intuitions that it would not be optimal for physicians to invest in the expertise needed to eliminate all risk of medical error.

Summary

Accordingly, empirical evidence reveals that, in order to determine the optimal structure of medical malpractice liability, we need to adopt a new economic model of medical malpractice liability. This new model is needed because the core framework of negligence underlying the classic model is not consistent with the understanding of the root causes of medical negligence that emerges from empirical scholarship. First, we need a model that permits the examination of errors committed by providers who do not know that they are providing poor care—errors that nevertheless are regulable through providers' ex ante investments in expertise, administrative systems, and other mechanisms to ensure that they have the capacity to diagnose accurately, select the right treatment, and provide the treatment without error. Second, the new model must recognize that physicians often care about their patients.[86] Employing this new model, we can examine the optimal structure of medical malpractice liability and evaluate various reform proposals.

The empirically grounded model of malpractice liability reveals that—contrary to the conclusions that emerge from the traditional law and economics view of medical malpractice—states seeking to optimally regulate healthcare markets cannot restrict their interventions to mechanisms designed to limit the practice of incompetent physicians. They need to intervene to ensure that competent licensed physicians have optimal incentives to invest in the expertise necessary to correctly diagnose patients, assess treatment options, and provide treatment.[87] Moreover, this framework reveals that states can achieve this goal by imposing malpractice liability on physicians who select and provide negligent treatment, even when they err accidentally. Indeed, this analysis shows that liability for accidental error is anything but a deadweight cost of tort liability. The threat of liability for accidental error is a valuable—indeed essential—mechanism for inducing medical providers to invest optimally in expertise. The fact that liability is imposed on competent providers who err accidentally is what we would expect were the system operating the way it should.[88]

As we will see in the next section, we can employ this model to reassess classic reform proposals, such as suggestions to permit contracting over liability. This model also can be modified to permit assessment of new proposals. The most important modification to be discussed below is incorporating the ways in which institutions make decisions that affect patient safety.

Reassessing classic reform proposals

The empirically grounded model reveals that malpractice liability has an important role to play in regulating the quality of medical care delivered by competent and incompetent providers alike. Moreover, this empirically grounded model provides new insights on the merits of a leading reform proposal—to permit contracting over liability[89]—showing that this reform would likely reduce social welfare. This model of medical malpractice reveals that this reform would harm patients because patients potentially derive more benefit from malpractice liability than from liability procured by contract. Thus, the solution to malpractice liability reform lies in making the system more effective, not in eliminating it.[90]

Empirical analysis also provides insights on the direction that alternative reforms should take. State legislatures have tended to adopt reforms designed to reduce malpractice liability, such as damage caps, collateral source rule reform, joint and several liability reform, contingency fee reform, and contractual malpractice liability. These reforms can best be justified if providers currently face excessive expected liability. Yet empirical analysis suggests that there may be too little malpractice liability. Moreover, there is far less erroneously imposed liability than standard political rhetoric would suggest. Indeed, the vast majority of medical malpractice settlements involve patients injured by genuine medical error.[91] Finally, empirical studies provide evidence that suggests important directions for reforms to take. Of particular importance, evidence shows that many medical errors can be attributed, at least in part, to decisions made by medical institutions, especially hospitals. Yet these institutions generally avoid bearing financial responsibility for the errors caused by their decisions; indeed, hospitals may be able to profit from error, to the extent that error results in additional treatment.[92] Empirical evidence thus provides support for proposals to impose liability on medical institutions, such as hospitals and MCOs.[93]

Contractual liability

As previously explained, scholars operating within the traditional framework have argued that states seeking to reform malpractice liability can best do so by allowing patients to contract over liability with their providers.[94] Proponents of this reform contend that contractual liability should be attractive to supporters and opponents of liability alike. This claim rests on the assumption that patients obtain the same benefit from liability (at the same cost) whether it is imposed by tort or contract. Given this assumption, patients cannot be hurt by being allowed to contract over liability because any patient who would have benefited from tort liability will impose it by contract—so long as patients are informed about the expected costs and benefits of liability, and contracting is voluntary.

The empirically grounded model of malpractice liability enables us to see why the classic economic argument for contractual liability is incorrect. To see this, we focus on negotiated contracting between patients and individual providers at the moment patients seek care.[95]

The claim that patients would not be harmed by the adoption of contractual liability rests on the conclusion that patients who benefit from tort liability necessarily would elect to contract into liability if offered the ability to pay for liability by their individual providers. This conclusion, in turn, rests on the premise that patients obtain the same deterrence benefit from liability procured through individual contracts as they do from liability imposed by the state. This premise appears reasonable if we accept the assumption of the traditional model that each patient's risk of injury depends on patient-specific investments in care by individual providers. In this framework, tort liability operates to increase these patient-specific investments in care—a function that could be served equally well by contractual liability.

This argument for contract collapses once we incorporate the insights of empirical analysis about the causes of medical error and the purposes of liability. The empirically grounded model of malpractice liability finds that a central purpose of malpractice liability is to induce optimal investment in "expertise"—defined as investments in information, personnel, healthcare technology, and systems that affect the probability that the provider is able to correctly diagnose the patient, select the correct treatment, and correctly provide any treatment that is selected.[96] These investments in expertise generally are not patient-specific; they affect a provider's ability to correctly diagnose, assess the treatments for, and provide care to, each of his patients. Accordingly, the expected benefit to a provider of investing in expertise depends not only on his expected liability to one patient, but instead on his expected liability to all of his patients.[97] This recognition undermines the economic argument for negotiable contractual liability because it reveals that malpractice liability is a collective good in that each medical provider's incentive to invest in expertise depends on his expected liability to all of his patients. Thus, each patient's expected safety depends not only on the patient's own liability decisions, but also on the liability choices of others. Moreover, no patient can reliably use liability to induce optimal investment in expertise unless all patients collectively impose liability.[98]

Because malpractice liability is a collective good, patients contracting individually over liability might rationally eschew liability even when all patients would be better off if liability were imposed. This is because each patient derives more benefit from any given liability rule when it is imposed collectively by all patients than when he imposes it individually. When liability is imposed collectively, each patient obtains the deterrence benefit of his provider's expected liability to all of his patients. By contrast, a patient imposing liability individually only benefits to the extent that his individual choice alters his provider's expertise. As a result, each patient gains less from imposing liability by contract than he gains from the imposition of malpractice liability collectively (by fiat). Thus, patients do not have optimal incentives to impose liability by contract in that a patient may rationally decide that it is not worthwhile to impose liability individually (holding constant the decision of other patients) even when all patients would be better off if they could impose liability collectively.[99]

Indeed, in the case of a medical provider with many patients, the decision of any one patient to impose liability may have too little effect on the provider's expected costs to induce the provider to increase his investment in expertise, personnel, administrative systems, or healthcare technology—even when the provider would materially increase his investments when facing liability to all of his patients (and in so doing confer a collective benefit on patients that exceeds the cost of care). In this situation, contracting over liability would encourage each patient to waive liability in order to reduce his healthcare expenses because he can do so without substantially reducing expected outcomes.[100] Of course, if each patient makes the same rational decision, none of them will impose liability even when all of them would have been better off if they imposed liability collectively.[101] As a result, patients who would have benefited from state-imposed liability will be harmed by the move to contractual liability because patients required to contract over liability lose the ability to easily regulate collective investments in care that is afforded by collectively imposed tort liability.[102] Empirical scholarship thus helps reveal the tremendous benefit to patients of the ability to impose liability collectively, and in turn helps us understand why states should not embrace contractual liability.

Empirical evidence on malpractice litigation and settlements

The conclusion that we cannot rely on contracting over liability to produce efficient malpractice liability rules implies that states must address the issue of malpractice liability reform directly. Accordingly, it is important to determine the appropriate goals of malpractice liability reform. Many politically popular reform proposals—such as damage caps, collateral source rule reform, joint and several liability reform, and contingency fee reform—were adopted to curtail malpractice litigation, often in the belief that medical providers face an excessive risk of frivolous litigation and that a substantial portion of settlement awards are paid in cases where the physicians did not commit medical error.[103] Empirical analysis of malpractice liability undermines the core justification for these malpractice liability reforms. The evidence suggests that reforms should be directed at enhancing expected liability for medical caregivers who deliver erroneous care and expanding the reach of medical malpractice to more thoroughly cover medical institutions when their policies and practices contribute to medical error.

Evidence reveals that: negligent doctors face too little litigation; juries tend to get it right, and when they err they are more likely to err in favor of doctors, not patients; the vast majority of malpractice cases that settle with positive (nonzero) payments involve instances where external review reveals the medical provider probably did err; and the enormous trial verdicts one sees generally do not result in equally enormous payments.

Evidence on claiming rates and settlement accuracy

Consider a standard claim that there are too many malpractice liability claims and that many, if not most, successful litigations occur in cases where there was no error. The evidence does not support these conjectures.

If we compare the malpractice settlements to the amount of medical error, we see that the number of medical errors exceeds the number of malpractice settlements. Empirical analysis reveals that patients who are injured by medical error rarely sue: indeed, only 2–3 percent of the patients injured by medical error file a claim.[104] Moreover, only one in three patients seriously injured (or killed) by medical error sues.[105]

Beyond this, patients with good claims do not always recover. Indeed, one study found that 27 percent of the victims of error who did sue did not recover.[106] Victims of error are particularly likely to be denied recovery if they proceed to trial.[107]

As for the quality of the settled cases, empirical studies do not support the oft-repeated claim that malpractice liability is random, falling on physicians regardless of whether they erred.[108] To the contrary, numerous studies show that the vast majority of patients who recover were in fact injured by medical negligence.[109] For example, a recent review of medical malpractice settlements found that 82 percent of the malpractice liability claims that resulted in payment involved situations where it is more likely than not that the physician erred. By contrast, patients who file nonmeritorious claims usually do not receive any money in settlement.[110] These findings are supported by other studies.[111]

Of course not all cases are resolved correctly. Almost 20 percent of malpractice cases with positive settlements involve claims where no error occurred. Yet many claims where patients do not recover also were resolved incorrectly. Indeed, if we examine the general direction of case-resolution-error, we find that erroneous claims resolutions are more likely to favor doctors than patients. Specifically, an examination of the claims that were resolved incorrectly found that 60 percent involved a pro-physician error (in which the patient lost even though his injuries probably were the result of physician error); only 40 percent of the erroneous decisions favored the patient. Jury trial errors were particularly likely to favor the physician, not the patient.[112] In addition, when patients do obtain a favorable settlement erroneously, settlements tend to be substantially smaller than in cases involving error.[113] Thus, the evidence does not support the view that the central problem facing the malpractice system is that patients are recovering too often for invalid claims. To the contrary, we find that patients regularly are injured by error and do not recover.

As for damages, empirical analysis provides evidence to suggest why medical professionals are concerned about malpractice awards, but nevertheless does not support the view that malpractice judgments either exceed the social cost of the injuries imposed or are spiraling upwards faster than the rate of medical inflation. A recent study of malpractice settlements found that 50 percent of paid claims involved awards of $206,400 or less. The median amount paid in settlement was less than $197,000, and the mean amount was less than $463,000.[114] As for the trend in damages, recent analysis suggests that medical malpractice settlements and verdicts have not increased significantly in real terms, once one accounts for the rate of medical inflation.[115] Claiming rates per capita also appear to be stable.[116]

Moreover, while juries periodically do award enormous damages, analysis of paid claims suggests that these verdicts rarely result in enormous payments by individual physicians. Patients who receive enormous damages against physicians rarely receive the full award because they tend to settle at the providers' policy limits to avoid an appeal. Providers only pay out of pocket in a small fraction of the cases.[117]

Summary

Empirical analysis highlights the importance of taking a fresh approach to malpractice liability by revealing the fallacy of conventional wisdom. Whereas the reforms embraced by many politicians and law and economic scholars focus on curtailing malpractice suits on the apparent assumption that most malpractice suits are frivolous or random, empirical analysis shows this is not correct. It shows that the core task of reform should not be to limit suits, but instead should be to ensure that medical institutions and medical providers who provide suboptimal care bear the full cost of their neglect, while insulating high-quality providers from the liability costs of their lower-quality peers.[118]

In addition, empirical analysis indirectly enabled scholars to reexamine the claim that states should permit contracting over liability. Empirical analysis led to the development of a more empirically grounded model of malpractice liability. This model deepens our understanding of the purposes and effect of malpractice liability. Specifically, by revealing the central importance of expertise, empirical scholarship led scholars to understand that malpractice liability is a collective good. This framework thus reveals the tremendous benefit to patients of the ability to impose liability collectively, and in turn reveals why states are right to reject contractual liability and to seek alternative mechanisms for reforming the malpractice liability system.[119]

The empirically grounded case for organizational liability

Empirical analysis has not only helped scholars understand why states should reject many favored reforms, it also illuminates the direction that malpractice liability reform should take. In particular, it reveals that we cannot optimally deter medical error unless liability is imposed on the medical organizations (e.g. hospitals and

MCOs) that affect patients' welfare. Empirically grounded analysis of medical error also highlights the critical importance of holding medical institutions liable for their own neglect, as well as for that of individual providers practicing under their purview.[120]

Empirical evidence on the role of medical institutions

Empirical analysis reveals that patients' welfare depends on choices made by medical institutions, specifically hospitals and MCOs. Both institutions affect patient welfare both directly, through interventions that directly affect the probability of a patient receiving erroneous care, as well as indirectly, through actions that affect the likelihood that a physician will commit actionable negligence. To optimally regulate medical care, liability must ensure that both institutions make decisions that minimize the joint cost of care and expected accidents, and not just decisions that minimize their own direct costs. To do this, we must expand hospital liability to ensure that they are liable for independent-contractor physicians practicing within them and also impose liability on MCOs for their decisions regarding what constitutes "medically necessary and appropriate" care, as well as for negligence in the care provided by the physicians and hospitals with whom they contract.

Hospitals

Empirical analysis of medical error reveals that states cannot hope to optimally safeguard patient safety unless they can induce hospitals to invest optimally in measures to reduce error. Many errors result when organizations (such as hospitals) fail to implement systems to reduce the probability and consequences of medical error. Indeed, one recent study suggested that most medical errors were attributable, at least in part, to systems problems; most of these systems are in the control of hospital administrators, not individual physicians.[121] For example, hospitals control equipment purchases and repairs.[122] They also determine whether inexperienced physicians are adequately supervised,[123] the probability that medical personnel know their patient responsibilities and are adequately informed about their patients' care, and the likelihood of patient infection. They also control whether their employees and affiliated physicians have access to information technology capable of alerting providers promptly when an error has been made.[124] Finally, hospitals establish the rules governing maximum (and required) shifts that determine whether patients are cared for by a physician whose judgment is potentially impaired by lack of sleep.[125] Indeed, we can get a sense of the importance of hospitals' decisions concerning internal systems from evidence indicating that the best hospitals impose expected error costs of only $42 per patient admission whereas the worst impose error costs per patient admission of $4,769.[126]

Thus, in order to protect patients, states must ensure that hospitals have sufficient incentives to invest optimally in systems and equipment that prevent and detect errors and adopt rules governing hospital practice in order to adequately care for patients.[127] Hospitals thus must internalize the cost of medical errors. This implies that we need to impose liability directly on institutions because individual provider liability will not ensure that institutions have optimal incentives to make systemic investments in care.

Hospital liability is needed for two reasons. First, evidence reveals that hospitals generally do not internalize the cost to their patients of injuries resulting from medical error, even when this produces actionable negligence.[128] Hospitals often are not liable for individual providers' negligence because they generally have an independent-contractor relationship with the surgeons, anesthesiologists, and radiologists who use their facilities.[129] Moreover, providers often purchase their own malpractice insurance. Finally, hospitals can benefit from nonactionable medical errors that require additional billable hospital services.[130] Thus, individual liability does not ensure that hospitals have optimal incentives to reduce the risk that individual providers will be negligent. Second, many deficiencies in hospital systems harm patients through their cumulative effect without producing a clear act of individual negligence that is actionable under our current system, which focuses on whether a given individual provider delivered substandard care.[131] Given this, malpractice liability does not provide either a direct or indirect incentive to remedy these problems, as the errors they produce will not be actionable.[132]

Accordingly, malpractice liability cannot provide hospitals with adequate incentives to safeguard their patients if liability is predicated primarily on individual provider negligence.[133] In order to optimally deter medical errors, we must hold hospitals directly liable for iatrogenic injuries, even when these cannot be attributed to any particular individual provider. We also must hold hospitals liable for the negligence of providers who use their facilities, even when these providers are independent contractors. This liability for patient injuries resulting from individual, institutional, and systemic errors will improve patient welfare.[134]

Managed care organizations

MCOs also affect patient welfare both directly and indirectly in ways that are not optimally regulated by individual malpractice liability.[135] Of particular importance, many MCOs affect care directly through the use of utilization review. Utilization review enables an MCO to deny coverage for treatments that the MCO deems not to be "medically necessary or appropriate" (or otherwise not covered). In the case of expensive treatments, this denial of coverage tends to result in a denial of treatment.[136] Moreover, evidence reveals that MCOs' authority to affect treatment choices not only affects the care their own subscribers receive, but also affects contracted providers' choice of treatment for patients with non-MCO insurance.[137]

MCO liability is needed to ensure that these organizations make optimal decisions about what treatments are "medically necessary and appropriate." The current regime of individual provider liability for malpractice is not sufficient. It does not deter MCOs from negligently denying coverage for treatments that were, in fact, medically necessary because individual providers are not liable if they recommend the treatment and the MCO denies it. Moreover, MCOs often can structure their decisions to deny coverage for recommended treatments in ways that leave them insulated by federal preemption from liability under state tort law. Optimal regulation of patient safety thus requires that MCOs be held liable for their own negligence, as well as that of individual physicians.[138]

Summary

Empirical analysis thus reveals that optimal malpractice liability reform must include reforms that increase medical entities' incentives to invest in care. This conclusion follows from evidence on the multitude of ways that institutions affect patient safety directly and indirectly,[139] as well as the degree to which they avoid bearing the cost of injuries resulting from their decisions.[140] Moreover, states should impose liability directly on hospitals and MCOs, even when physicians can be, and are, held liable for their medical negligence. One effective way to achieve this goal would be to impose liability for all malpractice claims on medical entities—MCOs or hospitals—and allow these entities to contract with physicians to shift liability to them. Malpractice liability would be more effective if liability were imposed on medical entities because much (if not most) medical error appears to result from decisions made by entities that either affect care directly or influence the quality of care that physicians can provide. Entity-level liability would provide the entities with financial incentives to use their influence to make optimal decisions regarding the costs and quality of care. Entity-level liability also would induce entities to make superior investments in systematic care and to better monitor the quality of providers with whom they contract. MCOs and hospitals would also have incentives to use their substantial data on health outcomes to develop protocols for physicians based on due consideration of treatment cost-effectiveness.[141]

Conclusion

Empirical legal studies have transformed our understanding of the economic functions of malpractice liability, thereby reshaping the debate over malpractice liability reform.

Many popular reforms are predicated on the assumption that the best way to reform malpractice liability is to curtail it. This belief finds support in the results of the classic model of accidents, which assumes that medical malpractice represents a knowing decision by a physician to select a suboptimal treatment in order to reduce his costs.

Empirical malpractice analysis undermines both the theoretical and empirical arguments supporting this approach. Empirical analysis reveals that scholars cannot rely on the classic model of accidents to analyze malpractice liability because it does not accurately capture the root causes of medical error. In contrast with the classic model, empirical analysis demonstrates that medical error does not generally result from a deliberate decision to economize on treatment costs, but instead results from insufficient expertise. Empirical analysis thus reveals that we cannot accurately understand the central functions of malpractice liability unless we employ a model that captures the effect of expertise on the probability of medical error. Theoretical models that incorporate expertise show that malpractice liability is vital to the effective operation of healthcare markets. Well-designed liability for medical negligence is among the most effective mechanisms for inducing medical providers to invest optimally in expertise—a primary determinant of patient welfare.

Empirical analysis also reveals that we cannot optimally regulate healthcare markets unless we take a dramatically different approach to malpractice liability reform. Many traditional reforms are predicated on the belief that malpractice liability provides little benefit because it is randomly imposed. Others press states to embrace contractual liability. Empirical analysis undermines the core assumptions of both reform proposals. Empirical analysis shows that malpractice liability is anything but random, and instead generally is imposed correctly on providers who erred. It also helps us understand why malpractice liability imposed collectively through the tort system is superior to other individual forms of liability, such as contractual liability: the primary benefit of malpractice liability flows from its ability to regulate a form of care—expertise—that is a collective good.

Finally, empirical analysis has helped scholars identify the most productive avenue for malpractice reform. Specifically, empirical combined with theoretical analysis has shown that states seeking to safeguard patient welfare can best do so by imposing malpractice liability directly on hospitals and MCOs, as they have the greatest ability to affect healthcare quality.

Thus, by understanding medical error and malpractice liability, we gain the insight needed to guide policymakers toward solutions that offer a genuine promise of saving patients' lives.

Notes

1 I benefited from the helpful comments of Yun-chien Chang, participants at the Conference on Empirical Legal Studies at Academia Sinica in Taiwan, June 2011, and two anonymous referees. I also want to thank my research assistant, Tristan Favro, for his excellent work on this project. I am grateful for the financial support of the D'Agostino/Greenberg Fund of the New York University School of Law.
2 *See* Steven Shavell, *Strict Liability Versus Negligence*, 9 J. Legal Stud. 1 (1980).
3 For a discussion of evidence suggesting that we cannot rely entirely on licensing and regulation to adequately address the problem of incompetent physicians, *see* Jennifer Arlen & W. Bentley MacLeod, *Malpractice Liability for Physicians and Managed Care Organizations*, 78 N.Y.U. L. Rev. 1929, 1960, n.108–09 (2003).
4 *See* Shavell, *supra* note 2 (reaching this result in the context of torts generally).
5 This conclusion is consistent with the classic model of accidents. Some scholars have extended this analysis to allow for the possibility that courts err in the standard of care. It has been shown that under reasonable assumptions about error, error in determining "due care" can lead to an equilibrium in which defendants take excessive care but are found liable nonetheless. *See* John E. Calfee & Richard Craswell, *Deterrence and Uncertain Legal Standards*, 2 J.L. Econ. & Org. 279 (1986). As is discussed later, this equilibrium also is inconsistent with the evidence that genuine medical error occurs regularly.

6 *See* Richard H. Thaler & Cass R. Sunstein, NUDGE: IMPROVING DECISIONS ABOUT HEALTH, WEALTH, AND HAPPINESS (2008); Richard A. Epstein, *Medical Malpractice: The Case for Contract*, 1 AM. B. FOUND. RES. J. 87 (1976); Richard A. Epstein & Alan O. Sykes, *The Assault on Managed Care: Vicarious Liability, ERISA Preemption, and Class Actions*, 30 J. LEGAL STUD. 625 (2001); Clark C. Havighurst, *Private Reform of Tort-Law Dogma: Market Opportunities and Legal Obstacles*, 49 LAW & CONTEMP. PROBS. 143 (1986); Glen O. Robinson, *Rethinking the Allocation of Medical Malpractice Risks Between Patients and Providers*, 49 LAW & CONTEMP. PROBS. 173 (1986).

7 Concerns also arise about high malpractice liability insurance premiums. Nevertheless, efforts to address this problem through measures that reduce recovery and litigation—such as non-economic damage caps and collateral source rule reform—suggest that state legislatures accept the view that perceived excessive premiums result from excessive damages and not from inefficiencies in malpractice liability insurance markets.

8 State legislatures have restricted damage awards directly by adopting caps on noneconomic damages and wrongful death awards. *See* Catherine M. Sharkey, *Unintended Consequences of Medical Malpractice Damages Caps*, 80 N.Y.U. L. REV. 391 (2005). They have limited damages indirectly through measures such as collateral source rule reform (under which patients injured by medical negligence cannot recover compensatory damages for damages covered by their first-party insurance, such as health insurance), joint and several liability reform, and measures that increase physicians' ability to shelter assets from patients. Early reforms include shortened statute of limitations and requirements that patients submit claims to a physician review board with authority to assess the validity of the claim. More recent indirect efforts include limitations on contingency fees. For a survey of reforms, *see* Ronen Avraham, *An Empirical Study of the Impact of Tort Reforms on Medical Malpractice Settlement Payments*, 36 J. LEGAL STUD. S183 (2007).

9 *See* Shavell, *supra* note 2. In the traditional model, injurers know the cost and benefits of care, the level of care that they take, and the standard of care. Thus, an injurer who decides to take suboptimal care ($x < x^*$, where x^* is due care) does so knowingly. The injurer does not knowingly cause harm; harm happens with probability $p(x)$. Yet the injurer does know he is being negligent. *See infra* Classical model of accidents and its implications.

10 Thus, while there is evidence that patients often receive negligent care, *see* sources cited *infra* note 11, this negligent care does not appear to be the result of a knowing decision to provide suboptimal care ($x < x^*$) in the way depicted in the classic model of accidents.

11 *See* Paul C. Weiler, MEDICAL MALPRACTICE ON TRIAL (1991); Lori B. Andrews, *Studying Medical Error in Situ: Implications for Malpractice Law and Policy*, 54 DEPAUL L. REV. 357 (2005); Michelle M. Mello & David M. Studdert, *Deconstructing Negligence: The Role of Individual and System Factors in Causing Medical Injuries*, 96 GEO. L.J. 599 (2008).

12 *See* Arlen & MacLeod, *supra* note 3.

13 *See id.*

14 *See* Jennifer Arlen & W. Bentley MacLeod, *Torts, Expertise, and Authority: Liability of Physicians and Managed Care Organizations*, 36 RAND J. ECON. 494 (2005). The framework actually employed assumes that doctors are compassionate and thus want to provide medically appropriate care. Nevertheless, the model is structured to permit analysis of situations where physicians might benefit from knowingly providing suboptimal care. This can happen under capitation insurance plans that give physicians a flat payment per patient and require physicians to pay all or most of the cost of any treatment provided.

15 *See* Arlen & MacLeod, *supra* note 3; *id.*

16 *Id.*

17 *Id.*

18 *Compare* Arlen & MacLeod, *supra* note 3, *with* Shavell, *supra* note 2, *and* Marcel Kahan, *Causation and Incentives to Take Care under the Negligence Rule*, 18 J. LEGAL STUD. 427 (1989).

19 Nevertheless, it is likely that we see regular error and litigation because malpractice liability is not optimally designed. Yet the core problem is not that there are too many settlements, but rather that the system does not impose sufficiently large expected liability on negligent providers and on the institutions responsible for patient safety to induce optimal investments in patient safety. *See* Jennifer Arlen, *Contracting Over Liability: Medical Malpractice and the Cost of Choice*, 158 U. PA. L. REV. 957 (2010); *see also* Michelle M. Mello & Troyan A. Brennan, *Deterrence of Medical Errors: Theory and Evidence for Malpractice Reform*, 80 TEX. L. REV. 1595 (2002).

20 *See* Arlen & MacLeod, *supra* note 3; Arlen & MacLeod, *supra* note 14.

21 *See* Arlen & MacLeod, *supra* note 14.

22 This empirically grounded model also reveals why we should not embrace contractual liability—which is a reform proposal favored by many scholars. *See, e.g.*, Epstein, *supra* note 6; Epstein & Sykes, *supra* note 6; Clark C. Havighurst, *Vicarious Liability: Relocating Responsibility for the Quality of Medical Care*, 26 AM. J.L. & MED. 7 (2000); Robinson, *supra* note 5; THALER & SUNSTEIN, *supra* note 6. This model reveals that liability imposed automatically by the state, on all patients, across all providers, benefits patients more, at lower cost, than liability imposed by contract, even when the precise liability rule is the same. Thus, states shifting to contractual liability would reduce many patients' welfare and would induce many patients to contract out of liability even when they would have been better off were liability imposed by fiat. *See* Arlen, *supra* note 19.

23 *See* David M. Studdert *et al.*, *Claims, Errors, and Compensation Payments in Medical Malpractice Litigation*, 354 NEW ENG. J. MED. 2024 (2006).

24 *See id.*

25 *See* Arlen, *supra* note 19.

26 *See* Epstein, *supra* note 6; Robinson, *supra* note 6; THALER & SUNSTEIN, *supra* note 6; Havighurst, *supra* note 6; Havighurst, *supra* note 22; Patricia M. Danzon, *Tort Liability: A Minefield for Managed Care?*, 26 J. LEGAL STUD. 491, (1997); *see also* Keith N. Hylton, *Agreements to Waive or to Arbitrate Legal Claims: An Economic Analysis*, 8 SUP. CT. ECON. REV. 209 (2000).

27 This is not the only reason why contracting over liability is inefficient. *See, e.g.*, Arlen, *supra* note 19; Jennifer Arlen, *Private Contractual Alternatives to Malpractice Liability*, *in* MEDICAL MALPRACTICE AND THE US HEALTH CARE SYSTEM: NEW CENTURY, DIFFERENT ISSUES (Rogan Kersh & William M. Sage eds., 2006); Arlen & MacLeod, *supra* note 2; *see also* Abraham Wickelgren, *The Inefficiency of Contractually-Based Liability with Rational Consumers*, 22 J.L. ECON. & ORG. 168 (2006) (arguing that contractual products liability is inefficient); *accord* Mark Geistfeld, *The Political Economy of Neocontractual Proposals for Products Liability Reform*, 72 TEX. L. REV. 803 (1994).

28 *See* Kenneth Abraham & Paul C. Weiler, *Enterprise Medical Liability and the Evolution of the American Health Care System*, 108 HARV. L. REV. 381 (1994).

29 *See* Arlen & MacLeod, *supra* note 3; Havighurst, *supra* note 6; William Sage, *Regulating Through Information: Disclosure Laws and American Health Care*, 99 COLUM. L. REV. 1701 (1999).

30 *See* Michelle M. Mello *et al.*, *Who Pays for Medical Errors? An Analysis of Adverse Event Costs, the Medical Liability System, and Incentives for Patient Safety Improvement*, 4 J. EMPIRICAL LEGAL STUD. 835 (2007); Arlen & MacLeod, *supra* note 3; Epstein & Sykes, *supra* note 6; Havighurst, *supra* note 6.

31 *See* John E. Rolph *et al.*, *Identifying Malpractice-Prone Physicians*, 4 J. EMPIRICAL

LEGAL STUD. 125 (2007).

32 *See* John Prather Brown, *Toward an Economic Theory of Liability*, 2 J. LEGAL STUD. 323 (1973); Shavell, *supra* note 2.

33 Initial empirical analysis challenging the "bad apple" view of medical error appeared in the early 1990s, prior to the rise of MCOs and associated institutions such as capitation. Thus, in discussing the traditional view we focus on the application of the traditional model to patients insured by fee-for-service insurers who cover all treatment costs (minus a deductible).

34 Of course, this situation can lead to excessive treatment, which can harm patients when higher-cost care is also riskier. This chapter does not focus on this issue because neither markets nor classic malpractice liability is particularly effective at addressing this problem. Classic malpractice liability does not effectively deter excessive treatment because the standard of negligence generally is based on medical custom, as measured by a national standard. Physicians tend to prevail if they can show adherence to an accepted custom, even if the plaintiff can get other physicians to testify that this is not the best practice. *See, e.g.*, Gary Schwartz, *Medical Malpractice, Tort, Contract, and Managed Care*, 3 U. ILL. L. REV. 885, 894–95 (1998). *But see* Helling v. Carey, 519 P.2d 981 (Wash. 1974). If due care is based on "customary care" and if custom is developed under fee-for-service insurance, then providers can be expected to err on the side of providing too much care, rather than substandard care. *See* Danzon, *supra* note 26 (observing that the tort standard for due care, which is based on customary care, likely sets due care equal to excessive care since medical custom developed under fee-for-service health insurance); *see* Arlen & MacLeod, *supra* note 14 (providing formal proof that informed doctors select the care that maximizes the benefit of treatment to patients, and not the care that maximizes the net benefit of treatment (optimal care), when insurers, not doctors, bear all treatment costs).

35 This view also led some to conclude that medical quality would be best addressed by licensing and similar regulations as these measures are targeted at controlling the few bad doctors who were assumed to be responsible for most medical errors. *See* Rolph *et al.*, *supra* note 31. As it happens, licensing and quality regulation currently do not adequately protect patients from incompetent physicians. Hospitals are often slow to report problem physicians to state review boards. Atul Gawande, COMPLICATIONS: A SURGEON'S NOTES ON AN IMPERFECT SCIENCE 88–106 (2003) (describing the slow response to problem physicians). State disciplinary review boards are reluctant to impose serious disciplinary sanctions (e.g. suspension, probation, or license revocation) on physicians. PUBLIC CITIZEN, HEALTH RESEARCH GROUP, RANKING OF STATE MEDICAL BOARD'S SERIOUS DISCIPLINARY ACTIONS IN 2001, PUBLICATION #1616 (2001), *available at* http://www.citizen.org/documents/1616table1.pdf (finding that, in 2001, review boards imposed fewer than two disciplinary actions per 1,000 physicians (.2 percent) in District of Columbia, Hawaii, Delaware, South Dakota, Illinois, South Carolina, Wisconsin, Minnesota, Maryland, Rhode Island, Indiana, Connecticut, Maine, and Wyoming).

36 *E.g.*, Brown, *supra* note 32; Shavell, *supra* note 2.

37 *See* Shavell, *supra* note 2; *see supra* note 34.

38 *See* Jennifer Arlen, Note, *An Economic Analysis of Tort Damages for Wrongful Death*, 60 N.Y.U. L. REV. 1113 (1985) (explaining that negligence liability does not provide adequate incentives to take care if damages for death and serious permanent injury are below the social costs imposed by the injurer, as they are at present).

39 In the classic economic model, injurers cannot both overinvest in care and produce an excessive risk of medical error. By contrast, with medical care, one can have overinvestment in treatment and excessive risk. This possibility is relevant to the design of an optimal malpractice liability, but is not relevant to the issues explored in this chapter. *See also supra* note 34.

40 *See* Shavell, *supra* note 2.

41 *See* Arlen & MacLeod, *supra* note 3.

42 Indeed, they arguably have incentives to provide excessive treatment (that maximizes patient benefit without regard to cost) if insured patients do not internalize the cost of treatment decisions but do obtain the benefits. *See* Arlen & MacLeod, *supra* note 14. If courts can distinguish excessive treatment that is risky from that which is not, then malpractice liability may be needed to deter physicians from selecting treatments that are high cost but excessively risky.

43 *See supra* note 42 (this conclusion changes when treatments can be both expensive and risky).

44 *See* Arlen & MacLeod, *supra* note 14; Sherry Glied, *Managed Care*, *in* 1A HANDBOOK OF HEALTH ECONOMICS 707 (Anthony J. Culver & Joseph P. Newhouse eds., 2000). This is because ex ante investments in care are unobservable and because many investments in medical quality occur after the patient contracts with the medical provider. *See* Arlen & MacLeod, *supra* note 14; Arlen, *supra* note 19 (discussing the empirical evidence that patients do not know the expected quality of the physicians or hospitals that provide them care). Indeed, most patients believe that healthcare regulation is sufficiently strong to eliminate any significant differences in physician or hospital quality. *See* Jacquelyn J. Jewett & Judith H. Hibbard, *Comprehension of Quality Care Indicators: Differences among Privately Insured, Publicly Insured, and Uninsured*, 18 HEALTH CARE FIN. REV. 75 (1996); KAISER FAMILY FOUNDATION & AGENCY FOR HEALTHCARE RESEARCH & QUALITY, AMERICANS AS HEALTH CARE CONSUMERS: AN UPDATE ON THE ROLE OF QUALITY INFORMATION 12, 15 (2000). Patients persist in this belief even though licensed medical providers differ dramatically in the expected quality of care they deliver. *See* Paul C. Weiler *et al.*, A MEASURE OF MEDICAL MALPRACTICE: MEDICAL INJURY, MALPRACTICE LITIGATION, AND PATIENT COMPENSATION (1993) (providing evidence on quality disparity); *accord* Mello *et al.*, *supra* note 30; Mark R. Chassin, *Benefits and Hazards of Reporting Medical Outcomes Publicly*, 334 NEW ENG. J. MED. 394, 394–97 (1996). Moreover, hospitals not only do not bear the full cost of errors they could prevent, they can even profit from them. Evidence suggests that medical error substantially increases the expected costs of hospitalized patients. Yet hospitals are able to pass on to insurers or patients almost 80 percent of these costs, bearing only 22 percent of the increased health care costs occasioned by their error. Mello *et al.*, *supra* note 30, at 835. While recent reforms have reduced this problem, it nevertheless persists.

45 *See* Shavell, *supra* note 2 (obtaining this result in a general model).

46 *Id.* While traditionally customary care probably was not optimal, *see supra* note 34 (discussing whether a customary standard of care equals optimal care when custom evolved under fee-for-service insurance), there are reasons to hope that the rise of evidence-based medicine and managed care has muted some of the distorting effects of fee-for-service insurance.

47 *Id.*

48 *See* Shavell, *supra* note 2 (obtaining this result in a general model).

49 *See* Robert D. Cooter, *Prices and Sanctions*, 84 COLUM. L. REV. 1523 (1984).

50 *See* Calfee & Craswell, *supra* note 5.

51 Specifically, the classic model of accidents assumes that injurers not only know the expected equilibrium levels of care for themselves and victims (when relevant), but also know the actual costs and benefits of care, thereby enabling them to precisely determine that marginal cost and benefit of any change in their care-taking. Injurers also have perfect control over their own actions. Thus, injurers can control whether they are negligent and are never negligent accidentally. *See* Shavell, *supra* note 2.

52 *Id.*

53 The possibility that due care may be set too high, *see supra* note 34, generally should not result in doctors being negligent in the sense of knowingly selecting the wrong treatment to avoid excessive costs. The reason for this is that doctors can recommend

the non-negligent treatment, even though it is excessively expensive, without bearing the extra cost when patients are insured. Moreover, even when patients are not insured, doctors would not risk negligence liability to avoid treatment costs when the patient is competent (and not indigent). Doctors generally have a duty to recommend the correct treatment, not to pay for it. A doctor can avoid liability by recommending the treatment that satisfies the legal standard; he need not provide it if a non-indigent patient does not want to pay for it (in a non-emergency context).

54 *See* Epstein & Sykes, *supra* note 6, at 642 (citing the Harvard Medical Practice Study for the claim that "courts are rather poor at identifying malpractice ... lawsuits often focus on cases where the physician did nothing wrong").

55 This extra cost does not inure to the benefit of most patients, in this view, since most patients seek care from competent physicians who, in this model, have no reason not to provide good quality care to insured patients.

56 Thus, states have focused on adopting reforms that curtail liability in general, and malpractice liability in particular, including damage caps, collateral source rule reform, joint and several liability reform, and limitations on damages that can be imposed on charitable organizations, such as many hospitals. *See generally* Avraham, *supra* note 8 (discussing malpractice liability reforms adopted from 1991–1998 and finding that they reduced the total number of malpractice cases but not the state-level average award or total payments).

57 *See* Thaler & Sunstein, *supra* note 6; Epstein, *supra* note 6; Havighurst, *supra* note 6; Robinson, *supra* note 6.

58 *E.g.*, Thaler & Sunstein, *supra* note 6; Epstein, *supra* note 6; Richard A. Epstein, *Contractual Principle Versus Legislative Fixes: Coming to Closure on the Unending Travails of Medical Malpractice*, 54 DePaul L. Rev. 503 (2005); Epstein & Sykes, *supra* note 6; Havighurst, *supra* note 22; Clark C. Havighurst, *Doctors and Hospitals: An Antitrust Perspective on Traditional Relationships*, 33 Duke L.J. 1071 (1984); Robinson, *supra* note 6; *see* Danzon, *supra* note 26.

59 *See* Arlen & MacLeod, *supra* note 3.

60 Moreover, evidence discussed later shows that the tort system is able to sort frivolous litigation from genuine negligence with sufficient accuracy that it could be employed to ensure that providers who deliver substandard care face substantially higher costs than those who do not, particularly if certain reforms were implemented. *See infra* notes 107–115 (discussing empirical evidence on malpractice liability litigation and settlements).

61 The low estimate (4 percent) comes from the Harvard Medical Malpractice Study, which reviewed written hospital records and found that 3.7 percent of the patients were victims of an error that caused significant harm. Weiler *et al.*, *supra* note 44, at 42–44, 137–39. The higher estimate (17.7 percent) is from a study involving on-site observation of hospital error. Most of the errors detected by on-site observation were not recorded in the hospital's written records. Andrews, *supra* note 11, at 362. Other studies of hospital error include Robert H. Brock *et al.*, *Effectiveness of Nonemergency Care Via an Emergency Room: A Study of 116 Patients with Gastrointestinal Symptoms*, 78 Annals of Internal Med. 333 (1973) (explaining that only 27 percent of one cohort of patients seeking care in an emergency room received "minimally adequate medical care"); Knight Steel *et al.*, *Iatrogenic Illness on a General Medical Service at a University Hospital*, 304 New Eng. J. Med. 638 (1981) (showing that 9 percent of 815 consecutive patients had an iatrogenic event that was life-threatening or produced disability). Indeed, evidence suggests that a larger percentage of hospital deaths may be attributable to medical error than many people would expect. One study of patients who died in hospitals found that 40 percent were misdiagnosed; one third would have been expected to live if properly diagnosed. *See* Gawande, *supra* note 35, at 197–98.

The rate of medical error in the Harvard Medical study is striking for several reasons. First, the study was conducted based on medical records from New York hospitals in 1984. This was a period when the vast majority of insured patients were enrolled in fee-for-service insurance plans, and not health management organizations (HMO). Jon Gabel *et al.*, *The Changing World of Group Health Insurance*, 7 HEALTH AFF. 48, 52 (1988) (examining subscribers with employer-provided health insurance in 1987 and finding that less than 30 percent of employees with group health insurance were enrolled in a managed care insurance plan in 1987; enrollment was strongest in the west but only 8 and 1 percent in the south and east respectively). Fee-for-service insurance tends to create incentives for excessive treatment, and not undertreatment. Second, the error rate is quite high given that the Harvard Medical Study was structured in ways that would understate the rate of medical error. *See infra* note 108.

62 Elizabeth A. McGlynn *et al.*, *The Quality of Health Care Delivered to Adults in the United States*, 348 NEW ENG. J. MED. 2635, 2641 (2003).

63 Mark A. Schuster *et al.*, *How Good Is the Quality of Health Care in the United States?*, 76 MILLBANK Q. 517, 521 (1998).

64 INSTITUTE OF MEDICINE, TO ERR IS HUMAN: BUILDING A SAFER HEALTH SYSTEM 26 (Linda T. Kohn, Janet M. Corrigan & Molla S. Donaldson eds., 2000). This probably underestimates the total cost of the medical "error" because it does not include many infections that probably result from poor hospital practices, but nevertheless generally cannot be treated as "medical error" because it is difficult to distinguish infections caused by substandard care from infections that are a background risk of the procedure. Nevertheless, it appears that preventable infections increase the overall cost of medical care by billions of dollars.

65 *See* Mello *et al.*, *supra* note 30. Another study found that patient safety events in hospitals result in excess hospital charges of almost $5 billion per year, in addition to the other costs they impose on victims. *See* Chunliu Zhan & Marlene R. Miller, *Excess Length of Stay, Charges and Mortality Attributable to Medical Injuries During Hospitalization*, 209 J. AMER. MED. ASSOC. 1868 (2003).

66 *See* AGENCY FOR HEALTHCARE RESEARCH AND QUALITY, NATIONAL HEALTH CARE QUALITY REPORT (2009) *available at* http://www.ahrq.gov/ research/findings/nhqrdr09/qrdr09.html.

67 *See* Shavell, *supra* note 2.

68 *See* Rolph, *supra* note 31.

69 *See* Mello & Studdert, *supra* note 11.

70 *Id.*; *see also* Lori B. Andrews *et al.*, *An Alternative Strategy for Studying Adverse Events in Medical Care*, 349 LANCET 309 (1997) (analyzing medical errors in three surgical units based on on-site observation of error and finding that many errors are attributable to lack of knowledge, often related to lack of adequate supervision); *accord* Thomas J. Krizek, *Surgical Error: Ethical Issues of Adverse Events*, 135 ARCHIVES OF SURGERY 1359, 1360–61 (2000).

71 *See* Weiler *et al.*, *supra* note 44, at 42–44, 137–39; Andrews, *supra* note 11; Andrews *et al.*, *supra* note 70; INSTITUTE OF MEDICINE, *supra* note 64; Mello & Studdert, *supra* note 11.

72 *See* Weiler *et al.*, *supra* note 44; Arlen & MacLeod, *supra* note 3; *see* Andrews *et al.*, *supra* note 70; Mello & Studdert, *supra* note 11; INSTITUTE OF MEDICINE, *supra* note 64.

73 *See* Arlen & MacLeod, *supra* note 3.

74 *See id.*; Arlen & MacLeod, *supra* note 14.

75 We make this assumption to simplify the analysis for purposes of this chapter. The full presentation of the model assumes that patients are insured and considers the effect of insurance on incentives to select treatment. *See* Arlen & MacLeod, *supra* note 14. We employ this simplifying assumption here to enable us to analyze the way liability affects patients' risk of being accidentally injured by their medical care, without the complexities introduced by health insurance markets.

76 *See* Arlen & MacLeod, *supra* note 3.

77 *See* Arlen & MacLeod, *supra* note 14, which considers the situation where patients are insured and thus bear expected treatment costs ex ante, but do not bear actual treatment costs ex post. In this situation, ex ante the patient wants the physician to maximize the net benefit of treatment, including costs, but ex post (after the patient is insured) the patient wants the physician to maximize the expected benefit of treatment *excluding* cost considerations. If the insurer, not the physician, bears treatment costs, the physician selects the treatment that maximizes the expected benefit of treatment excluding costs. This implies that the physician can provide more intensive treatment than the patient would prefer ex ante, and more intensive than is optimal. *Id.* A standard of care based on physician custom will thus push physicians to provide excessive care. *See* Danzon, *supra* note 26. We abstract away from this issue in this chapter but it is addressed in Arlen & MacLeod, *supra* note 14.

78 *See* Shavell, *supra* note 2.

79 *See* Arlen & MacLeod, *supra* note 14.

80 Observe that, unlike the classic model—in which care is either too expensive or too high-risk, but not both—this model produces an equilibrium in which physicians select treatments for insured patients that are both excessively costly and of insufficient quality. Treatments are excessively costly when compared to the treatment choice that maximizes social welfare because physicians endeavor to select the treatment that maximizes the patient's expected outcome (b) instead of the treatment that maximizes the net benefit of treatment, taking into account treatment costs ($b-c$). Medical care is excessively risky because physicians underinvest in expertise, imposing on patients an excessive risk of injury from medical negligence. Arlen & MacLeod, *supra* note 3, at 1978. Observe also that if physicians invest in care post-contract, then physicians will underinvest in expertise, even if patients accurately predict the quality of care ex ante. This is because if actual expertise is noncontractable, providers who want to invest more in expertise cannot reap any benefit of doing so because patients will not be willing to pay more ex ante for the hope that the provider will eventually invest more in expertise, if expertise is non-observable and noncontractable. Thus, patients will expect providers not to invest optimally in expertise. This expectation will be correct because providers cannot cover the costs of the added expertise through higher prices. Thus, expertise will be suboptimal even though patients correctly anticipate providers' care levels. *Id.* at 1979.

81 *See* Arlen & MacLeod, *supra* note 14.

82 *See* Arlen & MacLeod, *supra* note 3; Arlen & MacLeod, *supra* note 14.

83 *Id.*

84 *Id.*

85 *See* Shavell, *supra* note 2.

86 *See* Arlen & MacLeod, *supra* note 3.

87 *Id.* States should also intervene to alter the behavior of medical institutions that affect patients' welfare: specifically hospitals and MCOs. States can provide these incentives by subjecting physicians, hospitals, and MCOs to malpractice liability for medical negligence. *Id.*; *see* Arlen & MacLeod, *supra* note 14.

88 *See* Arlen & MacLeod, *supra* note 14. This is not to say that the current system functions perfectly. It is plagued with problems, as discussed in Arlen, *supra* note 19. But these problems do not include the fact that liability is imposed on competent providers who erred accidentally.

89 *See* Thaler & Sunstein, *supra* note 6; Epstein, *supra* note 6; Havighurst, *supra* note 58; Robinson, *supra* note 6; Hylton, *supra* note 26.

90 *See* Arlen, *supra* note 19.

91 *See* Studdert *et al.*, *supra* note 23.

92 *See* Mello *et al.*, *supra* note 30.

93 *See* Abraham & Weiler, *supra* note 28; Arlen & MacLeod, *supra* note 14; Havighurst, *supra* note 22; Mello & Brennan, *supra* note 19.

94 *See* Thaler & Sunstein, *supra* note 6; Epstein, *supra* note 6; Havighurst, *supra* note 6; Robinson, *supra* note 6.

95 This part only discusses one form of contracting. For a thorough discussion of why contractual malpractice liability is inefficient, showing that collective non-negotiable contracting through organizations also can be inefficient, *see* Arlen, *supra* note 19; *see also* Arlen & MacLeod, *supra* note 3; and compare Wickelgren, *supra* note 27 (discussing contracting over products liability).

96 *See* Arlen & MacLeod, *supra* note 14. Consistent with the results of this model, empirical analysis reveals that inadequate expertise—which is defined here as any investment that affects the probability that the provider is able to provide the quality of care she wants to provide, and thus includes inadequate knowledge, as well as errors attributable to healthcare technology and systems—is an important cause of medical error attributable to individual providers. *See* Mello & Studdert, *supra* note 11. The argument against contractual liability is enhanced when we recognize that, in the case of medical care occurring within hospitals, many if not most injuries due to medical error are at least partially the result of "systems" errors attributable to the hospital. *Id.* When properly designed, malpractice liability can redress these systems errors. Clearly, liability aimed at improving the systems of medical institutions is a collective good since hospital systems benefit patients collectively and thus hospitals' incentives to improve their systems for the benefit of any one patient depend on their liability to all patients.

97 *See* Arlen & MacLeod, *supra* note 3. These investments in collective care include investments in obtaining the expertise needed to correctly diagnose patients and select the right treatment, as well as pre- and post-contractual investments in healthcare technology, staffing, and supervision. These investments benefit all of a provider's patients because providers usually use their expertise, improved administrative systems, and good health information technology when treating all of their patients, not just a select few. For example, once a physician develops expertise in a particular illness or treatment choice, she uses this expertise to benefit all affected patients. She will not knowingly deny some patients the right to that expertise because they have not paid for premium care. Similarly, physicians who develop administrative systems or surgical procedures to reduce error generally apply them to all relevant patients, and do not limit them to a select few. The claim that providers tend to standardize collective aspects of care—such as expertise, treatment assessments, and systems—even when patients have paid for care of differing quality is supported by evidence that the quality of care a patient receives from her physician depends not only on whether that patient has decided to insure through an MCO (which will place pressure on the physician to reduce costs), but also on whether a high portion of the physician's other patients are insured through an MCO. *See* Sherry Glied & Joshua G. Zivin, *How Do Doctors Behave When Some (But Not All) of Their Patients Are in Managed Care?*, 21 J. Health Econ. 337, 352–53 (2002) (concluding that the quality of care a patient receives from her physician depends not only on whether the patient is enrolled in an MCO, but also on whether the physician's other patients are predominately managed care patients); Paul A. Heidenreich *et al.*, *The Relation Between Managed Care Market Share and the Treatment of Elderly Fee-for-Service Patients with Myocardial Infarction*, 112 Am. J. Med. 176 (2002) (providing evidence that a patient's expected outcome from treatment by a particular physician depends on the portion of the patients enrolled in managed care in the local market and not just on that patient's choice of insurer); *see also* Richard G. Frank & Richard Zeckhauser, *Custom-Made Versus Ready-to-Wear Treatments: Behavioral Propensities in Physicians' Choices*, 26 J. Health Econ. 1101, 1102 (2007) (finding that physicians tend to follow norms rather than customizing care for individual patients).

98 Arlen & MacLeod, *supra* note 3, at 2003. The interdependence of patients' liability choices is heightened by the fact that many important medical care investments are "lumpy"—the provider faces a discrete choice between making a substantial investment in a particular type of care or no investment at all. In many situations, the decision by one patient to impose liability will not provide a sufficient threat of liability to induce the provider to undertake the expensive, lumpy, investment. *See* Arlen, *supra* note 19.

99 *Id.* A similar argument applies to negotiable contracting over liability of medical institutions. *See supra* note 96.

100 *See* Arlen, *supra* note 19.

101 The free-rider problem is particularly great when liability is needed to induce providers to make substantial, discrete, collective investments that cannot be undertaken incrementally, such as healthcare technology, improvements in administrative systems or support staff, and substantial investments in expertise. In this situation, each patient knows that her medical provider will make the investment only if she faces liability for a substantial number of her patients. If she does face this liability, she will make the investment regardless of what any particular patient does. If she does not, she will not make it, also regardless of what any one patient does. Given this, each patient will rationally waive liability because she knows that her decision will have no effect on the provider's expected investment in discrete care. *Id.*

102 *Id.* This problem could be addressed by the use of contracting with commitment, as when patients are presented with take-it-or-leave-it standard form contracts under which all patients contracting with the provider are required to make the same choice regarding liability. While this would reduce the collective good problem it would introduce other problems, as discussed in Arlen, *supra* note 19. These issues are beyond the scope of this chapter since the analysis does not turn on insights from empirical analysis of malpractice liability.

103 Epstein & Sykes, *supra* note 6, at 642.

104 David M. Studdert *et al.*, *Negligent Care and Malpractice Claiming Behavior in Utah and Colorado*, 38 Med. Care 250, 253 (2000) (finding that only 2.5 percent of patients injured due to medical error filed a malpractice suit). A study of medical error at a Chicago hospital found that only 13 of the 175 patients who were the victims of medical error that caused serious injury filed suit. Andrews *et al.*, *supra* note 70, at 312; Krizek, *supra* note 70, at 1360–61. In an early study out of California, Patricia Danzon found that only 10 percent of patients injured by negligent adverse events filed a medical malpractice case. Only 40 percent of these resulted in payment. Patricia M. Danzon, Medical Malpractice: Theory, Evidence and Public Policy 23–24 (1985).

105 Weiler, *supra* note 11, at 12–13.

106 Studdert *et al.*, *supra* note 23, at 2038; *see* Weiler *et al.*, *supra* note 44.

107 *See* Mello & Studdert, *supra* note 11.

108 Those who claim tort liability is regularly imposed on doctors who did not err often cite the Harvard Medical Study, Epstein & Sykes, *supra* note 6, at 642 (citing to the Harvard Medical Study as evidence that courts often focus on cases where physicians did nothing wrong), and find additional support in a study of medical error in Utah and Colorado by the core members of the same research team. Studdert *et al.*, *supra* note 104. Both studies are excellent studies of medical error. Yet neither study should be used to provide evidence on the quality of the tort system. Each included too few observations in which a suit was filed to enable scholars to draw any statistically significant conclusions regarding the tort system. *See* Patricia M. Danzon, *Medical Malpractice*, *in* 2 The New Palgrave Dictionary of Economics and the Law 626 (Peter Newman ed., 1998); cf. Studdert *et al.*, *supra* note 104 (noting that only 18 patients in the Utah/Colorado sample filed a claim). Moreover, the methodology used in the Harvard Medical Study to identify error understates the amount of error for

several reasons. First, the Harvard Medical Study relied on written hospital medical records to evaluate the merits of each claim. Yet evidence reveals that written hospital records do not document most medical errors. Arlen & MacLeod, *supra* note 3, at 1940 n.36; *see* Andrews, *supra* note 11 (finding that most errors detected by on-site observation were not recorded in the hospital's written records). Second, the Harvard Medical Study focused on errors identified within the hospital, and thus undercounted errors which were not discovered until years later by other medical professionals. *See* William E. Encinosa & Fred J. Hellinger, *The Impact of Medical Errors on Ninety-Day Costs and Outcomes: An Examination of Surgical Patients*, 43 HEALTH SERVICES RES. 2067 (2008) (explaining that the existence and consequences of error can remain hidden for years). Finally, the Harvard Medical Study employed a methodology to identify error that was designed to rule out close cases (that might nevertheless satisfy the "more likely than not" standard of proof employed in tort cases). Specifically, the Harvard Medical Study had two physicians review each claim; claims were not coded as involving error unless both doctors agreed that error had occurred. *See* Tom Baker, *Reconsidering The Harvard Medical Practice Study Conclusions about the Validity of Medical Malpractice Claims*, 33 J.L. MED. & ETHICS 501 (2005). These design features served the purpose of the Harvard Medical Study, which was to provide a conservative, but in the end startling, estimate of the rate of medical error. This design does not yield a good measure of litigation accuracy, however. *See* Andrews *et al.*, *supra* note 70, at 312 (finding that on-site evaluation of medical error reveals that eleven out of thirteen patients who filed tort suits were the victims of treatment-induced adverse events). In subsequent work, David Studdert and co-authors modified the methodology to include many more claims filed, information about quality of care going beyond written hospital records, and a standard for determining whether there is error that more closely matches the preponderance of the evidence standard used in the tort system. *See* Studdert *et al.*, *supra* note 23.

109 *See* Phillip G. Peters, Jr., *What We Know about Malpractice Settlements*, 92 IOWA L. REV. 1783 (2007); Patricia M. Danzon & Lee Lillard, *Settlement Out of Court: The Disposition of Medical Malpractice Claims*, 12 J. LEGAL STUD. 345, 347 (1983).

110 Studdert *et al.*, *supra* note 23, at 2028 fig.1.

111 *See* Peters, *supra* note 109.

112 Studdert *et al.*, *supra* note 23, at 2028.

113 *Id.* at 2029; *see also* Michelle J. White, *The Value of Liability in Medical Malpractice*, 13 HEALTH AFF. 75 (1994) (discussing evidence that claims involving negligence resulted in average awards of $205,000, compared with $41,800 for those with no negligence). For example, conditional on recovery, expected damages are higher when the physician erred. Henry S. Farber & Michelle J. White, *A Comparison of Formal and Informal Dispute Resolution in Medical Malpractice*, 23 J. LEGAL STUD. 777, 799 (1994) ("Controlling for severity, settlements in cases with bad care are estimated to be almost four times larger than in cases with good care."); Henry S. Farber & Michelle J. White, *Medical Malpractice: An Empirical Examination of the Litigation Process*, 22 RAND J. ECON. 199, 204–05 (1991) (presenting "strong evidence" that negligence matters in the determination of liability). Nevertheless, physicians in some specialties may face an excessive risk of payouts even when there is no error. *See* Mello & Studdert, *supra* note 11 (suggesting that pro-plaintiff errors are more likely when plaintiffs are infants).

114 Studdert *et al.*, *supra* note 23, at 2027.

115 Bernard Black *et al.*, *Stability, Not Crisis: Medical Malpractice Claim Outcomes in Texas, 1988–2002*, 2 J. EMPIRICAL LEGAL STUD. 207, 209 (2005) (finding that, controlling for medical inflation, damages evidence reports an annual increase of only 0.1–0.5 percent per year, and this increase is either insignificant or marginally significant).

116 *Id.*

117 *See* David Hyman *et al.*, *Do Defendants Pay What Juries Award? Post Verdict Haircuts in Texas Medical Malpractice Cases*, 4 J. Empirical Legal Stud. 3 (2007).

118 Empirical evidence that collateral course rule reform, which curtails recovery, is associated with an increase in mortality rates among black infants is consistent with this conclusion. Jonathan Klick & Thomas Stratmann, *Medical Malpractice Reform and Physicians in High-Risk Specialties*, 36 J. Legal Stud. S121, S134 (2007).

119 *See* Arlen, *supra* note 19.

120 *See* Abraham & Weiler, *supra* note 28; Arlen & MacLeod, *supra* note 3; Epstein & Sykes, *supra* note 6; Havighurst, *supra* note 58; Mello & Brennan, *supra* note 19.

121 *See* Weiler, *supra* note 11; Andrews, *supra* note 11; Mello & Studdert, *supra* note 11.

122 *See* Andrews, *supra* note 11.

123 Hospitals' policies determine the likelihood that a patient will be treated by an inexperienced medical provider, such as an intern; they also determine whether that inexperienced provider is properly supervised. Lack of supervision has been shown to be a contributing factor in 20 percent of medical errors where claims were filed. *See* Mello & Studdert, *supra* note 11.

124 Hospitals also affect error rates through their investment in healthcare technology. For example, many patients are injured each year by drug errors. *See* Gawande, *supra* note 35, at 63. Yet, only a small percentage of hospitals have adopted computerized physician order entry systems to prevent such errors. Michael L. Millenson, *Moral Hazard vs. Real Hazard: Quality of Care Post-Arrow*, 26 J. Health Pol. Pol'y & L. 1069, 1076 (2001). Surgery patients also face a significant risk of injury from foreign objects left in them during surgery. Susan Burton, *The Biggest Mistakes of Their Lives*, N.Y. Times, Mar. 16, 2003, at 48 (explaining that foreign objects are left in at least 1,500 surgery patients); Barbara F. Ostrove & Julie S. Lyons, *Surgical Errors Alleged at Stanford Hospital*, San Jose Mercury News, Apr. 30, 2002, at 1B (finding that surgical gauze remains inside patients with sufficient frequency that some surgical gauze companies have incorporated materials into their gauze to make it detectable by X-ray post-surgery). Hospitals could reduce these problems through adopting surgical materials count procedures pre- and post-surgery.

125 Prior to 2003, work hour guidelines allowed interns in the United States to work very long shifts. The resulting exhaustion contributed to medical error. *See* Christopher P. Landrigan, *Effect of Reducing Interns' Work Hours on Serious Medical Errors in Intensive Care Units*, 351 New Eng. J. 1838 (2004) (explaining that residents on the traditional extended schedule made 39.5 percent more "serious medical errors" than did residents on a lighter schedule); J. Todd Arnedt, *Neurobehavioral Performance of Residents After Heavy Night Call vs. After Alcohol Ingestion*, 9 J. Am. Med. Ass'n 1025 (2005) (finding that pediatric residents on a "heavy call" schedule committed 40 percent more errors than those on a light call schedule, and that residents had limited ability to diagnose their own impairment); Drew Dawson & Kathryn Reid, *Fatigue, Alcohol, and Performance Impairment*, 388 Nature 235 (1997) (finding that after 24 hours of wakefulness, cognitive psychomotor performance decreased to a level equivalent to a person with a blood alcohol content of 0.10 percent). Maximum shifts were reduced to 24 consecutive hours by the American Council for Graduate Medical Education (ACGME), but these shifts still produce error-causing exhaustion. Moreover, physicians' hours remain unregulated, in contrast with the European Union, which limits the duration of shifts for all physicians to 13 hours. *See* Laura Berger *et al.*, *Extended Work Shifts and the Risk of Motor Vehicle Crashes among Interns*, 352 New Eng. J. Med. 125 (2005).

126 *See* Mello *et al.*, *supra* note 30.

127 For example, hospitals significantly affect errors through their rules and practices governing the supervision of inexperienced physicians, procedures to prevent patient infection, procedures governing the hand-off of patients between shifts, and rules

governing the maximum shift that physicians may work. *See, e.g.*, Mello & Studdert, *supra* note 11 (explaining that a lack of supervision partially explains 20 percent of medical errors where claims were filed); Kevin Sack, *Swabs in Hand, Hospital Cuts Deadly Infections*, N.Y. Times, July 27, 2007, at A1 (explaining that deadly hospital-induced infections in the US could be reduced by 68 percent through better procedures; those adopted by European hospitals have nearly eliminated the risk of antibiotic resistant staphylococcus); Landrigan *et al.*, *supra* note 125 (finding that residents on the traditional extended schedule made 39.5 percent more "serious medical errors" than did residents on a lighter schedule); Arnedt *et al.*, *supra* note 125 (explaining that pediatric residents on a "heavy call" schedule committed 40 percent more errors than those on a light call schedule); Dawson & Reid, *supra* note 125 (showing that after 24 hours of wakefulness, cognitive psychomotor performance decreased to a level equivalent to a person with a blood alcohol content of 0.10 percent); cf. Berger, *supra* note 125 (explaining that in the US, non-resident physicians' hours are unregulated; by contrast, the European Union limits all physicians to shifts of no more than 13 hours).

128 *See* Mello & Studdert, *supra* note 11.

129 *See* Mello & Brennan, *supra* note 19.

130 *See* Mello & Studdert, *supra* note 11.

131 *See* Mello & Brennan, *supra* note 19. Consider, for example, the problem of hospital infections. Patients often suffer serious injuries as a result of infections. Traditionally, malpractice liability has treated infection as a background risk, not properly attributable to suboptimal care. Yet, while it often will be the case that patient infection cannot be attributed to the error of any individual provider, a growing body of evidence suggests that hospitals can dramatically reduce, if not eliminate, the risk of many infections by adopting better procedures. US hospitals have not felt sufficient pressure to do so since patients generally cannot recover for infections under the current system of individual liability. While Medicare and some insurance companies are improving hospitals' incentives to control infections by refusing to reimburse hospitals for added medical expenses associated with certain infections, this is only a partial solution and does not ensure that hospitals bear the full cost of any insufficient attention to this issue. *See* Arlen, *supra* note 19.

132 *See* Abraham & Weiler, *supra* note 28; Arlen, *supra* note 19; Mello & Brennan, *supra* note 19; Sage, *supra* note 29.

133 *See* Weiler, *supra* note 11; Mello & Brennan, *supra* note 19; Mello & Studdert, *supra* note 11. For a discussion of the ways in which systems can cause preventable error without any one individual provider being clearly to blame, *see* Gawande, *supra* note 35.

134 *See* Abraham & Weiler, *supra* note 28; Arlen & MacLeod, *supra* note 3; Mello & Brennan, *supra* note 19; Sage, *supra* note 29.

135 *See* Arlen & MacLeod, *supra* note 3; Havighurst, *supra* note 58.

136 MCOs also affect quality through their authority to select the physicians and hospitals on their plans (to the extent permitted by state law), their ability to influence the treatment provided (through their ability to use utilization review to deny coverage for treatments deemed "unnecessary"), and through the financial incentives they give to providers to favor cost or quality. *See* Arlen & MacLeod, *supra* note 3.

137 *See* Glied & Zivin, *supra* note 97, at 352–53 (concluding that the quality of care a patient receives from her physician depends not only on whether the patient is enrolled in an MCO, but also on whether the physician's other patients are predominately managed care patients); Heidenreich *et al.*, *supra* note 97 (providing evidence that a patient's expected outcome from treatment by a particular physician depends on the portion of the patients enrolled in managed care in the local market and not just on that patient's choice of insurer); *see also* Frank & Zeckhauser, *supra* note 97, at

1102 (finding that physicians tend to follow norms rather than customizing care for individual patients).

138 *See* Arlen & MacLeod, *supra* note 3.

139 Many of these ways are not captured by the traditional model of vicarious liability. *See* Lewis A. Kornhauser, *An Economic Analysis of the Choice Between Enterprise and Personal Liability for Accidents*, 70 CALIF. L. REV. 1345 (1982); Alan O. Sykes, *The Economics of Vicarious Liability*, 93 YALE L.J. 1231 (1984).

140 *See* Arlen & MacLeod, *supra* note 3; Mello *et al.*, *supra* note 30; Mello & Brennan, *supra* note 19. The arguments favoring institutional liability go beyond the arguments presented here. The present analysis focuses on arguments that flow directly from empirical analysis. For a more detailed economic analysis of medical institution liability, *see, e.g.*, Arlen & MacLeod, *supra* note 3; Arlen, *supra* note 19; Mello & Brennan, *supra* note 19; *see also* Abraham & Weiler, *supra* note 28; Havighurst, *supra* note 58.

141 Malpractice liability would function better as a deterrent under entity-level liability because entity-level liability is not as distorted by liability insurance. Hospitals and MCOs either self-insure or purchase liability insurance that *is* experience-rated. *See, e.g.*, Arlen & MacLeod, *supra* note 3; Mello & Brennan, *supra* note 19, at 1617–18. Thus, entities subject to liability would have a strong incentive to reduce their risk of error. Entity-level liability also would reduce the distortions created by physician liability insurance because it would induce entities to use their rich data on physician quality to ensure that physicians who underinvest in quality bear more costs than those who do not. Finally, entity-level liability might improve the underclaiming problem because patients injured by medical care in a hospital would no longer be deterred from suit by the prospect of having to identify precisely the individual wrongdoer. These measures often would require MCOs and hospitals to invest in both equipment and changes in administrative systems to ensure broad monitoring of outcomes.

References

Abraham, Kenneth, and Paul C. Weiler. 1994. Enterprise Medical Liability and the Evolution of the American Health Care System. *Harvard Law Review* 108: 381–436.

Andrews, Lori B., Carol Stocking, Thomas Krizek, Lawrence Gottlieb, Claudette Krizek, Thomas Vargish, and Mark Siegler. 1997. An Alternative Strategy for Studying Adverse Events in Medical Care. *The Lancet* 349: 309–313.

——2005. Studying Medical Error in Situ: Implications for Malpractice Law and Policy. *DePaul Law Review* 54: 357–392.

Arlen Jennifer. 1985. Note, An Economic Analysis of Tort Damages for Wrongful Death. *New York University Law Review* 60: 1113–1136.

——2005. Torts, Expertise, and Authority: Liability of Physicians and Managed Care Organizations. *The RAND Journal of Economics* 36: 494–519.

——2006. Private Contractual Alternatives to Malpractice Liability. In *Medical Malpractice and the US Healthcare System: New Century, Different Issues*, edited by Rogan Kersh and William M. Sage. Cambridge, MA: Cambridge University Press, pp. 245–266.

——2010. Contracting Over Liability: Medical Malpractice and the Cost of Choice. *University of Pennsylvania Law Review* 158: 957–1023.

Arlen, Jennifer, and W. Bentley MacLeod. 2003. Malpractice Liability for Physicians and Managed Care Organizations. *New York University Law Review* 78: 1929–2006.

Arnedt, J. Todd, Judith Owens, Megan Crouch, Jessica Stahl, and Mary A. Carskadon. 2005. Neurobehavioral Performance of Residents after Heavy Night Call vs. after Alcohol Ingestion. *The Journal of the American Medical Association* 9: 1025–1033.

Avraham, Ronen. 2007. An Empirical Study of the Impact of Tort Reforms on Medical Malpractice Settlement Payments. *The Journal of Legal Studies* 36: S183–S229.

Baba-Akbari Sari, Ali, Trevor A. Sheldon, Alison Cracknell, Alastair Turnbull, Yvonne Dobson, Celia Grant, William Gray, and Aileen Richardson. 2007. Extent, Nature and Consequences of Adverse Events: Results of a Retrospective Case Note Review in a Large NHS Hospital. *British Medical Journal* 16: 434–439.

Baker, Tom. 2005. Reconsidering the Harvard Medical Practice Study Conclusions about the Validity of Medical Malpractice Claims. *The Journal of Law, Medicine & Ethics* 33: 501–514.

Berger, Laura K., Brian E. Cade, Najib T. Ayas, and John W. Cronin. 2005. Extended Work Shifts and the Risk of Motor Vehicle Crashes among Interns. *The New England Journal of Medicine* 352: 125–134.

Black, Bernard S., Charles M. Silver, David A. Hyman, and William M. Sage. 2005. Stability Not Crisis: Medical Malpractice Outcomes in Texas, 1988–2002. *Journal of Empirical Legal Studies* 2: 207–259.

Brook, Robert H., Morris H. Berg, and Philip A. Schechter. 1973. Effectiveness of Nonemergency Care Via an Emergency Room: A Study of 116 Patients with Gastrointestinal Symptoms. *Annals of Internal Medical* 78: 333–339.

Brown, John Prather. 1973. Toward an Economic Theory of Liability. *Journal of Legal Studies* 2: 323–349.

Calfee, John E., and Richard Craswell. 1986. Deterrence and Uncertain Legal Standards. *The Journal of Law, Economics and Organization* 2: 279–303.

Chassin, Mark R., Edward L. Hannan, and Barbara A. DeBuono. 1996. Benefits and Hazards of Reporting Medical Outcomes Publicly. *The New England Journal of Medicine* 334: 394–398.

Cooter, Robert D. 1984. Prices and Sanctions. *Columbia Law Review* 84: 1523–1560.

Danzon, Patricia M. 1985. *Medical Malpractice: Theory, Evidence and Public Policy*. Cambridge, MA: Harvard University Press.

——1997. Tort Liability: A Minefield for Managed Care? *The Journal of Legal Studies* 26: 491–519.

——1998. Medical Malpractice. In vol. 2 of *The New Palgrave Dictionary of Economics and the Law*, edited by Peter Newman. Hampshire: Palgrave Macmillan, pp. 626–635.

——2000. Liability for Medical Malpractice. In vol. 1B of *Handbook of Health Economics*, edited by Anthony J. Culyer and Joseph P. Newhouse. Amsterdam: North Holland, pp. 1339–1404.

Danzon, Patricia, and Lee Lillard. 1983. Settlement Out of Court: The Disposition of Medical Malpractice Claims. *The Journal of Legal Studies* 12: 345–377.

Dawson, Drew, and Kathryn Reid. 1997. Fatigue, Alcohol and Performance Impairment. *Nature* 388: 235–237.

Encinosa, William E., and Fred J. Hellinger. 2008. The Impact of Medical Errors on Ninety-Day Costs and Outcomes: An Examination of Surgical Patients. *Health Services Research* 43: 2067–2085.

Epstein, Richard A. 1976. Medical Malpractice: The Case for Contract. *American Bar Foundation Research Journal* 1: 87–149.

——2005. Contractual Principle Versus Legislative Fixes: Coming to Closure on the Unending Travails of Medical Malpractice. *DePaul Law Review* 54: 503–526.

Epstein, Richard A., and Alan O. Sykes. 2001. The Assault on Managed Care: Vicarious Liability, ERISA Preemption, and Class Actions. *The Journal of Legal Studies* 30: 625–659.

Farber, Henry S., and Michelle J. White. 1991. Medical Malpractice: An Empirical Examination of the Litigation Process. *The RAND Journal of Economics* 22: 199–217.

——1994. A Comparison of Formal and Informal Dispute Resolution in Medical Malpractice. *The Journal of Legal Studies* 23: 777–806.

Frank, Richard G., and Richard Zeckhauser. 2007. Custom-Made Versus Ready-to-Wear Treatments: Behavioral Propensities in Physicians' Choices. *Journal of Health Economics* 26: 1101–1127.

Gabel, Jon, Cindy Jajich-Toth, and Gregory de Lissovoy. 1988. The Changing World of Group Health Insurance. *Health Affairs* 7: 48–65.

Gawande, Atul. 2003. *Complications: A Surgeon's Notes on an Imperfect Science*. New York, NY: Picador.

Geistfeld, Mark. 1994. The Political Economy of Neocontractual Proposals for Products Liability Reform. *Texas Law Review* 72: 803–847.

Glied, Sherry. 2000. Managed Care. In vol. 1A of *Handbook of Health Economics*, edited by Anthony J. Culver and Joseph P. Newhouse. Amsterdam: North Holland, pp. 707–753.

Glied, Sherry, and Joshua G. Zivin. 2002. How Do Doctors Behave When Some (But Not All) of Their Patients Are in Managed Care? *Journal of Health Economics* 21: 337–353.

Havighurst, Clark C. 1984. Doctors and Hospitals: An Antitrust Perspective on Traditional Relationships. *Duke Law Journal* 1984: 1071–1162.

——1986. Private Reform of Tort-Law Dogma: Market Opportunities and Legal Obstacles. *Law and Contemporary Problems* 49: 143–172.

——2000. Vicarious Liability: Relocating Responsibility for the Quality of Medical Care. *American Journal of Law & Medicine* 26: 7–29.

Heidenreich, Paul A., Mark McClellan, Craig Frances, and Laurence C. Baker. 2002. The Relation Between Managed Care Market Share and the Treatment of Elderly Fee-for-Service Patients with Myocardial Infarction. *American Journal of Medicine* 112: 176–182.

Hylton, Keith N. 2000. Agreements to Waive or to Arbitrate Legal Claims: An Economic Analysis. *Supreme Court Economic Review* 8: 209–263.

Hyman, David, Charles Silver, Kathryn Zeiler, Bernard Black, and William Sage. 2007. Do Defendants Pay What Juries Award? Post Verdict Haircuts in Texas Medical Malpractice Cases. *Journal of Empirical Legal Studies* 4: 3–68.

Institute of Medicine. 2000. *To Err is Human: Building a Safer Health System*, edited by Linda T. Kohn, Janet M. Corrigan, and Molla S. Donaldson. Washington, DC: National Academies Press.

Jewett, Jacquelyn J., and Judith H. Hibbard. 1996. Comprehension of Quality Care Indicators: Differences among Privately Insured, Publicly Insured, and Uninsured. *Health Care Finance Review* 18: 75–94.

Kahan, Marcel. 1989. Causation and Incentives to Take Care under the Negligence Rule. *The Journal of Legal Studies* 18: 427–447.

Kaiser Family Foundation, and Agency for Healthcare Research and Quality. Dec. 2000. *National Survey on Americans as Health Care Consumers: An Update on the Role of Quality Information*. Rockville, MD: AHRQ.

Klick, Jonathan, and Thomas Stratmann. 2007. Medical Malpractice Reform and Physicians in High-Risk Specialties. *The Journal of Legal Studies* 36: S121–S142.

Kornhauser, Lewis A. 1982. An Economic Analysis of the Choice Between Enterprise and Personal Liability for Accidents. *California Law Review* 70: 1345–1392.

Krizek, Thomas J. 2000. Surgical Error: Ethical Issues of Adverse Events. *Archives of Surgery* 135: 1359–1366.

Landrigan, Christopher P., Jeffrey M. Rothschild, John W. Cronin, Rainu Kaushal, Elisabeth Burdick, Joel T. Katz, Craig M. Lilly, Peter H. Stone, Steven W. Lockley, David W. Bates, and Charles A. Czeisler. 2004. Effect of Reducing Interns' Work Hours on Serious Medical Errors in Intensive Care Units. *The New England Journal of Medicine* 351: 1838–1848.

McGlynn, Elizabeth A., Steven M. Asch, John Adams, Joan Keesey, Jennifer Hicks, Alison DeCristofaro, and Eve A. Kerr. 2003. The Quality of Health Care Delivered to Adults in the United States. *The New England Journal of Medicine* 348: 2635–2645.

Mello, Michelle M., and David M. Studdert. 2008. Deconstructing Negligence: The Role of Individual and System Factors in Causing Medical Injuries. *Georgetown Law Journal* 96: 599–623.

Mello, Michelle M., and Troyan A. Brennan. 2002. Deterrence of Medical Errors: Theory and Evidence for Malpractice Reform. *Texas Law Review* 80: 1595–1637.

Mello, Michelle M., David M. Studdert, Eric J. Thomas, Catherine S. Yoon, and Troyen A. Brennan. 2007. Who Pays for Medical Errors? An Analysis of Adverse Event Costs, the Medical Liability System, and Incentives for Patient Safety Improvement. *Journal of Empirical Legal Studies* 4: 835–860.

Millenson, Michael L. 2001. Moral Hazard vs. Real Hazard: Quality of Care Post-Arrow. *Journal of Health Politics, Policy and Law* 26: 1069–1080.

Peters, Philip G., Jr. 2007. What We Know About Malpractice Settlements. *Iowa Law Review* 92: 1783–1833.

Robinson, Glen O. 1986. Rethinking the Allocation of Medical Malpractice Risks Between Patients and Providers. *Law and Contemporary Problems* 49: 173–199.

Rolph, John E., John L. Adams, and Kimberly A. McGuigan. 2007. Identifying Malpractice-Prone Physicians. *Journal of Empirical Legal Studies* 4: 125–153.

Sage, William. 1999. Regulating through Information: Disclosure Laws and American Health Care. *Columbia Law Review* 99: 1701–1829.

Schuster, Mark A., Elizabeth A. Mcglynn, and Robert H. Brook. 1998. How Good is the Quality of Health Care in the United States. *The Milbank Quarterly* 76: 517–563.

Schwartz, Gary. 1998. Medical Malpractice, Tort, Contract, and Managed Care. *University of Illinois Law Review* 3: 885–907.

Sharkey, Catherine M. 2005. Unintended Consequences of Medical Malpractice Damages Caps. *New York University Law Review* 80: 391–512.

Shavell, Steven. 1980. Strict Liability Versus Negligence. *The Journal of Legal Studies* 9: 1–25.

Steel, Knight, Paul M. Gartman, Caroline Crescenzi, and Jennifer Anderson. 1981. Iatrogenic Illness on a General Medical Service at a University Hospital. *New England Journal of Medicine* 304: 638–642.

Studdert, David M., Eric J. Thomas, Helen R. Burstin, Brett I. W. Zbar, E. John Orav, and Troyen A. Brennan. 2000. Negligent Care and Malpractice Claiming Behavior in Utah and Colorado. *Medical Care* 38: 250–260.

Studdert, David M., Michelle M. Mello, Atul A. Gawande, Tejal K. Gandhi, Allen Kachalia, Catherine Yoon, Ann Louise Puopolo, and Troyen A. Brennan. 2006. Claims, Errors, and Compensation Payments in Medical Malpractice Litigation. *The New England Journal of Medicine* 354: 2024–2033.

Sykes, Alan O. 1984. The Economics of Vicarious Liability. *The Yale Law Journal* 93: 1231–1280.

Thaler, Richard H., and Cass R. Sunstein. 2009. *Nudge: Improving Decisions about Health, Wealth, and Happiness*. New York, NY: Penguin.

Weiler, Paul C. 1991. *Medical Malpractice on Trial*. Cambridge, MA: Harvard University Press.

Weiler, Paul C., Howard Hiatt, Joseph P. Newhouse, William G. Johnson, Troyen Brennan, and Lucian Leape. 1993. *A Measure of Medical Malpractice: Medical Injury, Malpractice Litigation, and Patient Compensation*. Cambridge, MA: Harvard University Press.

White, Michelle J. 1994. The Value of Liability in Medical Malpractice. *Health Affairs* 13: 75–87.

Wickelgren, Abraham. 2006. The Inefficiency of Contractually-Based Liability with Rational Consumers. *Journal of Law, Economics, and Organization* 22: 168–183.

Zhan, Chunliu, and Marlene R. Miller. 2003. Excess Length of Stay, Charges and Mortality Attributable to Medical Injuries During Hospitalization. *The Journal of the American Medical Association* 290: 1868–1874.

3 How do we decide how long to incarcerate?

David S. Abrams[1]

Introduction

With over 2.4 million Americans behind bars (as of 2008),[2] devising a more rational incarceration policy is of paramount importance for both crime control and economic reasons. The topic of depriving an individual of his freedom is one that arouses substantial moral intuitions and arguments. I take a different approach: an economic one. As with other important policy considerations, decisions about crime, punishment, and incarceration must be based on rational, fact-based studies and cannot be left to often ill-informed theorizing.

In this chapter, I build on some of my recent work and supplement this analysis with other research that shares one attribute: the careful analysis of empirical data sufficient to allow for causal inference. Unfortunately, the vast majority of criminal justice research lacks this character, and thus many studies yield unjustified or uncertain conclusions. Poor inputs lead to poor policy analysis, and thus until recently it was difficult to draw meaningful policy implications from academic research. This is not the first attempt to do so, but I hope it represents a more sophisticated attempt than has come before. It should certainly not be the last.

The goal is to use quantitative estimates of each of the principal effects of incarceration to provide guidance on when incarceration makes sense. Doing so requires the results of a number of recent studies on general deterrence, specific deterrence, incapacitation, and the cost of crime. There are certainly other important implications of incarceration that will not be accounted for, but I assume these to be the primary ones. I now explain why these are the mechanisms on which I focus in this chapter.

Incarceration (and other penalties) can reduce crime simply by its threatened use. This effect is called general deterrence by criminologists, and it has the advantage of potentially reducing crime without increasing costs at all (or even reducing them)—because crime reduction due to longer sentences is concomitant with a reduction of incarcerated individuals (although increase in duration of incarceration). There has been and continues to be much debate among economists and criminologists about the magnitude and even existence of general deterrence. I report some of the most recent findings from my own work and those of others that generally find a non-zero, but relatively small general deterrent effect.

Another pathway through which incarceration can impact crime is its effect on those who experience it. Does a prison term make an individual less likely to commit crime, having been chastened by the experience? Or do individuals learn to be better criminals while behind bars? Knowing the answers to these questions is clearly essential to understanding the overall impact of incarceration. The net effect of the experience of incarceration on crime is called specific deterrence. It is very difficult to obtain a causal estimate of it because this requires a situation approximating random assignment of sentences to offenders. In a recent paper, I use a natural experiment where offenders are randomly assigned to public defenders as a way to approximate the random assignment of sentences.

Incapacitation describes the simple, direct impact of incarceration on crime: the fact that offenders are unable to commit crimes (outside of prison) during their period of incarceration. While simple to state, incapacitation is not simple to estimate, and must account for replacement effects (the fact that locking up a criminal means another may very well take his place).

Incarceration carries explicit costs, including direct financial costs of feeding, clothing, housing, and monitoring prisoners. I use the most recent estimates from the literature to estimate these costs. In addition, there are costs to prisoners themselves, in terms of lost wages as well as lost freedom. I build on work with Chris Rohlfs in which we estimate the magnitude of these factors using individual bail decisions.[3] There are also costs incurred by relatives and friends of offenders, some of which may be incorporated into the bail decision.

In order to balance the costs and benefits of incarceration, it is necessary to choose one unit to measure everything. Putting everything in dollar terms is both necessary and difficult. Putting a dollar figure on crime victimization or freedom is an inherently challenging exercise. Fortunately, there have been some clever attempts to use individual choices as indicia of their valuations of these abstract quantities through the mechanism of revealed preference. I use work by Mark Cohen and others to estimate the cost of foregone crime via the various pathways of incarceration's impact.[4]

There are other ways in which incarceration may directly or indirectly affect crime and aggregate welfare. Reduced employment prospects for ex-inmates is one mechanism that will not be addressed in this chapter. While there is good evidence (see, e.g., Kling[5]) that earnings are reduced, if one assumes efficient labor markets, this should not have an overall welfare effect. I will also not attempt to value retribution in this chapter. Very little is known about this empirically, although there is some recent experimental evidence (see, e.g., Fehr *et al.*[6]) that indicates that individuals are willing to pay in order to punish others. Additionally, rehabilitation will not be explicitly valued in this chapter, except as it is incorporated into specific deterrence.

Because incarceration is by far the most widely used punishment for serious crime in most countries, it is the only mechanism for reducing crime that I consider in this chapter. This is not to say that changes in expenditures on imprisonment are the most effective way to increase the efficiency of the criminal justice system. A number of recent papers suggest that increasing the probability, as opposed to the magnitude of deterrence may be a more cost-effective way to decrease crime.[7] But since incarceration is likely to remain an important component of criminal justice expenditures for the foreseeable future, it is the focus of this chapter.

It is important to stress that this is one of the first attempts at a welfare analysis of incarceration and, as such, has a number of limitations. The results are based on the studies I rely on, each of which has important limitations. In addition, there is a limit to how much I am able to account for individual characteristics (race, sex, criminal history, socioeconomic status), differences by jurisdiction, by time, or by type of crime, although of course these are important in policy-making. My hope is that this will set out the framework for estimating the value of incarceration, and that the estimates will be substantially improved as our understanding of the underlying phenomena increases.

The rest of the chapter is structured as follows. In the next section, General deterrence, I discuss research and estimates about general deterrence. The following section does the same for specific deterrence and the section thereafter for incapacitation. In the section entitled Analysis and results, I introduce the cost of crime estimates that will be used and present the main results, combining all of the aforementioned factors. I discuss the policy implications and limitations on the results in the penultimate section and conclude in the final section.

General deterrence

Background

There has been a great deal of research on general deterrence over the past several decades, but a lack of consensus remains. Recent literature reviews on general deterrence have mixed conclusions. Nagin (1998) finds evidence for an overall deterrent effect in the criminal justice system, but believes more work is needed to better establish that increased sentences deter crime.[8] Doob and Webster (2003) review a handful of papers by economists and a large number by criminologists and conclude that the lack of strong evidence for deterrence is widespread enough to conclude that there is a null effect.[9] These authors, along with Frank Zimring (Webster, Doob, and Zimring 2006), pay particular attention to Kessler and Levitt's 1999 paper, which they do not finding convincing.[10] Robinson and Darley (2004) take a more nuanced view that there are circumstances in which increased sentences may deter, although they argue that the magnitude is insufficient to influence policy decisions.[11] In the *Handbook of Law and Economics*, Levitt and Miles (2007) discuss several economic studies that find evidence for general deterrence, but conclude that more research on the topic is necessary.[12]

Ehrlich (1981) performs some of the most publicized empirical work on deterrence by an economist and focuses to a great extent on murder.[13] In the past 15 years, greater attention has been paid to the careful identification of deterrence, as well as the separation of deterrence and incapacitation effects, as in Levitt (1998a).[14] Other examples include an investigation into the effects of California's three strikes law by Helland and Tabarrok (2007). They find a decrease in arrests of around 20 percent among felons with two strikes.[15] An Italian natural experiment that resulted in individual-level variation in sentencing is investigated in Drago, Galbiati, and Vertova (2009).[16]

Finding discontinuities in sentences is one of the primary obstacles to obtaining good empirical estimates of general deterrence; sentencing changes at the age of majority are perhaps the most commonly used type of discontinuity. Interstate differences in the relative harshness of adult sanctions versus those of juveniles are used in Levitt (1998b).[17] He finds that those states with larger jumps in punishment have larger decreases in adult crime relative to juvenile. Hjalmarsson (2009) examines offender perceptions of penalties and finds that they vary much less than actual changes at the age of majority. She also finds little evidence of deterrence in self-reported data.[18] Using high-frequency data from Florida, Lee, and McCrary (2009) look for a discontinuity in offending around the eighteenth birthday.[19] They find a drop in crime of 2 percent around this discontinuity and suggest that part of the low response might be due to myopic behavior.

The approach I describe below uses a similar methodology to that of Kessler and Levitt (1999) in which they make use of sentence enhancements in California enacted by the passage of Proposition 8 to estimate deterrence.[20] The authors use a difference-in-difference and triple-difference approach, using variation by time, type of crime, and state to isolate the effect of the California law change. They also separate deterrence from incapacitation by examining changes in short-term crime rates for serious offenses with lengthy underlying sentences and find the mean three-year deterrent effect to be 8 percent. Another paper close in subject matter to that described below is that of Marvell and Moody (1995) in which they examine the effect of gun laws on a range of outcomes.[21] Using a data set on firearm sentencing enhancements, prison population, and crime, the authors find little evidence for impact of firearm enhancements on either deterrence or incapacitation.

Methodology

Any convincing research on general deterrence has to approximate random variation of sentence length in order to determine the causal effect on crime. Absent random variation, one is not able to distinguish a correlation between sentence length and crime (perhaps due to an unobservable variable) from a causal impact of sentence length. This is a common problem that constantly recurs in social science research.[22] General deterrence is even more difficult to gauge because increased sentences may impact crime through both general deterrence and increased incapacitation. Several recent studies (mentioned above) take pains to distinguish these effects, using California ballot measures, changes in sentence length at the age of majority, and a natural experiment in Italian prisons in order to do so. I now describe the approach I make use of in a recent paper[23] to gain a causal estimate of general deterrence.

Add-on gun laws result in increased sentences for defendants convicted of possessing of a firearm while committing a crime. These laws grew popular in the United States in the 1970s and 80s, with 30 states adopting one of these laws by 1996 (Vernick and Hepburn 2003).[24] One may use add-on gun laws as a unique set of natural experiments in order to distinguish the deterrent effect of incarceration from the incapacitative effect. The key to the approach is the fact that add-on laws apply only to defendants who would otherwise receive sentences of incarceration. Thus the short-term impact of an add-on gun law should be purely deterrent.

Consider the change in the gun robbery rate between the month before and the month after an add-on gun law goes into effect, in a jurisdiction where robbery carries a sentence of six years and the add-on is two years. After the law change, criminals convicted of gun robbery will now receive sentences of eight years instead of six. If there is no deterrent effect of the add-on law, there will be no difference in the number of defendants newly incarcerated the month before the introduction of the add-on law and the month after. If there is a change in the number of gun robberies in the month after the law's introduction, it cannot be due to a change in incapacitation, and the change may be attributed to the deterrent effect of the increased sentence length.

Several characteristics of add-on gun laws make them ideal for isolating the deterrent effect of incarceration. First, add-on laws were adopted in many different states, yielding many separate experiments for the analysis. Thus, Abrams (2012) is able to expand on previous studies of deterrence, which usually focus on a single state (see, e.g., Loftin and McDowall 1984; Kessler and Levitt 1999).[25] Second, the laws are generally only applied in cases in which the underlying crime would merit a sentence of at least several years. This allows a good amount of time to detect the deterrent effect. Finally, add-on laws were adopted over a long time period (over 40 years), during which there was substantial variation in crime rates. The temporal and cross-sectional variation in adoption of add-on laws makes it possible to control for time trends and state fixed effects.

Empirical estimates

Using hand-cleaned Uniform Crime Reports (UCR) data, newly collected data on add-on gun laws, as well as that from the literature, Abrams (2012) reports estimates of the deterrent effect of increased sentences. The main empirical results are from a regression of reported-log gun robberies per capita on post add-on law dummies. Table 3.1 reproduces these results, with each column representing a separate regression. The log specification is preferred because it counts equivalent relative declines in per capita gun robberies equally. "Balanced panel" indicates that data points were included only if they were within seven years prior to, or six years after the effective date for an add-on law. This is the maximum range of data that is available for all states that passed add-on laws. In half of the specifications the data is restricted to years after 1974 because there is a discontinuity in several variables in a large number of agencies in 1975 in the UCR data. Panels A, B, and C differ in the number of years included in coding the post-add-on dummy. For example, in panel B, the add-on law dummy is one for the first two years following the add-on law effective date and zero otherwise. All errors reported allow for intrastate correlation and are weighted by state population. All specifications included state and year effects and the controls for poverty rate, unemployment rate, racial composition, age composition, lagged police population share, and lagged imprisoned population.

Table 3.1 Impact of add-on gun laws on gun robbery rates

	Panel A: One year impact							
	Annual reported gun robberies per 100,000 residents							
	(1)	*(2)*	*(3)*	*(4)*	*(5)*	*(6)*	*(7)*	*(8)*
Post add-on law	–0.04	–0.06	–0.05	–0.02	–0.06	–0.07	–0.04	–0.01
Effective date	(0.06)	(0.04)	(0.03)	(0.02)	(0.07)	(0.05)	(0.03)	(0.02)
Post MM law effective	–0.04	0.00	–0.12	–0.13	0.01	–0.07	–0.07	–0.10
date	(0.07)	(0.08)	(0.10)	(0.09)	(0.06)	(0.07)	(0.16)	(0.10)
State-specific time								
trends	n	y	n	y	n	y	n	y
Balanced panel	n	n	y	y	n	n	y	y
Restrict to post-1974	n	n	n	n	y	y	y	y
Observations	15,516	15,516	2,975	2,975	12,979	12,979	2,234	2,234
R-squared	0.17	0.18	0.18	0.19	0.16	0.18	0.18	0.19
	Panel B: Two year impact							
	Annual reported gun robberies per 100,000 residents							
	(1)	*(2)*	*(3)*	*(4)*	*(5)*	*(6)*	*(7)*	*(8)*
Post add-on law	–0.12	–0.14**	–0.11**	–0.08**	–0.14	–0.15**	–0.10**	–0.06*
Effective date	(0.07)	(0.04)	(0.03)	(0.02)	(0.07)	(0.05)	(0.02)	(0.02)
Post MM law effective	–0.03	0.02	–0.10	–0.11	0.02	–0.05	–0.05	–0.09
date	(0.07)	(0.07)	(0.10)	(0.09)	(0.06)	(0.07)	(0.15)	(0.10)
State-specific time								
trends	n	y	n	y	n	y	n	y
Balanced panel	n	n	y	y	n	n	y	y
Restrict to post-1974	n	n	n	n	y	y	y	y
Observations	15,516	15,516	2,975	2,975	12,979	12,979	2,234	2,234
R-squared	0.17	0.18	0.18	0.19	0.17	0.18	0.18	0.19

Continued

Table 3.1 (Continued)

	Panel C: Three year impact							
	Annual reported gun robberies per 100,000 residents							
	(1)	*(2)*	*(3)*	*(4)*	*(5)*	*(6)*	*(7)*	*(8)*
Post add-on law	–0.14	–0.17**	–0.13**	–0.09**	–0.17	–0.18**	–0.11**	–0.05*
Effective date	(0.08)	(0.05)	(0.04)	(0.02)	(0.09)	(0.06)	(0.03)	(0.02)
Post MM law effective	–0.02	0.04	–0.10	–0.10	0.04	–0.04	–0.04	–0.10
date	(0.07)	(0.07)	(0.10)	(0.09)	(0.06)	(0.06)	(0.15)	(0.10)
State-specific time trends	n	y	n	y	n	y	n	y
Balanced panel	n	n	y	y	n	n	y	y
Restrict to post-1974	n	n	n	n	y	y	y	y
Observations	15,516	15,516	2,975	2,975	12,979	12,979	2,234	2,234
R-squared	0.17	0.18	0.18	0.19	0.17	0.18	0.18	0.19

* Significant at 5 percent; ** significant at 1 percent.

Source: Abrams (2012, pp. 44–53).

Note: The data consists of agency-year level observations. Standard errors reported in parentheses are clustered at the state level to allow for intra-state correlation in error structure. State and year effects are included in all specifications. Controls include poverty rate, unemployment rate, racial composition, age composition, lagged police population share, and lagged imprisoned population share.

Log per capita crime rate is the preferred dependent variable in Abrams (2012) and this preference may be illustrated by the following example. Assume Albany has a pre-gun-law level of 200 gun robberies per 100,000 residents and Seattle has a pre-gun-law level of 100 gun robberies per 100,000 residents. We might believe that the severity of the impact of a marginal crime decreases with level of crime, so a reduction from 100 to 50 gun robberies per 100,000 residents is more meaningful than one from 200 to 150 per 100,000 residents. If this belief about social preferences is accurate, it is appropriate to focus on the logarithm of the per capita rate of gun robberies as the outcome of interest.

Across specifications there appears to be a consistent finding that gun robbery rates decline after add-on gun laws go into effect. The impact is insignificant in the first year, but is significant at the 1 percent level after two or three years. The coefficients in Table 3.1 provide an estimate of the magnitude of the impact. Although the coefficients vary somewhat across specifications, there is a decline of 6–14 percent within the first two years and 5–18 percent within the first three years of introduction of the law. In the preferred specification (column 8), which is the most conservative, with a balanced panel restricted to post-1974 data and including state-specific time trends, there is an impact which seems to level off to 6 percent within two years, and 5 percent within three years. Note that the addition of state-specific time trends does not affect the coefficient substantially. This provides some support for the notion that the timing of add-on gun laws is exogenous.

In order to gain more information on the timing of the impact of the law change, Abrams (2012) estimates a regression of log per capita gun robberies on dummy variables for year relative to the date of passage of the law change in a particular

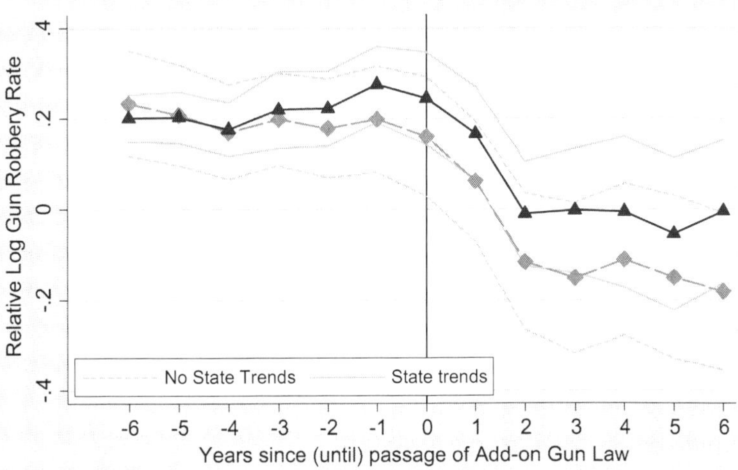

Figure 3.1 Gun robbery rate relative to add-on gun law passage date

Notes: All regressions control for state and year fixed effects. For details, see tables.
Source: Abrams (2012, p. 45).

state. The results, reported in Figure 3.1, support the findings discussed above. Gun robberies rates (both with and without controlling for state trends) are fairly stable in the years preceding implementation of an add-on gun law, then decline for approximately two years, and then level out.

The evidence from UCR data on gun robberies supports the notion that criminals are deterred by the implementation of add-on gun laws. There are a number of important confounds that could be belie this interpretation, and they are addressed at length in Abrams (2012). But it is important to take note of the strength of the evidence presented here. By using panel data with state and time fixed effects, the attempt is made to rule out that spurious results could be obtained due to an overall national time trend in crime, or cross-sectional endogeneity in passage of add-on gun laws. Adding state trends increases the strength of the exogeneity assumption by ruling out endogenous response in law passage not just to levels, but also to state trends in crime. Making use of timing dummies relative to the law effective date allows for the detection of the dynamic response of crime relative to implementation of the law.

Other papers use sentencing changes that are substantially different from those in this chapter, and so a comparison of elasticities is more illuminating. A quick back-of-the-envelope calculation yields an elasticity of approximately –0.10 in Abrams (2012).[26] This magnitude is consistent with that found by Lee and McCrary (2009).[27] They found allowable elasticities consistent with their data and model to have a magnitude no greater than –0.13, although their preferred parameter values yield elasticities close to 0. The largest recent empirical elasticity estimates come from Drago, Galbiati, and Vertova (2009) using Italian data, where they find a magnitude of –0.74 for seven months.[28] This may be an indication that the substantially lower incarceration rate in Italy makes it difficult to extrapolate to the United States. A back-of-the-envelope calculation using Helland and Tabarrok's (2007) results from examining three-strikes-induced change yields an elasticity around –0.07.[29]

Specific deterrence

Background

Another important way in which incarceration may impact crime is through the effect of incarceration on subsequent criminal behavior. A number of studies of specific deterrence have been made, but a large fraction of them suffer from omitted variables bias. For that reason, I focus on recent studies that make use of techniques that allow them to obtain causal estimates of the impact of incarceration on subsequent recidivating behavior.

Recent reviews of work on specific deterrence and recidivism (Nagin, Cullen, and Jonson 2009; Bushway and Paternoster 2009) point out the wide spread of findings in the field.[30] One of the reasons this is the case is that authors are frequently investigating slightly different questions. For example, one may investigate the extensive margin (the experience of any incarceration at all) or the intensive margin (the length of incarceration). In either case, one may examine jail or prison, first-time offenders, or recidivists. Whether examining either margin, obtaining some kind of randomization in the likelihood and length of incarceration is difficult. Once these definitions are clarified, and identification obtained, there is still the matter of defining and measuring recidivism, a subject about which entire books have been written (Maltz 2001).

Perhaps the best study on the subject is one of the earliest, a field experiment carried out in California in the 1970s (Berecochea and Jaman 1981). The California Department of Corrections chose a treatment group of prisoners to be released six months earlier than the control group. They followed the two groups for two years after the final release dates and compared recidivism rates. While the paper reports no significant difference in recidivism, in fact a simple t-test on the data shows that the early-release group has a significantly higher recidivism rate.

Kuziemko (2013) also looks at an early release of prisoners, in this case from a Georgia prison in 1981. That release was not part of a field experiment, so there is not a natural control group. Instead of a simple comparison of recidivism rates, Kuziemko uses variation in when prisoners' sentences began as an instrument for the amount of time ultimately served. She finds that an extra month in prison yields a 7 percent decline in recidivism, a substantial effect.

In 2006, Italy introduced a dramatic policy change where all inmates receive a sentence commutation of up to three years. As part of the policy change, prisoners with longer commutations also receive greater penalties if they are re-arrested. Drago, Galbiati, and Vertova (2009) study this policy change and find a substantial impact on re-arrest rates.[31] They find that prisoners that receive longer commutations have larger drops in recidivism.

While the experiment is significant, and although they find substantial changes in re-arrest rates, the interpretation is difficult. Because prisoners both have sentences shortened and penalties lengthened, the effect they estimate is a combination of specific and general deterrence. If, as some of the other studies discussed here suggest, the impact of specific deterrence is negative (less crime after longer incarceration) then general deterrence must dominate in the Italian experiment since defendants who received greater commutations had larger drops in recidivism. Another recent paper using a European natural experiment (Maurin and Ouss 2009) uses the 1996 Bastille Day pardon in France to estimate the effect of sentence reductions on recidivism.[32] They find that a greater sentence reduction via the pardon leads to an increase in expected future recidivism, consistent with a number of the other studies.

Turning back to American data, Hjalmarsson (2009) uses a regression discontinuity approach made possible by the Washington State juvenile sentencing guidelines to investigate the extensive margin of incarceration on juveniles.[33] She finds that juveniles who are incarcerated have a lower probability of recidivism than those who receive a local (non-incarceration) sanction.

A Maryland law change in 2001 is the natural experiment that Bushway and Owens (2012) exploit to examine how perception of sentence length impacts recidivism. Their paper is not directly comparable to other papers on specific deterrence because they propose a behavioral response of prisoners in which the frame of the sentence has an important impact on recidivism.[34] They find that shorter sentences relative to a reference point lead to higher recidivism rates.

In the next two sections I discuss recent work by this author (Abrams 2013) investigating specific deterrence using an instrument for sentence served. There are several recent papers that use a similar IV approach to the question, three of which use instruments based on judicial identity.[35] Loeffler (2013) uses judge-specific sentencing tendencies and random case assignment to obtain exogenous variation in sentence length.[36] This study, using data from Essex County, New Jersey, focuses on the extensive margin and does not find a strong relationship between incarceration and the likelihood of recidivism.

Berube and Green (2007) and Green and Winik (2010) use a very similar approach to that used by Loeffler.[37] The Green co-authored papers both make use of data from the DC superior court and both find little relationship between sentence length and recidivism. They find a negative and statistically significant relationship between incarceration length and recidivism when doing ordinary least squares regressions. But the sign becomes positive and the effect statistically insignificant when 2SLS or LIML estimation is performed (although the standard errors are larger).

The closest approach to that discussed below is found in Turner (2009).[38] Using the Clark County data set used here, Turner instruments for sentence length using random assignment to attorney and heterogeneity in attorney performance. She finds a mostly insignificant relationship between sentence length and recidivism, although one that varies somewhat by the recidivism window.

Methodology

As discussed above, much early research on specific deterrence was plagued by unobservables that could potentially confound findings. The studies mentioned above use several different approaches to address this problem. Here, I report a recent study in which I use a new approach to estimating the effect of sentencing length on recidivism. It is the first study that has the advantage of being fully non-parametric and allowing for a heterogeneous deterrent effect as a function of sentence length.

In a previous paper (Abrams and Yoon 2007) I investigate the impact of individual attorneys on case outcomes using data from the Public Defender's Office of Clark County (Las Vegas), Nevada.[39] One of the central findings of this paper is that there is substantial heterogeneity in attorney ability. Because public defenders are randomly assigned to first-time offenders and there is substantial heterogeneity in expected sentence by attorney, I use attorney assignment as an instrument for sentence length. Based on attorney assignment, I then estimate the impact of time served on recidivism.[40]

One challenge present in this context is that the relationships investigated are complicated and may not be well suited to a single coefficient as in an OLS or probit regression. I estimate both OLS and IV regressions, using different assumptions about the sentencing distribution. Depending on the model for the sentencing distribution, I find either a negative relationship or, more frequently, no significant relationship between recidivism and sentence length. The relationship between the variables is not always monotonic, and I further explore it through non-parametric techniques.

Empirical estimates

Table 3.2 presents the main regression results from the IV strategy, although, as I will discuss shortly, linear regression tells a very incomplete story in this context. Using an IV approach is important in this context to avoid the unobserved variables problem since unobserved criminal propensity is likely to bias the coefficient on sentence upward. This is borne out by examining the results reported in column 2 of Table 3.2, where the coefficient on sentence length is almost twice the magnitude as that in the OLS regression, where the first stage is linear. The coefficient is little changed when adjusting for the recidivism-age profile.

In the IV regressions, I find a statistically insignificant relationship between recidivism and sentence length. The relationship is actually more complicated: it is negative for relatively low sentence lengths and a flat relationship thereafter. The IV results are similar when any incarceration is the endogenous independent variable. Again, there appears to be a declining relationship for low probabilities of incarceration that flattens out as probability of incarceration exceeds about 40 percent.

Because of a potential weak instruments concern, I also perform a LIML IV regression, which should be consistent even with weak instruments. The point estimate from this specification is negative, but smaller in magnitude and statistically insignificant. An examination of two- or three-year recidivism finds negative coefficients, ones that are larger in magnitude than OLS (not reported here), and statistically indistinguishable from zero. Offender age is significantly negatively related to recidivism while black and male offenders have higher recidivism rates.

Another approach is to use a Tobit model for the first stage, which leads to somewhat distinct results, but ones that are consistent with the OLS first-stage results. The coefficient on sentence length is more positive for each of the three time windows examined, and all are still statistically insignificant. An examination of Figures 3.2 and 3.3 provides the visual analog of these regressions. While the IV approach is key to getting an unbiased measure of specific deterrence, the coefficients are not meaningful if the relationship between deterrence is not linear, as has been assumed thus far.

Besides examining point estimates, it is illuminating to make a visual inspection of the relationship between recidivism and sentence length. Figures 3.2 and 3.3 show a complicated relationship between recidivism and sentence length, one that is not well captured in a monotonic regression as reported in Table 3.2. The relationship between recidivism and sentence length is generally negative, but does not appear to be very linear (this may explain the insignificant regression results). The evidence seems to suggest that increasing sentences may reduce recidivism for short sentence lengths, but that the effect rapidly diminishes.

Table 3.2 IV regression results

Variables	One year recidivism					Two year recidivism		Three year recidivism	
	First stage OLS			First stage tobit	IV LIML	First stage OLS	First stage tobit	First stage OLS	First stage tobit
	(1) First stage sentence length	*(2) No age control*	*(3) Recidivism-age profile adjustment*	*(4) Recidivism-age profile adjustment*	*(5) Control for age at offense*	*(6) Recidivism-age profile adjustment*	*(7) Recidivism-age profile adjustment*	*(8) Recidivism-age profile adjustment*	*(9) Recidivism-age profile adjustment*
Sentence		–0.0148	–0.0157	–0.00478	–0.00715	–0.0126	0.00123	–0.00757	0.00514
		(0.00519)**	(0.00525)**	(0.00425)	(0.00434)	(0.00741)	(0.00544)	(0.0103)	(0.00824)
Sex (1 = male)	1.081	0.0735	0.0744	0.0624	0.0695	0.107	0.0923	0.1000	0.0901
	(0.123)**	(0.0101)**	(0.0103)**	(0.00965)**	(0.00873)**	(0.0142)**	(0.0128)**	(0.0171)**	(0.0161)**
Black offender	0.0516	0.0359	0.0359	0.0355	0.0338	0.0622	0.0622	0.0803	0.0791
	(0.110)	(0.00831)**	(0.00844)**	(0.00844)**	(0.00744)**	(0.0111)**	(0.0111)**	(0.0134)**	(0.0134)**
Hispanic offender	–0.0235	–0.0200	–0.0265	–0.0261	–0.0328	–0.0302	–0.0285	–0.0246	–0.0251
	(0.106)	(0.00888)*	(0.00886)**	(0.00887)**	(0.0105)**	(0.0124)*	(0.0123)*	(0.0156)	(0.0157)
Drug offense	0.896	0.0199	0.0240	0.0209	–0.0530	0.0392	0.0217	0.0214	–0.00385
	(0.187)**	(0.0145)	(0.0147)	(0.0164)	(0.0149)**	(0.0210)	(0.0228)	(0.0288)	(0.0330)
Violent offense	1.397	–0.0169	–0.0171	–0.0288	–0.0949	–0.0160	–0.0402	–0.0533	–0.0796
	(0.233)**	(0.0165)	(0.0166)	(0.0177)	(0.0157)**	(0.0237)	(0.0246)	(0.0311)	(0.0337)*
EFT	1.631	0.0357	0.0359	0.0223	–0.0437	0.0468	0.0215	0.0113	–0.0181
	(0.171)**	(0.0158)*	(0.0159)*	(0.0177)	(0.0167)**	(0.0220)*	(0.0235)	(0.0302)	(0.0325)
Sex offense	1.207	–0.0135	0.000429	–0.00687	–0.0807	–0.0369	–0.0481	0.0202	0.00150
	(0.361)**	(0.0276)	(0.0294)	(0.0307)	(0.0238)**	(0.0397)	(0.0411)	(0.0512)	(0.0532)
Age at offense	0.000453								
	(0.00425)								

Continued

Table 3.2 (Continued)

	One year recidivism					*Two year recidivism*		*Three year recidivism*	
	First stage OLS			*First stage tobit*	*IV LIML*	*First stage OLS*	*First stage tobit*	*First stage OLS*	*First stage tobit*
Variables	*(1) First stage sentence length*	*(2) No age control*	*(3) Recidivism-age profile adjustment*	*(4) Recidivism-age profile adjustment*	*(5) Control for age at offense*	*(6) Recidivism-age profile adjustment*	*(7) Recidivism-age profile adjustment*	*(8) Recidivism-age profile adjustment*	*(9) Recidivism-age profile adjustment*
Constant	–0.884	0.233	0.214	0.230	0.271	0.363	0.375	0.514	0.519
	(0.386)*	(0.0485)**	(0.0463)**	(0.0461)**	(0.0174)**	(0.0514)**	(0.0510)**	(0.0504)**	(0.0500)**
Observations	13,573	13,573	13,557	13,557	13,725	10,087	10,087	7,146	7,146
Adjusted *R*-squared	0.165	0.024	0.022	0.021	0.022	0.043	0.042	0.074	0.074

** $p<0.01$, * $p<0.05$. Robust standard errors in parentheses.

Note: Offender-level data obtained from the Clark County Public Defender Office for the years 2001–2008. Monthly time dummies included to allow for time variation in overall crime rates. Sentence is the minimum sentence measured in months. EFT = embezzlement, fraud, theft. Data includes 78 Public Defenders, each with a minimum of 50 cases and 51 judges. Recidivism is defined as reappearance as a Public Defender client with in the indicated time after release from incarceration (if sentenced to incarceration).

Source: Reproduced from Abrams (2013).

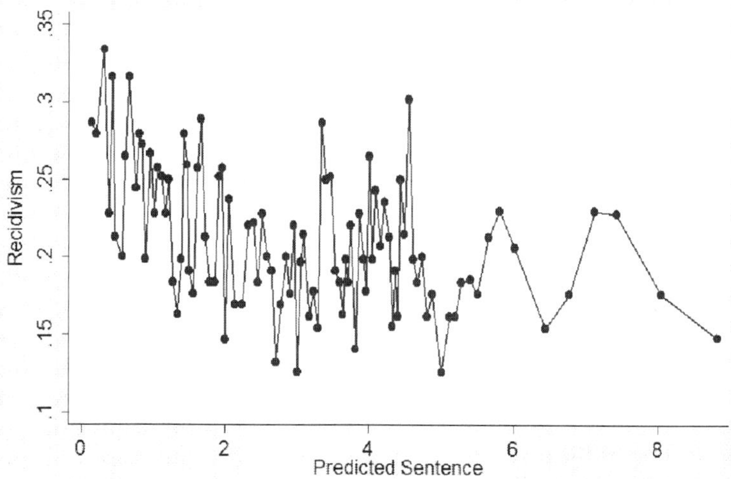

Figure 3.2 One-year recidivism rate vs. predicted sentence
Source: Abrams (2013).

In addition to the impact of a longer sentence on recidivism, I also investigated the extensive margin: the effect of a change in likelihood, rather than length, of incarceration on future recidivism. The results are reported in Table 3.3 and Figure 3.4. The OLS results here also appear to be upward-biased, as with the intensive margin. This likely results from the fact that there is a higher rate of judicial sentencing

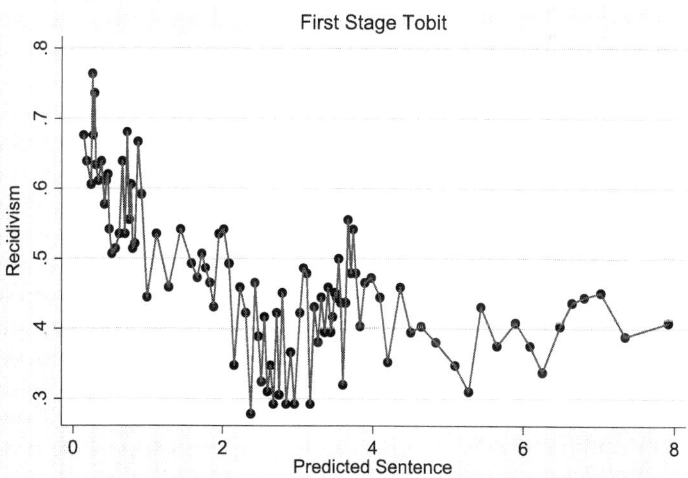

Figure 3.3 Three-year recidivism rate vs. predicted sentence
Source: Abrams (2013).

Table 3.3 Recidivism and incarceration

	One year recidivism		*Two year recidivism*		*Three year recidivism*	
Variables	*(1) OLS*	*(2) IV*	*(3) OLS*	*(4) IV*	*(S) OLS*	*(6) IV*
Incarceration	0.0335	0.00396	0.114	0.0148	0.159	0.0889
	(0.00774)**	(0.0437)	(0.0106)**	(0.0521)	(0.0131)**	(0.0804)
Sex (1 = male)	0.0543	0.0574	0.0807	0.0910	0.0777	0.0861
	(0.00836)**	(0.00954)**	(0.0115)**	(0.0126)**	(0.0146)**	(0.0162)**
Black	0.0333	0.0345	0.0565	0.0591	0.0706	0.0734
offender	(0.00832)**	(0.00839)**	(0.0108)**	(0.0109)**	(0.0130)**	(0.0134)**
Hispanic	–0.0272	–0.0257	–0.0325	–0.0289	–0.0311	–0.0288
offender	(0.00901)**	(0.00907)**	(0.0124)**	(0.0126)*	(0.0156)*	(0.0162)
Drug offense	0.00782	0.00995	0.00777	0.0161	–0.0257	–0.0358
	(0.0140)	(0.0186)	(0.0189)	(0.0259)	(0.0238)	(0.0436)
Violent	–0.0409	–0.0393	–0.0443	–0.0393	–0.0799	–0.0959
offense	(0.0147)**	(0.0188)*	(0.0201)*	(0.0261)	(0.0254)**	(0.0403)*
EFT	0.00654	0.00914	0.0115	0.0192	–0.0284	–0.0405
	(0.0134)	(0.0191)	(0.0179)	(0.0257)	(0.0222)	(0.0404)
Sex offense	–0.0254	–0.0223	–0.0510	–0.0500	–0.0164	–0.0337
	(0.0270)	(0.0309)	(0.0367)	(0.0407)	(0.0466)	(0.0563)
Age at	–0.00159	–0.00157	–0.00288	–0.00282	–0.00303	–0.00294
release	(0.000340)**	(0.000340)**	(0.000457)**	(0.000460)**	(0.000575)**	(0.000588)**
Constant	0.296	0.290	0.487	0.467	0.633	0.608
	(0.0490)**	(0.0498)**	(0.0535)**	(0.0546)**	(0.0532)**	(0.0545)**
Observations	13,573	13,540	10,103	10,059	7,156	7,110
Adjusted R-squared	0.026	0.025	0.060	0.050	0.100	0.082

** $p<0.01$, * $p<0.05$. Robust standard errors in parentheses.

Note: This table reports the results of OLS and 2SLS regressions or recidivism on a binary incarceration indicator. Offender-level data obtained from the Clark County Public Defender Office for the years 2001–2008. Monthly time dummies induded to allow for time variation in overall crime rates. EFT = embezzlement, fraud, theft. Data includes 81 Public Defenders, each with a minimum of 50 cases and 50 judges. A tobit regression is used for the first stage of the IV regressions reported in this table.

Source: Abrams (2013).

of individuals that appear more prone to commit crime based on characteristics unobservable to the researcher to incarceration. The point estimates for all time ranges are positive and statistically significant for OLS, but not for IV. It is possible that there could be a substantial positive impact of incarceration on recidivism of up to 10 percentage points, but due to the large standard errors in the IV specifications it is not possible to distinguish an effect of this magnitude from a null effect.

Incapacitation

My estimates of the effects on incapacitation are taken not from my own research, but from several recent papers that produce credible estimates of the crime-reduction effect of incapacitating the marginal offender. I review some of these papers and then use their estimates in calculations below.

There are several important challenges inherent in incapacitation research. First, the relationship between incapacitation length and crime is a complicated one, with the causal arrow almost certainly going in both directions. This has led to two main types of attempted solutions: structural modeling of the relationship and use of instrumental variables to break the simultaneity. The aim of either approach is to find a causal estimate of the elasticity of crime with respect to incarceration rate (usually denoted ε or η) and/or the distribution of offenses averted due to incapacitation (λ in the criminology literature).

Levitt (1998a) attempts to separate incapacitation from deterrence by comparing the impact of arrest rates for one crime-on-crime rates for that crime with crime

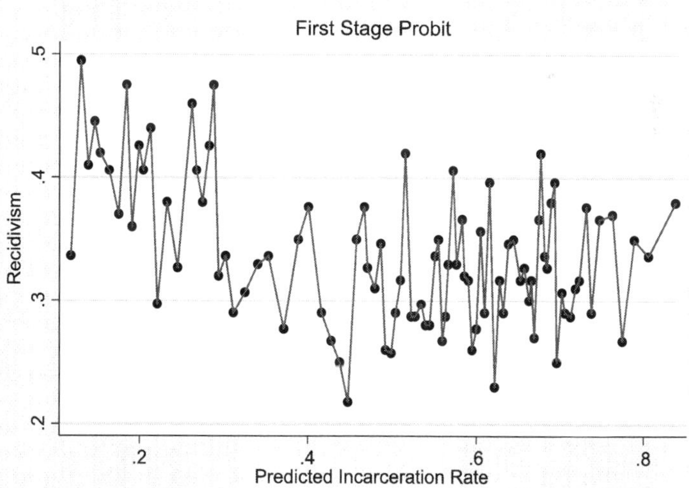

Figure 3.4 Two-year recidivism rate vs. predicted incarceration rate
Source: Abrams (2013).

rates for other crimes.[41] While there are endogeneity concerns with this approach, Levitt finds deterrence has a larger impact than incapacitation. His incapacitation estimates suggest that an additional person-year of incapacitation reduces or prevents 5.1 to 8.2 index crimes, depending on category. He notes that these numbers are somewhat lower than self-reports of 12 to 15 estimated crimes per year. This disparity could be due to multiple offender commission of single crimes. Offender reports also do not account for "replacement" effects—in other words, that the foregone crimes not committed by incarcerated offenders are likely to be at least partially replaced by non-incarcerated individuals.

Some of the best recent work on incapacitation was published in an issue of the *Journal of Quantitative Criminology* (JQC) organized by Shawn Bushway and Peter Reuter (Reuter and Bushway 2007). The papers in this issue both summarize much previous work from both the economic and criminology perspective, and add some new estimates. Piquero and Blumstein (2007) survey much of the recent literature and report on estimates of elasticity of crime with respect to incarceration:

> Estimates of the crime-reduction potential of incapacitation are both numerous and diverse, reflecting different assumptions made by different researchers (Cohen 1983; Visher 1987). Most incapacitation studies suggest that prison exerts a significant suppression effect on crime; however, the estimated effects vary markedly from study to study depending on the extent of incapacitation, how much the prison population is increased, and the values of the model parameters used (Spelman 2000a; Weatherburn *et al.* 2006). In an early review, Cohen (1978, pp. 219–221) estimated elasticities of –0.05 to –0.70, while Spelman's (1994, p. 220) estimates ranged from –0.12 to –0.20, with a best guess estimate of –0.16. DiIulio and Piehl (1991), using Wisconsin prisoner data from 1989, report an elasticity estimate of –0.22, while Piehl and DiIulio's (1995) analysis of New Jersey offender data indicates an elasticity estimate of –0.26. Likewise, Weatherburn and colleagues (2006) carried out an analysis of burglary offenders from New South Wales and obtained an adjusted elasticity of burglary with respect to imprisonment of –0.3. These various estimates cover a reasonable range of elasticity of about –0.2, or a requirement for a 5 percent increase in the prison population to achieve a 1 percent reduction in crime.

Table 3.4 Incapacitation estimates from previous work

Paper	*λ (crimes/ year avoided)*	*Elasticity*
Marvell and Moody (1995)		0.16
Levitt (1996)	5–8	0.31
Sweeten Apel (2007)	4.9–8.4	
Bhati (2007)—person	1.93	0.93
Bhati (2007)—property	9.47	0.69
Owens (2009)	1.5	
Johnson and Raphael (2011)—property	9	0.15–0.21
Johnson and Raphael (2011)—violent	0.15	0.06–0.11

Piquero and Blumstein include a number of studies that do not overcome the endogenous relationship between incarceration rates and crime. Still, the range of elasticities (–0.3 to –0.2) estimated in these studies are not far off from others that attempt to more explicitly deal with this problem. I summarize the elasticity estimates from the most reliable studies in Table 3.4.

Bhati (2007), in the same issue of JQC, uses a structural model of the offending process to estimate the incapacitation effect. His information-theoretic model is estimated using data from about a dozen state prisons on inmates released in 1994. He finds mean crimes averted in line with other studies. For property crimes, an average of 8.5 are averted per year of incarceration; the mean is 1.9 for crimes against persons. Bhati's elasticity estimates are substantially larger in magnitude than those of much other work, with a mean of –0.93 for crimes against persons and –0.69 for property crimes.

Owens (2009) uses a natural experiment to attempt to estimate the magnitude of the incapacitation effect. A law change in 2001 in Maryland reduced sentences for young offenders with juvenile records. She is thus able to gain a causal estimate of incapacitation on crime for this group. She finds a comparatively low impact of the foregone incarceration: about 1.5 crimes per year, a number several times lower than other estimates. This may be because the affected group is a particularly low-offending one.

Most recently, Johnson and Raphael (2011) use the fact that incarceration rates adjust to permanent shocks with a dynamic lag in order to estimate incapacitation effects. They find elasticities of between –0.06 and –0.11 for violent crime and between –0.15 and –0.21 for property crime. Moreover, they present evidence that the magnitude of the elasticities has declined in more recent years.

Analysis and results

Previous work (Donohue 2009; DiIulio and Piehl 1991) has focused on answering the hypothetical question "what would be the effect of incarcerating an additional individual?"[42] This omits the mechanism by which the additional incarceration is achieved. The potential mechanisms are numerous, including increased sentencing standards, policing, detection rates, prosecution rates, or reduced parole rates, among other possibilities. The mechanism by which incarceration is increased will almost certainly affect its overall impact and welfare effects.

This chapter attempts to determine the impact of a very specific policy change: a marginal increase in sentence lengths. As discussed above, the first-order effects of sentence length increase will likely accrue due to general and specific deterrence and incapacitation. These effects can be quantified using cost of crime estimates and weighed against direct costs of incarceration. I now proceed with this calculation.

The equation for the total elasticity of crime is:

$$\eta_{crime} = \eta_{GD} + \int_0^{life} \eta_{SD} f(sent)dsent + \eta_{Inc} \tag{3.1}$$

where η_{GD} is the elasticity of crime with respect to sentence length due to general deterrence, η_{SD} is the elasticity of crime with respect to sentence length due to specific deterrence, and η_{Inc} is the incapacitation elasticity. This equation assumes negligible discounting, which allows crime-reducing effects that will be realized at different times (like specific deterrence and incapacitation) to be added directly. It would be simple to incorporate a discount factor into the equation.

The net annual benefit (or cost) of a doubling of sentence lengths will be:

$$\text{Net Benefit} = \eta_{crime} * crime * c_{crime} - c_{prison} * prisoners \tag{3.2}$$

where c_{crime} is the cost of the mean crime, c_{prison} is the cost of a year of prison, *crime* is the number of crimes committed annually, and *prisoners* is the number of offenders incarcerated.[43]

I have discussed appropriate estimates for some of these parameters above. For η_{GD} I will use –0.10 estimated in Abrams (2012) and consistent with a number of other recent studies. Estimates of incapacitation elasticities were discussed above and summarized in Table 3.4. There is substantial variation in these estimates, but there seems to be a growing view that some of the more consistent estimates are toward the lower end, between –0.05 and –0.30 (Donohue 2009). I will focus on this range and examine the impact of allowing some variation.

The recidivism study discussed above is somewhat difficult to directly relate to an elasticity. Fortunately, it is not necessary to calculate this directly, since what is desired is actually the number of foregone crimes. Using the empirical recidivism crime profile (Figure 3.3) I estimate the increase in recidivism from a 1 percent sentence length increase. Using the sentencing distribution, $f(sent)$, from the same dataset, I can compute the number of expected additional crimes via the specific deterrence pathway. I find a 1 percent increase in sentence length should lead to a decrease in recidivism of about 0.1 percentage points.

Thus I now have a total impact on crime from a 1 percent increase in sentence length, a range from –0.25 percent to –0.50 percent depending on the value used for the incapacitation elasticity. All that remains is to use this information in the cost–benefit analysis (Equation (3.2)). For this, a few more parameters are necessary. For *crime* I use the 2005 level adjusted for underreporting of 28,892,802 as in Donohue (2009). Mean sentence length is derived from National Judicial Reporting Program data (Rosenmerkel *et al.* 2009) and found to be 37.2 months for all convicted felons sentenced to a jail or prison sentence in 2006.

Since much of the cost of crime may be indirect (e.g. crime prevention, behavioral response) or intangible (e.g. emotional distress), estimating its cost is quite challenging. Several approaches have been used, including: survey data (contingent valuation), jury awards, and hedonic pricing. The last of these is in many ways most appealing, because it is the only one that relies on actual expenditure decisions by individuals. I use cost estimates from Cohen and Piquero (2009) (reproduced in Table 3.5) that derive from both contingent valuation ("bottom up") and hedonic pricing ("WTP") approaches. These build on earlier work by

Cohen and co-authors, including the most comprehensive "bottom up" study to date, reported in Miller, Cohen, and Wiersema (1996).

The final parameter necessary is the cost of incarceration. Ideally, this should include direct costs of feeding, housing, and monitoring prisoners, as well as indirect costs like the value of lost freedom, foregone wages, impact on families, and capital costs. I estimate direct annual imprisonment costs at $25,000, which is in line with data from Hill and Harrison (2005), and Bierie (2007). In addition, I use the value of freedom calculated in Abrams and Rohlfs (2011) adjusted for the higher overall employment rate in the general offender population, relative to the sample they used (Cohen and Piquero 2009). This augments the cost of imprisonment by about $10,600 and should incorporate some of the impact on families and friends, as well as on foregone wages and lost freedom. I add $3,000 for capital costs, as in Donohue (2009), for a total incarceration cost of $38,600 per prisoner per year.

I now combine the various parameters to yield an aggregate social benefit/cost under these different assumptions. The results are reported in Table 3.6. As with other attempts at similar calculations, the results are quite sensitive to crime cost and also vary substantially as a function of elasticity. I discuss implications and limitations of these results below.

Policy implications and discussion

The exercise above yields a wide range of potential costs and benefits from a 1 percent increase in all felony incarceration sentences. At the low end, assuming

Table 3.5 Estimated "bottom-up" and WTP for crimes (2007 US dollars)

	Victim costs	*CJ costs*	*Offender*	*Total productivity*	*WTP estimate*
Murder	4.6 million	300,000	140,000	5.00 million	11.80 million
Rape	135,000	8,300	4,500	150,000	290,000
Armed robbery	29,000	14,700	8,000	50,000	280,000
Robbery	12,000	7,400	4,000	23,000	39,000
Aggravated assaults	37,000	13,500	6,400	55,000	85,000
Simple assaults	4,500	5,000	1,300	11,000	19,000
Burglary	2,000	2,300	1,000	5,000	35,000
Motor vehicle theft	5,500	2,900	1,000	9,000	17,000
Larceny	450	1,700	700	2,800	4,000
Drunk driving	28,000	1,700	700	30,000	60,000
Arson	57,000	1,700	700	60,000	115,000
Vandalism	370	630	–	1,000	2,000
Fraud	1,100	1,700	700	3,500	5,500
Other offenses (prostitution, loitering, false statements, etc.)	500	–	500	1,000	

Source: Reproduced from Cohen and Piquero (2009, p. 33).

Table 3.6 Net benefit calculation from inreasing sentence lengths

		Total crime elasticity				
		0.25	*0.3*	*0.35*	*0.45*	*0.5*
Low crime cost ($5,860)	Benefit (millions of dollars)	423	508	593	762	847
	Cost (millions of dollars)	1,355	1,355	1,355	1,355	1,355
	Net benefit (millions of dollars)	–932	–847	–762	–593	–508
High crime cost ($26,400)	Benefit (millions of dollars)	1,907	2,288	2,670	3,432	3,814
	Cost (millions of dollars)	1,355	1,355	1,355	1,355	1,355
	Net benefit (millions of dollars)	552	933	1,315	2,078	2,459

Notes: Benefits and costs from a 1 percent overall increase in sentence lengths of felony offenders sentenced to incarceration. See text for details.

Source: Author's calculations.

a total elasticity of 0.25 and a low cost of the average crime, the costs of the sentence increase would exceed the benefits by over $900 million. At the other extreme, using the high cost of crime estimate and the high range of the elasticity estimates implies the sentence increase would yield a net benefit of almost $2.5 billion.

Given the sensitivity to the cost of crime, what is a policymaker to take from these results? First, there is the obvious implication that greater research on costs of crime is necessary in order to narrow this very wide range of estimates. If any sort of rational criminal justice policy is to be possible, it will require more precise estimates of how much an averted crime is worth.

The cost of crime is a hugely understudied area by economists, who have tended to focus more on estimates of deterrence. This is not wholly surprising since many recent empirical advances have to do with carefully drawn causal inference. Methodologies to measure the cost of crime, like contingent valuation or using jury awards, have not advanced as much in the past two decades. The cost–benefit calculation makes it clear just how important it is to have more precise costs of crime. My hope is that this chapter will spur more research on this topic.

But even though the policy implications are ambiguous when considered in the aggregate, there is something more than can be derived from this work. Thus far, I have ignored variation by type of crime, location, criminal background, and other sources of variation. In reality, criminal justice policies vary according to all of these factors, as they should. It is a fool's errand to attempt a single unified incarceration policy for all crimes, criminals, and locales. Nevertheless, this study can help inform the realistically tailored incarceration policies.

For a given elasticity, one can calculate the cost of crime where costs of increased incarceration exactly balance the benefits, the break-even point. That is, where

$$\eta_{crime} * crime * c_{crime} = c_{prison} * prisoners \tag{3.3}$$

I solve this for c_{crime} using my preferred elasticity estimate of 0.35, implying an elasticity of about 0.15 for incapacitation. The break-even point under these assumptions is $13,400 per crime; assuming an overall elasticity of 0.30 yields a break-even of $15,600.

Now the break-even point can be used as a concrete criterion for considering changes in sentence lengths for particular crimes. For example, larceny or drug possession almost certainly imposes a societal cost of less than these amounts. Of course, they also (generally) currently carry lower sentences than the mean, so the calculation would need to be adjusted for this as well. But there will almost certainly be examples where the cost from certain crimes or offenders is well below the break-even point, and lower sentences would be warranted. I hope to further develop this crime-specific approach in future work.

Conclusion

Determining the appropriate level of punishment for crimes is one of the most important functions of society, government, and the criminal justice system. Recent advances in data availability and analysis have made a scientific approach to these questions possible. In this chapter I have attempted to build on my own recent work and that of others to help further this goal.

Unlike previous studies, I have attempted to account for general deterrence, specific deterrence, incapacitation, as well as a variety of indirect costs of incarceration, including lost freedom and capital costs. For general deterrence, I use elasticity estimates from my study that makes use of add-on gun laws adopted in different states. For specific deterrence, I use estimates from my study using random assignment of cases to public defenders as an instrument for sentence served. For incapacitation, I survey some of the most recent, sophisticated studies on the topic. In addition, I use estimates of the cost of crime, cost of incarceration, value of freedom, and other parameters from my own work and that of other economists working in the field.

Because I incorporate more mechanisms by which sentencing affects crime, I use larger elasticities than some other studies, although not substantially larger. I find that the results are very dependent on the cost of crime estimates. For low cost of crime, shorter sentences are welfare enhancing, while for high cost of crime, the reverse is true. This points to the need for more study and more precision on the cost of crime. However, the approach used here may still be useful as it yields break-even points that can give some guidance for appropriate sentences by type of crime.

Notes

1 Thanks to participants in The Second International Conference on Empirical Studies of Judicial Systems and two anonymous referees for helpful comments. Eric Hague and Kathy Qian provided excellent research assistance.

2 See the Bureau of Justice Statistics website for recent data on incarceration rates: US Dep't Just., *Bureau of Justice Statistics*, OFFICE OF JUSTICE PROGRAMS, http://www. ojp. usdoj.gov/bjs/ (last visited Mar. 27, 2012).

3 *See* David S. Abrams & Chris Rohlfs, *Optimal Bail and the Value of Freedom: Evidence from the Philadelphia Bail Experiment*, 49 ECON. INQUIRY 750 (2011).

4 *See* Mark A. Cohen & Alex R. Piquero, *New Evidence on the Monetary Value of Saving a High Risk Youth*, 25 J. QUANTITATIVE CRIMINOLOGY 25 (2009).

5 *See* Jeffrey R. Kling, *Incarceration Length, Employment, and Earnings*, 96 AM. ECON. REV. 863 (2006).

6 Ernst Fehr & Urs Fischbacher, *Third Party Punishment and Social Norms*, 25 EVOLUTION & HUMAN BEHAVIOR 63 (2004).

7 *See* Jonathan Klick & Alexander Tabarrok, *Using Terror Alert Levels to Estimate the Effect of Police on Crime*, 48 J.L. & Econ. 267 (2005); Jonathan Klick & Alexander Tabarrok, *Police, Prisons, and Punishment: The Empirical Evidence on Crime Deterrence*, *in* HANDBOOK ON THE ECONOMICS OF CRIME 127, 127–44 (Bruce L. Benson & Paul R. Zimmerman eds., 2010).

8 *See* Daniel S. Nagin, *Criminal Deterrence Research at the Outset of the Twenty-First Century*, 23 CRIME & JUST. 1.

9 *See* Anthony N. Doob & Cheryl M. Webster, *Sentence Severity and Crime: Accepting the Null Hypothesis*, 30 CRIME & JUST. 143 (2003).

10 *See* Cheryl M. Webster, Anthony N. Doob & Franklin E. Zimring, *Proposition 8 and Crime Rates in California: The Case of the Disappearing Deterrent*, 5 CRIM. & PUB. POL'Y 417 (2006).

11 *See* Paul H. Robinson & John M. Darley, *Does Criminal Law Deter? A Behavioural Science Investigation*, 24 OXFORD J. LEGAL STUD. 173 (2004).

12 *See* Steven D. Levitt & Thomas J. Miles, *Empirical Study of Criminal Punishment, in* 1 HANDBOOK OF LAW AND ECONOMICS 457 (A. Mitchell Polinsky & Steven Shavell eds., 2007).

13 *See* Isaac Ehrlich, *On the Usefulness of Controlling Individuals: An Economic Analysis of Rehabilitation, Incapacitation and Deterrence*, 71 AM. ECON. REV. 307 (1981).

14 *See* Steven D. Levitt, *Why Do Increased Arrest Rates Appear to Reduce Crime: Deterrence, Incapacitation, or Measurement Error?*, 36 ECON. INQUIRY 353 (1998a).

15 *See* Eric Helland & Alex Tabarrok, *Does Three Strikes Deter: A Non-Parametric Estimation*, 42 J. HUM. RESOURCES 309 (2007).

16 *See* Francesco Drago, Roberto Galbiati & Pietro Vertova, *The Deterrent Effects of Prison: Evidence from a Natural Experiment*, 117 J. POL. ECON. 257 (2009).

17 *See* Steven D. Levitt, *Juvenile Crime and Punishment*, 106 J. POL. ECON. 1156 (1998b).

18 *See* Randi Hjalmarsson, *Crime and Expected Punishment: Changes in Perceptions at the Age of Criminal Majority*, 11 AM. L. & ECON. REV. 209 (2009).

19 *See* David S. Lee & Justin McCrary, *The Deterrence Effect of Prison: Dynamic Theory and Evidence* (Princeton U. Ctr. for Econ. Policy Studies, Working Paper No. 189, 2009).

20 *See* Daniel P. Kessler & Steven D. Levitt, *Using Sentence Enhancements to Distinguish between Deterrence and Incapacitation*, 42 J.L. & ECON. 343 (1999).

21 *See* Thomas B. Marvell & Carlisle E. Moody, *The Impact of Enhanced Prison Terms for Felonies Committed with Guns*, 33 CRIMINOLOGY 247 (1995).

22 In general, changes in prison populations are correlated with a number of variables and thus isolating the effect of a single causal mechanism is difficult. For example, states with higher prison populations tend to have higher crime. This does not mean that incarceration causes crime, but rather a third factor (an "omitted variable," for example a bad economy) likely causes both. In order to obtain a clear causal effect of the variable of interest (here sentence length) it is necessary to employ a research design that approximates a randomized experiment. That is what most of the papers discussed here attempt to do.

23 *See* David S. Abrams, *Estimating the Deterrent Effect of Incarceration using Sentencing Enhancements*, 4 AMERICAN ECONOMIC JOURNAL: APPLIED ECONOMICS (2012) 32–56.

24 *See* Jon S. Vernick & Lisa M. Hepburn, *State and Federal Gun Laws: Trends for 1970–99, in* EVALUATING GUN POLICY: EFFECTS ON CRIME AND VIOLENCE 345 (Jens Ludwig ed., 2003).

25 *See* Colin Loftin & David McDowall, *The Deterrent Effects of the Florida Felony Firearm Law*, 75 J. CRIM. L. & CRIMINOLOGY 250 (1984); Kessler & Levitt, *supra* note 20.

26 This elasticity is calculated by simply dividing the percentage change in crime (about –5 percent) by the average percentage change in sentence length (about 50 percent) due to the add-on gun laws.

27 *See* Lee & McCrary, *supra* note 19.

28 *See* Drago, Galbiati & Vertova, *supra* note 16.
29 *See* Helland & Tabarrok, *supra* note 15.
30 *See* Daniel S. Nagin, Francis T. Cullen & Cheryl L. Jonson, *Imprisonment and Reoffending*, 38 Crime & Just. 115 (2009); Shawn Bushway & Raymond Paternoster, *The Impact of Prison on Crime*, *in* Do Prisons Make Us Safer? The Benefits and Costs of the Prison Boom 119 (Steven Raphael & Michael A. Stoll eds., 2009).
31 *See* Drago, Galbiati & Vertova, *supra* note 16.
32 *See* Eric Maurin & Aurelie Ouss, *Sentence Reductions and Recidivism: Lessons from the Bastille Day Quasi Experiment* (IZA, Discussion Paper No. 3990, 2009), *available at* http://papers.ssrn.com/sol3/papers.cfm?abstract_id=1351154.
33 *See* Hjalmarsson, *supra* note 18.
34 *See* Shawn D. Bushway & Emily G. Owens, *Framing Punishment: Incarceration, Recommended Sentences, and Recidivism* (Working Paper, 2012), *available at* http://www.human.cornell.edu/pam/people/upload/Framing-JLawEc-Final.pdf.
35 See David S. Abrams, *Building Criminal Capital vs. Specific Deterrence: The Effect of Incarceration Length on Recidivism* (Working Paper, 2013), *available at* https://www.law.upenn.edu/cf/faculty/dabrams/workingpapers/AbramsRecidivism.pdf.
36 *See* Charles Loeffler, *Does Imprisonment Alter the Life Course? Evidence on Crime and Employment from a Natural Experiment*, 51 Criminology 137 (2013).
37 *See* Danton A. Berube & Donald P. Green, *The Effects of Sentencing on Recidivism: Results from a Natural Experiment* (2nd Annual Conference on Empirical Legal Studies Paper, 2007), *available at* http://ssrn.com/abstract=999445; Donald P. Green & Daniel Winik, *Using Random Judge Assignments to Estimate the Effects of Incarceration and Probation on Recidivism among Drug Offenders*, 48 Criminology 357 (2010).
38 *See* Emily Turner, *Using Random Case Assignment and Heterogeneity in Attorney Ability to Examine the Relationship Between Sentence Length and Recidivism* (2009) (unpublished dissertation, University of Pennsylvania).
39 *See* David S. Abrams & Albert H. Yoon, *The Luck of the Draw: Using Random Case Assignment to Investigate Attorney Ability*, 74 U. Chi. L. Rev. 1145 (2007).
40 Recidivism is defined here as reappearance in the public defender data set. This means that, at a minimum, offenders have been re-arrested and charges have not been immediately dropped.
41 *See* Levitt, *supra* note 14.
42 *See* John Donohue, *Assessing the Relative Benefits of Incarceration: The Overall Change Over the Previous Decades and the Benefits on the Margin*, *in* Do Prisions Make Us Safer? The Benefits and Costs of the Prison Boom 269 (Steven Raphael & Michael Stoll eds., 2009).
43 Assuming (counterfactually) a stationary distribution of sentence lengths.

References

Abrams, David S. 2012. Estimating the Deterrent Effect of Incarceration using Sentencing Enhancements. *American Economic Journal: Applied Economics* 4: 32–56.

Abrams, David S. 2013. Building Criminal Capital vs. Specific Deterrence: The Effect of Incarceration Length on Recidivism. Working Paper.

Abrams, David, and Chris Rohlfs. 2011. Optimal Bail and the Value of Freedom: Evidence from the Philadelphia Bail Experiment. *Economic Inquiry* 49: 750–770.

Abrams, David, and Albert Yoon. 2007. The Luck of the Draw: Using Random Case Assignment to Investigate Attorney Ability. *University of Chicago Law Review* 74: 1145–1177.

Berecochea, J. and Jaman, D. 1981. *Time Served in Prison and Parole Outcome: An Experimental Study. Report 2.* Sacramento, CA: California Department of Corrections.

Berube, Danton A., and Donald P. Green. 2007. The Effects of Sentencing on Recidivism: Results from a Natural Experiment. 2nd Annual Conference on Empirical Legal Studies Paper Working Paper.

Bhati, Avinash. 2007. Estimating the Number of Crimes Averted by Incapacitation: An Information Theoretic Approach. *Journal of Quantitative Criminology* 23(4): 355–375.

Bierie, David M. 2007. Cost Matters: Application and Advancement of Economic Methods To Inform Policy Choice in Criminology 157 tbl.11 (unpublished Ph.D. dissertation, University of Maryland), available at http://drum.lib.umd.edu/bitstream/1903/6786/1/umi-umd-4271.pdf.

Bushway, Shawn, and Emily G. Owens. 2012. Framing Punishment: Incarceration, Recommended Sentences, and Recidivism. Working Paper.

Bushway, Shawn, and Raymond Paternoster. 2009. The Impact of Prison on Crime. In *Do Prisions Make Us Safer? The Benefits and Costs of the Prison Boom*, edited by Steven Raphael and Michael Stoll. New York, NY: Russell Sage Foundation, pp. 119–150.

Cohen, Mark A., and Alex R. Piquero. 2009. New Evidence on the Monetary Value of Saving a High-Risk Youth. *Journal of Quantitative Criminology* 25: 25–49.

Donohue, John J. 2009. Assessing the Relative Benefits of Incarceration: The Overall Change Over the Previous Decades and the Benefits on the Margin. In *Do Prisions Make Us Safer? The Benefits and Costs of the Prison Boom*, edited by Steven Raphael and Michael Stoll. New York, NY: Russell Sage Foundation, pp. 269–341.

Doob, Anthony M., and Cheryl Webster. 2003. Sentence Severity and Crime: Accepting the Null Hypothesis. *Crime and Justice* 23: 143–195.

Drago, Francesco, Roberto Galbiati, and Pietro Vertova. 2009. The Deterrent Effects of Prison: Evidence from a Natural Experiment. *Journal of Political Economy* 117: 257–280.

Ehrlich, Isaac. 1981. On the Usefulness of Controlling Individuals: An Economic Analysis of Rehabilitation, Incapacitation and Deterrence. *The American Economic Review* 71: 307–322.

Fehr, Ernst, and Urs Fischbacher 2004. Third Party Punishment and Social Norms. *Evolution and Human Behavior* 25: 63–87.

Green, Donald P., and Daniel Winik. 2010. Using Random Judge Assignments to Estimate the Effects of Incarceration and Probation on Recidivism Among Drug Offenders. *Criminology* 48: 357–387.

Helland, Eric, and Alexander Tabarrok. 2007. Does Three Strikes Deter: A Non-Parametric Estimation. *Journal of Human Resources* 42(2): 309–330.

Hill, George, and Paige Harrison. 2005. *Sentenced Prisoners under State or Federal Jurisdiction.* Washington, DC: Bureau of Justice Statistics.

Hjalmarsson, Randi. 2009. Crime and Expected Punishment: Changes in Perceptions at the Age of Criminal Majority. *American Law and Economics Review* 11: 209–248.

Johnson, Rucker, and Steven Raphael. 2011. How Much Crime Reduction Does the Marginal Prisoner Buy? *Journal of Law and Economics* 55(2): 275–310.

Kessler, Daniel P., and Steven D. Levitt. 1999. Using Sentence Enhancements to Distinguish between Deterrence and Incapacitation. *Journal of Law and Economics* 42: 343–364.

Klick, Jonathan, and Alexander Tabarrok. 2005. Using Terror Alert Levels to Estimate the Effect of Police on Crime, *The Journal of Law & Economics* 48: 267–279.

Klick, Jonathan, and Alexander Tabarrok. 2010. Police, Prisons, and Punishment: The Empirical Evidence on Crime Deterrence. In *Handbook on the Economics of Crime*, edited by Bruce L. Benson and Paul R. Zimmerman. Northampton, MA: Edward Elgar, pp. 127–144.

Kling, Jeffrey. 2006. Incarceration Length, Employment, and Earnings. *American Economic Review* 96: 863–76.

Kuziemko, Ilyana. 2013. How Should Inmates Be Released from Prison? An Assessment of Parole Versus Fixed Sentence Regimes. *The Quarterly Journal of Economics* 128(1): 371–424.

Lee, David S., and Justin McCrary. 2009. The Deterrence Effect of Prison: Dynamic Theory and Evidence, CEPS Working Paper No.189.

Levitt, Steven D. 1996.The Effect of Prison Population Size on Crime Rates: Evidence from Prison Overcrowding Litigation. *Quarterly Journal of Economics* 111(2): 319–351.

Levitt, Steven D. 1998a. Why Do Increased Arrest Rates Appear to Reduce Crime: Deterrence, Incapacitation, or Measurement Error? *Economic Inquiry* 36: 353–372.

Levitt, Steven D. 1998b. Juvenile Crime and Punishment. *Journal of Political Economy* 106: 1156–1185.

Levitt, Steven D., and Thomas J. Mills. 2007. Empirical Study of Criminal Punishment. In vol. 1 of *Handbook of Law and Economics*, edited by A. Mitchell Polinsky and Steven Shavell. Amsterdam: Elsevier, pp. 457–494.

Loeffler, Charles. 2013. Does Imprisonment Alter the Life Course? Evidence on Crime and Employment from a Natural Experiment. *Criminology* 51: 137–166.

Loftin, Colin, and David McDowall. 1984. The Deterrent Effects of the Florida Felony Firearm Law. *The Journal of Criminal Law and Criminology* 75: 250–259.

Maltz, Michael D. 1984. *Recidivism*. Orlando, FL: Academic Press, Inc.; Internet version: 2001. Available at http://www.uic.edu/depts/lib/forr/pdf/crimjust/recidivism.pdf.

Marvell, Thomas B., and Carlisle E. Moody, Jr. 1994. Prison Population Growth and Crime Reduction. *Journal of Quantitative Criminology* 10: 109–133.

Marvell, Thomas B., and Carlisle E. Moody. 1995. The Impact of Enhanced Prison Terms for Felonies Committed with Guns. *Criminology* 33: 247–281.

Maurin, Eric, and Aurelie Ouss. 2009. Sentence Reductions and Recidivism: Lessons from the Bastille Day Quasi Experiment, IZA Discussion Paper.

Miller, R., Mark A. Cohen, and Brian Wiersema. 1996. Natational Institute of Justice, Victim Costs and Consequences: A New Look 1. Available at https://www.ncjrs.gov/pdffiles/victcost.pdf.

Nagin, Daniel S., 1998. Criminal Deterrence Research at the Outset of the Twenty-First Century. *Crime and Justice* 23: 1–42.

Nagin, Daniel S., Francis T. Cullen, and Cheryl L. Jonson. 2009. Imprisonment and Reoffending. *Crime & Justice: A Review of Research* 38: 115–200.

Owens, Emily G. 2009. More Time, Less Crime? Estimating the Incapacitative Effect of Sentence Enhancements. *Journal of Law and Economics* 52(3): 551–579.

Piquero, Alex, and Alfred Blumstein. 2007. Does Incapacitation Reduce Crime?. *Journal of Quantitative Criminology* 23: 267–285.

Reuter, Peter, and Shawn Bushway. 2007. Available at http://www.deepdyve.com/browse/journals/journal-of-quantitative-criminology/2007/v23/i4?numPerPage=10.

Robinson, Paul H., and John M. Darley. 2004. Does Criminal Law Deter? A Behavioural Science Investigation. *Oxford Journal of Legal Studies* 24: 173–205.

Rosenmerkel, Sean *et al.* 2009. Bureau of Justice Statistics, Felony Sentences in State Courts, 2006—Statistical Tables 7 tbl.1.4. Available at http://bjs.ojp.usdoj.gov/content/pub/pdf/fssc06st.pdf.

Sweeten, Gary, and Robert Apel. (2007). Incapacitation: Revisiting an Old Question with a New Method and New Data. *Journal of Quantitative Criminology* 23: 303–326.

Turner, Emily. 2009. Using Random Case Assignment and Heterogeneity in Attorney Ability to Examine the Relationship Between Sentence Length, and Recidivism. Unpublished dissertation. University of Pennsylvania.

Vernick, Jon S., and Lisa M. Hepburn. 2003. State and Federal Gun Laws: Trends for 1970–99. In *Evaluating Gun Policy: Effects on Crime and Violence*, edited by Jens Ludwig. Washington, DC: Brookings Institution Press, pp 345–411.

Webster, Cheryl M., Anthony N. Doob, and Franklin E. Zimring. 2006. Proposition 8 and Crime Rates in California: The Case of the Disappearing Deterrent. *Criminology and Public Policy* 5: 417–448.

4 Does appellate precedent matter?

Stock price responses to appellate court decisions on FCC actions

Daniel L. Chen, Susan Yeh, and Alberto G. Araiza

Introduction

Do courts matter? Scholars are of two minds. Some view courts as critical in being able to effect widespread social change. Others believe momentous judicial decisions may be caused by, rather than be causes of, political or socioeconomic changes. Generally, the empirical evidence is mixed and a heated debate has arisen on the impact of the decisions of the highest courts.[1] Part of the difficulty in reaching definitive conclusions is that courts make decisions in different ways, depending to some extent on external factors, be they litigant strategy, developments in legal doctrine, or social trends. This chapter examines the stock market response to appellate Federal Communications Commission (FCC) decisions to test whether the market pays attention to the arrival of new legal precedent. We use the random assignment of judges to appellate cases to make the causal inferences that would be difficult in the case of Supreme Court decisions. We focus on the FCC because we can construct a natural control group. FCC decisions pertain to media companies. We can therefore use non-media companies as control. If courts have no effect whatsoever, then we should not see any differential impact on stock markets.

The FCC is interesting in and of itself as it sets licensing policies based "on the theory that diversification of mass media ownership serves the public interest by promoting diversity of program and service viewpoints."[2] To promote diverse programming and viewpoints, Congress sets limits on the number of media outlets a firm can own.[3] In the last decade, federal Courts of Appeals demonstrated their "broader goal of First Amendment policy to prevent"[4] an "inordinate effect on public opinion,"[5] achieve "vigorous debate"[6] and ensure access to "controversial issues,"[7] and "suitable access to social, political, aesthetic, moral and other ideas and experiences."[8]

There are two competing theories about the effects of diversification of media ownership on the diversity of programming and viewpoints.[9] One theory posits that media monopolies frustrate diversity because a firm owning multiple media outlets will provide homogenous programming and viewpoints.[10] A competing theory by Peter Steiner posits that media monopolies encourage diverse programming and viewpoints because they will seek to cater to an entire market.[11]

That is, homogenous programming and viewpoints result from the diversification of media ownership because firms will only compete for the most popular type of programming.[12]

Previous studies have examined the effects of media monopolies on format variety (e.g. country, rock, talk, sports), amount of news programming, advertising revenue, commercial versus noncommercial ratings, and listenership.[13] Existing literature has shown that *decreased* media competition causes an increase in format variety and advertising revenue.[14] Thus, determining what causes changes in media competition is an important concern.

This study examines the impact of federal appellate court decisions on FCC actions ("appellate court decisions") on media stock prices. Specifically, this study examines how appellate court decisions affect media stock prices when a court rules in favor of the public interest, granting relief against media businesses.[15] Although existing studies have examined the relationship between relaxing media ownership rules and the diversity of programming offered by media firms,[16] there are no empirical studies examining how appellate court decisions on FCC actions affect stock prices or media competition.

An increase in media stock prices caused by appellate court decisions may suggest an increase in media competition.[17] Prior studies indicate that firms in highly concentrated industries experience less stock price variability.[18] Further, firms experience a "decrease in profit and return volatility" and a reduction in expected returns when there is less competition.[19] These results are consequences of stock prices being more informative because there is "improved accuracy of public information" of firms.[20] Thus, an increase in media stock prices caused by appellate court decisions can suggest an increase in media competition.[21]

A caveat should be noted when interpreting our study. Our study is not an event study, which is an empirical method often used in other research in empirical finance. We look at long-term changes, not immediate changes.[22] Nor is our study examining the impact of winning or losing a lawsuit on a firm's stock prices. This chapter illustrates two empirical methods: one using differences-in-differences and a second using the random assignment of judges to ascertain the causal impact of judicial precedent.[23] Specifically, this study demonstrates how appellate court decisions against media businesses affect stock prices in the media industry.

The next section provides an overview of FCC policies and procedures. The following section describes how media firms may be exposed to the appellate court decisions. The penultimate section describes the design of the study and presents the basic results from a differences-in-differences analysis and a two-stage least squares (instrumental variables) analysis. The last section concludes.

FCC policies and procedures

Congress vests broad discretion in the FCC to regulate interstate and international communications services.[24] The FCC is assigned the responsibility to "prescribe such rules and regulations as may be necessary in the public interest."[25] The FCC is authorized to adopt rules that "are not an unreasonable means" to achieve "permissible public-interest goals."[26] Congress specifically requires the FCC to provide "biennial review[s] of regulations" to "repeal or modify any regulation it determines to be no longer necessary in the public interest."[27]

The FCC revises its rules in response to new laws, including both legislation and court decisions. For example, the Telecommunications Act of 1996 increased radio station ownership limits within markets and eliminated restrictions on the number of stations firms can own nationwide.[28] This statute gave rise to FCC efforts to modify cross-ownership restrictions on the extent to which a single firm may own multiple media entities in a market, which set off a series of legal actions. In particular, the Third Circuit's decision in *Prometheus Radio Project v. FCC* blocked the FCC's initial proposal to lift existing restrictions on ownership rule changes in 2003.[29] After several rounds addressing court challenges, however, the FCC recently relaxed a ban on media outlet cross-ownership that had been in effect for more than 30 years.[30] The FCC now evaluates a proposed cross-ownership combination on a case-by-case basis to determine whether it is in the public interest and promotes competition, localism, and diversity.[31]

To analyze how appellate court decisions matter to the market using the example of FCC cases, it is informative to understand the types of FCC actions that are challenged in courts. FCC responsibilities include "processing applications for licenses and other filings; analyzing complaints; conducting investigations; developing and implementing regulatory programs; and taking part in hearings."[32] The FCC may grant or deny a license to a firm for a media outlet including, inter alia, TV, radio, newspapers, the Internet, movies, cable TV, billboards, magazines, and the like.[33] The appellate court decisions utilized in this study are challenges to FCC actions.[34] For example, in *Pappas v. FCC*, the FCC denied the petitioner a media license and the court upheld that FCC action.[35] The FCC based its action on its interpretation of a statute and the court held that the FCC did not abuse its discretion.[36]

This study examines whether federal appellate court decisions matter and whether the market pays attention to their rulings. Stock prices in the media industry may respond to federal appellate courts' rulings on challenges to FCC actions because these court decisions create legal precedent affecting media competition. Many FCC actions begin by distinguishing between different media markets.[37] In larger markets, the FCC presumes that a combination of some media outlets is in the public interest, whereas in smaller markets, the FCC presumes that the same combination is against public interest.[38] These presumptions are rebuttable.[39] Combinations are reviewed under a four-factor analysis, in which the FCC considers:

1 how much the combination will increase local news in the market;
2 whether each outlet will exercise independent news judgment;
3 market concentration; and
4 the financial condition of the outlets.[40]

Although the FCC might not have fully justified how awarding one firm several licenses in a market could serve the public interest and promote competition, some scholars have argued that less media competition leads to diversity of programming and viewpoints.[41]

Many of the appellate court decisions in this study are challenges to FCC actions based on specific FCC rules, including those that directly regulate market concentration. For example, a rule provides that the number of TV stations a firm may license nationwide is limitless, so long as it is not more than 39 percent of all US households.[42] Another FCC rule prohibits a merger among two or more of the television networks ABC, CBS, Fox, and NBC.[43] According to the FCC, a firm may license two TV stations in the same market if their service areas do not overlap or at least one station is not among the top four in the market, and at least eight independently licensed stations remain in the market after the combination.[44] In the largest markets, a firm may own two TV stations and six radio stations.[45] Such rules also impose restrictions on the number of local radio stations a firm may license, based on a sliding scale that depends on the size of a market.[46] For example, in a market with forty-five stations, a firm may license eight stations.[47]

In addition to those cases relating to market competition,[48] a number of court decisions concern certain aspects of viewpoint diversity in media markets. Indeed, a prominent public interest purpose of the FCC statute is to establish rules to ensure that media communications are "ma[d]e available, so far as possible, to all the people of the United States."[49] This statutory purpose has been cited, for example, in challenges to the employment practices of broadcast licensees (*National Black Media Coalition v. FCC*).[50] Litigation on diversity also concern bidding procedures for broadband licenses that favored minority-owned businesses,[51] as well as challenges to the FCC's renewal of licenses for television stations on the grounds that the stations failed to offer close captioning of programs for hearing-impaired viewers.[52]

Firms' exposure to appellate court decisions

Underlying the effect of appellate court decisions on media industry stock prices are the questions of whether firms anticipate effects on media competition and whether they change their policies in response to the decisions. Firms may learn of court decisions from in-house or outside counsel, through news reports, or the like. This study utilizes news reports discussing federal appellate court decisions as a proxy for determining how readily media firms were exposed to the decisions. Publications examined in this study were *The New York Times*, *Los Angeles Times*, *Chicago Tribune*, Dow Jones News Service, and *Wall Street Journal*. News reports discussing the appellate court decisions from our dataset of cases[53] were retrieved from the electronic database LexisNexis.com by using a custom search string.[54] The aggregate news reports for each year are included in the "Combined News" column of Table 4.1.

Table 4.1 Newspaper reports of appellate decisions on FCC actions

Year	*Cases decided*	*Combined news*	The New York Times	Los Angeles Times	Chicago Tribune	*Dow Jones News Service*	Wall Street Journal	*Case discussed in randomly selected publications. "False" indicates the case is not part of the dataset.*
1985	3	2	0	1	0	0	**1**	*Storer Communications v. FCC*
1986	4	1	**1**	0	0	0	0	False
1987	6	3	0	2	**1**	0	0	False
1988	5	2	0	1	0	**1**	0	*News America Pub. v. FCC*
1989	1	3	2	0	**1**	0	0	False
1990	1	0	0	0	0	0	0	–
1991	0	0	0	0	0	0	0	–
1992	4	5	0	2	1	**1**	1	*AT&T v. FCC*
1993	0	1	0	0	**1**	0	0	False
1994	0	1	0	**1**	0	0	0	False
1995	6	4	1	0	0	**2**	1	False; *Cincinnati Bell Tel. Co. v. FCC*
1996	5	2	0	0	0	**2**	0	*Iowa Utils. Bd. v. FCC*
1997	8	7	**1**	1	1	4	0	*Bell Atl. Tel. Cos. v. FCC*
1998	5	6	2	0	0	**1**	3	*Southwestern Bell Tel. Co. v. FCC*
1999	14	11	0	0	0	**4**	7	*US West, Inc. v. FCC; 3X* False
2000	20	5	0	**2**	0	3	0	*AT&T Corp. v. FCC; Dup.*
2001	5	9	4	2	0	**1**	2	False
2002	2	9	2	2	1	3	**1**	False
2003	9	12	2	3	2	3	**2**	2X False
2004	6	11	0	4	0	4	**3**	2X False; *Prometheus Radio Project v. FCC*
2005	5	2	1	0	0	**1**	0	False

Note: The bold numbers indicate that at least one of the news articles was selected for review. The right-hand column indicates the case name if the case mentioned in the news article is also found in our database. "2X False" indicates two of the articles examined did not mention a case included in our database.

Figure 4.1 compares the total annual number of appellate court decisions and news reports. News reports were randomly selected for review to determine if they were false positives, i.e. the search yielded a report of a decision that was not among the dataset's cases that substantively rule on FCC actions regarding competition. The randomly selected reports are shown in bold font in Table 4.1 and reviewed in the far right column. If a news report identified the case name or the circuit and the facts match the corresponding case's from the same year in the dataset, then that case is identified in the rightmost column in Table 4.1. News reports are labeled "false" in the rightmost column if they were false positives. Some years had more news reports than appellate court decisions. This is likely due to more intense media attention to those cases over the course of the year. Or, perhaps publishers generated more articles that continued to discuss appellate court decisions from prior years, or the search string was imperfect. Overall, it is plausible for firms to have been exposed to relevant appellate decisions through news reports in the years the cases were decided.

Do firms change their policies in response to appellate court decisions? Because specific data on the competition policies of media firms are not readily available, we reviewed the cases in our dataset to determine whether or not monetary damages were awarded (Table 4.2). Theories on the deterrence effects of damages and fines suggest that reported judgments awarding monetary damages against businesses are more likely to induce media firms to change their policies to avoid similar judgments.[55] Of the 109 cases in the dataset, 38 include the terms "damage" or "award." A thorough examination of the details of these cases reveals that only two cases from 2003 were related to awarding or denying monetary damages to a party. The majority of the cases dealt with a challenge to an FCC decision awarding a license to a firm. Thus, because of the limited number of cases awarding damages, the existence of deterrent effects on media firms remains an open question.

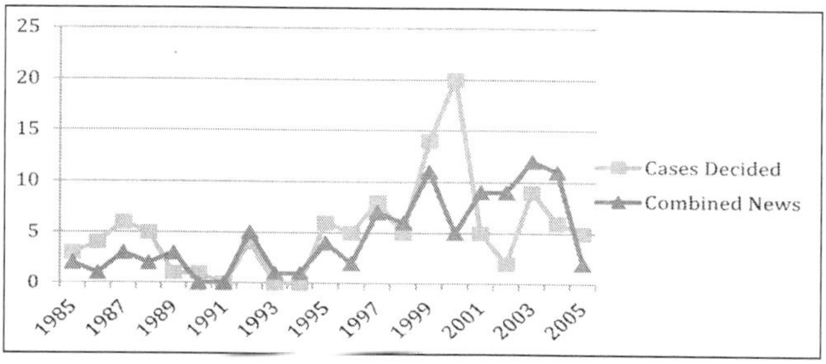

Figure 4.1 Annual numbers of appellate decisions on FCC actions and combined newspaper reports of appellate decisions

Table 4.2 Monetary damages and awards in appellate cases on FCC actions

Year	*Circuit*	*Citation*	*Term found*	*Explanation of award*
1985	12	249 US App. D.C. 292	Award	Decided against FCC's awarding a license without having held a hearing and without imposing heightened reporting obligations.
1986	12	257 US App. D.C. 104	Award	Denied challenge to FCC for not giving preference to awarding licenses to women as a minority group.
1987	12	259 US App. D.C. 191	Award	Denied challenge to FCC for forbidding cable franchisors from imposing standards of their own.
1987	12	259 US App. D.C. 481	Award	Denied challenge to FCC's practice of awarding certain licenses.
1987	12	262 US App. D.C. 244	Award	Discusses awarding franchises.
1987	12	264 US App. D.C. 85	Damages	Where "application favored when 'fines or damages' are assessed and agency imposes new liability 'for past actions which were taken in good-faith reliance on [agency] pronouncements.'"
1988	12	267 US App. D.C. 1	Award	Granted review of FCC's practice of awarding certain licenses.
1988	12	268 US App. D.C. 208	Award	Denied challenge to FCC's practice of awarding certain broadcast licenses.
1992	12	294 US App. D.C. 377	Award	Discusses a franchising authority awarding franchises within its jurisdiction.
1992	12	978 F.2d 727	Damages	AT&T sought both damages and a cease and desist order against a ruling by the FCC favoring MCI. The court remanded to the FCC.
1995	6	69 F.3d 752	Award	Granted review of FCC's practice of awarding certain wireless communications licenses.
1995	12	310 US App. D.C. 256	Damages	Discussed damages in a statute that was inconsistent with legislative history to make a point about statutory interpretation.
1995	12	310 US App. D.C. 90	Damages	Granted review of FCC decision and. vacated a tariff order discussed how persons have a right claim damages from the FCC.
1996	12	316 US App. D.C. 220	Award	Remanded to FCC to review preference for developers of new technology awarded licenses without competition or charges.
1997	12	324 US App. D.C. 72	Award	Denied challenge to FCC's practice of awarding certain Direct Broadcasting Satellite (DBS) channels.

Continued

Table 4.2 (Continued)

Year	*Circuit*	*Citation*	*Term found*	*Explanation of award*
1997	12	327 US App. D.C. 133	Damages	Used in reference to another case where a petitioner sought damages.
1998	12	134 F.3d 1143	Award	Denied challenge to FCC's practice of awarding certain licenses.
1999	12	335 US App. D.C. 54	Award	Used in reference to overruling the awarding of a license and rejecting a proposed settlement.
1999	12	337 US App. D.C. 78	Award	Remanded to FCC to award Qualcomm a "pioneer's preference" (license of their choice without payment).
1999	12	333 US App. D.C. 253	Award	Cited a case where "injunctive remedy [was] awarded."
1999	12	334 US App. D.C. 178	Award	Used in reference favoring the FCC awarding a license.
2000	5	201 F.3d 608	Award	Denied challenge to how subsidies awarded by the FCC.
2000	10	201 F.3d 1264	Award	Affirming FCC decision. Discussion about awarding local exchange carriers a competitive advantage.
2000	11	208 F.3d 1263	Award	The rate formula denies just compensation when wires are overlashed because no additional compensation is awarded.
2000	12	341 US App. D.C. 404	Award	Denied challenge to FCC's practice of awarding certain licenses.
2000	12	343 US App. D.C. 138	Award	Cited case in a footnote ("Awarding reparation for the past and fixing rates for the future").
2000	12	342 US App. D.C. 290	Award	Denied challenge to FCC's practice of awarding certain licenses.
2000	12	343 US App. D.C. 17	Award	Denied challenge to FCC's practice of awarding certain licenses.
2001	10	258 F.3d 1191	Damages	Court found no reason to require petitioner to seek review of FCC action before it can know whether it will be damaged by the action.
2002	8	299 F.3d 949	Damages	Indicating, "any damage" and "liability of any kind" include all damages from a government project, not just property damage.
2003	12	357 US App. D.C. 134	Award	Denied challenge to FCC's practice of awarding certain licenses.
2003	12	358 US App. D.C. 369	Damages	Denied challenge awarding monetary damages for breach of contract.
2003	12	354 US App. D.C. 325	Damages	Atlas must pay damages to AT&T.
2004	3	373 F.3d 372	Award	Discussed "industry awards" indicating quality of stations.
2004	12	360 US App. D.C. 202	Damages	Indicating FCC was not arbitrary or capricious thinking any damage to

Continued

Table 4.2 (Continued)

Year	*Circuit*	*Citation*	*Term found*	*Explanation of award*
				broadband competition from denying unbundled access to the broadband capacities of hybrid loops is likely to be mitigated by the availability of alternatives.
2004	12	361 US App. D.C. 139	Damages	Upheld FCC decision that local telephone companies owe payphone providers damages, but providers barred from collecting.
2005	12	2005 US App. LEXIS 11804	Award	Granted challenge to FCC's practice of awarding certain licenses.
2005	12	402 F.3d 205	Damages	Discussed damages, petitioners' financial interests, and their inability to recover additional costs.

Study design

The data

This empirical study draws on multiple sources of appellate courts data. The first dataset consists of substantive federal appellate court decisions on FCC actions between 1985 and 2005, totaling 109 cases.[56] This study focuses on published opinions to investigate established precedent that is readily available to firms. Appellate courts determine a significant portion of cases that shape the law in the US. This effective making of law occurs because decisions become precedents for decisions in future cases. The FCC rendered actions favoring businesses or public interests, which were then challenged in appellate courts. Decisions favoring business interests would make it easier, on the margin, for subsequent business decisions to be approved by the courts. More specifically, the sample of FCC cases comes from shepardizing *Chevron v. Natural Resources Defense Council*[57] and searching for challenges to FCC decisions. A vote was coded as pro-public interest if it favored upholding an agency's decision that was against industry attack, or if it favored striking down an agency's decision in the face of a challenge by a public interest group. A typical case of this sample is *Cellco Partnership v. FCC* (D.C. Cir. 2004) (denying industry petition for review of FCC action). This study estimates the responses of media stock prices, providing evidence on whether firms and investors pay attention to appellate precedent.[58]

We analyze a stock as a media industry stock if the firm's Standard Industrial Classification (SIC) Code[59] identifies its business type as print, broadcast, film, or other media as listed in Table 4.3.

The changes in media stock prices of these specific SIC coded stocks were obtained from the Center for Research in Security Prices (CRSP), which maintains

Table 4.3 Media industries and SIC codes

2711	NEWSPAPERS: PUBLISHING OR PUBLISHING & PRINTING
2721	PERIODICALS: PUBLISHING OR PUBLISHING & PRINTING
2731	BOOKS: PUBLISHING OR PUBLISHING & PRINTING
2741	MISCELLANEOUS PUBLISHING
3663	RADIO & TV BROADCASTING & COMMUNICATIONS EQUIPMENT
3669	COMMUNICATIONS EQUIPMENT, NEC
4812	RADIOTELEPHONE COMMUNICATIONS
4813	TELEPHONE COMMUNICATIONS (NO RADIOTELEPHONE)
4822	TELEGRAPH & OTHER MESSAGE COMMUNICATIONS
4832	RADIO BROADCASTING STATIONS
4833	TELEVISION BROADCASTING STATIONS
4841	CABLE & OTHER PAY TELEVISION SERVICES
4899	COMMUNICATIONS SERVICES, NEC
7812	SERVICES-MOTION PICTURE & VIDEO TAPE PRODUCTION
7841	SERVICES-VIDEO TAPE RENTAL
7310	SERVICES-ADVERTISING
7331	SERVICES-DIRECT MAIL ADVERTISING SERVICES

Source: http://www.sec.gov/info/edgar/siccodes.htm.

large, comprehensive, proprietary, historical databases of security prices.[60] Summary statistics of the key dependent variables are below in Table 4.4, which includes data from CRSP for both media and non-media stock prices from 1985 through 2005. The prices used in the analysis are closing prices for the period.[61] In our analyses, we use log prices, which would automatically exclude missing values and zeros that were recorded when closing prices were unavailable.

Differences-in-differences

How do markets respond to momentous court decisions? To answer this question, a first step is to identify a small period during which an unusually high number of appellate decisions were issued. Indeed, appellate court decisions in favor of the public interest, and against anticompetitive actions, may be concentrated within a period of time. For example, during the period 1985 to 2005, an unusually high number of pro-public-interest legal precedents occurred in the year 2000. In 2000, 20 relevant appellate cases were decided. In about 75 percent of those cases, courts did not provide relief to businesses. An example of a pro-public-interest decision is *Orion Comm. Ltd. v. FCC*, where a communications company challenged the FCC's application of an anticollusion rule.[62] In *Orion*, the D.C. Circuit denied the petition for review and held the FCC's action was not arbitrary and capricious.[63]

One might estimate the impact of the year's appellate court decisions on media stock prices by conducting a simple before and after comparison of prices. This may be informative of how the appellate court decisions about FCC actions changed media stock prices. That raw difference in prices, however, would mask the possibility of stock price trends and make it difficult to determine if appellate court decisions or trends caused any of the observed changes.

Table 4.4 Summary statistics of stock prices

	Observations	*Mean*	*Standard Deviation*	*Min.*	*Max.*
Stock prices	479,086	20.85882	659.498	–2,315	130,250
Log of stock prices	408,954	2.418702	1.157762	–4.50986	11.77721

Our analysis examines the period before and after the year 2000 because that year had the greatest number of appellate court decisions on FCC actions during the period 1985–2005. In the year 2000, there was a visible spike of 20 FCC appellate decisions, in contrast to an average of 4.45 per year for the other years. Choosing the year with the greatest number of decisions is based on a constant linear effects assumption, which is standard in the literature. Our measure of appellate decisions follows from previous studies that also measure the impact of law by counting the number of court decisions or the number of statutes.[64]

To isolate the effect of appellate court decisions on media stock prices, we run a differences-in-differences (DID) analysis. In a DID analysis, the effect of a treatment (such as pro-public-interest appellate decisions) is examined by comparing a treatment group with a control group in a particular period. A DID analysis measures the change induced by a particular treatment, although the estimates may remain subject to certain biases. Here, media industry stocks are the "treatment" and the other stocks are the "control" group. A comparison of their respective changes reveals the effect of appellate decisions from the year 2000.

To visualize the responses to appellate decisions in 2000, we show the raw data before and after 2000. Figure 4.2 plots the mean media and non-media stock prices (in logarithmic units), and Figure 4.3 plots their median prices. Here, both media and non-media stocks have parallel price trends before the "treatment" of appellate decisions in 2000, with media stocks having higher prices. After 2000,

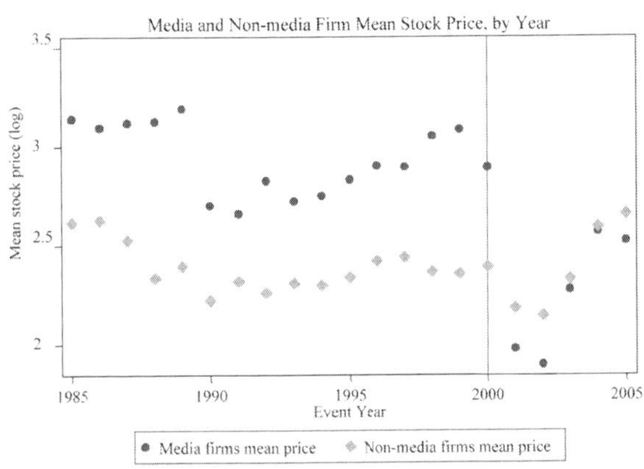

Figure 4.2 Mean stock prices before and after 2000

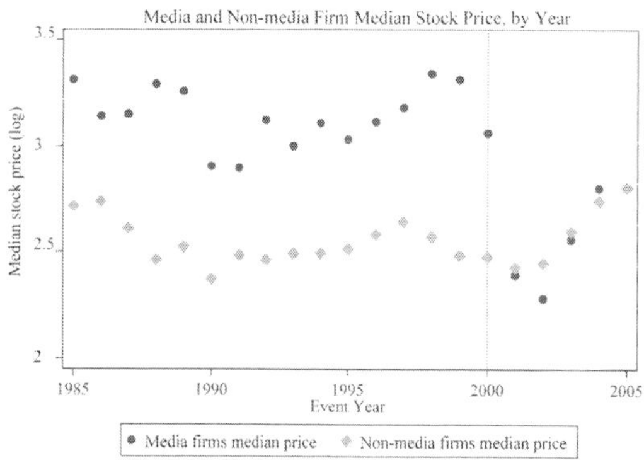

Figure 4.3 Median stock prices before and after 2000

media stock prices show a dramatic drop below non-media stock prices. These raw plots suggest that it is plausible for media stocks, the treatment group, to respond to FCC appellate precedent.

The following linear regression specification depicts the effects of appellate decisions on media stock prices:

$$Y_{it} = \beta_0 + \beta_1 \,.\, Post_t + \beta_2 \,.\, Media_i + \beta_3 \,.\, (Media_i \,.\, Post_t) + \varepsilon_{it} \quad (4.1)$$

where Y_{it} is the media stock price for each firm i at time period t, $Post_t$ is a dummy indicating that the stock price is observed in the period after the appellate decisions occur, M_i is a dummy for media stocks, and ε_{it} is the error term representing omitted factors that determine Y_{it}. The key coefficient of interest is β_3, which corresponds to the interaction between the post-period and media stocks. Table 4.5

Table 4.5 A brief primer on differences-in-differences calculations

Coefficient	*Calculation*
β_0	a
β_1	$c - a$
β_2	$b - a$
β_3	$(d - b) - (c - a)$

where a, b, c, d correspond to:

	Non-media stocks	*Media stocks*
Year 1	a	b
Year 2	c	d

summarizes in an alternative format how the β coefficients in Equation (4.1) are calculated.

The coefficient β_0 is the baseline average for media stock prices. β_1 represents the change over time for the control group, β_2 represents the differences between media and non-media stocks in year 1, and β_3 represents the difference in the changes over time of media and non-media stocks. Assuming both types of stocks have the same trends over time, this regression controls for a possible trend in all stocks using the trend of the control group. Thus, the DID analysis will more accurately provide the impact of appellate court decisions on media stock prices.

Table 4.6 shows the DID results. The baseline average for the log prices of non-media stocks, β_0, is 2.668. The time trend for this control group, β_1, is –0.0713 but is not statistically significant at the 10 percent level; this indicates that non-media stock prices did not differ before and during the year 2000. On average, in the year 2000, the log prices of media stocks were greater than the log prices of non-media stocks by $\beta_2 = 0.559$ with 5 percent statistical significance. Finally, on average, the difference in the changes between the log prices of media and non-media stocks over time, β_3, is –0.710 with 1 percent significance.

These results show that the appellate courts' decisions from the year 2000, which mostly ruled against media businesses, caused the log prices of media stocks to *decrease* by 0.710 with 1 percent significance relative to a baseline of 2.668 for non-media stock prices. This DID analysis suggests that the surge of decisions against media businesses caused a corresponding negative response by stakeholders in the media industry.[65] In other words, the markets were aware of the surge of appellate decisions and the media stock prices reflected this information.

The decreased media competition may correspond to an increase in format variety.[66] Thus, when deciding against media businesses, the courts may have effectively reinforced the purpose of the FCC to "serve … the public interest by promoting diversity of program and service viewpoints."[67]

Table 4.6 Differences-in-differences estimates

Coefficient	*Change in log stock prices*
β_3 (on *Media$_i$*Post$_t$*)	–0.710**
	(–0.132)
β_2 (on *Media$_i$*)	0.559**
	(–0.154)
β_1 (on *Post$_t$*)	–0.0713
	(–0.0668)
β_0 (on a constant)	2.668**
	(–0.0415)
N	408,954
R-squared	0.023

Note: Standard errors in parentheses; $+p < 0.10$; * $p < 0.05$; ** $p < 0.01$.

Two-stage least squares

Determining the effect of appellate court decisions on media stock prices is difficult because reverse causality may exist, or there may be omitted variables influencing media stock prices but correlated with these appellate court decisions.[68] The main specification in this study considers changes in media stock prices measured with respect to appellate decisions establishing legal precedent that differ across circuits and years. The main specification, shown in Equation (4.2), is an ordinary least squares (OLS) model that studies the effects of these appellate decisions on media stock prices over time. This OLS model estimates the unknown parameters in a linear regression model by minimizing the sum of squared distances between the observed data and that predicted by a linear approximation. Equation (4.2) gives the basic OLS specification:

$$Y_{it} = \beta_0 + \beta_1 \,.\, Year_t + \beta_2 W_t + \beta_3 W_t \,.\, Media_i + \beta_4 Media_i + \beta_5 Law_t + \beta_6 Law_t \,.\, Media_i + \varepsilon_{it} \quad (4.2)$$

where Y_{it} represents media stock prices of firm i in year t. ε_{it} is the error term representing omitted factors that determine Y_{it}. Law_t represents the number of pro-public-interest appellate decisions in year t, averaged across all federal appellate circuits. $Year_t$ represents year fixed effects. W_t represents characteristics of the pool of judges available to be assigned and docket size (the number of appellate terminations minus the appellate court decisions) in year t, averaged across the nation. $Media_i$ is a dummy variable indicating whether or not firm i belongs to the media industry.[69] The key coefficient of interest is β_6, on the interaction of Law_t and $Media_{it}$. Since stock prices are serially correlated, ε_{ict} is not independent and identically distributed. Hence, to alleviate this problem, all specifications cluster standard errors at the two-digit industry level.[70]

Despite its controls, the OLS model is susceptible to biases from reverse causality and omitted variables. Therefore, a two-stage least squares (TSLS) framework, more generally known as an instrumental variable (IV) framework, was employed to analyze the effect of relevant appellate court decisions on media stock prices. The first stage of the TSLS model is an OLS regression of pro-public-interest appellate court decisions on judicial attributes, which are randomly assigned. The second stage of the TSLS model is to estimate a regression of media stock prices on the appellate court decisions, based on the coefficients from the first stage regression. In this second stage, an instrumental variable (or "instrument") is used to estimate the causal effect of the appellate decisions on our main outcome of interest, stock prices. The instrumental variable must be correlated with appellate decisions but not directly correlated with the stock prices themselves. In other words, the instrument affects the outcome (stock prices) only through the instrument's effect on the appellate court decisions.

Below, we further illustrate why merely relying on an OLS regression of media stock prices on appellate decisions could lead to biased estimates. A correlation between appellate court decisions and media stock prices may result from

Appellate Decisions

⇓ ⇑ ***[reverse causality]***

Media Stock Prices

⇑

Omitted Variables

Figure 4.4 Illustration of reverse causality

reverse causality or variables influencing media stock prices may be omitted.[71] For example, the FCC pays attention to industry trends when deciding whether to take action against industry or not. This practice can lead to more pro-business actions as well as higher stock prices. It is possible that disproportionately higher stock prices in the media industry would lead to more pro-public-interest appellate decisions because the higher prices can be interpreted as evidence of anticompetitive practices. When a regression model fails to account for omitted variables and reverse causality, the estimate of the effect of pro-business appellate decisions may be biased. The roles of reverse causality and omitted variables in the relationship between appellate decisions and stock prices are represented in Figure 4.4.

To determine the causal effect of appellate court decisions on FCC actions on media stock prices, this study utilizes a TSLS (instrumental variables) empirical method where the instruments are specific personal attributes of judges on federal appellate court panels. The diagram below summarizes the links in the TSLS method:

Judicial Attributes ⇒ Appellate Decisions ⇒ Media Stock Prices

Thus, the instrument must isolate media stock prices to ensure that there is no reverse causality between appellate decisions and media stock prices. Though the randomized controlled trial would generate the most reliable results, it is impossible to conduct controlled experiments that randomly administer appellate court decisions on the media industry stock market. Instead, this study estimates the causal effect of the decisions on media stock prices from observational data by using instrumental variables of judicial attributes.

Since media stock prices (Y_{ict}) may simultaneously affect appellate court decisions (*Law*) for unknown reasons, this study exploits the fact that appellate judges are randomly assigned to three-judge panels, that Democratic appointees are more likely to decide pro-public interest, and that black appointees are more likely to vote pro-business. A number of papers have documented the relationship between judges' demographic backgrounds and their voting behavior in federal appellate courts.[72] Previous research has found mixed evidence of statistically significant differences in decision-making between black and white judges.[73] However, the number of cases analyzed in prior studies was limited, which constricted the potential for behavioral analyses.[74]

To address the concern that Y_{it} and Law_t may be correlated for unknown reasons, we utilize the relationship between a judge's personal attributes and legal decision-making to instrument for appellate court decisions. Given that there are 12 federal appellate circuits in the US, we considered exploiting variation in the number of decisions that arose across these circuits due to the random assignment of judges within each jurisdiction. However, using across-circuit variation is impractical. Decisions on FCC actions are concentrated in the D.C. Circuit. Moreover, stock price responses to those decisions are likely to transcend jurisdictions and occur nationwide. For these reasons, we analyze the results nationally rather than locally. Nevertheless, we acknowledge that circuit-specific characteristics do exist and it is important to observe the variation at the judge, panel, and circuit-year level before utilizing the aggregate variation at the national level. Equation (4.3) gives the first stage regression, which also controls for differences across the 12 circuits:

$$Law_{ct} = \varphi_0 + \varphi_1 Z_{ct} + \varphi_2 C_c + \varphi_3 T_t + \varphi_4 C_c \,.\, Year_t + \varphi_5 W_{ct} + \eta_{ct} \qquad (4.3)$$

where Z_{ct} represents the instruments, *supra*, in circuit c and year t. The identification assumption is $E(\varepsilon_{ict}Z_{ct}) = 0$, meaning that the instruments are orthogonal (uncorrelated) with the error term in the stock price regression of Equation (4.2). A threat to this assumption is that the instruments may be correlated with omitted factors that affect media stock prices. For example, a jurisdiction may have a reputation for favoring private industries, given a higher number of Republican judges who sit in its courts. This may attract fewer public interest litigants and therefore fewer cases appear in that jurisdiction. To minimize omitted variable bias, this study controls for the composition of the judicial pool and the docket size by circuit, which will be aggregated to the national level when conducting the TSLS analysis. This addresses unobserved factors influencing the quantity of litigation and influencing how often judges with a particular demographic background are assigned to these cases.

For our study, data on federal appellate courts were collected from several sources.[75] The composition of circuits and years with Democratic appointees and black judges was calculated using data from the Federal Judicial Center.[76] A measure of annual circuit workload—the number of federal appeals terminated in each fiscal year—was obtained from the Federal Court Management Statistics.[77] The appellate judge and court decisions data span the years 1985 to 2005.

Table 4.7 documents the relationship between pro-public-interest appellate court decisions on FCC actions and the composition of judicial panels.[78] In our main results, we use estimates of the relationship at the national level in the first stage in our two-stage least squares estimation We verify that in addition to being strong at the national level, the relationship between judicial attributes and appellate FCC decisions is robust at the judge, case, and circuit levels, and include

Table 4.7 First stage: relationship between pro-public-interest FCC appellate decisions and the composition of judicial panels, 1985–2005

Panel A: Judge level	*Pro-public-interest decision*		
	(1)	(2)	(3)
Democrat judge	0.0622*		0.127**
	(0.0257)		(0.0222)
Black judge		–0.0618**	–0.151**
		(0.0107)	(0.0131)
N	327	327	327
R-sq	0.324	0.324	0.334

Notes: Heteroskedasticity-robust standard errors are in parentheses. Observations are clustered at the circuit level. Judge-level regressions control for circuit fixed effects, year fixed effects, and the probability of a panel being assigned a judge of the type under consideration: Democrat appointee (columns 1, 3), black (columns 2, 3).

Panel B: Case level	*Pro-public-interest decision*		
	(1)	(2)	(3)
Panel has at least two Democrat judges	0.176**		0.257**
	(0.0261)		(0.0304)
Panel has at least one black judge	–0.0886*	–0.191**	
	(0.0302)	(0.0379)	
N	109	109	109
R-sq	0.385	0.369	0.407

Notes: Heteroskedasticity-robust standard errors are in parentheses. Observations are clustered at the circuit level. Case-level regressions control for circuit fixed effects, year fixed effects, and the probability of a panel being assigned at least two Democrat appointees (columns 1, 3), or at least one black appointee (columns 2, 3).

Panel C: Circuit-year level	*Number of pro-public-interest appellate decisions*					
	(1)	(2)	(3)	(4)	(5)	(6)
Number of FCC panels with at least two Democrat judges	1.278**		0.497**	0.179*		0.334**
	(0.216)		(0.149)	(0.0693)		(0.0868)
Number of FCC panels with at least two Democrat judges		0.994**	0.716**		–0.168+	–0.322**
		(0.0586)	(0.0620)		(0.0840)	(0.0918)
Normalization	Docket	Docket	Docket	Panels	Panels	Panels

Continued

Table 4.7 (Continued)

Panel C: Circuit-year level	*Number of pro-public-interest appellate decisions*					
	(1)	(2)	(3)	(4)	(5)	(6)
N	240	240	240	252	252	252
R-sq	0.776	0.818	0.830	0.923	0.922	0.928

Notes: Heteroskedasticity-robust standard errors are in parentheses. Observations are clustered at the circuit level. Circuit-year-level regressions control for circuit fixed effects, year fixed effects, circuit-specific time trends, the probability of a panel being assigned at least two Democrat appointees, the probability of being assigned at least one black appointee, a dummy for whether there were no cases in that circuit year to minimize mechanical correlation, and docket size in Columns 1–3 or the number of FCC panels in Columns 4–6. Docket size is the number of appellate terminations in the circuit year minus the number of FCC decisions. + Significant at 10 percent, * 5 percent, ** 1 percent.

controls for circuit-specific characteristics. Panels A and Panel B display the relationship at the judge level and the case level, respectively. Panel C displays the relationship at the circuit-year level.

In Panel A of Table 4.7, each of the regressions of a judge's decision on the judge's party affiliation and race clusters the standard errors at the circuit level and controls for circuit fixed effects, year fixed effects, and the probability of being assigned a judge with the attribute under consideration. Column 1 shows that Democratic appointees are 6.22 percent more likely to vote pro-public interest. This is statistically significant at the 5 percent level. Meanwhile, black judges are 6.18 percent more likely to vote pro-business, which is statistically significant at the 1 percent level (column 2). When controlling for whether or not the judge was also a Democratic appointee, black judges are 15.1 percent more likely to vote pro-business in cases about FCC actions (column 3).

The patterns at the judge level are also observed at the case level. Table 4.7, Panel B shows the relationships at the case level. Having at least one black judge on a three-judge panel reduces the chances of a pro-public-interest decision by 8.86 percent, but having at least two Democratic appointees (one judge may influence a colleague's decision, but two judges would win by the force of majority) increases the chances of a pro-public-interest decision by 17.6 percent, which is statistically significant at the 1 percent level.

The circuit-year level results to be used in the first stage of our TSLS model are displayed in Panel C of Table 4.7. At the circuit-year level, the relationship is between the number of panels with a judge attribute and the number of pro-public-interest decisions. Regressions at the circuit-year level control for circuit-specific time trends in addition to circuit fixed effects, year fixed effects, and the probability of a panel being assigned the judge attributes of interest.

Columns 1, 2, and 3 show estimates at the circuit-year level that control for docket size. An additional panel with at least one black judge resulted in 0.994 more cases decided in favor of the public interest, when controlling for docket size. Similarly, an additional panel with at least two Democratic appointees resulted in 1.278 more cases decided in favor of the public interest. Column 3 shows estimates when including both instruments in the same regression. When controlling for panels with two or more Democratic appointees, an additional panel with a black judge results in 0.716 more pro-public-interest decisions. And controlling for the number of panels with black judges, having more panels with majority Democratic appointees also leads to 0.497 more pro-public-interest appellate decisions.

Columns 4, 5, and 6 show estimates that control for the number of cases regarding FCC actions instead of docket size. These regressions include a dummy for whether there were no cases in that circuit year to minimize mechanical correlation.[79] Here, an additional panel with at least one black judge led to 0.168 (10 percent significance) fewer cases favoring the public interest. An additional panel with at least two Democratic appointees resulted in 0.179 more pro-public-interest decisions in a circuit and year on average. Column 6 shows the estimates when including both instruments (number of panels with at least two Democratic appointees and number of panels with at least one black judge) in the same regression; these estimates also control for panel effects. When controlling for panels with two or more Democratic appointees, an additional panel with a black judge corresponds to 0.322 fewer decisions that favor the public interest. Likewise, when controlling for the number of panels with black judges, having more panels with majority Democratic appointees leads to 0.334 more pro-public-interest appellate decisions (Table 4.7, Panel C).

When we aggregate the decisions and panel characteristics to the national level by averaging, we obtain qualitatively similar estimates as in Panel C. When controlling for the number of panels, the assignment of Democratic appointees and black judges to judicial panels have opposite effects on the average number of public interest decisions. The F-statistics of joint significance are very high. When we collapse decisions and panel characteristics data to be one observation per year, the joint F-statistic is 14 when we control for docket size and 4 when we control for number of panels.

To summarize the above, we exploit the fact that Democratic judges and black judges have a predicted relationship with the number of pro-public-interest decisions on FCC actions. The judges' personal attributes are instruments to determine the effect of appellate court decisions on media stock prices. These instruments identify exogenous variation in appellate decisions in the media stock prices regression. For the TSLS strategy to be valid, these instrumental variables must affect media stock prices only by affecting appellate decisions (holding other variables in the model fixed). A correlation between the judge panel composition and media stock prices would be evidence that appellate decisions cause changes in media stock prices.[80] Note that changes in media stock prices do not change judicial characteristics. Thus, the randomized assignment of judges and the resulting judicial panel composition provide a causal experiment to study the effects of appellate court decisions on media stock prices. Put in another way, to implement the TSLS empirical strategy:

1 We begin by estimating Equation (4.3), which is the first-stage regression of the relationship between appellate laws (Lawt) and judicial attributes

(or instruments Zt). Panel C of Table 4.7 shows these results from the first-stage regression.

2 After running the first-stage regression, we then estimate the second-stage regression, shown in Equation (4.4). We use the estimated coefficients from the first-stage regression (Equation (4.3)) to predict $L\hat{a}w_t$, which we then use when estimating the coefficients in the second stage regression in Equation (4.4):

$$Y_{it} = \beta_0 + \beta_1\, Year_t + \beta_2 W_t + \beta_3 W_t \cdot Media_i + \beta_4\, Media_i + \beta_5\, L\hat{a}w_t + \beta_6 L\hat{a}w_t \cdot Media_i + \varepsilon_{it}. \tag{4.4}$$

This two-stage least squares method overcomes the problems of reverse causality and omitted variables that bias the basic OLS estimates of Equation (4.2). The TSLS method allows us to estimate the causal effect of appellate court decisions on media stock prices. Note that as long as judges are randomly assigned to appellate panels, the validity of our method does not rely on the specific set of judicial characteristics used as the instruments.[81] Wooldridge (2001) indicates that the choice of instrument should not affect the 2SLS result for a linear model if the model is well identified under standard assumptions.[82]

The results are in Table 4.8. Each column provides the changes in log stock prices. In each table, column 1 provides OLS coefficient estimates controlled for docket size ("OLS Docket"), and column 2 provides IV estimates that control for docket size ("IV Docket"). Columns 3 and 4 provide OLS and IV estimates that control for the number of FCC cases adjudicated, respectively. In Table 4.9, columns 1–4 include estimates for specifications similar to those in columns 1–4 of Table 4.8, except Table 4.9 applies to lead data and Table 4.8 applies to lag data. Note that in these results we examine *when* appellate court decisions on FCC actions ("appellate court decisions") affected media stock prices. The lag calculations concern the effect one year and two years after the decisions were issued. The lead calculation concerns one year before the decisions issued; we examine the lead to verify that our instrument, the appellate decisions, is random and uncorrelated with preexisting trends in stock prices.

The values of interest are the coefficients on the interaction between the variables *Law* and *Media*. In Tables 4.8 and 4.9, these values are represented by $Media * Law_t$, $Media * Law_{t-1}$, $Media * Law_{t-2}$, and $Media * Law_{t+1}$, where the subscripts t, $t-1$, $t-2$, and $t+1$ denote a zero-year lag, one-year lag, a two-year lag, and a one-year lead, respectively.

The lag values for the interaction between law and media industry stocks suggest that the appellate courts' pro-public-interest decisions caused a *decrease* in the log prices of media stocks. The OLS estimates that control for docket size show a negative correlation (column 1 of Table 4.8). One year after the pro-public-interest appellate decisions, media stock prices were lower by 0.0160 log points relative to non-media stock prices. After two years, media stock prices were lower by 0.0206 log points. These differences are statistically significant at the 10 percent level.

Table 4.8 Effects of appellate decisions over time on log (media stock prices)

	(1)	(2)	(3)	(4)
Pro-public-interest decisions (*t*)	–0.0260** (0.00522)	0.00573 (0.00822)	–0.0888** (0.0208)	–0.104** (0.0217)
Media*pro-public-interest decisions (*t*)	–0.0366 (0.0232)	0.0319** (0.0117)	–0.0420 (0.0409)	–0.0499 (0.0460)
Pro-public-interest decisions (*t* – 1)	–0.0147** (0.00481)	–0.00766* (0.00377)	–0.0876** (0.0154)	–0.0947** (0.0155)
Media*pro-public-interest decisions (*t* – 1)	–0.0223** (0.00456)	–0.0315** (0.00750)	–0.0186 (0.0265)	–0.0158 (0.0292)
Pro-public-interest decisions (*t* – 2)	–0.0447** (0.0123)	–0.0189** (0.00662)	0.0228** (0.00675)	0.0165** (0.00600)
Media*pro-public-interest decisions (*t* – 2)	–0.0475 (0.0423)	–0.0336** (0.0116)	–0.00701 (0.0254)	–0.00272 (0.0390)
Media indicator	0.323 (1.984)	0 (0.111)	2.037 (1.235)	2.004+ (1.178)
Pr(panel has 2+ Democrat appointees) (*t*)	1.599 (1.054)	0 (1.382)	7.569** (0.722)	7.828** (0.798)
Pr(panel has 1+ black appointees) (*t*)	–5.759+ (2.942)	0 (0.396)	4.667** (1.453)	3.404* (1.516)
Media*Pr(panel has 2+ Democrat appointees) (*t*)	3.002 (3.780)	0 (0.0406)	5.043* (1.943)	5.235* (2.248)
Media*Pr(panel has 1+ black appointees) (*t*)	–21.67** (7.720)	0 (0.00274)	–15.09** (4.656)	–14.75* (6.601)
Pr(panel has 1+ black appointees) (*t* – 1)	10.91** (3.896)	0 (0.334)	–8.188** (1.374)	–6.885** (1.141)
Pr(panel has 2+ Democrat appointees) (*t* – 1)	3.074 (3.442)	0 (0.583)	–11.43** (0.827)	–11.74** (0.905)
Media*Pr(panel has 1+ black appointees) (*t* – 1)	15.37 (18.04)	0 (0.00923)	0.399 (4.388)	0.848 (5.307)
Media*Pr(panel has 2+ Democrat appointees) (*t* – 1)	9.013 (12.87)	0 (0.0373)	–1.566 (3.150)	–1.900 (3.785)
Pr(panel has 1+ black appointees) (*t* – 2)	–6.699* (3.362)	0 (0.106)	6.647** (1.845)	6.420** (1.840)

Continued

Table 4.8 (Continued)

	(1)	(2)	(3)	(4)
Pr(panel has 2+ Democrat appointees) (t – 2)	–1.223 (1.624)	0 (0.570)	4.103** (0.800)	4.191** (0.794)
Media*Pr(panel has 1+ black appointees) (t – 2)	–11.44 (12.14)	0 (0.0116)	1.356 (4.624)	0.582 (5.079)
Media*Pr(panel has 2+ Democrat appointees) (t – 2)	–6.226 (5.313)	0 (0.0412)	–2.406 (2.156)	–2.243 (2.348)
Docket size (t) – number of FCC cases (t)	–0.00000525** (0.00000133)	–0.00000190 (0.00000249)		
Media industry*(docket size (t) – number of FCC cases (t))	–0.00000649 (0.00000493)	0.00000228* (0.000000935)		
Docket size (t – 1) – number of FCC cases (t – 1)	0.0000115** (0.00000300)	0.00000213 (0.0000139)		
Media industry*(docket size (t – 1) – number of FCC cases (t – 1))	0.0000190 (0.0000121)	–0.00000349 (0.00000346)		
Docket size (t – 2) – number of FCC cases (t – 2)	–0.00000115 (0.00000127)	0.00000134 (0.0000190)		
Media industry*(docket size (t – 2) – number of FCC cases (t – 2))	–0.00000673+ (0.00000363)	0.00000325 (0.00000655)		
Year had no FCC cases (t)	–0.144 (0.0979)	0.0497 (0.646)	0.207** (0.0403)	0.186** (0.0352)
Media industry*year had no FCC cases (t)	–0.184 (0.340)	0.0211 (0.186)	0.123 (0.0867)	0.120 (0.0753)
Year had no FCC cases (t – 1)	0.0705* (0.0322)	0.0638 (0.384)	0.153* (0.0655)	0.161* (0.0660)

Continued

Table 4.8 (Continued)

	(1)	(2)	(3)	(4)
Media industry* year had no FCC cases ($t-1$)	0.0589 (0.0732)	–0.129 (0.138)	0.136 (0.192)	0.161 (0.199)
Year had no FCC cases ($t-2$)	0.0449 (0.0388)	–0.0190 (0.571)	0.266** (0.0924)	0.293** (0.0926)
Media industry* year had no FCC cases ($t-2$)	0.210 (0.179)	0.00224 (0.135)	0.198 (0.246)	0.215 (0.213)
Number of FCC cases (t)			0.0399** (0.0141)	0.0498** (0.0143)
Media industry* number of FCC cases (t)			0.0327 (0.0227)	0.0374 (0.0284)
Number of FCC cases ($t-1$)			0.0606** (0.0113)	0.0665** (0.0110)
Media industry* number of FCC cases ($t-1$)			0.0000891 (0.0184)	–0.00148 (0.0197)
Number of FCC cases ($t-2$)			–0.0337** (0.00841)	–0.0297** (0.00764)
Media industry* number of FCC cases ($t-2$)			–0.00397 (0.0334)	–0.00884 (0.0439)
Constant	0.434 (0.371)	1.936** (0.461)	1.293** (0.320)	1.281** (0.321)
N	313,387	313,387	313,387	313,387
R-sq	0.014	0.011	0.015	0.015

Note: Robust standard errors are clustered by industry and displayed in parentheses below each coefficient; +*p*-value < 0.10; **p*-value < 0.05; ***p*-value < 0.01. *Law* is the number of appellate decisions ruling in favor of the public interest in FCC actions.

Next, the TSLS (IV) estimates demonstrate that the negative relationship is causal (column 2 of Table 4.8). One year after the pro-public-interest decisions, the log prices of media stocks decreased by 0.0268, which is statistically significant at the 1 percent level. Two years after the decisions, the log prices decreased to 0.0346, which is statistically significant at the 5 percent level.[83] Thus, relative to non-media stocks, media stocks generally *decreased* in their log prices over a longer period after appellate courts issued their decisions against businesses.[84]

Table 4.9 Log (media stock prices) one year before appellate decisions

	(1)	(2)	(3)	(4)
Pro-public-interest decisions (*t*)	0.00413 (0.00516)	–0.00253 (0.00488)	0.0152* (0.00716)	0.0232* (0.0113)
Media*pro-public-interest decisions (*t*)	0.0179 (0.0128)	0.0321* (0.0156)	–0.0312 (0.0254)	–0.0234 (0.0329)
Pro-public-interest decisions (*t* + 1)	–0.00785* (0.00357)	–0.00687 (0.00550)	0.0221** (0.00463)	0.0118+ (0.00634)
Media*pro-public-interest decisions (*t* + 1)	0.0204+ (0.0106)	0.0282** (0.00757)	–0.0367 (0.0347)	–0.0499 (0.0311)
Media indicator	3.334** (0.743)	0 (0.0147)	2.892** (0.556)	2.874** (0.542)
Pr(panel has 1+ black appointees) (*t* + 1)	–3.562** (0.992)	0 (0.324)	2.587** (0.772)	1.261 (1.037)
Pr(panel has 2+ Democrat appointees) (*t*)	–0.654 (0.815)	0 (1.858)	–1.552+ (0.884)	–1.637+ (0.880)
Pr(panel has 1+ black appointees) (*t*)	–1.205 (2.273)	0 (0.517)	–5.775* (2.288)	–4.433 (2.875)
Media*Pr(panel has 2+ Democrat appointees) (*t*)	–2.895 (4.334)	0 (0.0426)	–4.781 (3.821)	–4.807 (3.770)
Media*Pr(panel has 1+ black appointees) (*t*)	–17.37** (3.745)	0 (0.0159)	–17.36** (2.791)	–15.72** (3.623)
Pr(panel has 2+ Democrat appointees) (*t* + 1)	2.031** (0.742)	1.799 (20.51)	0.978 (0.806)	0.933 (0.827)
Media*Pr(panel has 1+ black appointees) (*t* + 1)	1.980 (3.557)	0 (0.00755)	1.088 (2.451)	–0.434 (2.820)
Media*Pr(panel has 2+ Democrat appointees) (*t* + 1)	3.063 (3.904)	0 (0.852)	4.134 (4.079)	4.173 (4.112)
Docket size (*t*) – number of FCC cases (*t*)	0.00000177 (0.00000129)	–0.000000105 (0.00000734)		
Media industry*(docket size (*t*) – number of FCC cases (*t*))	–0.00000417+ (0.00000237)	0.00000174 (0.00000264)		
Docket size (*t* + 1) – number of FCC cases (*t* + 1)	–0.00000213** (0.000000348)	–0.00000132 (0.00000210)		
Media industry*(docket size (*t* + 1) – Number of FCC cases (*t* + 1))	0.00000101 (0.000000748)	0.000000754 (0.00000140)		
Year had no FCC cases (*t*)	0.0342 (0.0231)	0.0144 (0.505)	0.118** (0.0283)	0.129** (0.0323)
Media industry* year had no FCC cases (*t*)	0.200* (0.0917)	–0.237 (0.224)	0.260* (0.102)	0.270** (0.105)

Continued

Table 4.9 (Continued)

	(1)	(2)	(3)	(4)
Number of FCC cases (*t*)			–0.00959	–0.0128
			(0.00845)	(0.0103)
Media industry* number of FCC cases (*t*)			0.0372+	0.0334
			(0.0193)	(0.0217)
Year had no FCC cases (*t* + 1)	0.105**	0.0272	0.264**	0.241**
	(0.0368)	(0.486)	(0.0363)	(0.0436)
Media industry* year had no FCC cases (*t* + 1)	0.209**	–0.363**	0.208**	0.172**
	(0.0625)	(0.139)	(0.0649)	(0.0608)
Number of FCC cases (*t* + 1)			–0.0176**	–0.0102+
			(0.00316)	(0.00568)
Media industry* number of FCC cases (*t* + 1)			0.0301+	0.0399**
			(0.0159)	(0.0147)
Constant	2.684**	2.065**	2.828**	2.867**
	(0.526)	(0.255)	(0.406)	(0.391)
N	317,607	317,607	317,607	317,607
R-sq	0.013	0.006	0.009	0.009

Recall that some appellate decisions were reported in major newspapers.[85] The period between decisions and when firms are exposed to corresponding news reports may explain the lag effect. For example, the issued decisions may have caused a decrease in stock prices for all firms sometime after they received corresponding news reports. With this situation, then, the media stock prices may have continued to decrease into the second year because media firms altered their policies in response to the decisions.

We now consider a falsification check: If our identification strategy truly approximates a random experiment, then no outcome occurring before the treatment has taken place should respond to the randomly administered treatment. The treatment in our situation is the random assignment of judges. This falsification check helps ensure that our results have a causal interpretation instead of being only a correlation. Our next table, Table 4.9, presents an analysis of the data that conducts this check.

The lead values in columns 1–4 of Table 4.9 suggest a potential issue with the current identification strategy. Namely, the number of appellate decisions on FCC actions could be endogenous to previous years' assignment of judicial panels. If this is the case, then attenuation bias is introduced in lags but not in the most advanced lead. However, when we collapse our data to be the yearly average stock price with one observation each for media and non-media stocks, the lead coefficients are no longer statistically significant while the two-year lag coefficient is statistically significant at the 10 percent level. This provides further evidence supporting the hypothesis that stock prices respond to appellate taking decisions on

FCC actions. Our subsequent work on appellate takings decisions improves upon the identification strategy presented in this chapter and further addresses concerns about endogeneity.[86]

The primarily goal of this study is to document the responses of media stock prices to appellate decisions regarding FCC actions. Our findings on stock price responses directly inform whether appellate decisions matter to the market. In view of the broader literature linking stock prices with competition,[87] it is plausible that decreases in media stock prices might imply greater media competition. Still, we caution that media stock prices do not necessarily measure media competition, which is more commonly measured by the revenue of the largest four media owners in a market,[88] audience size of local programming, the variety of programming options,[89] the "percentage of circulation of newspapers, the number of publications owned, the advertising share of radio stations, or the number of journals in a discipline."[90] Further studies are needed to more thoroughly understand the impacts of appellate FCC decisions on media competition and ideological diversity in media markets.

Conclusion

This study utilized a DID analysis and a TSLS framework to test the effects of appellate court decisions on FCC actions on media competition. Changes in media stock prices were used as a proxy for changes in media competition because industry competition may directly affect stock prices. The chapter exploited the random assignment of appellate judges to three-judge panels to identify the instruments of a judge's party affiliation and race, which predict outcomes in appellate decisions. The instruments were used to demonstrate a causal relationship between appellate decisions and changes in media stock prices, as a proxy for changes in media competition.

The DID analysis shows the appellate court decisions against media businesses decreased media stock prices relative to non-media stock prices. Similarly, the TSLS analysis shows the appellate court decisions decreased stock prices among media firms one and two years after the decisions. The relative decrease in media stock prices could be consistent with greater competition in the media market and could correspond to an increased variety of programming. If so, appellate decisions on FCC actions that increase competition and programming variety would suggest that the courts effectively reinforced the purpose of the FCC to serve the public interest by promoting a diversity of viewpoints.

Doctrinal appendix

Communications Act of 1934, 47 U.S.C. §§ 151 *et seq.* (1934) (creating the FCC to regulate broadcasting content after the unregulated growth of the radio industry began booming).

FCC v. Nat'l Citizens Comm. for Broad., 436 US 775, 779, 796 (1978) (alleging certain regulations exceeded the FCC's authority under the Communications Act of 1934, 47 U.S.C. § 151 *et seq.*, and that the FCC exceeded its authority in determining the divestiture under the Administrative Procedure Act, 5 U.S.C. § 706. The court upheld the FCC regulations barring common ownership of a radio or television broadcast station and a daily newspaper in the same community. A co-owner has to divest, within five years, either its newspaper or station holdings to comply with the regulations. The court reversed the lower court's order vacating the limited divestiture requirement because the divestiture rules "enhance the possibility of achieving greater diversity of viewpoints").

Telecommunications Act of 1996, Pub. L. No. 104–104, 110 Stat. 56 (1996) (increasing radio station ownership limits within markets and eliminating restrictions on the number of stations firms can own nationwide. Defines how the FCC grants and licenses the broadcast spectrum to media outlets. Requires a biennial review by the FCC of regulations, provides regulatory forbearance, regulatory relief, and for the elimination of unnecessary regulations).

Cellco P'ship v. FCC, 357 F.3d 88, 99 (D.C. Cir. 2004) (construing the FCC's regulatory power broadly and finding that the FCC does not need to establish that a regulation is absolutely "necessary" in order to comply with a statutory provision requiring necessity for the agency to regulate).

Prometheus Radio Project v. FCC, 373 F.3d 372, 402–03 (3d Cir. 2004) (ruling against FCC action from 2003 to raise the limits of cross-ownership of media outlets, which would have allowed for more media concentration. The court held that a "diversity index" used by the FCC to weigh cross-ownership of media outlets employed "several irrational assumptions and inconsistencies"). The Supreme Court later turned down an appeal for *Prometheus Radio Project v. FCC*, so the decision stands. *See FCC v. Prometheus Radio Project*, 545 US 1123 (US 2005).

In 2007, the FCC proposed a scaled-down version of the consolidation proposal that still contained loopholes allowing for larger media monopolies. However, the Third Circuit placed a stay on the FCC to prevent enforcement. *See Prometheus Radio Project v. FCC*, No. 08–3078, 2009 US App. LEXIS 28819 (3d Cir. June 12, 2009).

In March 2010, during the FCC's 2010 quadrennial review, the Third Circuit removed the stay. *See Prometheus Radio Project v. FCC*, No. 08–3078, 2010 US App. LEXIS 20436 (3d Cir. Mar. 23, 2010). Thus, the 2007 rules are in effect.

Notes

1 *See generally* Gerald N. Rosenberg, The Hollow Hope: Can Courts Bring about Social Change? (1991).
2 *See* FCC v. Nat'l Citizens Comm. for Broad., 436 US 775, 780 (1978).
3 *See* Peter DiCola, *FCC Regulation and Increased Ownership Concentration in the Radio Industry* (Northwestern U. Sch. Law, Faculty Working Papers No. 33, 2010) *available at* http://ssrn.com/abstract=1553483.
4 Larry A. Blosser *et al.*, *Introduction in* The Case Against Media Consolidation, Evidence on Concentration, Localism and Diversity 1, 6 (Mark N. Cooper ed., 2007), *available at* http://www.fordham.edu/images/undergraduate/communications/caseagainstmediaconsolidation.pdf.
5 Assoc. Press v. United States, 326 US 1, 28 (1945).

6 Red Lion Broadcasting Co., Inc. v. FCC, 395 US 367 (1969).
7 *Id.*
8 *Id.* at 390.
9 *See* DiCola, *supra* note 3, at 3.
10 *Id.* ("Firms that own multiple radio stations may find it less costly to offer the same or at least similar programming on all of their stations.").
11 *See id.* at 4–5.
12 *See id.*
13 *Id.* at 17.
14 *See id.* at 3.
15 *See, e.g.*, Cellco P'ship v. FCC, 357 F.3d 88 (D.C. Cir. 2004) (denying industry petition for review of FCC action).
16 *See generally* DiCola, *supra* note 3.
17 *See* Eugene P.H. Furtado & Michael S. Rozeff, *The Wealth Effects of Company Initiated Management Changes*, 18 J. Fin. Econ. 147, 147–160(1987) (noting an increase in stock prices may indicate *more* competition because firm valuations increase from increased efficiencies). *But see* Aditya Todawal, *Effect of Mergers and Acquisitions on Stock Markets*, EzineArticles.com, http://ezinearticles.com/?Effect-of-Mergers-and-Acquisitions-on-Stock-Markets&id=3208748 (last visited June 7, 2010) (noting an increase in stock prices may indicate *less* media competition since stock prices usually increase after mergers).
18 *See, e.g.*, Kewei Hou & David T. Robinson, *Industry Concentration and Average Stock Returns*, 61 J. Fin. 1927, 1928 (2006).
19 Joel Peress, *Product Market Competition, Insider Trading, and Stock Market Efficiency*, 65 J. Fin. 1, 18 (2010), *available at* http://faculty.insead.edu/peress/ personal/Peress_competition.pdf.
20 *Id.* at 5.
21 *See* Furtado & Rozeff, *supra* note 17. *But see* Todawal, *supra* note 17.
22 We also lack the data to make comparison portfolios for each stock. This is a fruitful direction for future work.
23 Another difference between our study and other empirical finance studies is that we do not calculate excess returns, which is the calculation of stock price differences once key observable characteristics are controlled for. These observable characteristics would be uncorrelated, however, with the random assignment of judges.
24 *See* FCC, *About the FCC*, Federal Communications Commission, http://www.fcc. gov/aboutus.html (last visited June 7, 2011) [hereinafter *About the FCC*].
25 Telegraphs, Telephones, and Radiotelegraphs, 47 U.S.C. § 201(b) (2006).
26 FCC v. Nat'l Citizens Comm. for Broad., 796 (1978).
27 47 U.S.C. § 161(b) (1996).
28 Telecommunications Act of 1996, Pub. L. No. 104–104, 110 Stat. 56 (1996). *See also* DiCola, *supra* note 3, at 9.
29 *See generally* Prometheus Radio Project v. FCC, 373 F.3d 372 (3d Cir. 2004).
30 *See* 47 CFR § 73.3555; *see also* Stephen Labaton, *Plan Would Ease Limits on Media Owners*, N.Y. Times, Oct. 18, 2007, *available at* http://www.nytimes.com/2007/10/ 18/business/media/18broadcast.html.
31 *See* FCC, *FCC's Review of the Broadcast Ownership Rules*, Federal Communications Commission, http://www.fcc.gov/cgb/consumerfacts/reviewrules. pdf [hereinafter *FCC's Review*].
32 *See About the FCC*, *supra* note 24.
33 *See FCC's Review*, *supra* note 31.
34 *See infra*, Study design.
35 Pappas v. FCC, 807 F.2d 1019, 1022 (D.C. Cir. 1986).
36 *Id.* at 1025.
37 *See FCC's Review*, *supra* note 31.

38 *Id.*
39 *Id.*
40 *Id.*
41 *See* DiCola, *supra* note 3; *see also supra* Introduction. *But see* Ted Turner, *Monopoly or Democracy?* WASH. POST, May 30, 2003, at A23 (discussing the concern that media concentration prevents new media entrepreneurship).
42 *See FCC's Review*, *supra* note 31, at 2.
43 *Id.*
44 *Id.*
45 *Id.*
46 *Id.*
47 *Id.*
48 *See, e.g.*, Prometheus Radio Project v. FCC, *supra* note 29; Astroline Communications Co. v. FCC, 857 F.2d 1556, 1558 (D.C. Cir. 1988) (observing that "the one-to-a-market rule reflects the Commission's commitment to diversity in ownership and control of broadcast licenses in order to maximize competition, as well as to promote variety in programming sources and viewpoints"); Sinclair v. FCC, 284 F.3d 148 (D.C. Cir. 2002) (holding in part that the FCC's local ownership rule, which restricted common ownership of television stations in a market, "furthered diversity at the local level and was necessary in the public interest").
49 47 U.S.C. § 151.
50 775 F.2d 342 (D.C. Cir. 1985).
51 Omipoint Corp. v. FCC, 78 F.3d 620 (D.C. Cir. 1996).
52 California Ass'n of the Physically Handicapped v. FCC, 840 F.2d 88 (D.C. Cir. 1988).
53 *See infra* Part Study design.
54 "(FCC OR 'F.C.C.' OR 'Federal Communications Commission') w/100 (judgment OR 'court ruling') AND circuit AND NOT 'Supreme Court'."
55 *See, e.g.*, Richard A. Posner, *Optimal Sentences for White-Collar Criminals*, 17 AM. CRIM. L. REV. 409, 410 (1980) (arguing that fines are an economically efficient deterrence measures); *but see* Darlene R. Wong, *Stigma: A More Efficient Alternative to Fines in Deterring Corporate Misconduct*, 3 CAL. CRIM. L. REV. 3, ¶ 2 (Oct. 2000), *available at* http://www.boalt.org/CCLR/v3/v3wongnf.htm ("The combination of these findings indicates that fines are limited in their applicability as an economically fair and efficient deterrence measure.").
56 *See* Cass R. Sunstein *et al.*, ARE JUDGES POLITICAL? AN EMPIRICAL ANALYSIS OF THE FEDERAL JUDICIARY (2006).
57 467 US 837 (1984).
58 The efficient markets hypothesis would suggest that information contained in legal precedent would affect stock prices. The impact of stock prices need not be immediate, however. *See, e.g.*, Stefano DellaVigna & Joshua Pollet, *Demographics and Industry Returns*, 97 AM. ECON. REV. 1667–1702 (2007). In addition, we note that media stock price effects can also be indicative of changes in media competition; studies indicate that firms in highly concentrated industries experience decreased stock price variability, profit, and return volatility. *See supra* Introduction.
59 *See* Division of Corporation Finance: Standard Industrial Classification (SIC) Code List, SEC, http://www.sec.gov/info/edgar/siccodes.htm (last visited Dec. 7, 2010).
60 *See* CRSP, *History*, CENTER FOR RESEARCH IN SECURITY PRICES, http://www.crsp. com/crsp/about/history.html (last visited Nov. 24, 2010).
61 Table 4.1 reveals that some stock prices from CRSP have "negative" signs. A price preceded by a negative sign indicates that the price recorded is the "bid/ask average and not an actual closing price." Furthermore, "[i]f neither closing price nor bid/ask average is available, Price or Bid/Ask Average is set to zero." CRSP, *Price, End of Period*, CENTER FOR RESEARCH IN SECURITY PRICES, http://www.crsp.com/documentation/product/stkind/

definitions/price_end_of_period.html (last visited May 26, 2011). These observations are dropped in our log price regressions.

62 Orion Comm. Ltd. v. FCC, 213 F.3d 761 (D.C. Cir. 2000) (*per curiam*).

63 *Id.*

64 *See, e.g.*, Matthew J. Baker & Brendan Michael Cunningham, *Court Decisions and Equity Markets: Estimating the Value of Copyright Protection,* 49 J.L. & Econ. 567 (2006) (counting the number of court decisions that broadened copyright protection and the number of decisions that narrowed copyright protection and taking the difference as an index of the law); Kenneth J. Meier *et al.*, *The Impact of State-Level Restrictions on Abortion*, 33 Demography 307, 310 (1996) (summing the number of abortion laws to estimate the impact of abortion restrictions on abortion incidence); John C. Moorhouse & Brent Wanner, *Does Gun Control Reduce Crime or Does Crime Increase Gun Control?* 26 Cato J. 103 (2006) (using the Open Society Institute's index of laws consisting of a weighted sum of gun control statutes as the measure of gun control laws); Ingrid Verheul *et al.*, Regional Opportunities and Policy Initiatives for New Venture Creation (Erasmus Research Institute of Management Report Series, December 2007) (using the number of laws promoting firm formation as a measure of policy).

65 *See* Hou & Robinson, *supra* note 18. *But see* Marianne Bertrand *et al.*, *How Much Should We Trust Differences-in-Differences Estimates?* 119 Q. J. Econ. 249 (2004) (noting that a DID "estimation as it is commonly performed grossly under-states the standard errors around the estimated intervention effect").

66 *See* DiCola, *supra* note 3, at 3.

67 *See* FCC v. Nat'l Citizens Comm. for Broad., 780.

68 See Daniel L. Chen & Jasmin K. Sethi, Insiders and Outsiders: Does Forbidding Sexual Harassment Exacerbate Gender Inequality? 13 (Nov., 2011) (unpublished manuscript) (on file with the ETH Zurich), *available at* http://nber.org/~dlchen/ papers/SexHarass.pdf.

69 We do not include firm fixed effects because that would absorb the media dummy.

70 In doing so, we follow Bertrand *et al.*, *See* Bertrand *et al.*, *supra* note 65, at 272–73.

71 *Id.*

72 *See, e.g.*, Christina L. Boyd *et al.*, *Untangling the Causal Effects of Sex on Judging*, 54 Am. J. Pol. Sci. 398 (2010).

73 Thomas G. Walker & Deborah J. Barrow, *The Diversification of the Federal Bench: Policy and Process Ramifications*, 47 J. Pol. 596, 598–99 (1985).

74 *Id.* at 615.

75 *See* Chen & Sethi, *supra* note 68, at 12.

76 *See* FJC, *History of the Federal Judiciary*, Federal Judicial Center, *available at* http:// www. fjc.gov/history/home.nsf (last visited Dec. 17, 2010).

77 *See* USC, *Federal Court Management Statistics*, United States Courts, *available at* http://www. uscourts.gov/fcmstat/index.html (last visited Dec. 17, 2010).

78 Coefficients are shown in each column, with standard errors in parentheses.

79 A dummy variable indicating whether there were no cases in that circuit year was included to minimize mechanical correlation, since both the number of pro-public-interest decisions and the number of panels with a particular judicial composition would equal zero.

80 Other papers have documented the effectiveness of using judicial characteristics as instruments. *See, e.g.*, Chen & Sethi, *supra* note 68, at 14–21.

81 The LASSO technique, which selects optimal instruments from a large set of potential instrumental variables, addresses this concern. *See* Alexandre Belloni *et al.*, *Sparse Models and Methods for Optimal Instruments with an Application to Eminent Domain* (MIT Department of Economics Working Paper No. 11–19, Aug. 15, 2011), *available at* http://papers.ssrn.com/sol3/ papers.cfm?abstract_id=1910169.

82 Jeffrey R. Wooldridge, Econometric Analysis of Cross Section and Panel Data 201 (2002). *See also* Esther Duflo, *MIT Lecture Notes, Empirical Methods (2002)*, at 21, *available at* http://web.mit.edu/14.771/www/emp_handout.pdf.

83 Table 4.8 reveals multicollinearity in a number of control variables when including all interactions with two years of lags. The estimates on the main coefficients are robust when estimating the specification on 25 percent and 75 percent samples, and when estimating separate regressions for media and non-media stocks (robustness results available upon request).

84 The same decline is observed for non-logged stock prices but is less statistically significant.

85 *See supra* Firms' exposure to appellate court decisions.

86 *See* Daniel L. Chen & Susan Yeh, The Economic Impacts of Eminent Domain, (Aug., 2012a) (unpublished manuscript) (on file with the Duke University School of Law), *available at* http://www.duke.edu/~dlc28/papers/EminentDomain.pdf; Daniel L. Chen & Susan Yeh, State Response to Expanding Government Capacity: Evidence from Takings Law, (2012b) (unpublished manuscript) (on file with the Duke University School of Law), *available at* http://www.duke.edu/~dlc28/papers/State. pdf; Daniel L. Chen & Susan Yeh, *Distinguishing Between Custom and Law: Empirical Examples of Endogeneity in Property and First Amendment Precedents*, 21 Wm & Mary Bill Rts J. 1081 (2013).

87 *See*, *e.g*., Hou & Robinson, *supra* note 18 (showing that in the United States firms in more concentrated industries have lower returns because they have lower risks than firms in more competitive industries). A further study develops a model of how the interaction between competition, production, and investment and shows that consistent with Hou and Robinson's risk hypothesis, higher demand and growth can result in a negative relationship between industry competition and stock price returns. Felipe L. Aguerrevere, *Real Options, Product Market Competition, and Asset Returns*, 64 J. Fin. 957 (2009). In the United States it is unlikely that these higher returns would imply a monopoly in the media industry. Studies have established that the US media industry is unlikely to be a monopoly. *See*, *e.g*., Robert B. Horwitz, *On Media Concentration and the Diversity Question*, 21 Info. Soc'y 181 (2005); Benjamin M. Compaine, The Media Monopoly Myth: How New Competition Is Expanding Our Sources of Information and Entertainment (2005).

88 Compaine, *supra* note 87, at i.

89 *Id.* at 1.

90 *Id.* at 6.

References

Aguerrevere, Felipe L. 2009. Real Options, Product Market Competition, and Asset Returns. *The Journal of Finance* 64: 957–983.

Baker, Matthew J., and Brendan Michael Cunningham. 2006. Court Decisions and Equity Markets: Estimating the Value of Copyright Protection. *The Journal of Law and Economics* 49: 567–596.

Belloni, Alexandre, Daniel L. Chen, Victor Chernozhukov, and Christian Hansen. 2011. Sparse Models and Methods for Optimal Instruments with an Application to Eminent Domain. Working Paper No. 11–19. Massachusetts Institute of Technology Department of Economics, Cambridge, MA. Available at http://papers.ssrn.com/sol3/papers.cfm?abstract_id=1910169.

Bertrand, Marianne, Esther Duflo, and Sendhil Mullainathan. 2004. How Much Should We Trust Differences-in-Differences Estimates? *Quarterly Journal of Economics* 119: 249–275.

Boyd, Christina L., Lee Epstein, and Andrew D. Martin. 2010. Untangling the Causal Effects of Sex on Judging. *American Journal of Political Science* 54: 398–411.

Blosser, Larry A., Ben Scott, Jeannine Kenney, Gene Kimmelman, and Glenn B. Manishin. 2007. Introduction. In *The Case Against Media Consolidation, Evidence on Concentration, Localism and Diversity*, edited by Mark N. Cooper. New York, NY: Donald McGannon Center for Communications Research, Fordham University Press, pp. 1–20. Available at http://www.fordham.edu/images/undergraduate/ communications/caseagainstconsolidation.pdf.

Chen, Daniel L., and Jasmin K. Sethi. 2011. Insiders and Outsiders: Does Forbidding Sexual Harassment Exacerbate Gender Inequality? Unpublished manuscript. Duke University, Department of Law, November. Available at http://www.duke.edu/~ dlc28.

Chen, Daniel L., and Susan Yeh. 2012a. The Economic Impacts of Eminent Domain. Unpublished manuscript. Duke University, Department of Law, August. Available at http://www.duke.edu/~dlc28/papers/ EminentDomain.pdf.

——. 2012b. State Response to Expanding Government Capacity: Evidence from Takings Law. Unpublished manuscript. Duke University, Department of Law. Available at http://www.duke.edu/~ dlc28/papers/State.pdf.

——. 2013. Distinguishing Between Custom and Law: Empirical Examples of Endogeneity in Property and First Amendment Precedents. *William and Mary Bill of Rights Journal* 21: 1081–1106.

Compaine, Benjamin M. 2005. The Media Monopoly Myth: How New Competition is Expanding Our Sources of Information and Entertainment. New Millennium Research Council. Available at http://www.thenmrc.org/archive/Final_Compaine_Paper_050205. pdf.

DellaVigna, Stefano, and Joshua Pollet. 2007. Demographics and Industry Returns. *American Economic Review* 97: 1667–1702.

DiCola, Peter. 2010. FCC Regulation and Increased Ownership Concentration in the Radio Industry. Working Paper No. 10–05. Northwestern University School of Law, Law and Economics Research, Northwestern, Washington, DC. Available at http://ssrn.com/abstract=1553483.

Duflo, Esther. 2002. *Empirical Methods* (Lecture Notes), Cambridge, MA: MIT.

Furtado, P.H., and Michael S. Rozeff. 1987. The Wealth Effects of Company Initiated Management Changes. *Journal of Financial Economics* 18: 147–160.

Horwitz, Robert B. 2005. On Media Concentration and the Diversity Question. *The Information Society Journal* 21: 181–204.

Hou, Kewei, and David T. Robinson, 2006. Industry Concentration and Average Stock Returns. *The Journal of Finance* 61: 1927–1956.

Meier, Kenneth J., Donald P. Haider-Markel, Anthony J. Stanislawski, and Deborah R. McFarlane. 1996. The Impact of State-Level Restrictions on Abortion. *Demography* 33: 307–312.

Moorhouse, John C., and Brent Wanner. 2006. Does Gun Control Reduce Crime or Does Crime Increase Gun Control? *Cato Institute* 26: 103–124.

Peress, Joel. 2010. Product Market Competition, Insider Training, and Stock Market Efficiency. *The Journal of Finance* 65: 1–43.

Posner, Richard A. 1980. Optimal Sentences for White-Collar Criminals. *American Criminal Law Review* 17: 409–418.

Rosenberg, Gerald N. 1991. *The Hollow Hope: Can Courts Bring about Social Change*. 2d ed. Chicago, IL: University of Chicago Press.

Sunstein, Cass R., David Schkade, Lisa M. Ellman, and Andres Sawicki. 2006. *Are Judges Political? An Empirical Analysis of the Federal Judiciary*. Washington, DC: The Brookings Institution.

Todawal, Aditya. 2010. Effect of Mergers and Acquisitions on Stock Markets. Available at http://ezinearticles.com/?Effect-of-Mergers-and-Acquisitions-on-Stock-Markets&id=3208748.

Turner, Ted. 2003. Monopoly or Democracy? *Washington Post* May 30: A23.

Verheul, Ingrid, Martin Carree, and Enrico Santarelli. 2007. Regional Opportunities and Policy Initiatives for New Venture Creation. *International Small Business Journal* 27(5): 608–625.

Walker, Thomas G., and Deborah J. Barrow. 1985. The Diversification of the Federal Bench: Policy and Process Ramifications. *Journal of Politics* 47: 596–617.

Wong, Darlene R. 2000. Stigma: A More Efficient Alternative to Fines in Deterring Corporate Misconduct. *California Criminal Law Review* 3: 3–29.

Wooldridge, Jeffrey R. 2001. *Econometric Analysis of Cross Section and Panel Data.* Cambridge, MA: MIT Press.v

5 Do police reduce crime?

A reexamination of a natural experiment

John J. Donohue, Daniel E. Ho, and Patrick Leahy[1]

Introduction

Do police reduce crime? Assessing the policing effect has vexed scholars for generations. Governments may deploy police to areas with expected high crime, seriously confounding observational inference. To break the simultaneity of crime and police, one approach has been to exploit natural experiments that affect police levels in ways unrelated to expected crime. Researchers, for example, have studied electoral cycles,[2] tsunamis,[3] terror alert levels,[4] terrorist attacks,[5] and federal grants to police agencies as inducing plausibly exogenous variation in policing to credibly assess its effect.[6]

We reexamine one such natural experiment first studied by Di Tella and Schargrodsky (DS) (2004).[7] On July 18, 1994, a Renault van loaded with explosives detonated in front of a major Jewish community center in Buenos Aires, Argentina. Eighty-five individuals were killed, hundreds were injured, and the five-story building ultimately collapsed. In the aftermath of the attack, the government began providing 24-hour police protection for 287 Jewish and Muslim institutions in Buenos Aires Province (for fear of reprisals, in the latter case).[8]

DS used the government's response to assess the causal effect of police on crime. Since the assignment of police officers was plausibly exogenous to underlying crime levels, this policy provides a potential opportunity to identify the causal effect of a "fixed and observable police presence" on criminal behavior.[9] Employing a difference-in-differences (DID) approach, DS compared ordinary car theft rates before and after the attack on (1) city blocks with buildings under 24-hour protection ("protected" or "treatment" blocks) and (2) blocks that did not receive special protection ("unprotected" or "control" blocks). They found "a large deterrent effect of observable police on crime" but that "[t]he effect is local, with no appreciable impact outside the narrow area in which the police are deployed."

In this chapter, we revisit this evidence. We argue that there are three mechanisms that may invalidate the experiment. First, the reassignment of police officers to protection details may have reduced police levels in unprotected blocks. Second, the 24-hour police presence on protected blocks may have displaced car thieves from protected to unprotected blocks. Third, a federal order prohibiting parking near potential targets confounds the intervention. Each of these invalidates the assumption that control blocks are independent from the treatment blocks. We provide evidence consistent with displacement, although ultimately we conclude that the existing data do not lead to firm inferences.

The chapter proceeds as follows. The first section provides an overview of the Buenos Aires data and the original DS analysis. The second section discusses threats to validity of the DID design. The third section describes an alternative DID approach that (a) disaggregates control blocks into "near" blocks that are likely subject to displacement and "far" blocks that are not, and (b) matches treatment, near blocks and far blocks exactly on all pretreatment covariates, including neighborhood and pretreatment crime trends. Results are consistent with displacement. Crime trends on protected and far blocks are indistinguishable, while crime increases on near blocks. The final section concludes with a general note of caution about qualitative assumptions underpinning natural experiments.

Buenos Aires data and DS analysis

The Buenos Aires data consist of monthly car thefts from April to December 1994 in three neighborhoods with a substantial number of Jewish institutions, out of a total of 48 city neighborhoods.[10] The units of analysis are 876 city blocks, 37 of which contained protected buildings. Figure 5.1 shows maps of the three neighborhoods (Belgrano, Villa Crespo, and Oncé), as well as the locations of blocks with protected buildings (solid dots).[11] The core of the DS analysis focused on the following model, estimated using ordinary least squares:

$$E(y_{it}) = \alpha T_{it} + M_t + F_i,$$

where y_{it} is the number of thefts on block i in month t (with fractional thefts when the exact location was unclear); $T_{it} = 1$ block i contained a protected building and $t > 7$ (i.e. after July), and zero otherwise; M_t is a month fixed effect; and F_i is a block fixed effect. The coefficient α represents the deterrent effect of police protection on the rate of car thefts. DS found that police protection caused a statistically significant reduction of approximately 0.08 car thefts per month on protected blocks.[12] To test whether the protective halo extended to other blocks (but not to test for displacement), DS also tested models with indicators for blocks that were one to two blocks away from protected institutions, but found no evidence for a diffusion of benefits.

Figure 5.2 conveys the intuition of the original findings, plotting average monthly car thefts per block from April to December 1994. The top panel presents theft rates for protected blocks—i.e. blocks that would receive added police protection beginning in August—while the middle panel presents theft rates for unprotected blocks—i.e. blocks serving as the control group. The bottom panel shows monthly averages and 95 percent pointwise confidence bands for protected blocks (light gray) and unprotected blocks (dark gray). Mean car theft levels on protected and unprotected blocks are somewhat comparable prior to the attack.

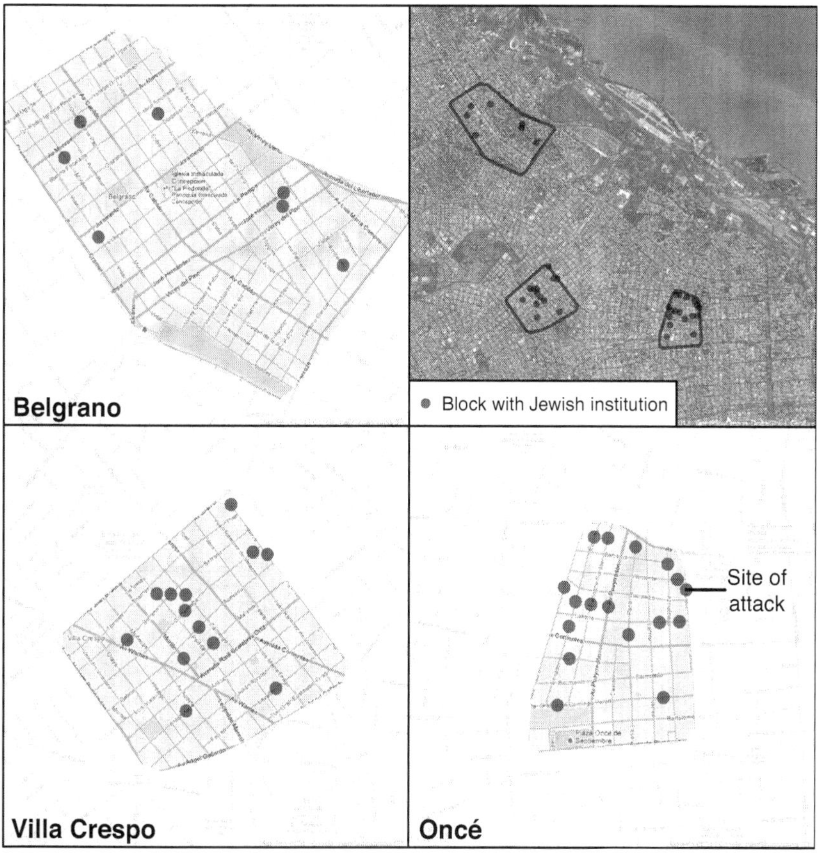

Figure 5.1 Neighborhoods included in Buenos Aires data

Note: The top right panel shows the location of the three neighborhoods within Buenos Aires. The other three panels zoom in on individual neighborhoods. Gray dots indicate blocks with Jewish institutions, which are disproportionately located in Villa Crespo and Oncé.

After the attack, the mean rate decreases for protected blocks, but also increases for the large group of unprotected blocks.

Credibility of identifying assumptions

The central question is whether the decrease in crime on protected blocks can be attributed to deterrence—i.e. whether police protection prevented crimes that otherwise would have occurred. The DID design theoretically allows one to answer this question by using the control group (of unprotected blocks) to estimate counterfactual potential outcomes for protected blocks (absent the protection policy). Unprotected blocks must still satisfy two conditions, however, in order to serve

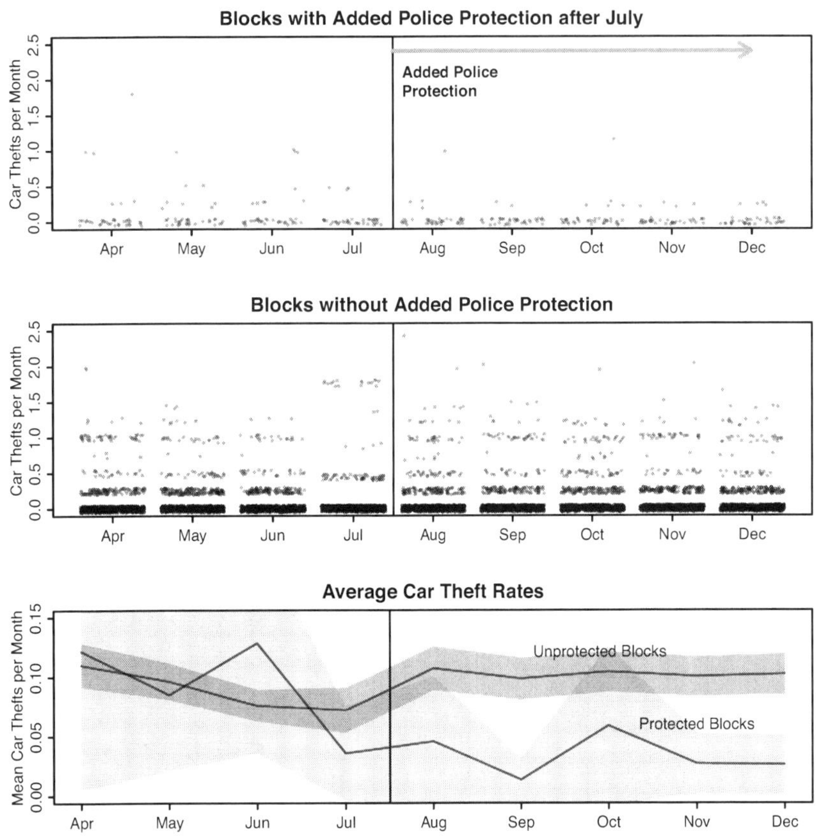

Figure 5.2 Monthly car theft rates

Note: The top panel plots car theft rates for protected blocks (those that received police protection after July) in each month from April to December 2004. The middle panel shows theft rates for unprotected blocks (those that did not receive additional protection after July). Each dot represents one block. Dots are jittered for visibility. The bottom panel plots mean monthly car theft rates for each group of blocks, with pointwise 95 percent confidence bands. Car thefts occurring between July 18 and July 31 are excluded, as in DS. Theft rates are normalized to 30-day months.

as a valid control group: they must (a) be independent of the treatment received by the protected blocks, and (b) exhibit *homogeneity* in time trends with protected blocks. We argue that both of these assumptions are likely not met.

Independence

One general difficulty in attributing changes to the protection policy is that it did not occur in isolation: the city had just weathered the deadliest terrorist attack in Argentina's history,[13] which could have affected crime in many other ways. Terrorist attacks have been noted to have a wide and unpredictable impact on economic activity and human behavior.[14] Ignoring broader social effects, we identify three ways in which the government's response might have impacted crime on unprotected blocks, violating the assumption of independence.

First, the attack almost certainly affected police levels on unprotected blocks. Officers cannot be drawn from thin air. The provision of 24-hour police protection on certain blocks likely decreased the police resources available to others. According to DS, "the police forces made a serious effort to maintain previous levels of police presence in the rest of the neighborhoods," but "more than one-third of approximately 200 police officers stationed in Once [sic] … had to be reassigned to protection duties."[15] Other security measures may have absorbed additional police resources in these neighborhoods,[16] and there may also have been a large-scale shift in police priorities from combatting street crime to preventing terrorism.[17] Independent of any shift in criminal activity, a reduction in police levels—or a decreased emphasis on apprehending ordinary criminals—would theoretically lower the risks associated with crime and thereby incite car thieves to act with greater frequency.[18] Alternatively, of course, it is possible that police levels *increased* throughout these neighborhoods as the government tightened security and shifted police resources toward neighborhoods with a large Jewish population. Either scenario, however, would result in biased estimates of the deterrent effect. Without data on police levels, it is impossible to know what effects we are actually measuring when comparing protected and unprotected blocks.

Second, criminals may have responded to the police presence on protected blocks by refocusing their activities on unprotected blocks. Spatial displacement is a common concern with crime prevention measures that focus on particular locations: increasing enforcement efforts in one area may displace criminals to others (or to other types of crime, a possibility that we have no way of examining).[19] Empirical findings about the prevalence of displacement have been mixed,[20] but in the current case it is doubtful that thieves would be limited by a lack of opportunity on other blocks, given the ubiquity of vehicles. In the four months prior to the attack, a car theft was reported on or at the intersection of 51 percent of the blocks under observation, suggesting that opportunities for theft are not geographically restricted to a few hot spots. This possibility is especially likely if police levels decreased—or even were perceived to decrease—on blocks without Jewish institutions. It is thus conceivable that crime would, as the authors of one study on displacement put it, literally "move around the corner."[21]

Last, the intervention may have altered the distribution of vehicles themselves, leading to changes in car theft patterns. In the wake of the attack, the government imposed parking restrictions on the streets of protected institutions, potentially dislocating cars and traffic and reducing the number of available targets on protected blocks.[22] The 24-hour police protection is fundamentally confounded with the parking prohibition. While DS estimate that a small fraction of parking space on protected blocks was affected by the prohibition,[23] little evidence exists to corroborate its scope. In any case, the number of vehicles on blocks with Jewish institutions may also have decreased if they were perceived as potential terrorist targets.[24] And there would have been an acute parking disruption in the area around the site of the bombing itself, which is included in the DS analysis.

Homogeneity

Random assignment of protection would guarantee that protected and control blocks follow (in expectation) comparable underlying time trends. The assignment of police protection, however, was determined by the location of Jewish (and Muslim) institutions. As a result, there may be systematic differences between the control and treatment groups. One obvious difference, as Figure 5.1 shows, is that protected blocks are disproportionately located in Oncé and Villa Crespo (and are often clustered together within neighborhoods as well), while Belgrano contains the majority (55 percent) of unprotected blocks under observation. Crime varies considerably across neighborhoods, however: in the pretreatment period, Oncé, Villa Crespo, and Belgrano had 0.04, 0.08, and 0.11 thefts per block (F-test p-value < 0.0001). The imbalance means that crime trends—estimated largely from Belgrano—may not be homogeneous across treatment and control groups, potentially biasing results.[25] Indeed, the pretreatment time series itself suggests a lack of homogeneity, as protected and unprotected blocks appear to diverge even in the pretreatment period.[26]

Natural experiments require assumptions that must be defended. In the Buenos Aires case, there are strong substantive reasons to think that the independence assumption is violated. Displacement, rather than deterrence, may drive the decrease in crime that DS observe. While the available data may not allow us to learn much more, we demonstrate one possible research design that attempts to account for displacement effects, weaken model sensitivity, and establish more homogeneous treatment and control groups. We emphasize, however, that the primary purpose of this chapter is to raise questions about the deterrence effect in the Buenos Aires data.

An alternative approach

Constructing a plausible control group

We modify DS's approach in two ways to address the implausibility of the independence and homogeneity assumptions.

First, we disaggregate unprotected blocks into two groups: "near" blocks, which are within one to three blocks of a protected institution, and "far" blocks, which are located four or more blocks away. Near blocks are presumably more likely to be affected by at least two of the three mechanisms discussed above: crime-shifting in response to the police presence and the parking prohibition. There is of course no obvious threshold between near and far blocks, but it seems plausible that drivers unable to park on protected blocks and thieves displaced by 24-hour patrols would be displaced in only a localized way. Our cutoff classifies 557 blocks as near and 279 as far.[27] (We exclude the block where the attack occurred and all adjacent blocks, which were impacted in a more drastic way by cleanup and building reconstruction.[28])

Second, to make the homogeneity assumption more credible (and to reduce model dependence), we preprocess the data by matching protected, near, and far blocks that are identical in all pretreatment covariates.[29] In essence, we construct strata with identical values on eight covariates: the neighborhood; thefts rates in each of the pretreatment months (March to the beginning of July); and the presence of a bank, gas station, or public institution.[30] The latter three, as DS note, may have an independent deterrent effect on car thefts.[31] Matching on the neighborhood ensures that groups are physically proximate, and avoids using the large number of high-crime, control blocks in Belgrano to estimate counterfactual outcomes for protected blocks disproportionately in the other neighborhoods. Matching units with identical pretreatment car theft time series means that any post-treatment deviation between groups can be more plausibly attributed to the intervention.

Matching produces nine strata (listed in Appendix A) with common support, containing 307 blocks (21 protected, 218 near, and 68 far). To estimate the (in-sample) treatment effect on the protected blocks, we construct matching weights proportional to the number of protected blocks in each stratum (e.g. a stratum with i protected, j near, and k far blocks results in weights of 1, i/j, and i/k, respectively).

Table 5.1 summarizes covariate balance for the raw and matched samples. Protected, near, and far blocks have different neighborhood distributions in the raw sample. Moreover, the average June theft rate is substantially higher for protected blocks than near or far blocks. By construction, exact matching results in perfect covariate balance in these dimensions.

Removing observations for unmatched blocks (i.e. observations with no common support), we estimate the effects of the intervention via weighted least squares, minimizing:

$$\sum_{i,t} w_i \, [y_{it} - (\alpha T_{it}^{prot} + \beta T_{it}^{near} + M_t + F_i)],$$

where w_i is the weight assigned to block i, T_{it}^{prot} is an indicator variable for protected blocks in months after the intervention, T_{it}^{near} is an indicator for near blocks in months after the intervention, and fixed effects are as before. The coefficient α represents the effect of the intervention on protected blocks and β its effect on unprotected nearby areas, relative to the control group of far blocks. We might interpret negative and positive values of these coefficients as deterrent and displacement effects, respectively. (In the discussion that follows, we use the term "displacement" somewhat loosely to refer to an increase in crime driven by proximity to protected blocks, regardless of the precise mechanism responsible.)

Results

Table 5.2 reports estimates of these effects, with robust standard errors in parentheses. The first column presents results for the full matched sample, with treatment

Table 5.1 Covariate balance in the raw and matched samples

	Raw sample			*Matched sample*		
	Protected	*Near*	*Far*	*Protected*	*Near*	*Far*
Neighborhood						
Belgrano	0.20	0.41	0.82	0.19	0.19	0.19
Villa Crespo	0.37	0.36	0.16	0.33	0.33	0.33
Oncé	0.43	0.23	0.03	0.48	0.48	0.48
Crime rates						
April	0.13	0.13	0.08	0.00	0.00	0.00
May	0.09	0.10	0.10	0.03	0.03	0.03
June	0.14	0.07	0.08	0.08	0.08	0.08
July	0.04	0.07	0.07	0.02	0.02	0.02
Buildings						
Bank	0.06	0.08	0.08	0.10	0.10	0.10
Gas station	0.03	0.02	0.03	0.00	0.00	0.00
Public inst.	0.06	0.04	0.02	0.00	0.00	0.00
Blocks	35	557	279	21	218	68

Note: Columns summarize the covariates used for matching in each group of blocks—protected, near, and far—within the full sample and matched sample. The rows under "Neighborhood" contain the average value of dummy variables indicating whether each block is in a particular neighborhood. (Due to rounding, the three values may not sum to 1.00.) The rows under "Crime rates" contain the average monthly theft rate in each month prior to the attack. The rows under "Buildings" contain the average value of dummy variables indicating the presence of each building type. For the matched sample, all figures are weighted averages. By construction, covariates have the same mean value across all groups in the matched sample.

effects pooled across neighborhoods. The deterrent effect (for protected blocks) is statistically indistinguishable from zero. The displacement effect (for near blocks) is positive and statistically significant. We estimate that the added police patrols caused an increase in 0.06 car thefts per block per month, plus or minus 0.04, at the 95 percent confidence level. This amounts to roughly 13 thefts per month across all near blocks in the matched sample. The next three columns of Table 5.2 present results for matched blocks within a single neighborhood. Displacement effects appear in Villa Crespo and Oncé, but not in Belgrano. Deterrence effects are never statistically significant.

Figure 5.3 illustrates these findings, plotting months on the x-axis against car theft rates on the y-axis, separately for protected, near, and far blocks in the matched sample. The three lines represent monthly weighted averages of the theft rate in each group, with 95 percent pointwise confidence intervals.[32] By construction, the three groups have identical trends before the attack. In the aftermath of the terrorist attack, the theft rate rises in near blocks, diverging sharply from the other two groups, while protected and far blocks remain indistinguishable in the months immediately after the attack.

What explains the discrepancy between these results and the deterrence effect that DS found? The DS model restricts the coefficient on nearby blocks by pooling

Table 5.2 Effects of the protection policy

	Pooled	*Belgrano*	*Villa Crespo*	*Oncé*
Protected × Post	–0.014	–0.087	0.008	0.000
	(0.017)	(0.076)	(0.016)	(0.010)
Near × Post	0.061	0.033	0.072	0.065
	(0.019)**	(0.089)	(0.013)***	(0.013)***
N	2,763	450	1,296	1,017
Adjusted R^2	0.10	0.10	0.08	0.10

Note: The first column presents weighted least squares regression results for the full matched sample. The remaining columns present results for the model when fitted using only matched observations in a single neighborhood. "Protected × Post" is the effect of the intervention on treated blocks; "Protected × Near" is the effect on near blocks. The dependent variable is the number of car thefts per month per block. All regressions include block and month fixed effects. Robust standard errors are given in parentheses.

** = significant at the 0.01 level. *** = significant at the 0.001 level.

near and far blocks[33] and assigns a weight of 1 to each observation. This has two effects. First, pooling nearby blocks (where crime rises) and far blocks (where crime stays the same as in protected blocks) in the control group inflates the estimated deterrent effect since the difference is just as plausibly due to displacement effects. Second, equal weighting means that Belgrano, which has a higher baseline rate of car thefts, has a disproportionate influence on the results, despite the fact it has the smallest number of protected blocks. Villa Crespo and Oncé, conversely, have relatively low theft rates, such that there is not much crime to deter. Indeed, Belgrano drives DS's original findings: if Belgrano is omitted from their models, the estimated deterrent effect is a statistically *insignificant* decrease of roughly 0.05 car thefts per month (compared to a 0.18 decrease in Belgrano[34]).

To visualize these neighborhood differences, Figure 5.4 plots outcomes in the matched sample before and after the intervention for each neighborhood. Black

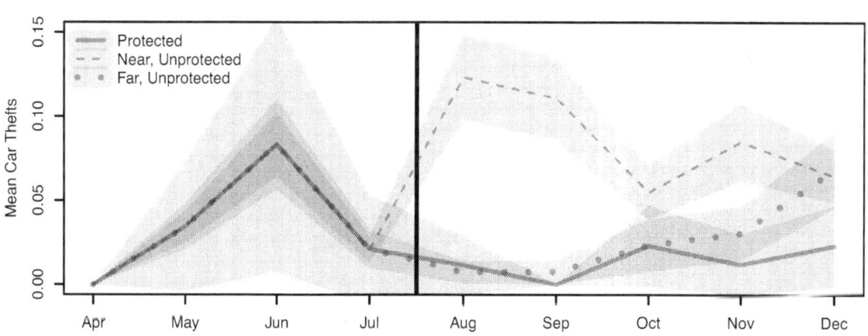

Figure 5.3 Monthly car theft rates in the matched sample

Note: The three lines show weighted averages of the monthly car theft rate in each group of blocks in the matched sample (using the weights described in the section entitled An alternative approach). Thefts from July 18 to July 31 are excluded from the July averages. Theft rates are normalized to a 30-day month. By construction, the three trend lines are identical in months before the attack. After the attack, the theft rate rises among near unprotected blocks.

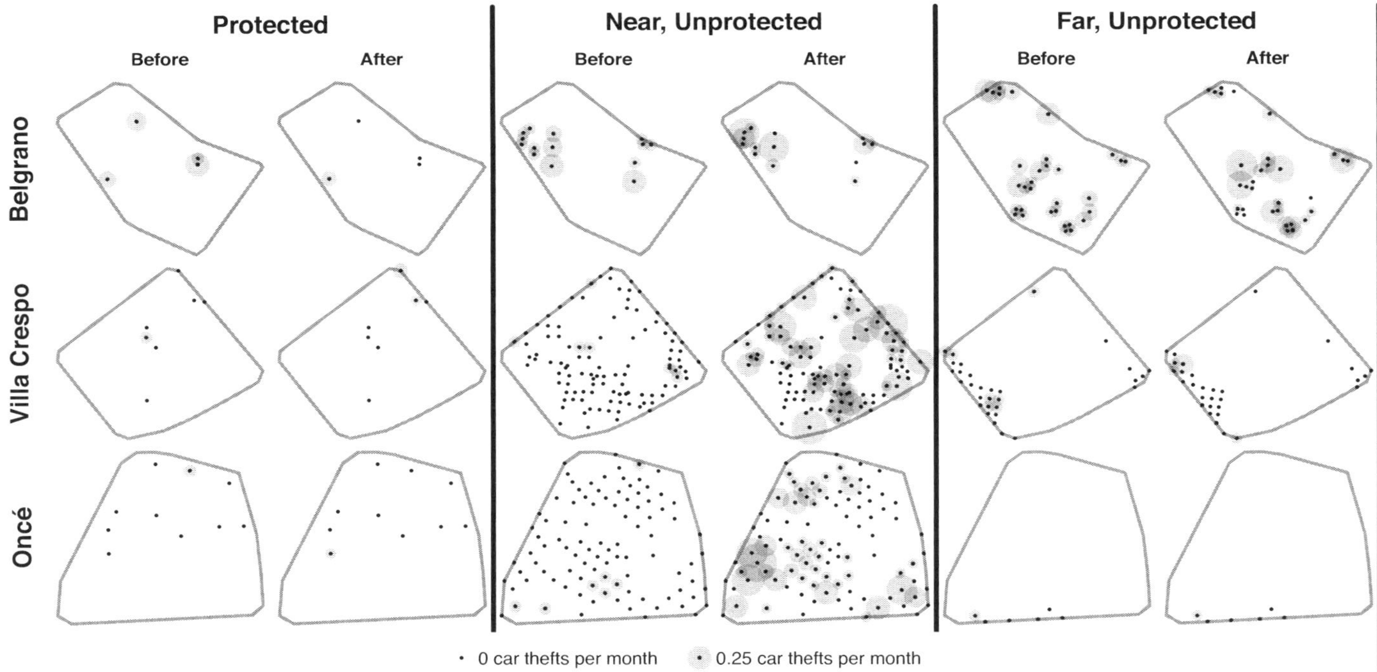

Figure 5.4 Car theft rates on matched blocks before and after the attack

Note: Each vertical panel shows outcomes for one of the groups in the matched sample. Within each panel, the two columns show average monthly crime rates for individual blocks in that group before and after the attack. Black dots indicate the location of matched blocks. The gray circles are sized in proportion to the overall theft rate for that period.

dots indicate the location of matched blocks while the gray circles are proportional to the car theft rate for the pre- and post-period. In Belgrano, matched blocks each experience thefts pre-attack; afterward, thefts decline somewhat in protected blocks but remain roughly constant in the two unprotected groups. In the other two neighborhoods, by contrast, we see a sharp increase in near blocks and virtually no change in far blocks. Because matched blocks in these neighborhoods mostly had no car thefts prior to the attack, we might expect thefts to increase by regression to the mean. But the increase is concentrated almost entirely in areas closer to protected blocks, suggesting that displacement may be driving these car thefts.

Lastly, we offer some evidence of displacement in the raw sample. Figure 5.5 presents 30-day moving averages of the crime rate across all near and far unprotected blocks. The theft rates are remarkably consistent, crisscrossing frequently, for most of the observation period, but diverge in the two months after the attack. This divergence appears consistent, at least with the displacement of car theft to near blocks.

With a few seemingly innocuous modifications to the original approach—aimed to make more credible the independence and homogeneity assumptions—we find evidence inconsistent with pure deterrence. Of course, the affirmative evidence of displacement is also limited: there are fewer units with common support; the time series is very short, making it difficult to establish homogeneity in the pretreatment period; and without further knowledge about the precise mechanisms at work, far blocks, as we have defined them, may not be a persuasive control group. At minimum, however, this reanalysis establishes that the conclusions one draws from the data depend considerably on the qualitative assumptions one is willing to make.

Figure 5.5 30-day moving averages of theft rate in near and far blocks

Note: The two lines represent daily time series for near and far blocks. For a given day the height of each line corresponds to the average number of thefts on near or far blocks within a 30-day window centered on that day.

Conclusion

Our reexamination of the Buenos Aires experiment questions DS's finding of a deterrent effect. There are strong reasons to suspect that the 24-hour police protection policy displaced crime to other blocks. The Argentinian natural experiment may be less a story of the deterrent effect of police than of the complex and inadvertent impact of antiterrorism measures on street crime.

Firmer conclusions would require both (a) more precise data and (b) deeper institutional and historical knowledge.

Better data

First, we would ideally have block-level data on police activity. The analyses above use the presence of a protected institution as a proxy for police presence, but "protected" and "unprotected" blocks are better characterized as blocks on which at least one officer was stationed and blocks about which we have no information on police levels. Police levels may have decreased on unprotected blocks, but the devastation caused by this terrorist attack may also have heightened police vigilance throughout the city. Second, data on parking availability and traffic flows would potentially enable one to separate the effects of police protection from those of the parking prohibition. Third, to establish DID as a credible identification strategy, crime data from a longer observation period would be invaluable, allowing the researcher to examine (and better adjust for) seasonal trends in car thefts. As Appendix B documents, however, obtaining such historical data from Buenos Aires is challenging. Finally, for the research design we propose, additional block-level information on factors that may influence thefts—such as street size, lighting, foliage, and activity levels—would help in establishing more credible matches.

Institutional knowledge

Qualitative institutional knowledge is invaluable in assessing the credibility of assumptions and specific causal mechanisms. What was the nature of the added police protection? What precisely were the officers' duties? How visible were they to would-be thieves? Did protection vary by institution or over time? How widely publicized was the protection policy? What types of car thieves operate in these neighborhoods, and how far might they reasonably travel in search of targets?

Obviously, it is not always feasible to acquire all the data and qualitative information that a researcher desires. DS deserve much credit for identifying a case where police assignment was plausibly exogenous to crime, obtaining these data, and conducting interviews with high-level officials. But the DID research design requires the assessment of the credibility of key assumptions that may not be justified in this case.

While DS's evidence may not be persuasive, we see promise in the use of natural experiments and granular crime data to evaluate police effects. Conventional observational studies in this area often rely on geographically aggregated data, such as police size and budgets and city- or county-level crime rates.[35] While such studies encompass many jurisdictions, causal inference is difficult in such observational settings.[36] Moreover, aggregated data may provide less insight into *how* police reduce crime, given the myriad ways in which police resources can be deployed. The Buenos Aires natural experiment, by contrast, in principle permits researchers to assess the impact of a specific mechanism, namely the observable presence of stationary police officers. As local law enforcement agencies increase the scope, quality, and accessibility of the data they collect, research in this vein will undoubtedly reveal greater nuances in the relationship between police and crime.

Appendix A: composition of the matched sample

Table 5.3 presents covariates of each of the matched strata, along with stratum-specific DID estimates in the right two columns. For example, the first row represents seven protected blocks in Oncé that have no car thefts, no banks, gas stations or public institutions before the attack, which are matched to seventy-eight near and three far blocks in the same neighborhood with the same covariates. The DID estimate between these near and protected blocks is 0.04, meaning that thefts increased in near blocks relative to the protected blocks. The DID estimate between these far and protected blocks is –0.01, meaning that thefts decreased in far blocks relative to protected blocks. The estimates reported above are essentially a weighted average of these conditional effects over strata: generally near blocks experience increases relative to protected blocks, while the far blocks are not statistically distinguishable from protected blocks.

Appendix B: seasonality

In the absence of a proper control group, an alternative approach for estimating counterfactual outcomes might be to establish a seasonal baseline trend based on several years' worth of data. Figure 5.6 illustrates what such data might reveal. Each panel reproduces the mean car theft trends from Figure 5.1, with the thick line showing a hypothetical baseline trend. In the left panel, unprotected blocks follow the normal seasonal trend, suggesting that the protection policy has a purely deterrent effect. In the middle panel, however, it is protected blocks that follow the baseline trend, which suggests the increase in crime among unprotected blocks is due to displacement. In the right panel, there is minimal seasonality, implying a mixture of deterrence and displacement.

To assess seasonality in Buenos Aires car thefts, we attempted to collect data for a longer period of time. Using insurance reports from the *Superintendencia de*

Table 5.3 Unique strata in the matched sample

Covariates												
Neighborhood	*April Thefts*	*May Thefts*	*June Thefts*	*July Thefts*	*Bank*	*Gas station*	*Public Inst.*	*No. Protected*	*No. Near*	*No. Far*	*DID: Near - Protected*	*DID: Far - Protected*
Oncé	0	0	0	0	0	0	0	7	78	3	0.04	–0.01
Villa Crespo	0	0	0	0	0	0	0	6	100	23	0.06	–0.01
Oncé	0	0	0	0	1	0	0	2	12	2	0.13	–0.00
Belgrano	0	0	0.25	0	0	0	0	1	10	22	0.10	0.09
Villa Crespo	0	0	0.25	0	0	0	0	1	7	7	0.05	–0.00
Oncé	0	0	0.25	0	0	0	0	1	7	1	0.10	0.05
Belgrano	0	0	1	0	0	0	0	1	2	4	0.07	0.15
Belgrano	0	0.5	0	0	0	0	0	1	1	5	–0.10	0.01
Belgrano	0	0.25	0	0.25	0	0	0	1	1	1	0.39	0.10

Note: Each row corresponds to a stratum in the matched sample. The first eight columns indicate the unique combination of covariate values that define each stratum: the neighborhood; the theft rates in April, May, June, and July; and the presence of a bank, gas station, or public building. The next three columns indicate the number of protected, near, and far blocks contained in each stratum. The last two columns present conditional DID estimates for each stratum, comparing protected blocks to near blocks and far blocks.

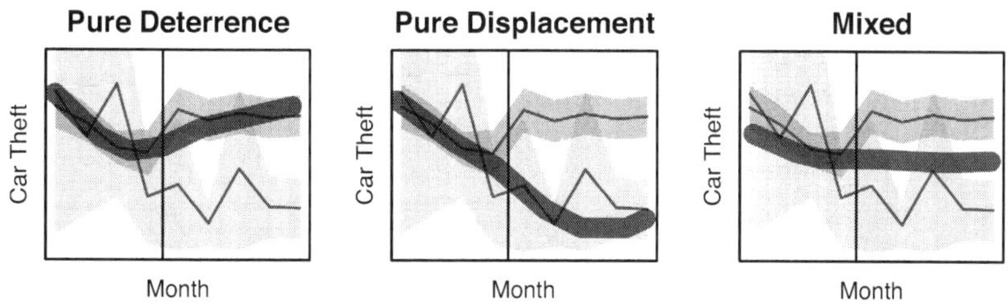

Figure 5.6 Hypothetical baseline trends

Note: Each panel plots actual mean car theft rates for protected (lighter gray) and unprotected (darker gray) blocks, as shown in the bottom panel of Figure 5.1. The thick black lines indicate hypothetical baseline trends. In the left panel, the observed data is most consistent with pure deterrence; in the middle panel, with pure displacement; and in the right panel, with both deterrence and displacement.

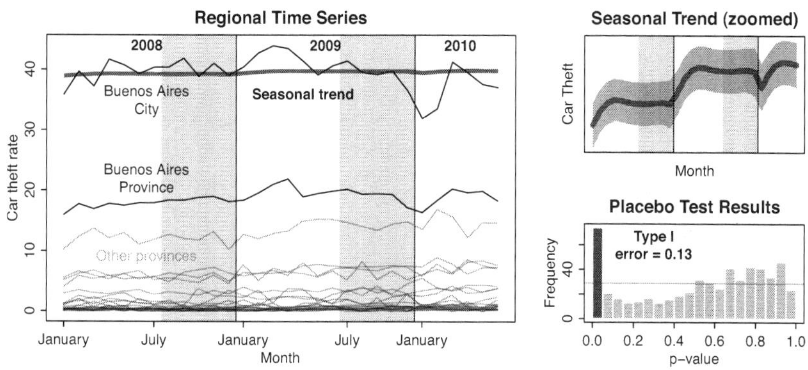

Figure 5.7 Car theft trends in Argentina, 2008–10

Note: The left panel shows monthly car theft rates in Argentinian provinces. The thick black line indicates the estimated seasonal trend (using a generalized additive model smoothing over months). The top right panel zooms in on the seasonal trend. The bottom right panel plots p-values from placebo DID estimates, showing a 13 percent Type I error rate at the 0.05 significance level.

Seguros de Nación, we were able to obtain monthly province-level data only from 2008 to mid-2010. Figure 5.7 presents the car theft time series for each province, with the city and province of Buenos Aires. The vertical black line indicates a new calendar year and the gray bands indicate the August–December period, the months corresponding to the treatment period in the DS data. The individual times series exhibit considerable noise: comparing trends in the city of Buenos Aires before and after July would indicate an increase in 2008 but a decrease in 2009. To leverage information from the other provinces, we fit a generalized additive model with year and province fixed effects, allowing for a smooth time trend over the calendar year. The dark gray line in the left panel of Figure 5.7 represents the seasonal trend for Buenos Aires. While the months of January and February generally exhibit decreased car theft (see the top right panel), such systematic seasonality is small compared to the month-to-month noise in car theft: the line is effectively flat. This would seem to point toward the possible presence of both displacement and deterrence in the DS data, but given the large gap in time between the two datasets, it is probably unreasonable to extrapolate time trends from one to the other.

While there is no evidence of strong seasonality, the additional car theft data does point to one danger in the use of DID estimators. When serial correlation is present, estimated standard errors will be smaller than their true values, which may result in the detection of significant effects where none exist.[37] Here, for example, a placebo DID test where we activate the treatment in each possible province at each possible month yields a 13 percent false positive rate (at a 0.05 significance level), as shown in the bottom right panel of Figure 5.7.

Notes

1 We thank Andrea Chin, Alex Holtzman, Rebecca Morris, Tim Shapiro, and Olga Zverovich for research assistance, Rafael Di Tella and Ernesto Schargrodsky for data, and Jennifer Arlen, Yun-chien Chang, Daniel Chen, Ming-Jen Lin, Dan Rubinfeld, two anonymous referees, and participants at the International Conference on Empirical Studies of Judicial Systems at Academia Sinica for helpful comments.

2 *See* Steven D. Levitt, *Using Electoral Cycles in Police Hiring to Estimate the Effects of Police on Crime*, 87 Am. Econ. Rev. 270 (1997). *See also* Justin McCrary, *Using Electoral Cycles in Police Hiring to Estimate the Effects of Police on Crime: Comment*, 92 Am. Econ. Rev. 1236 (2002); Steven D. Levitt, *Using Electoral Cycles in Police Hiring to Estimate the Effects of Police of Crime: Reply*, 92 Am. Econ. Rev. 1244 (2002).

3 *See* Panu Poutvaara & Mikael Priks, *The Effect of Police Intelligence on Group Violence: Evidence from Reassignments in Sweden*, 93 J. Pub. Econ. 403 (2009).

4 *See* Jonathan Klick & Alexander Tabarrok, *Using Terror Alert Levels to Estimate the Effect of Police on Crime*, 48 J.L. & Econ. 267 (2005).

5 *See* Mirko Draca, Stephen Machin & Robert Witt, *Panic on the Streets of London: Police, Crime, and the July 2005 Terror Attacks*, 101 Am. Econ. Rev. 2157 (2011).

6 *See* William N. Evans & Emily G. Owens, *COPS and Crime*, 91 J. Pub. Econ. 181 (2007).

7 *See* Rafael Di Tella & Ernesto Schargrodsky, *Do Police Reduce Crime? Estimates Using the Allocation of Police Forces After a Terrorist Attack*, 94 Am. Econ. Rev. 115 (2004).

8 Di Tella & Schargrodsky, *supra* note 7, at 117.

9 *Id.* at 123.

10 For many car thefts the reported location is an intersection, rather than a particular block; in these cases DS assigned 0.25 car thefts to each of the adjacent blocks.

11 The original data contain the street name and first address for each block, but no coordinate information. We used the Google Geocoding API to obtain coordinates for the approximate midpoint of each block.

12 DS employed a variety of robustness tests, such as estimating separate treatment effects for each month after the intervention, activating police dummies in earlier months to test whether crime trends in protected blocks were already diverging, and excluding

blocks with no thefts in any month under observation. *See* Di Tella & Schargrodsky, *supra* note 7, at 124. None of their checks account for displacement, however.

13 *See* Michael Warren, *Israel Concerned over Argentina-Iran Meetings*, SEATTLE TIMES, Sept. 28, 2012, http://seattletimes.com/html/nationworld/2019291408_apltargentinairanisrael.html.

14 *See, e.g.*, Seymour Spilerman & Guy Stecklov, *Societal Responses to Terrorist Attacks*, 35 ANN. REV. SOC. 167 (2009); Zvi Eckstein & Daniel Tsiddon, *Macroeconomic Consequences of Terror: Theory and the Case of Israel*, 51 J. MONETARY ECON. 971 (2004); Gary S. Becker & Yona Rubinstein, Fear and the Response to Terrorism: An Economic Analysis (Feb. 2011) (unpublished manuscript) (on file with authors).

15 Di Tella & Schargrodsky, *supra* note 7, at 117.

16 The government also instituted air patrols and heightened security at media buildings and airports, for instance. *See* British Broad. Corp., *Government Adopts Security Measures in View of Possible Terrorist Attack*, BBC SUMMARY OF WORLD BROADCASTS, Aug. 15, 1994.

17 Soon after the attack, for instance, Argentina's president created a new security agency "to oversee police and quasi-military institutions." Martin Andersen, *A New Security Force Rises from the Ashes in Argentina*, WASH. TIMES, Aug. 22, 1994. *See also* Calvin Sims, *Argentina's New Secret Security Agency Raises Fear of Repression*, HOUSTON CHRON., Sept. 11, 1994.

18 A redistribution of police has been noted in a few cases to at least be correlated with an increase in crime: rates of street crime in London, for example, peaked in the month after the September 11 attacks, when police were redeployed to secure potential terrorist targets. Reportedly, robberies also increased in London when police were redeployed during a visit by President Bush in 2003. Kathryn Curran *et al.*, CRIME AND DRUGS DIVISION, GOVERNMENT OFFICE FOR LONDON, STREET CRIME IN LONDON: DETERRENCE, DISRUPTION, AND DISPLACEMENT (2005).

19 *See, e.g.*, Thomas A. Reppetto, *Crime Prevention and the Displacement Phenomenon*, 22 CRIME & DELINQUENCY 166 (1976).

20 *See* Rob T. Guerette & Kate J. Bowers, *Assessing the Extent of Crime Displacement and Diffusion of Benefits: A Review of Situational Crime Prevention Evaluations*, 47 CRIMINOLOGY 1331 (2009).

21 David Weisburd *et al.*, *Does Crime Just Move Around the Corner? A Controlled Study of Spatial Displacement and Diffusion of Crime Control Benefits*, 44 CRIMINOLOGY 549 (2006).

22 According to one press report, "the Federal Police has been ordered not to allow the parking of vehicles outside any objective on any account." British Broad. Corp., *supra* note 17.

23 *See* Di Tella & Schargrodsky, *supra* note 7, at 124.

24 This was a reasonable fear given that the 1994 attack was not an isolated incident: a similar bombing had occurred at the Israeli Embassy in Buenos Aires two years earlier, and in August 1994 the government received warnings that yet another attack was imminent, leading to heightened security—bomb-sniffing dogs and armored vehicles—at some Jewish institutions. *Menem Warns Argentinians Against Bomb Panic*, JERUSALEM POST, Aug. 14, 1994.

25 Consider the following simplified scenario: neighborhood A has 100 control blocks and 5 treated blocks, while neighborhood B has 20 control and 20 treated. If crime increases by 1 unit on every block in neighborhood A, and does not change at all in neighborhood B, the average increase across all control blocks is 100/120 = 0.83 units, while across all treated

blocks it is 20/40 = 0.5 units. Even though there is no deterrent effect in either neighborhood, we observe an apparent one when outcomes are averaged across neighborhoods.

26 For instance, with a conventional DID approach for just the June and July data, we would reject the null hypothesis of no deterrence effect at a 10 percent level, despite the fact that the test is conducted on data exclusively prior to the police intervention.

27 Since DS include controls for observations at a distance of one or two blocks, our threshold only extends the radius of possible influence by a block. Roughly 20 percent of the sample is three blocks away from a protected institution, however, so this expansion removes a large number of blocks from the control group.

28 The block where the attack occurred is also an invalid treatment unit because the Jewish Community Center was under police protection prior to the terrorist attack, due to a similar bombing at the Israeli embassy in 1992. According to a news report, "a police car was permanently stationed in front of the building." The car was destroyed in the explosion and two police officers were killed. Federico Ferber, *Argentina: Bombed Jewish Building Had Poor Security*, INTER PRESS SERV. (July 19, 1994).

29 See Daniel E. Ho *et al.*, *Matching as Nonparametric Preprocessing for Reducing Model Dependence in Parametric Causal Inference*, 15 POL. ANALYSIS 199 (2007); Stefano M. Iacus, Gary King & Giuseppe Porro, *Causal Inference with Balance Checking: Coarsened Exact Matching*, 20 POL. ANAL. 1 (2012).

30 This procedure is a form of coarsened exact matching, where we "coarsen" the time series for each block to the month level to facilitate matches. *See* Iacus, King & Porro, *supra* note 30.

31 *See* Di Tella & Schargrodsky, *supra* note 7, at 128.

32 As in DS, the averages for July include only the first 17 days of the month.

33 To be precise, DS in some specifications test for a protective halo by including controls for units one to two blocks away, but find these to be statistically insignificant. The key pooling assumption is for blocks that are three blocks away and more than three blocks away.

34 The Belgrano effect is statistically significantly different from 0 and the effect outside of Belgrano.

35 *See* Hyeyoung Lim, Hoon Lee & Steven J. Cuvelier, *The Impact of Police Levels on Crime Rates: A Systematic Analysis of Methods and Statistics in Existing Studies*, 8 ASIA PAC. J. POLICE & CRIM. JUST. 49 (2010).

36 *But see* Aaron Chalfin & Justin McCrary, The Effect of Police on Crime: New Evidence from US Cities, 1960–2010 (Oct. 1, 2012) (unpublished manuscript) (on file with authors).

37 *See* Marianne Bertrand *et al.*, *How Much Should We Trust Differences-in-Differences Estimates?*, 119 Q. J. ECON. 249 (2004).

References

Becker, Gary S., and Yona Rubinstein. 2011. Fear and the Response to Terrorism: An Economic Analysis. Working paper.

Bertrand, Marianne, Esther Duflo, and Sendhil Mullainathan. 2004. How Much Should We Trust Differences-in-Differences Estimates? *Quarterly Journal of Economics* 119: 249–275.

Chalfin, Aaron, and Justin McCrary. 2012. The Effect of Police on Crime: New Evidence from US Cities, 1960–2010. Working paper.

Curran, Kathryn, Michael Dale, Mark Edmunds, Mike Hough, Andrew Millie, and Melissa Wagstaff. 2005. *Street Crime in London: Deterrence, Disruption, and Displacement.* London: Government Office for London.

Di Tella, Rafael, and Ernesto Schargrodsky. 2004. Do Police Reduce Crime? Estimates Using the Allocation of Police Forces After a Terrorist Attack. *American Economic Review* 94: 115–133.

Draca, Mirko, Stephen Machin, and Robert Witt. 2011. Panic on the Streets of London: Police, Crime, and the July 2005 Terror Attacks. *American Economic Review* 101: 2157–2181.

Eckstein, Zvi, and Daniel Tsiddon. 2004. Macroeconomic Consequences of Terror: Theory and the Case of Israel. *Journal of Monetary Economics* 51: 971–1002.

Evans, William N., and Emily G. Owens. 2007. COPS and Crime. *Journal of Public Economics* 91: 181–201.

Guerette, Rob T., and Kate J. Bowers. 2009. Assessing the Extent of Crime Displacement and Diffusion of Benefits: A Review of Situational Crime Prevention Evaluations. *Criminology* 47: 1331–1368.

Ho, Daniel E., Kosuke Imai, Gary King, and Elizabeth A. Stuart. 2007. Matching as Nonparametric Preprocessing for Reducing Model Dependence in Parametric Causal Inference. *Political Analysis* 15: 199–236.

Iacus, Stefano M., Gary King, and Giuseppe Porro. 2012. Causal Inference with Balance Checking: Coarsened Exact Matching. *Political Analysis* 20: 1–24.

Jerusalem Post. 1994. Menem Warns Argentinians Against Bomb Panic. Aug. 14.

Klick, Jonathan, and Alexander Tabarrok. 2005. Using Terror Alert Levels to Estimate the Effect of Police on Crime. *Journal of Law and Economics* 48: 267–279.

Levitt, Steven D. 1997. Using Electoral Cycles in Police Hiring to Estimate the Effects of Police on Crime. *American Economic Review* 87: 270–290.

Levitt, Steven D. 2002. Using Electoral Cycles in Police Hiring to Estimate the Effects of Police on Crime: Reply. *American Economic Review* 92: 1244–1250.

Lim, Hyeyoung, Hoon Lee, and Steven J. Cuvelier. 2010. The Impact of Police Levels on Crime Rates: A Systematic Analysis of Methods and Statistics in Existing Studies. *Asian Pacific Journal of Police & Criminal Justice* 8: 49–82.

McCrary, Justin. 2002. Using Electoral Cycles in Police Hiring to Estimate the Effects of Police on Crime: Comment. *American Economic Review* 92: 1236–1243.

Poutvaara, Panu, and Mikael Priks. 2009. The Effect of Police Intelligence on Group Violence: Evidence from Reassignments in Sweden. *Journal of Public Economics* 93: 403–411.

Reppetto, Thomas A. 1976. Crime Prevention and the Displacement Phenomenon. *Crime & Delinquency* 22: 166–177.

Spilerman, Seymour, and Guy Stecklov. 2009. Societal Responses to Terrorist Attacks. *Annual Review of Sociology* 35: 167–189.

Weisburd, David, Laura A. Wyckoff, Justin Ready, John E. Eck, Joshua C. Hinkle, and Frank Gajewski. 2006. Does Crime Just Move Around the Corner? A Controlled Study of Spatial Displacement and Diffusion of Crime Control Benefits. *Criminology* 44: 549–592.

6 To tear down or not to tear down?

An empirical study of boundary encroachment cases in Taiwan

Yun-chien Chang[1]

Introduction

In civil law countries, unlike in common law jurisdictions, boundary encroachment and adverse possession are different issues,[2] as many civil codes contain separate doctrines for them. In 2009, the Taiwan Civil Code, including its stipulations for boundary encroachment (Articles 796, 796–1, and 796–2), was amended. Specifically, the current doctrines are as follows: the entitlement of the neighbor (whose land is trespassed) is generally protected by "the property rule"[3] when the encroachment is intentional or grossly negligent. The entitlement, however, is only protected by "the liability rule"[4] if the neighbor fails to promptly notify the negligent trespasser of her disapproval upon being aware of the trespass. And under the liability rule, the neighbor can either request that the encroacher purchase "the part of the trespassed land" and "the odd lot caused by the trespass" at a "reasonable price," or request payment for her losses. Pursuant to the newly enacted Article 796–1, if the trespass is unintentional, the court, after taking into account the public interests and the interests of the two parties, may switch from the property rule (removal) to the liability rule (preservation). The boundary encroachment doctrines apply to residential buildings and apply *mutatis mutandis* to other types of construction that are "similarly valuable" (Article 796–2).

This chapter empirically investigates how district courts in Taiwan employ the discretion provided by Article 796–1—specifically, whether courts tend to make efficiency-enhancing decisions. The property rule is generally preferred in property law.[5] From an ex ante viewpoint,[6] this makes economic sense[7] as security of property rights encourages owners to make investments, and voluntary transactions backed by the property rule generally ensure Pareto efficiency. Nonetheless, if the property rule is enforced to its logical limit, ex post inefficiency may occur. For instance, suppose a homeowner's house encroaches over the boundary by an inch due to an error made by a surveyor; in that case, the encroaching part of her house (often where the pillars are located) will be torn down by court officers upon request of her neighbor after a judgment that strictly enforces the property rule. As the value of the house is often much higher than that of one square inch of land, from an ex post viewpoint[8] the removal decision is inefficient. Courts in various jurisdictions are likely to draw on good faith or equity doctrines to preserve the encroaching building, perhaps ordering the no-fault trespasser to compensate her neighbor instead.[9] Henry Smith calls it the "safety valve" of private law.[10] Taiwan's law is unique in that the legislators have tailor-made a safety valve in the boundary encroachment context. This chapter examines whether courts have used the safety valve power to make welfare-improving decisions.

My study can be put into the broader context of exploring whether career judges in a civil law jurisdiction tend to make efficient decisions. Whether common law courts tend to make efficient laws is famously considered in Judge Posner's first edition of *Economic Analysis of Law*,[11] and discussed in many works in the past several decades.[12] Civil law courts have less rule-making discretion than their common law counterparts do,[13] but judges in civil law countries still have room to interpret the civil code, and oftentimes have discretion in determining the outcomes of the cases at hand, for example, in a boundary encroachment dispute. In my other works, I have found mixed evidence of the efficiency-mindedness of judges in Taiwan. On the one hand, in co-ownership partition cases, judges in Taiwan tend to take post-partition land value into account and wisely choose between partition by sale and partition in kind.[14] On the other hand, in unjust enrichment cases, judges in Taiwan do not use market value as a benchmark, and they suffer from the anchoring effect.[15] This study provides further evidence of judicial behaviors in Taiwan.

Using the population of boundary encroachment cases in Taiwan during over three years in logistic regression models, I find that the size of the encroached land and the culpability of the trespasser are the major determinants of judicial decisions to remove or preserve the encroaching buildings. Specifically, when the size of encroached land is small, judges tend to preserve the buildings and order compensation. In the eight cases in which the trespassers were found to be grossly negligent, courts ordered removal. In the only case in which the trespasser was found not to be at fault, the house was preserved. The statistical significance of the first factor (land size) suggests that courts in Taiwan emphasize efficiency-relevant factors when using their discretion.

This chapter is structured as follows. The next section, Research questions and methodologies, elaborates the research questions and sets out the specifications of the logistic regression models. The following section, Data, summarizes the pertinent data. The section thereafter, Findings and discussions, reports the findings and discusses their implications. The final section concludes.

Research questions and methodologies

Judicial behaviors in boundary encroachment cases

A boundary encroachment dispute by definition involves at least two parcels of land. In this chapter, I shall call the trespasser's land "encroacher's land," and "neighbor's land" refers to the adjacent land that has been encroached on. They are designated as A and B, respectively, in Figure 6.1. The encroacher's building generally does not cover the whole plot (A). The part of the land upon which the building is erected is called "building site" and marked as C. The specific part of land B where the building has encroached is called the "encroached land" and marked as D.

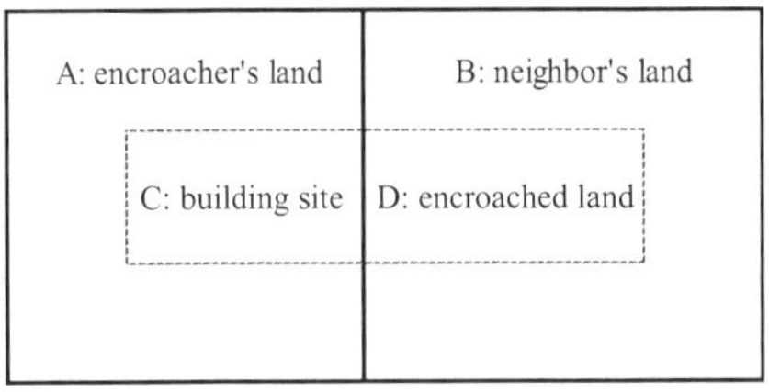

Figure 6.1 Illustration of terms used in boundary encroachment disputes

Pursuant to the stipulations in the Taiwan Civil Code, when Article 796–1 of the Taiwan Civil Code applies, the default is removal. In other words, judges must consider public interests and both parties' interests when determining whether to switch track from removal to preservation. There could be public interests for removal or preservation,[16] but courts do not always discuss both the pros and cons of removal. As a result, a dummy variable on "removal (or preservation) for the public interest" would suffer from a serious endogeneity problem. A similar problem would arise regarding the private interests of the two parties. Consequently, in the regression models I use to tease out the determinants of the judicial decisions, I cannot rely on the reasoning offered in the judgments. Rather, more objective factors like the value and size of the encroached land will be used. That being said, in the penultimate section I will analyze and discuss briefly how judges reason regarding the public and private interests.

My first conjecture regarding the determinants of the removal–preservation decision is that the (relative) sizes of *A*, *B*, *C*, and *D* (in Figure 6.1) matter. Specifically, the size of the encroached land (*D*) should be critical. The ratio of $C/(C + D)$ should also concern the judges, as a low ratio may suggest negligence, or even gross negligence In addition, the ratio of *B/D* should also matter. To paraphrase regulatory takings parlance, a high ratio suggests that the trespasser is going too far, or, the trespass may have deprived all the "economically viable use" of the neighbor's land. As it turns out, courts in Taiwan have focused predominantly on the size of the encroached land (*D*), as information regarding the land size of *A*, *B*, and *C* is available in only three, twenty-seven, and eight observations, respectively. As a result, the ratios of *B/D* are known in only 24 observations, and the ratios of $C/(C + D)$ are available in only a handful of observations. I will thus only be able to use the size of D (available in all but one observations) in the regression models.[17] In Figure 6.4, however, I will plot the judicial decisions by the ratio of *B/D* to see whether my conjecture might hold.

Article 796–1 of Taiwan Civil Code prescribes that interests of both parties have to be considered. From the law-and-economics standpoint, this rule could be interpreted as asking judges to compare the changes in value of the encroaching building and the encroached land under removal and preservation. Put differently, assuming that the expense of tearing down the encroaching part of the building is negligible, preservation is warranted only if the decrease in building value (resulting from removal) is larger than the alternative use value of the encroached land.[18]

If judges in Taiwan aim to increase ex post social welfare, they will take into account the values of the encroaching buildings and the encroached land. Nonetheless, while every registered building in Taiwan is assigned a tax value, courts appear to never consider the tax value or the market value of the encroaching buildings. Information regarding land value is available in the judgments, and presumably courts are consciously and subconsciously affected by the land value. My second hypothesis is thus that the higher the land value, the more judges are inclined to order removal. I will not be able to test the effect of building value on judicial behaviors, but I suspect that building value influences judges' decisions only in marginal cases (e.g. extremely shabby or luxurious buildings). That being said, as a rough proxy of building value my regression models include four dummy variables that control for the type of construction (more on this below).

The third hypothesis is that the level of culpability on the trespasser's side (no fault, negligence, and gross negligence) influences the courts' decisions. Civil law judges generally prioritize the pursuit of fairness and justice in cases. It is thus reasonable to posit that a grossly negligent trespasser is unlikely to persuade the judge to preserve her house, while it is easier for a no-fault trespasser to do so. As it turns out, in 71 percent of the observations, the courts do not specify in the judgments whether the trespasser is (grossly) negligent or without fault. Hence, this hypothesis cannot receive the examination that I have hoped for.

Logistic regression models

To test the above hypotheses, I run several logistic regression models. The dependent variable is whether courts order removal (=0) or preservation (=1).[19] The independent variables include: size of the encroached land (in natural log); the official land value of the encroached land (in natural log);[20] the numbers of plaintiff and defendant lawyers (both in square root); four dummy variables controlling for construction types: residential buildings, residential buildings and fixtures, non-residential buildings, and non-residential buildings and fixtures, with "fixtures only" as the baseline variable; three dummy variables controlling the culpability of the trespassers:[21] grossly negligent, negligent, and no fault, with "courts not taking into account the culpability" as the baseline variable.[22] My models try to control for the variances in economic development. Instead of using town fixed effects that would deplete the degree of freedom or county fixed effects that would mix rich towns with poor towns, I deal with this issue in two ways. First, I include a continuous variable that captures the population density (persons per square kilometer in natural log) of the town where the land is located. Alternatively, following Hou *et al.*[23] I categorize towns and boroughs (under counties and cities, respectively) in Taiwan into seven tiers based on sociodemographic variables (including age, education, industrial structure, occupation, and personal income). Stratum 1 is the most developed, while stratum 7 is the least. My data have few observations in strata 6 and 7, so I combine them and use this as the baseline. Five other dummy variables capture strata 1, 2, 3, 4, and 5, which represent central business district, industrial and business districts, growing towns, towns with traditional industries, and less-developed towns, respectively. Year fixed effects are also included. The models take the following form:

$$\boldsymbol{D} = \alpha + \beta \boldsymbol{PT} + \delta \boldsymbol{LD} + \theta \boldsymbol{CL} + \eta \boldsymbol{TY} + \rho \boldsymbol{YR} + \gamma \boldsymbol{ST} + \varepsilon$$

where ***D*** is the judicial decisions; ***PT*** is two variables controlling the number of lawyers on the two sides; ***LD*** is size and value of the encroached land; ***CL*** are three variables capturing the culpability of the trespassers; ***TY*** is a group of dummy variables controlling for the type of construction; ***YR*** are dummy variables indicating the year of the case. ***ST*** is the strata of the towns/cities where the land in question is located (or, alternatively, the population density variable). The coefficients to be estimated are α, β, δ, θ, η, ρ, and γ; ε is an error term.

Data

I collected and coded all district court cases between July 22, 2009 (when Article 796–1 of Taiwan Civil Code came into effect), and November 4, 2012. After irrelevant cases are discarded, my data set contains 157 observations. I focus on decisions by the court of first instance, because, as emphasized by Guthrie, Rachlinski, and Wistrich (2007: 4), most cases are handled by district/trial courts and many of these decisions are final.[24]

As Figure 6.2 and Table 6.1 show, the area of most encroached land parcels is between 1 square meter and 100 m^2. The mean is 17 m^2.

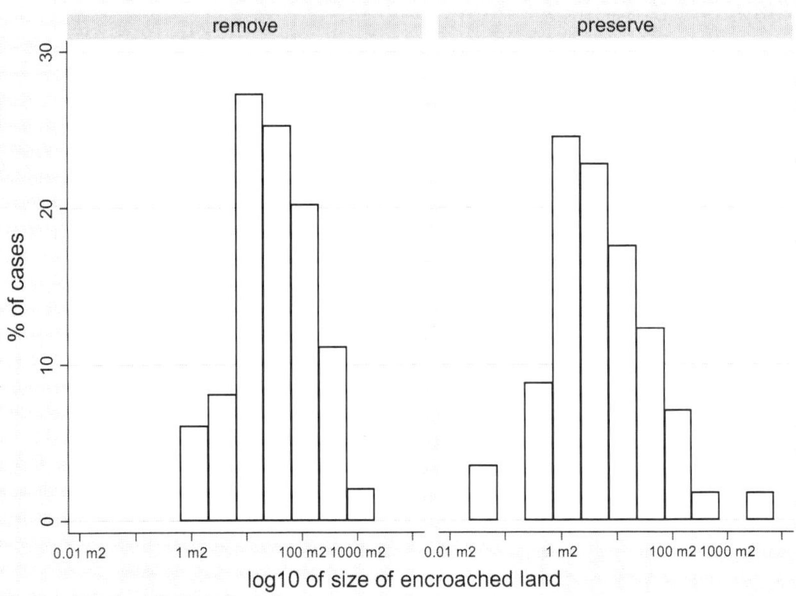

Figure 6.2 Court decision and size of encroached land

Note: N = 156. The left figure contains 99 observations, whereas the right figure contains 57 observations.

Table 6.1 Summary statistics of variables used in logistic regression models
Panel A Area of encroached land, by court decision

	Median	*25 percentile*	*75 percentile*	*Mean*	*St. dev.*	*Minimal 3 obs.*	*Maximal 3 obs.*	*N*
Remove	33	11	97	93	157	0.65; 1.01; 1.2	857; 848; 532	99
Preserve	4	2	16	98	536	0.02; 0.06; 0.32	4,035; 526; 158	57
All cases	17	4	63	95	345	0.02; 0.06; 0.32	4,035; 857; 848	156

Panel B Other continuous variables

Variable names	*Mean*	*St. dev.*	*Max.*	*Min.*
Population density (persons/km^2)	4,051	6,064	40,671	17
Number of plaintiffs' lawyers	0.95	0.82	4	0
Number of defendants' lawyers	0.89	1.10	7	0

Note N = 157.

Panel C Categorical variables

Variable types and names	*Percentage*
Culpability	
N/A	71.3
No fault	0.6
Negligent	23.0
Grossly negligent	5.1
Construction types	
residential buildings	32.5
residential buildings and fixtures	11.5
non-residential buildings	39.5
non-residential buildings and fixtures	10.8
other fixtures	5.7
Strata	
1	8.6
2	13.8
3	27.6
4	19.8
5	21.6
6	4.3
7	4.3
Year	
2009	7.0
2010	25.5
2011	42.0
2012	25.5

Note N = 157.

Findings and discussion

Table 6.2 reports results of four regression models. Models (1) and (3) include the official value of the encroached land as an independent variable, while Models (2) and (3) do not because information on official land value is missing in one-third of the observations. In addition, Models (1) and (2) use population density to control for variance in economic development, while Models (3) and (4) use strata dummies. Strata dummy variables are not used in all models because information on the exact location of the land (and thus the stratum of the town where the land parcel is located) is not available in 26 percent of the observations.

The regression results clearly indicate that the major determinant of the judicial decision to remove or preserve is the size of the encroached land. The size variable is statistically significant at the 0.05, 0.01, and 0.001 levels, and the sign of its coefficient is negative, suggesting that courts tend to preserve the encroaching buildings when the encroached land is small. This finding is foreshadowed in Figure 6.2: in the removal cases, the size of most parcels range from 10 to 100 m^2 or larger, while in the preservation cases, the size of most parcels range from 1 to 10 m^2 or smaller.

Moreover, the culpability of trespassers appears to matter a lot. All (eight) grossly negligent trespassers see their encroaching house removed, whereas the trespasser who encroaches through no fault of his own is rewarded by a preservation verdict. The variable negligence is statistically significant at the 0.05, 0.01, and 0.001 levels. The message it conveys, however, is ambiguous. The baseline variable is "culpability unknown from judgments." Thus, the interpretation of this result is that courts tend to preserve the encroaching building when the trespassers are negligent, as compared to when their culpability is unclear in the judgments. This is not a very informative finding.

The variable that captures the official value of land is not statistically significant, and the signs of the coefficient of this variable in Models (2) and (4) are different. As suggested above, official land value matters when compared to building value. Considering land value alone would not produce sound cost–benefit analysis. Given that my models (and the judicial decisions themselves) do not take into account building value, it is not surprising that official land value does not have a clear and strong impact on judicial decisions.

Figure 6.3 plots the relationships among size of encroached land, culpability, and judicial decisions. It shows that, first, the minimum size of encroached land in gross negligence cases is 14 m^2, while in the only no-fault case the encroached land size is 0.02 m^2. In addition, in a majority of cases where the size of encroached land is around 1 m^2, the courts order preservation.

Above I have conjectured that the ratio of *D/B* should have concerned judges. It is unclear whether most judges have the ratio in mind when determining whether to preserve the building. In only 24 observations do the judgments provide enough information about the ratio. Figure 6.4 plots the ratio with the judicial decision and culpability. It demonstrates that in the majority of cases the ratios are below 20 percent. Two out of three observations with greater than 75 percent ratio are

Table 6.2 Results of logistic regression models

	Dependent variable: court's decisions regarding the encroaching construction 0 = remove; 1 = preserve			
Variable names	*(1)*	*(2)*	*(3)*	*(4)*
Size of encroached land	–0.550***	–0.564**	–0.658***	–0.635*
(in natural log)	(0.138)	(0.202)	(0.183)	(0.320)
Official value of the encroached		–0.145		0.498
land (in natural log)		(0.266)		(0.581)
Population density (in natural log)	–0.0875	–0.182		
	(0.146)	(0.285)		
No. of plaintiff lawyers	0.166	0.226	0.189	0.341
(in square root)	(0.423)	(0.594)	(0.540)	(1.013)
No. of defendant lawyers	–0.326	–0.121	–1.088+	–1.201
(in square root)	(0.365)	(0.504)	(0.558)	(0.908)
Culpability of the trespasser				
Grossly negligent	Predict removal perfectly			
Negligent	2.100***	2.458**	2.460**	5.437*
	(0.532)	(0.831)	(0.753)	(2.154)
No fault	Predict preservation perfectly			
Type of construction				
Residential buildings	1.029	0.183	0.974	–0.509
	(1.188)	(1.571)	(1.544)	(2.349)
Residential buildings and fixtures	0.881	–1.134	0.925	–3.831
	(1.321)	(1.932)	(1.736)	(3.154)
Non-residential buildings	1.440	0.0974	1.370	–1.079
	(1.167)	(1.528)	(1.527)	(2.238)

Continued

Table 6.2 (Continued)

Variable names	*(1)*	*(2)*	*(3)*	*(4)*
Non-residential buildings and fixtures	0.227 (1.404)	Predict removal perfectly	–1.214 (2.011)	Predict removal perfectly
Year fixed effects	Yes	Yes	Yes	Yes
Strata fixed effects	No	No	Yes	Yes
Constant	0.165 (1.683)	1.944 (2.549)	–3.610 (2.204)	–4.385 (5.356)
N	147	80	108	58
Pseudo R^2	0.274	0.319	0.397	0.507
Rate of correct prediction	76%	78%	83%	83%

Note: Coefficients in cells; standard errors in parentheses.
***$p < 0.001$, **$p < 0.01$, *$p < 0.05$, +$p < 0.1$

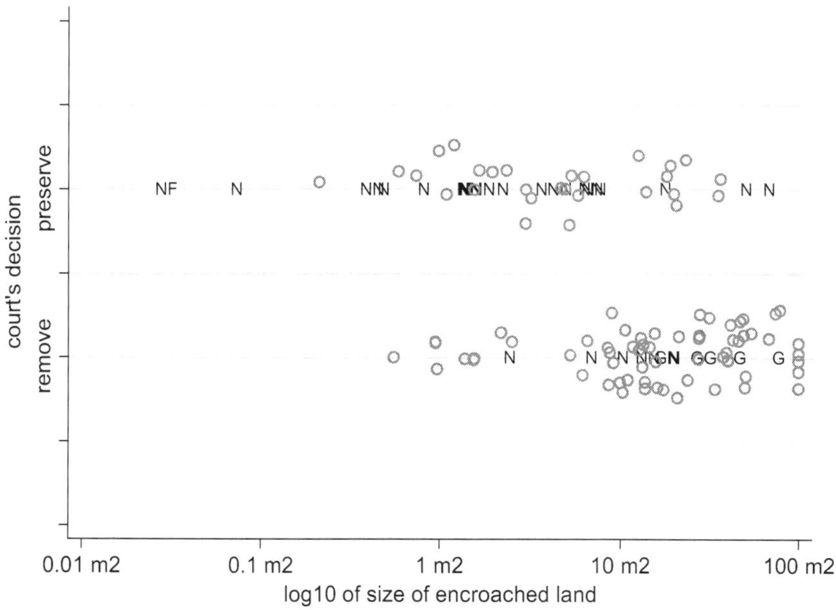

Figure 6.3 Size of encroached land, culpability, and court decisions

Note: N = 126. NF means the trespasser has no fault; N means the trespasser is negligent; G means the trespasser is grossly negligent. The open circles represent cases where the culpability of the trespasser is not revealed in the judgments. Observations in which the area of the encroaching land parcel is more than 100 m^2 are omitted from this figure. In 51 of the 57 preservation cases, the encroaching land areas are less than 100 m^2.

explicitly identified as gross negligence by the court. The top-right case leads to preservation because the area of encroached land is only 2 m^2.

Finally, as mentioned above, Article 796–1 of the Taiwan Civil Code requires that courts take into account public interests and interests of both parties when determining whether to remove or preserve the encroaching buildings. (Read: courts please conduct cost–benefit analysis.) While the two types of interests cannot be put in the regression models, it is still worth analyzing the pattern of judicial discourse in preservation cases. These cases are more interesting because removal is the default; thus, courts would need to find strong pro-preservation evidence to change the default option. As Table 6.3 shows, preservation is seldom (3/57 = 5 percent) due to concerns over public interest. Rather, in 75 percent (43/57) of the cases (Cell B), the preservation decision is at least partially based on the fact that preservation will cause the encroached party little harm. A typical case in Cell B concerns a small encroached land parcel. In the 11 observations in Cell A, there is no pro-preservation public interest, and harm to the plaintiff caused by the preservation may not be small. The court orders preservation because removal would cause great harm to the trespassers.

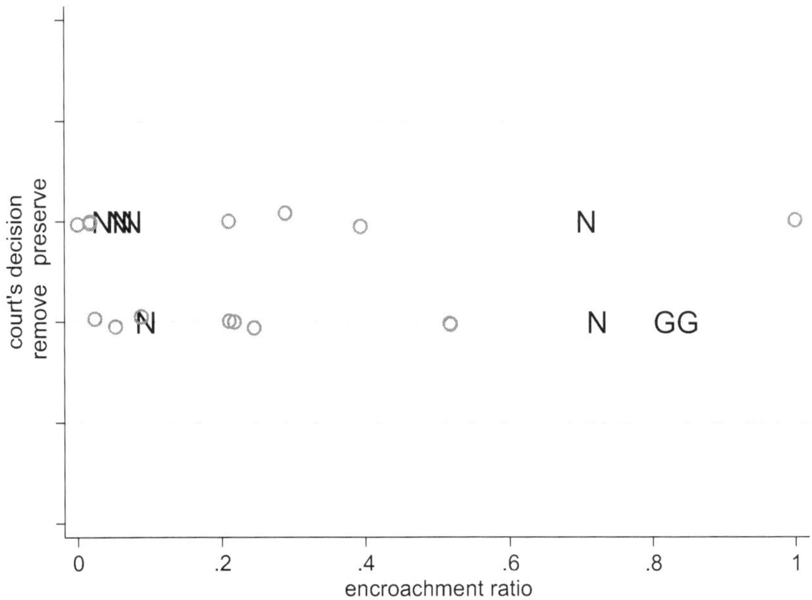

Figure 6.4 Encroachment ratio, culpability, and court decisions

Note: $N = 24$. N means the trespasser is negligent; G means the trespasser is grossly negligent. The open circles represent cases where the culpability of the trespasser is not revealed in the judgments. Encroachment ratio = B/D (see Figure 6.1).

Table 6.3 Private and public interests in preservation cases

Preservation is pro-public interest?	*Preservation does little harm to the plaintiff* — *No*	*Yes*	*Total*
No	(A) 11	(B) 43	54
Yes	(C) 1	(D) 2	3
Total	12	45	57

Conclusion

This chapter finds that in determining whether to remove or preserve an encroaching building, the size of the encroached land is the key determinant. That is, limited infringement is likely to lead to preservation and compensation (from the trespasser to the landowner), rather than an injunction to tear down the building. While I do not have data on the value of the encroaching buildings and how much their value will decline due to removal, given that the areas of encroached land in preservation cases are mostly below 10 m^2, it is highly likely that the value of alternative use of the land is less than the lost value of the building following removal. Hence, at least from an ex post viewpoint, courts in Taiwan appear to make social-welfare-enhancing decisions. This is another piece of evidence that career judges in civil law countries, while rarely open advocates of economic analysis and efficiency, make efficiency-compatible adjudications.

Notes

1 This book chapter draws on two previous articles of mine in Chinese: Yun-chien Chang, *An Economic Analysis of Boundary Encroachment Law in Taiwan*, 12 Academia Sinica Law Journal 153–201 (2013); Yun-chien Chang, *An Empirical Study of Boundary Encroachment Litigation*, 14 Academia Sinica Law Journal, *forthcoming* (2014).

2 American scholars generally discuss boundary encroachment in the context of adverse possession. *See, e.g.*, Lee Anne Fennell, *Efficient Trespass: The Case for "Bad Faith" Adverse Possession*, 100 Nw. U. L. Rev. 1037, 1077 (2006); Thomas J. Miceli & C.F. Sirmans, *An Economic Theory of Adverse Possession*, 15 Int'l Rev. L. & Econ. 161 (1995). For a comparative and economic analysis of the boundary encroachment doctrines in Europe and the US, see Matteo Rizzolli, *Building Encraochments*, 5 Rev. L. & Econ. 661, 679–91 (2009).

3 The definition of the property rule is that "the state guarantees property right assignments against infringement through the threatened use of its police powers." Louis Kaplow & Steven Shavell, *Property Rules Versus Liability Rules: An Economic Analysis*, 109 Harv. L. Rev. 713, 715 (1996).

4 "A liability rule gives at least one party an option to take an entitlement non-consensually and pay the entitlement owner some exercise price." Ian Ayres & J. M. Balkin, *Legal Entitlements as Auctions: Property Rules, Liability Rules, and Beyond*, 106 Yale L.J. 703, 704 (1996).

5 *See, e.g.*, Henry E. Smith, *Property and Property Rules*, 79 N.Y.U. L. Rev. 1719, 1722 (2004); Richard A. Epstein, *A Clear View of the Cathedral: The Dominance of Property Rules*, 106 Yale L.J. 2091, 2092 (1997); Richard R.W. Brooks, *The Relative Burden of Determining Property Rules and Liability Rules: Broken Elevators in the Cathedral*, 97 Nw. U. L. Rev. 267 (2002); Robert C. Ellickson, *Adverse Possession and Perpetuities Law: Two Dents in the Libertarian Model of Property Rights*, 64 Wash. U. L. Q. 723 (1986); Carol M. Rose, *The Shadow of the Cathedral*, 106 Yale L.J. 2175 (1997).

6 Economic analysis of law mainly uses the ex ante viewpoint. *See* Richard R.W. Brooks & Warren F. Schwartz, *Legal Uncertainty, Economic Efficiency, and the Preliminary Injunction Doctrine*, 58 Stan. L. Rev. 381 (2005); Henry E. Smith, *Law and Economics: Realism or Democracy?* 32 Harv. J.L. & Pub. Pol'y 127 (2009).

7 *See* Yun-chien Chang, *Optional Law in Property: A Theoretical Critique*, working paper; Smith, *supra* note 6; Rose, *supra* note 6.

8 For comparison of the ex ante and ex post viewpoints, *see* Lucian Arye Bebchuk, *Property Rights and Liability Rules: The Ex Ante View of the Cathedral*, 100 Mich. L. Rev. 601, 603 (2001).

9 In the US, for example, a judicial doctrine called the relative hardship doctrine resembles the stipulation in Article 796–1. *See* Stewart Sterk, *Strict Liability and Negligence in Property Theory*, 160 U. Pa. L. Rev. 2129, 2146 (2012).

10 *See* Henry E. Smith, *Institutions and Indirectness in Intellectual Property*, 157 U. PA. L. REV. 2083, 2128–29 (2009); Henry E. Smith, *An Economic Analysis of Law versus Equity* (working paper, available at http://extranet.isnie.org/uploads/isnie2010/smith.pdf).
11 *See generally* Richard A. Posner, ECONOMIC ANALYSIS OF LAW (1973).
12 *See, e.g.*, Paul H. Rubin, *Why Is the Common Law Efficient?* 6 J. LEGAL STUD. 51 (1977); George L. Priest, *Common Law Process and the Selection of Efficient Rules*, 6 J. LEGAL STUD. 65 (1977).
13 *See* Benito Arruñada & Veneta Andonova, *Common Law and Civil Laws as Pro-Market Adaptations*, 26 WASH. U. J.L. & POL'Y 81, 86 (2008).
14 *See* Yun-Chien Chang, *Tenancy in "Anticommons"?: A Theoretical and Empirical Analysis of Co-Ownership*, 4 J. LEGAL ANALYSIS 515 (2012).
15 *See* Yun-Chien Chang *et al.*, *Mimicking the Market or Seduced by Anchors? An Empirical Study of Judicial Behaviors in Real Litigation*, working paper.
16 For example, there are cases where the encroaching buildings are also blocking public roads; thus, removal is consistent with the public interest. Conversely, there is a case where the encroaching construction is a facility installed by a power company, the removal of which might expose people in the community to radiation. In that case, the court reasons that preservation of the encroaching fixtures enhances the public interest.
17 The null hypothesis is that the size of D does not matter, while the alternative hypothesis is that a larger D pushes courts to maintain the position of removal.
18 There might be external costs and benefits—they fall in the domain of public interests. They can be easily added to the equation.
19 Among the fifty-seven preservation cases, seven of them are "partial preservation and partial removal." I have run regression models with only the 50 "100 percent preservation" cases, and the results are essentially the same.
20 To be more exact, the official land value used here is the Publicly Announced Land Value (PALV). In most cases, the court uses 80 percent of the PALV as the land value, as it is the landowners' Declared Land Value (DLV). In some cases, courts use PALV or Assessed Current Land Value (ACLV), another official land value. To compare property values across cases, I compute the PALV of the land parcels in all cases, and use the PALV in the regression models. For an introduction of how this official land value is assessed and how it differs from ACLV and DLV, see Yun-Chien Chang, PRIVATE PROPERTY AND TAKINGS COMPENSATION: THEORETICAL FRAMEWORK AND EMPIRICAL ANALYSIS 61–67, 90–98 (2013).

It is also reasonable to use the land value as perceived by courts. I have run all the regression models with an alternative independent variable that reflects the land value used by courts in each case. The results are essentially the same.

21 There might be an endogeneity problem with the culpability variables. The judgments do not always contain enough facts for me to independently determine whether the trespassers are grossly negligent. There are certainly gray areas between the two types of negligence, as well as between negligence and no fault. Courts may first decide whether to preserve the construction and then declare in passing whether the trespassers are to blame. Perhaps this is why in most cases the courts do no bother to rule on the culpability of the trespassers—recall that Article 796–1 of Taiwan Civil Code does not specifically require courts to take into account the culpability. I have tried running all the regression models after discarding the culpability dummy variables. Again, the

results are essentially the same, as the variable on land size remains highly statistically significant and other variables insignificant.

22 Recall that Article 796–1 of the Taiwan Civil Code is not applicable in intentional boundary encroachment cases.

23 *See* Pei-Chun Hou *et al.*, *The Typology of Townships in Taiwan: The Analysis of Sampling Stratification of the 2005–2006 "Taiwan Social Change Survey"*, 23 SURVEY RESEARCH—METHOD AND APPLICATION 7 (2008).

24 *See* Guthrie, Chris, Jeffrey J. Rachlinski, and Andrew J. Wistrich. 2007. Blinking on the Bench: How Judges Decide Cases. *Cornell Law Review* 93: 1–43.

References

Arruñada, Benito, and Veneta Andonova. 2008. Common Law and Civil Laws as Pro-Market Adaptations. *Washington University Journal of Law & Policy* 26: 81–130.

Ayres, Ian, and J.M. Balkin. 1996. Legal Entitlements as Auctions: Property Rules, Liability Rules, and Beyond. *Yale Law Journal* 106: 703–750.

Bebchuk, Lucian Arye. 2001. Property Rights and Liability Rules: The Ex Ante View of the Cathedral. *Michigan Law Review* 100: 601–639.

Brooks, Richard R.W. 2002. The Relative Burden of Determining Property Rules and Liability Rules: Broken Elevators in the Cathedral. *Northwestern University Law Review* 97: 267–317.

Brooks, Richard R.W., and Warren F. Schwartz. 2005. Legal Uncertainty, Economic Efficiency, and the Preliminary Injunction Doctrine. *Stanford Law Review* 58: 381–410.

Chang, Yun-chien. 2012. Tenancy in "Anticommons"?: A Theoretical and Empirical Analysis of Co-ownership. *Journal of Legal Analysis* 4: 515–553.

———2013. *Private Property and Takings Compensation: Theoretical Framework and Empirical Analysis.* Northampton, MA: Edward Elgar.

———2013. Optional Law in Property: A Theoretical Critique. Working paper.

Chang, Yun-chien, Kong-pin Chen, and Yu-sheng Liu. 2013. Mimicking the Market or Seduced by Anchors? An Empirical Study of Judicial Behaviors in Real Litigation. Working paper.

Ellickson, Robert C. 1986. Adverse Possession and Perpetuities Law: Two Dents in the Libertarian Model of Property Rights. *Washington University Law Quarterly* 64: 723–737.

Epstein, Richard A. 1997. A Clear View of the Cathedral: The Dominance of Property Rules. *Yale Law Journal* 106: 2091–2120.

Fennell, Lee Anne. 2006. Efficient Trespass: The Case for "Bad Faith" Adverse Possession. *Northwestern University Law Review* 100: 1037–1096.

Guthrie, Chris, Jeffrey J. Rachlinski, and Andrew J. Wistrich. 2007. Blinking on the Bench: How Judges Decide Cases. *Cornell Law Review* 93: 1–43.

Hou, Pei-chun, Su-Hao Tu, Pei-shan Laio, Yung-Tai Hung, and Ying-Hwa Chang. 2008. The Typology of Townships in Taiwan: The Analysis of Sampling Stratification of the 2005–2006 "Taiwan Social Change Survey." *Survey Research—Method and Application* 23: 7–3.

Kaplow, Louis, and Steven Shavell. 1996. Property Rules Versus Liability Rules: An Economic Analysis. *Harvard Law Review* 109: 713–790.

Miceli, Thomas J., and C.F. Sirmans. 1995. An Economic Theory of Adverse Possession. *International Review of Law and Economics* 15: 161–173.
Posner, Richard A. 1973. *Economic Analysis of Law*. Boston: Little, Brown.
Priest, George L. 1977. The Common Law Process and the Selection of Efficient Rules. *The Journal of Legal Studies* 6: 65–82.
Rizzolli, Matteo. 2009. Building Encroachments. *Review of Law and Economics* 5: 661–693.
Rose, Carol M. 1997. The Shadow of the Cathedral. *Yale Law Journal* 106: 2175–2200.
Rubin, Paul H. 1977. Why Is the Common Law Efficient? *The Journal of Legal Studies* 6: 51–63.
Smith, Henry E. 2002. Exclusion Versus Governance: Two Strategies for Delineating Property Rights. *Journal of Legal Studies* 31: S453–S487.
———2004. Property and Property Rules. *New York University Law Review* 79: 1719–1798.
———2009. Institutions and Indirectness in Intellectual Property. *University of Pennsylvania Law Review* 157: 2083–2133.
———2009. Law and Economics: Realism or Democracy? *Harvard Journal of Law & Public Policy* 32: 127–145.
———2012. An Economic Analysis of Law versus Equity. Working paper.
Sterk, Stewart E. 2012. Strict Liability and Negligence in Property Theory. *University of Pennsylvania Law Review* 160: 2129–2156.

7 Judicial activism and government practices in litigation in the Israeli High Court of Justice 1970–2000

Yoav Dotan

Introduction

The object of this chapter is to describe and analyze the rise of judicial activism in the Israeli High Court of Justice (HCJ) during the past three decades.

"Judicial activism" is far from being a precise scientific concept that can be accurately defined and empirically quantified. In fact, the term is notorious for being amorphous and slippery.[1] As one scholar noted, "as the term has become more commonplace, its meaning has become increasingly unclear."[2] One reason for the lack of agreement regarding the content of "activism" is that the term has acquired many distinct, even contradictory, meanings.[3] The other principal reason is that the term "activist" always involves some value-based judgment on behalf of the one making the observation, and it usually carries negative connotations.[4]

Those difficulties in defining and measuring activism do not necessarily mean that efforts to examine judicial institutions by using the concept of activism are futile or worthless. In this chapter I seek to study developments in the activism of the Israeli Supreme Court by reference to one dimension of judicial activism: the readiness of the Court to intervene in and influence decisions made by governmental agencies in Israel. The frequency with which judicial institutions reverse decisions of the elected branches is considered "the most common standard for judicial activism."[5] Accordingly, the present research examines the practices of the HCJ, applying this conventional standard.

The conventional standard for judicial activism is by no means a perfect measurement for activism and it has an inherent major difficulty: it lacks a baseline that refers to the content and nature of the decisions reversed by the court. Thus, arguably, if the relevant judicial decision reverses legislative (or administrative) actions that are patently unconstitutional, it cannot be classified as activist.[6] However, for reasons explained below, such difficulties are largely negligible in the context of the present study.

The jurisprudence of Israel's Supreme Court has undergone significant changes during the past three decades. While the doctrine of the Court formerly followed the path of the traditional common law model, like most UK progenies, this Court is considered today as one of the most activist judicial institutions in the world. It is also an accepted proposition among commentators that the major shift in the

Court policies took place during the 1980s.[7] Those changes have been the subject of numerous works by lawyers and social scientists alike. Interestingly though, the rise of judicial activism in Israel has never been studied systematically from a quantitative perspective.

This chapter presents some preliminary results of a large-scale quantitative study of HCJ files. In the course of this research, we sampled about 10 percent of the files in the Court's archives and coded them by various factors that include, among others (see below), the outcomes of the litigation. The files sampled were from 1970 to 1979, and from 1990 to 1998, to enable us to compare the practices of the Court before and after "the activist revolution" of the 1980s.

The course of the discussion is as follows: in the next section I provide an overview of the development of the doctrines of the HCJ during the research period. The section thereafter discusses the methodology of the current research, and its outcomes are presented in the section after that. In the penultimate section, Analysis, I discuss the outcomes and analyze their significance for the understanding of the HCJ, and studies of high court litigation in general.

Judicial review in Israel—background

Israel has no formal constitution and during the early days of the state judicial review was limited only to administrative actions (rather than to legislation by the Knesset (Israel's parliament)). Accordingly, Israeli public law is almost entirely judge-made law, created and shaped by decisions of the Supreme Court. The principal forum for judicial review is the Supreme Court itself, sitting as the HCJ.[8]

Despite the lack of a formal constitutional text, the Supreme Court developed a rich jurisprudence of human rights during the early days of the state. It created the concept of an "unwritten" bill of rights that was cited by the Supreme Court on many occasions.[9] While the concept was not presented as a justification for the courts to invalidate parliamentary legislation, it did have a vital role in developing a rich jurisprudence of human rights that allowed the courts to adopt a vigorous interpretative doctrine in favor of human rights, and was a strong vehicle for controlling administrative actions infringing on human rights.[10]

During the 1960s and 1970s, the HCJ imposed strict limitations on litigants' ability to raise political issues in court. For meeting the requirement of standing, the petitioner had to show direct and genuine personal interest in the state action at stake. Moreover, the petitioner's standing was likely to be endangered if the same action caused similar harm to a large group of people, or to an entire sector of which she formed a part. This narrow concept allowed the Court to refrain from interfering in sensitive issues such as law enforcement with respect to high-ranking political figures.[11]

Another concept with similar effects on the courts' accessibility interest groups was justiciability. Until the late 1970s, the Supreme Court adopted a narrow conception of justiciability. Under this concept, the Court decided that petitions involving issues of foreign policy, military actions, or other questions concerning sensitive political issues were considered "unsuitable" for judicial determination and therefore non-justiciable.[12] The Court also adhered to a narrow concept of judicial review. In particular, the HCJ revealed an unwillingness to take a close look at certain areas of highly important state activity, such as actions taken by military agencies[13] and prosecutorial discretion.[14]

The 1980s saw a major shift in almost all the aspects of judicial review above mentioned. There was a dramatic change in the principles concerning access to the courts. In the early 1980s, the Court was already willing to acknowledge the standing of a petitioner who was substantially harmed by a certain state action even if she belonged to a larger group of people who suffered similar harm.[15] The scope of judicial review was further expanded in the landmark decision in Ressler v. Minister of Defense. There, the Supreme Court reversed its prior rulings on the issues of both standing and justiciability. On justiciability, Justice Aharon Barak (who became the Chief Justice) said: "Any [human] action is susceptible of determination by a legal norm, and there is no action to which there is no legal norm determining it."[16]

Similar revisions were made on the issue of standing. In Ressler, the Court presented a new and ambitious concept of standing, completely revising the older case law. The Court decided that whenever a petition raises an issue of important constitutional merit, or when there is suspicion of serious executive violations of the principle of the rule of law, any person is entitled to bring the petition into court, regardless of her personal interest in the outcome of the litigation.[17]

The reform of the rules concerning access to court was followed by a similar revision of the rules of judicial review. During the 1980s and 1990s, the courts showed a growing tendency to expand the scope of judicial review. They developed new tools for judicial review and imposed new requirements on administrative authorities, such as the duty of reasonableness,[18] rationality of the decision-making process,[19] and proportionality.[20] The courts also showed willingness to review actions of institutions that were previously held to be partly or wholly immune from judicial supervision, such as the military and the security services.[21] The Court also reversed its previously restricted policy in other fields, such as prosecutorial decisions, by beginning to review decisions made by the Attorney General and other prosecutorial agencies.[22] In addition, toward the end of 1980s, the Court began to exercise review in several areas related to the activities of the political system that were previously considered outside the ambit of judicial review. It ruled that it has the power to review and invalidate agreements made by political parties and candidates.[23] It also ruled that petitions related to alleged violations of the internal rules of the Knesset are justiciable, thus opening the door to various petitions on behalf of Knesset members with regard to parliamentary procedures, such as non-confidence vote etc.[24] Last, but not least, the rapid development of the requirement of reasonableness during the 1980s, and the broad definition of that concept, led the Court to treat appointments to governmental positions as a subject for judicial scrutiny. Thus, in the early 1990s the Court struck down appointments for senior governmental posts[25] and shortly thereafter the Court ordered the Israeli prime minister to dismiss a deputy minister and a cabinet member immediately after their indictment for charges of corruption.[26]

One significant result of all these developments is that Israeli courts became quite a tempting option for all kinds of political and social groups, trying to further their agenda through litigation, as well as for other players in the public arena, such as public interest groups.[27]

It should be noted that all the above-mentioned significant reforms in judicial review were carried out by the Court without any constitutional change during that period. Nor was there any significant change in the statutory basis for judicial review during the 1980s. In 1992, however, the Knesset (which holds the power to grant constitutional status to some of its laws)[28] enacted two new basic laws, of which the Basic Law: Human Dignity and Liberty is the most significant.[29] This basic law contained—for the first time in Israeli history—reference to some fundamental human rights, such as human dignity, privacy, and property.

The scope of the rights included in the Basic Law was limited. The law did not mention fundamental rights such as the right to speech, association, or religion, and did not espouse the concept of equality. In addition, its constitutional superiority over regular legislation was not entrenched in the text.[30] The Supreme Court, however, was quick to acknowledge its 'higher' constitutional status. In the landmark decision of Bank Ha'mizrachi v. Migdali, the Court ruled that the new Basic Law constitutes the "bill of rights" for Israel, and that the judiciary is authorized to invalidate regular legislation that infringes on the rights entrenched by the Basic Law.[31] Later, in 1994, the Court used various interpretative techniques to broaden the list of rights protected by the bill and to bolster its constitutional status.[32] While the enactment of the new Basic Law was titled 'a constitutional revolution' by various scholars,[33] the scope of review of legislation by the Court remained relatively limited. To date, the Court has invalidated only a handful of statutes enacted by the Knesset after 1992.[34] Accordingly, while the constitutional developments of the early 1990s have had a significant influence on the doctrine of judicial review, the HCJ's docket is still composed principally of "regular" administrative law cases. In other words, the great reforms in judicial review during the 1980s seem to have had a stronger impact on the Court's day-to-day practices than the 'constitutional revolution' of the 1990s.

Data and methodology

In order to study the quantitative impact of the rise of judicial activism in the HCJ, we sampled court files from two periods: 1970–79 and 1990–98.[35] The reason we choose to address these years is that, because the activist reform in the Supreme Court began in the early 1980s and was completed (to large extent) toward the end of that decade (see above), we sought to study outcomes of litigation over the decade before that process began and after it was completed. Accordingly we sampled around 10 percent of all court files for each year. Following previous research on the HCJ, we sampled actual court files in the Court's archives, rather than HCJ decisions as published in electronic databases. The reason for this is that—as previous research has established—most HCJ files do not reach final judicial dispositions but are settled out of court. Previous research has established that there may be significant differences between outcomes of final judicial decisions and out-of-court settlements, so that an understanding of the HCJ practices necessitates the study of all files, not only those that reach final judicial decision.[36] Existing electronic databases, however, contain little information about litigation that did not reach final judicial disposition. Therefore, we sampled court files in the HCJ archives.

For each year in the research period, we sampled about 10 percent of all files (i.e. around 50–70 cases for each year during the 1970s and around 100–140 cases for each year during the 1990s). Each file was coded with reference to a large number of factors including the petitioner's status (individual, corporation, interest group, etc.), her ethnic and civil affiliation (Jewish, Arab-Israeli, Palestinian from the territories, etc.), legal representation of both parties, the subject matter of the petition, the duration of the litigation, legal arguments raised by the parties, judicial writs issued throughout the litigation (interim injunctions, etc.), the position taken by the state (if involved as a third party or *amicus* in the litigation, see below), and so forth (see Tables 7.1 and 7.2). We also codified the outcomes of the litigation. The codification of outcomes referred to outcomes both in final judicial decisions (i.e. whether writs on behalf of all, or some, of the petitioners were issued) and in out-of-court settlements. This means that in cases where there were settlements, we studied and codified the content of the settlement between the parties. We also codified writs for expenses if issued by the court as the result of the litigation.

For the purpose of the present study we used the following working hypotheses:

Table 7.1 Descriptive statistics of variables

Variable	*N*	*Percentage*
Year		
1990s	1,064	63
1970s	626	37
Petitioner by institution		
Private	1,306	79
Public organization	14	0.8
Institution/corporation	229	13.8
State/authority/elected officials	105	6.3
Petitioner by ethnicity		
Jew	920	72.2
Arab-Israeli	178	14
Palestinian	176	13.8
Petitioner's lawyer		
Private	1,082	65.5
Organization	126	7.6
Self-representation	444	26.9
Respondent		
State	1,198	71
Corporation and tribunal	234	13.9
Private[47]	38	2.3
Local authority	217	12.9
State position		
Opposed	627	63.8
Supported petition	32	3.3

Continued

Table 7.1 (Continued)

Variable	*N*	*Percentage*
Offered settlement	200	20.3
No position	124	12.6
Subject of petition		
Civil	1,304	77.2
Prisoners and detainees	194	11.5
Occupied Territories/ security related	75	4.4
Constitution	117	6.9
Conditional order[48]		
Issued	457	27.1
Not issued	1,229	72.9

Table 7.2 Description statistics by period (bivariate analyses)

Variable	*1970s*	*1990s*
Petitioner by institution	$X^2 = 40.96$, $df = 3$ $p < 0.000$	
Private	84.1%	75.9%
Public organization	0.3%	1.2%
Institution/corporation	14%	13.8%
State/authority/elected officials	1.6%	9.2%
Petitioner by ethnicity	$X^2 = 101.78$, $df = 2$ $p < 0.000$	
Jew	88.5%	62.4%
Arab-Israeli	6.1%	18.7%
Palestinian	5.4%	18.9%
Petitioner's lawyer	$X^2 = 105.30$, $df = 2$ $p < 0.000$	
Private	60.8%	68.2%
Organization	1%	11.5%
Self-representation	38.2%	20.2%
Respondent	$X^2 = 15.19$, $df = 3$ $p < 0.01$	
State	%73	69.8%
Corporation or tribunal	8.9%	16.3%
Private	2.6%	2.1%
Local authority	14.6%	11.8%
State position	$X^2 = 171.51$, $df = 3$ $p < 0.00$	
Opposed	61%	64.8%
Supported petition	2%	3.7%
Offered settlement	3.2%	26.2%
No position	33.9%	5.3%
Subject of petition	$X^2 = 233.06$, $df = 3$ $p < 0.00$	
Civil	63.7%	66.8%
Prisoners and detainees	25.2%	3.4%
Occupied Territories/security related	5.8%	21.9%
Constitution	5.3%	7.9%
Conditional order	$X^2 = 49.74$, $df = 1$ $p < 0.00$	
Issued	37.1%	21.3%
Not issued	62.9%	78.7%

Hypotheses

1 The absolute number of petitions disposed by the HCJ has significantly increased over the years, and so did the relative number of cases that were settled out-of-court.
2 The rise of judicial activism during the 1980s brought about an increase in the number of cases in which the HCJ interfered to strike down decisions made by the other branches (i.e. success rates of petitions during the 1990s are expected to be higher than those in the 1970s).
3 The increase in the rate of success is reflected both in final judicial dispositions and in out-of-court settlements.

Outcomes

Caseload

As Figure 7.1 demonstrates, during the research period there was a gradual increase in the number of petitions on the HCJ's docket. During the early 1970s the number of petitions to the HCJ was around 400 per year. The number doubled toward the end of that decade, and crossed the 1,000 bar in late 1980s. The number of petitions continued to climb sharply during the early 1990s.[37] During the 1990s, the average number of petitions per year exceeded 1,000 and came close to 1,500 petitions per year toward the end of that decade. One obvious implication

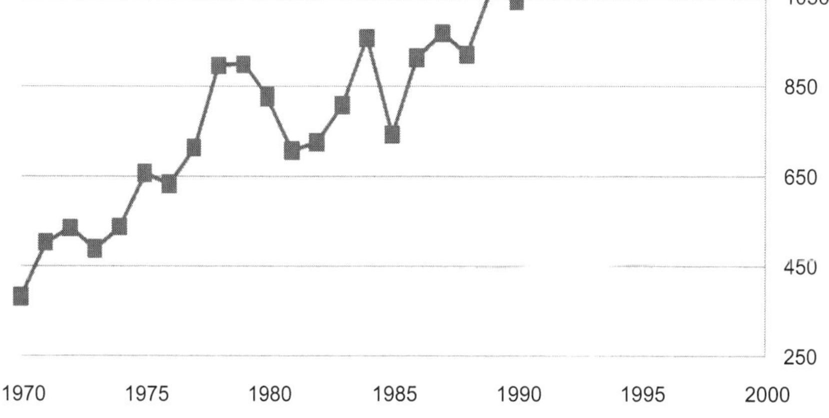

Figure 7.1 Petitions to the HCJ 1970–2000

of the rise in the number of cases is that it places a severe workload on the court. In fact, caseload pressures on the Supreme Court are even stronger than Figure 7.1 demonstrates because the HCJ is only one of the functions of the Supreme Court: it also functions as a court of appeals for civil and criminal cases and as a court of cassation for a certain number of other cases.[38] This means that the 15 justices of the Supreme Court are required to cope with thousands of cases per year.[39]

Outcomes in litigation

As the statistics show, there was a significant shift in the outcomes in litigation in the HCJ during the 1980s. This shift, however, does not refer to outcomes in litigation in final judicial decisions. The success rates of petitions in that respect remained constant. Only 4 percent of the petitions to the HCJ concluded with judicial decisions that allowed the petition (fully or partially). This is the case for the 1970s, and also for the 1990s (see Figure 7.2). In this respect, the practices of the Court seem to have remained quite similar. There is a significant difference, however, in the success rate of petitions that were settled out of court. During the 1970s, only 36 percent of all petitions in our sample concluded in settlements (see Figure 7.3), and the settlement was categorized as a success (complete or partial) for the petitioners in only 20 percent of the cases. During the 1990s, however, the rate of settlement jumped to 58 percent of all petitions (see Figure 7.4), and of these, 37.7 percent (of the overall number of petitions) concluded in success for the petitioners (see Figure 7.2).[40] These shifts in

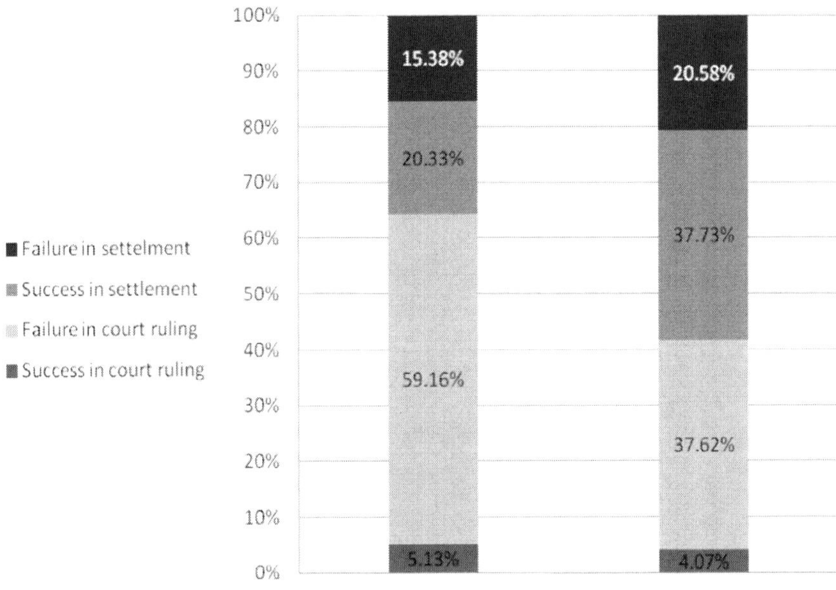

Figure 7.2 Outcomes in litigation—1970s vs. 1990s

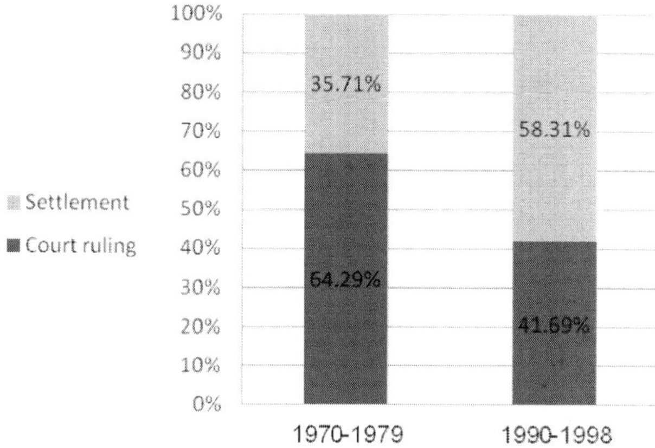

Figure 7.3 Outcomes in litigation—1970s vs. 1990s

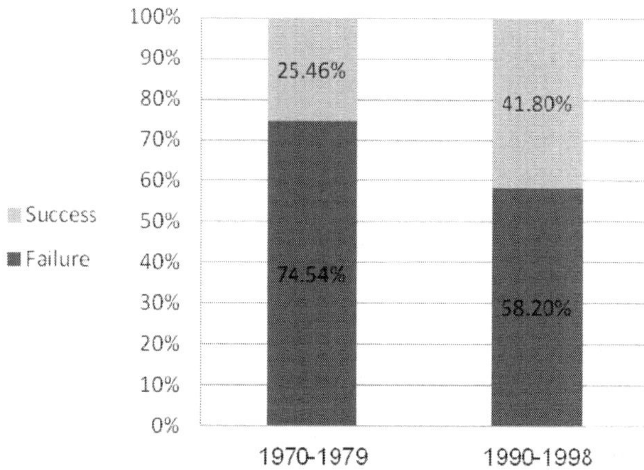

Figure 7.4 Outcomes in litigation—1970s vs. 1990s

the patterns of litigation are corroborated by logistic regression. As Table 7.3 demonstrates, the likelihood of petitioners' success during the 1990s is significantly higher than the likelihood of success during the 1970s (odd ratio 0.58 see Table 7.3), while the likelihood that the case would settle instead of being disposed by judicial decision also significantly increased (odd ratio 1.67 see Table 7.4).

Outcomes in litigation in "regular" administrative issues

An important fact regarding the comparison between the practices of the HCJ during the research period is that the subject matter of the petitions changed over the time. Thus, for example, during the 1970s a significant number of the petitions to the HCJ were prisoners' petitions that at the time were under the Court's jurisdiction. This changed during the 1980s as the caseload pressure on the Court grew. Similarly, during the 1990s a significant portion of the Court's docket consisted of petitions issued by Palestinian residents of the Occupied Territories (such petitions were relatively rare until the late 1970s, see Table 7.2). We present here the success rates of petitions that dealt with "regular" administrative matters such as regulation, licensing, state subsidies, etc. This category of cases remained largely unchanged during

Table 7.3 Logistic regression coefficients for predicting success in the outcome of the petition[49]

Variable	*Exp(B) odds ratio*	*Standard error*	*B*
Constant			–1.08***
Year (0 = 1990s)			
1970s	0.58**	0.17	–0.55
Petitioner, by institution (0 = Private)			
Public	1.99	0.66	0.69
Institution/corporation	1.29	0.2	0.25
State/authority/elected officials	2.27**	0.28	0.82
Petitioner, by ethnicity (0 = Jew)			
Arab-Israeli	1.63*	0.24	0.49
Palestinian	1.11	0.27	0.1
Petitioner's lawyer (0 = Private)			
Organization	3.33***	0.29	1.2
Respondent (0 = State)			
Corporation or tribunal	1.02	0.21	0.02
Private	0.91	0.41	–0.09
Local authority	0.82	0.22	–0.2
State position (0 = Support petition)	0.3***	0.19	–1.22
Opposed petition	23.41***	0.32	3.15
Offered settlement	1.32	0.24	0.27
No position			
Subject of petition (0 = Civil)	0.43**	0.31	–0.85
Prisoners and detainees	1.52	0.35	0.42
Occupied Territories/security related	1.15	0.25	0.14
Constitution	5.14***	0.16	1.64
Conditional order (0 = Not issued)			
Issued			
Dependent variable—outcome of petition (0 = failure; 1 = success)			
N = 1,477			
Chi-square = 582.76***			
Cox and Snell R^2 = 0.33 / Nagelkerke R^2 = 0.45			

Note: *$p < 0.05$, **$p < 0.01$, ***$p < 0.001$.

Table 7.4 Logistic regression coefficients for predicting the type of proceeding—if the petition ended in a settlement or in court

Variable	*Exp(B) odds ratio*	*Standard error*	*B*
Constant			–0.04
Year (0 = 1990s)			
1970s	1.67***	0.14	0.51
Petitioner, by institution (0 = Private)			
Public	0.90	0.60	–0.10
Institution/corporation	0.85	0.18	–0.17
State/authority/elected officials	1.14	0.26	0.13
Petitioner, by ethnicity (0 = Jew)			
Arab-Israeli	0.62*	0.21	–0.48
Palestinian	1.03	0.24	0.03
Petitioner's lawyer (0 = Private)			
Organization	0.77	0.27	–0.26
Respondent (0 = State)			
Corporation or tribunal	0.82	0.17	–0.20
Private	0.84	0.37	–0.17
Local authority	0.56**	0.18	–0.57
State position (0 = Opposed petition)	0.12***	0.51	–2.08
Supported petition	0.03***	0.40	–3.57
Offered settlement	0.33***	0.22	–1.10
No position			
Subject of petition (0 = Civil)	2.17**	0.23	0.78
Prisoners and detainees	0.71	0.31	–0.34
Occupied Territories/ security related	1.51	0.24	0.41
Constitution	0.74*	0.14	–0.29
Conditional order (0 = Not issued)			
Issued			
Dependent variable—type of proceeding (0 = settlement; 1 = court)			
N = 1,477			
Chi-square = 365.77***			
Cox and Snell R^2 = 0.22 / Nagelkerke R^2 = 0.29			

Note: *p < 0.05, **p < 0.01, ***p < 0.001.

the research period (in terms of legal doctrine, jurisdictional aspects, and general legal practices with regard to this category of cases. The outcomes are presented in Figure 7.5.

As the figures show, the general shifts in litigation patterns during the 1980s are also reflected with regard to regular administrative petitions, albeit in lesser magnitudes. In this group, the general percentage of proceedings that ended up in settlement was 45 percent during the 1970s, rising to 57 percent during the 1990s (see Figure 7.6). The overall success rate of petitions in this group rose slightly, from 32 percent to

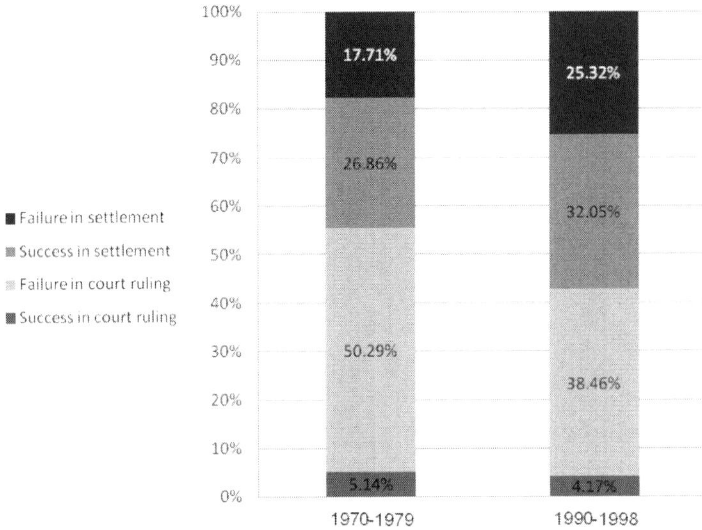

Figure 7.5 Outcomes in "regular" administrative matters 1970s vs. 1990s

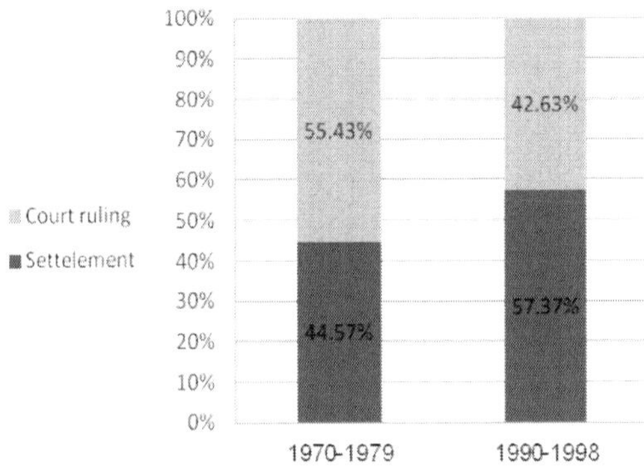

Figure 7.6 Outcomes in "regular" administrative matters 1970s vs. 1990s

36 percent (see Figure 7.7). These results suggest that the above tendencies of the HCJ to dispose petitions by out-of-court settlements, instead of final court decisions, differ in their magnitude according to the subject matter of the petitions. Future analysis is thus needed to accurately explain them.

Analysis

The most significant finding from the above data set is the changing pattern of litigation in the HCJ between the 1970s and the 1990s. To the extent that one

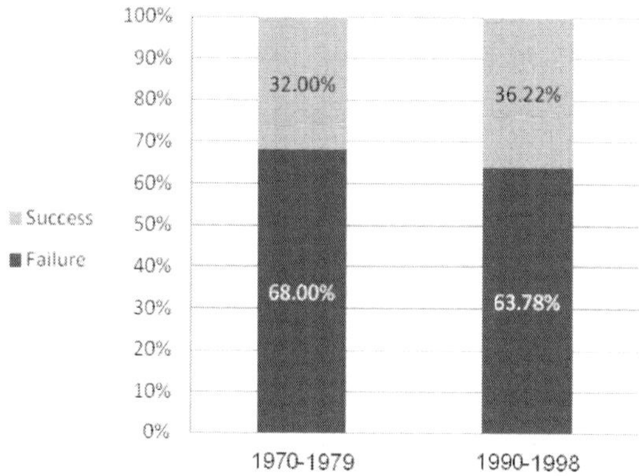

Figure 7.7 Outcomes in "regular" administrative matters 1970s vs. 1990s

examines final judicial decisions, it seems that the rise of judicial activism during the 1980s did not bring about any notable change in the relative rate of judicial intervention in governmental decision-making. There was, however, a very significant change in the relative portion of cases in which governmental agencies settled cases during litigation in a way that allowed petitioners to achieve their goals (wholly or partly). In other words, to the extent that the rise of judicial activism in the HCJ is reflected in numbers, it is the numbers of cases settled by litigation, rather than the numbers of cases decided by the Court.

These findings raise some new and intriguing questions. The rise in the rate of judicial interventions in governmental decisions does not, in itself, provide conclusive evidence of an increase in the level of judicial activism. Alternative explanations include the possibility that the subject matter of the petitions changed over the years (in Figure 7.5 and Table 7.3, we negated this alternative, at least in part) and the possibility that the true change was in governmental policies, which became more intrusive or more frequently illegal (which seems unlikely given the large number of cases and the variety of governmental agencies and activities covered by the HCJ's judicial review jurisdiction). Thus, the rise in the rate of judicial interventions does seem to provide quantitative support for the general observation by legal scholars that—at the doctrinal level—the Court became more activist over the research period, at least to the extent that activism is measured in terms of the relative number of cases in which the petitioners succeed in changing the original administrative decision by resorting to judicial review.

Still, there are persistent questions about where that rise in judicial activism took place. Why is the rise in the relative number of interventions reflected only in out-of-court settlements, not in final judicial decisions? Common academic wisdom with regard to litigation assumes some kind of correlation between cases that are disposed by courts and cases that are settled out of court.[41] In the case of the HCJ, this correlation does not seem to exist: while the rate of judgments in favor of petitions against government agencies stayed constant, the rate of cases in which the government settled rose significantly throughout the 1990s.

Out-of-court settlements have some important advantages from the point of view of the reviewing court. First, and probably most importantly, they save the court's time and resources. This is particularly the case for an extremely busy court, such as the HCJ during the 1990s. Accordingly, one simple explanation for the rise in the number of settled case is docket pressures. Another significant advantage of settlements over final judicial dispositions is lower visibility. Settlements are not officially published and tend to be less reported by the general media. Even in cases where settlements are reported, they are not regarded as interventions by the court in governmental policies. This is particularly significant when judicial review is exerted in sensitive areas, such as state security or the civil rights of Palestinians.[42] It is one thing if the Court decides to strike down governmental decision on such sensitive matters. The court is likely to be criticized by the proponents of governmental policy, and pay the full political price for its activist practices. It is another thing if the government agrees to settle the case. In such a case it would be more difficult to blame the court for the consequences. It should, therefore, not come as a surprise that the justices of the HCJ tend to exert pressure on the parties (particularly on the government agencies in the litigation) to settle a large proportion of the petitions to the Court.

Such pressures on behalf of the Court, standing alone, cannot fully explain why government agencies agree to settle so many cases (given the extremely high rate of success they have in final judicial dispositions). In order to explain the outcomes, one must explain why the Israeli government is willing to absorb the judicial pressure to settle so many petitions. A possible explanation relates to the centralized structure of the representation of the Israeli government before the HCJ.

Government agencies in Israel are represented in the HCJ by one, relatively small, department in the Office of the Attorney General (OAG), known as the High Court of Justice Department (HCJD).[43] This means that all departments of the central government in Israel are represented in court by a small group of lawyers who are not directly controlled (in terms of bureaucratic hierarchy) by the offices of their clients. Rather, they are part of the apparatus of the Ministry of Justice and the OAG. This means that the HCJD enjoys a considerable level of independence vis-à-vis their clients.[44] In addition, as previous research suggests, the lawyers in the department developed close working relationships with the justices of the Supreme Court (before whom they appear almost every day). These lawyers also develop a strong professional ethos of "officers of the court" who are committed to the ideal of the rule of justice no less than to the immediate interests of their clients in the specific litigation at hand.[45] This strong commitment by HCJD lawyers toward the Court can also be explained by their career structure, since many of them pursue a judicial career immediately after leaving their post at the OAG, and a notable number of them have been appointed as justices of the HCJ itself, immediately after leaving the OAG.[46] The structure of governmental representation in the HCJ seems to provide an additional explanation for outcomes in litigation during the 1990s.

The shift in governmental policies of representation in the HCJ throughout the research period is quantitatively reflected in our database.

As Figure 7.8 demonstrates, there has been a significant increase in the number of cases in which the government proposed settlement as the initial reaction to the petition. While during the 1970s the government proposed settlements in less than 5 percent of the cases, during the 1990s the government proposed settlement in more than a quarter of petitions to the HCJ.

As Figure 7.9 makes clear, government response to petitions issued to the HCJ seems to have had considerable impact on the outcomes in litigation. In over 90 percent of the cases in which the government proposed settlement in the HCJ, the case was successfully settled in favor of the petitioner (see also Table 7.3 that demonstrates that when the government proposed settlements the chances of the petitioners succeeding rose significantly, odd ratio 23.41). Thus, the rise in the relative number of cases in which the government proposed settlement during the 1990s can explain patterns of change in outcomes of litigation.

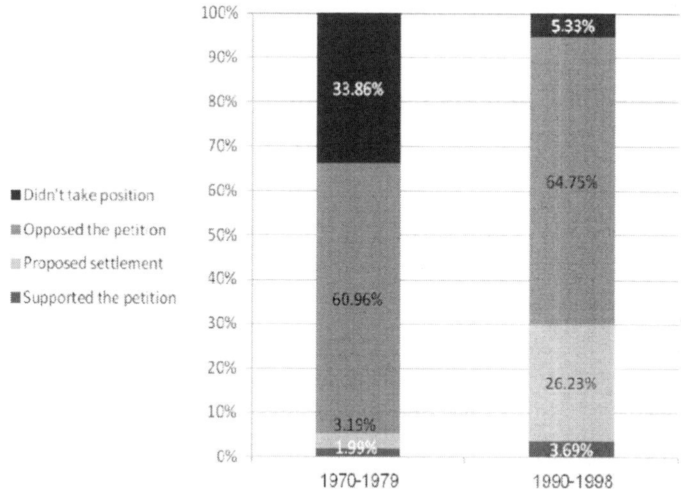

Figure 7.8 Government response to petitions to the HCJ: 1970s vs. 1990s

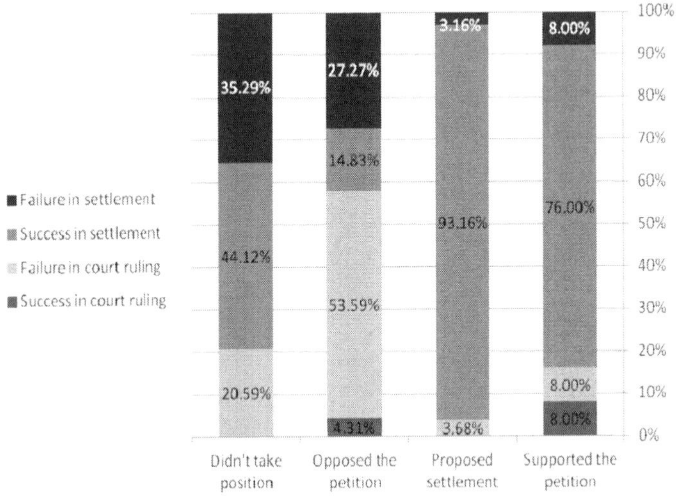

Figure 7.9 Success rates by government response 1990–98

Conclusion

We provide here some preliminary findings regarding patterns of judicial decision-making in the Israeli Supreme Court during the era of intensifying judicial activism in the 1980s. As this chapter demonstrates, an understanding of judicial behavior necessitates the study not only of the court itself, but also of other players in litigation: lawyers, organized petitioners, and governmental agencies. These insights should serve for the continuation of the current research, as well as for future research on judicial behavior.

Notes

1 *See* Frank H. Easterbrook, *Do Liberals and Conservatives Differ in Judicial Activism?* 73 U. Colo. L. Rev. 1401 (2002); *See* Keenan D. Kmiec, *The Origin and Current Meanings of "Judicial Activism"*, 92 Cal. L. Rev. 1441 (2004).

2 Kmiec, *supra* note 1, at 1442.

3 *See* Bradley C. Canon, *Defining the Dimensions of Judicial Activism*, 66 Judicature 236 (1983); William P. Marshall, *Conservatives and the Seven Sins of Judicial Activism*, 73 U. Colo. L. Rev. 1217 (2002); Ernest A. Young, *Judicial Activism and Conservative Politics*, 73 U. Colo. L. Rev. 1139 (2002). Among the various meanings of the terms, scholars include the following: (1) second-guessing the federal political branches or state governments; (2) departing from text and/or history; (3) departing from judicial precedent; (4) issuing broad or "maximalist" holdings rather than narrow or "minimalist" ones; (5) exercising broad remedial powers; and (6) deciding cases according to the judges' partisan political preferences, *see*, *e.g.*, Young, *id.* 1142.

4 *See* Cass R. Sunstein, Radicals in Robes 42 (2005); Frank B. Cross & Stefanie A. Lindquist, *The Scientific Study of Judicial Activism*, 91 Minn. L. Rev. 1752 (2006).

5 *See* Cross & Lindquist, *supra* note 4, at 1759.
6 *Id.* at 1760; *see* Margit Cohn & Mordechai Kremnitzer, *Judicial Activism: A Multidimensional Model*, 18 CAN. J. L. & JUR. 333 (2005).
7 *See generally*, for example, Ruth Gavison, Mordechai Kremnitzer & Yoav Dotan, JUDICIAL ACTIVISM AT THE HIGH COURT OF JUSTICE: FOR AND AGAINST (2000).
8 The High Court of Justice (HCJ) is one of the functions of the Supreme Court of Israel. When a civil or criminal dispute arises in Israel, it normally makes its way into a county court and then—on appeal—to a district court. Only a handful of such cases reach the Supreme Court as a third instance of cassation. The Supreme Court also sits as an appellate court for cases involving serious criminal offenses, or civil disputes where the value of the claim is very high. Such cases are referred directly to a district court and then, on appeal, to the Supreme Court. Most cases involving public agencies exercising their legal powers are brought directly before the Supreme Court and resolved by this Court with no possibility of appeal. Therefore, the Supreme Court in Israel serves, in fact, in three different functions: as a court of cassation, as a court of appeal, and as a court of first (and last) instance for judicial review cases (HCJ). In 2000 a reform was conducted to the structure of public law litigation, and various categories of litigation were placed under the jurisdiction of the district courts (The Administrative Affairs Court Act, 5760-2000 (Isr.)). However, the HCJ still serves as the principal court for judicial review in Israel.
9 *See* HCJ 1/49 Bejerano v. Minister of Police 2 IsrSc 80 [1949]; HCJ 73/53 Kol Ha'am v. Interior Minister 7 IsrSc 871 [1953]; Daphne Barak-Erez, *From an Unwritten Constitution to a Written Constitution: The Israeli Challenge in American Perspective*, 26 COLUM. HUM. RTS. L. REV. 309 (1995).
10 *See* Barak-Erez, *supra* note 9, at 315–17.
11 *See* HCJ 26/76 Bar-Shalom v. Zore'a 31(1) IsrSc 796 [1977] and controversies related to religion and state HCJ 287/69 Meiron v. Minister of Labor 24(1) IsrSc 337 [1970]; HCJ 11/79 Mirkin v. Minister of Interior 33(1) IsrSc 502 [1979]. *Cf.* in the US where the doctrine of standing is still kept within similar boundaries (*e.g.*, Simon v. Eastern Kentucky Welfare Right Organization, 426 U.S 26 (1976); Lujan v. Defenders of Wildlife, 504 U.S 555, 560 (1992); Anthony Clark Arend & Catherine B. Lotrionte, *Congress Goes to Court: The Past, Present, and Future of Legislator Standing*, 25 HARV. J. L. & PUB. POL'Y 209, 210–18 (2001)).
12 *See* HCJ 185/65 Reiner v. The Prime Minister of Israel 19(2) IsrSc 485 [1965]; HCJ 561/75 Ashkenazi v. Minister of Defense 30(3) IsrSc 309 [1976]. The doctrine of judiciability was applied by Israeli courts in a way that was roughly equivalent to the use of the doctrine of equitable discretion in regard to congressional suits in some federal cases in the US, *see, e.g.*, Riegle v. Federal Open Market Committee 656 F.2d 873, 882 (D.C. Cir. 1981); Arend & Lotrionte, *supra* note 11, at 236 and n.149.
13 *See* HCJ 46/50 El Aiubi v. Minister of Defense 4(1) IsrSc 222 [1950].
14 *See* HCJ 156/56 Schor v. Attorney General 11(1) IsrSc 285 [1957].
15 *See* HCJ 217/80 Segal v. Minister of Interior 34(4) IsrSc 429 [1980].
16 HCJ 910/86 Ressler v. Minister of Defense 42(2) IsrSc 441, 477 [1988].
17 *Id.*
18 *See* HCJ 389/80 Dapei Zahav v. Broadcasting Authority 35(1) IsrSc 421 [1980].
19 *See* HCJ 297/82 Berger v. Minister of Interior 37(3) IsrSc 29 [1983].
20 *See* HCJ 5510/92 Turkeman v. Minister of Defense 48(1) IsrSc 217 [1993]; Itzhak Zamir, *Unreasonableness, Balance of Interests and Proportionality*, in PUBLIC LAW IN ISRAEL 327 (Itzhak Zamir & Allen Zysblat eds., 1996).

21 *See* HCJ 680/88 Schnitzer v. Chief Military Censor 42(4) IsrSc 617 [1989]; HCJ 428/86 Barzilai v. the Government of Israel 40(3) IsrSc 505 [1986]; *see* Yoav Dotan & Menachem Hofnung, *Legal Defeats – Political Wins: Why Do Elected Representatives Go to Court*, 38 Comp. Pol. Stud. 75 (2005) [hereinafter Dotan & Hofnung 2005].

22 *See* HCJ 935/89 Ganor v. Attorney General 44(2) IsrSc 485 [1989]; HCJ 425/89 Tzofan v. General Military Attorney 43(4) IsrSc 718 [1989]; *see* Yoav Dotan, *Judicial Review and Political Accountability: The Case of the High Court of Justice in Israel*, 32 Isr. L. Rev. 448 (1998).

23 *See* HCJ 669/86 Rubin v. Berger 41(1) IsrSc 73 [1987]; HCJ 1635/90 Zarzavski v. Prime Minister 45(1) IsrSc 749 [1991]; HCJ 5364/94 Volner v. Chairman of the Labor Party 49(1) IsrSc 758 [1995].

24 *See* H.C 652/81 Sarid v. Chairman of the Knesset 36(1) IsrSc 197 [1982]; *see* Dotan & Hofnung 2005, *supra* note 21, at 86.

25 *See* HCJ 6163/92 Eisenberg v. Minister of Housing 47(2) IsrSc 229 [1993].

26 *See* HCJ 4267/93 Amitai – Citizens for Decent Government v. Prime Minister of Israel 47(5) IsrSc 441 [1993]; HCJ 3094/93 The Movement for Quality in Government v. State of Israel 47(5) IsrSc 404 [1993].

27 *See* Yoav Dotan & Menachem Hofnung, *Interest Groups in the Israeli High Court of Justice: Measuring Success in Litigation and in Out-of-Court Settlements*, 23 Law & Pol'y 1 (2001) [hereinafter Dotan & Hofnung 2001]. Since 1980 there has been a dramatic rise in the number of petitions issued by interest groups. While in 1980 only 1.5 percent of the petitions to the HCJ were issued by interest groups, by 1989 their share of the HCJ docket had reached 5.9 percent, and 12.4 percent by 1995 (Dotan & Hofnung 2001, at 16).

28 At the Declaration of Establishment of Israel (which was solemnly read to the people of the state on the date of establishment on 15 May 1948), the founders of the state provided that the people of Israel will elect a "Constituting Assembly" that will form a constitution for Israel. After the Assembly was elected, however, it soon decided to change its name to the First Knesset, and to postpone the preparation of the constitution for a later stage. Later, a decision (known as the Harari Resolution of 1950) was taken by the Knesset to postpone the adoption of a constitution as one document, and instead to prepare it piecemeal chapter-by-chapter in a series of basic laws that would eventually be brought together to form the constitution. Accordingly, the Israeli Knesset has two functions: one as a constitutional assembly, and the other as regular legislature, *see* Barak-Erez, *supra* note 9, at 323–30; Allen Zysblat, *Introduction: The System of Government*, *in* Public Law in Israel 1 (Itzhak Zamir & Allen Zysblat eds., 1996).

29 The other new basic law was Basic Law: Freedom of Occupation that referred to only one right: the right to pursue one's trade, *see* Barak-Erez, *supra* note 9, at 324.

30 *See* Barak-Erez, *supra* note); Yoav Dotan, *The Spillover Effect of Bills of Rights: A Comparative Assessment of the Impact of Bills of Rights on Courts in Canada and Israel*, 53 Am. J. Comp. L. 293 (2005).

31 *See* CA 6821/93 Bank Ha'mizrachi Hameuchad v. Migdal 49(4) IsrSc 221 [1994].

32 *See* HCJ 5394/92 Hopfert v. Yad Vashem 48(3) IsrSc 353 [1994]; HCJ 453/94 Israel Women's Network v. The Government of Israel 48(5) IsrSc 501 [1994].

33 *See*, for example, David Kretzmer, *The New Basic Laws on Human Rights: A Mini-Revolution in Israeli Constitutional Law*, 26 Isr. L. Rev. 238 (1992); Aharon Barak, *A Constitutional Revolution: Israel's Basic Laws*, 4 Const. Forum 83 (1993); Ran Hirschl, *Israel's 'Constitutional Revolution': The Legal Interpretation of Entrenched Civil Liberties in an Emerging Neo-Liberal Order*, 46 Am. J. Comp. L. 427 (1998).

34 Amnon Rubinstein & Barak Medina, The Constitutional Law of Israel 256 (2005). Under section 10 of the Basic Law: Human Dignity and Freedom, all legislation enacted prior to the Basic Law is not subject to invalidation, even if it does not correspond with the requirements of the basic law, but the section also provides that such prior legislation should be interpreted in accordance with the rights entrenched in the Basic Law. While the Constitutional Revolution could potentially have impacted on outcomes of litigation throughout the 1990s we found no evidence oo such influence in our database and therefore we do not discuss this issue here (*see* Yoav Dotan, Judicial Activism and Government Practices in Litigation in the Israeli High Court of Justice 1970–2000 (Jun. 2–5, 2011) (unpublished paper) (on file with author). And *cf.* Keren Weinshall-Margel, *Attitudinal and Neo-Institutional Models of Supreme Court Decision Making: An Empirical and Comparative Perspective from Israel*, 8 J. Empirical Legal Stud. 556 (2011) (suggesting that the Constitutional Revolution did have some impact on judicial behavior in regars to constitutional cases in the field of freedom of religion).

35 For technical reasons 1999 was not sampled.

36 *See* Yoav Dotan, *Judicial Rhetoric, Government Lawyers, and Human Rights: The Case of the Israeli High Court of Justice during the Intifada*, 33 Law & Soc'y Rev. 319 (1999).

37 Presumably due to the first Palestinian Intifada, *id.*

38 *See* supra note 8.

39 Unlike the Supreme Court of the US, the Supreme Court of Israel (as well as the HCJ) normally sits in panels of three justices and only rarely sits *en banc* or in panels larger than three. Moreover, the above-mentioned number of cases brought to the Supreme Court is somewhat misleading because a great portion of these cases are applications for leave for appeals and other "miscellaneous requests" that are normally disposed by one judge. Even in appeal cases, not all cases are fully disposed by all three justices on the bench because in some types of case there are procedures that allow the Court to shift most of the burden of such cases to one justice, while limiting the amount of work that the other two members of the panel need to invest in those cases. Even so, the burden that this caseload places on the justices is extraordinary.

40 In 12 percent of the cases in our sample, the outcome was categorized as "other" (that is, neither as success nor as failure). The data presented in following figures are the net numbers after the subtraction of this group.

41 *See*, for example, Robert Cooter, Stephen Marks & Robert Mnookin, *Bargaining in the Shadow of the Law: A Testable Model of Strategic Behavior*, 11 J. Legal Stud. 225 (1982).

42 *See* Dotan, *supra* note 36.

43 The number of lawyers in the HCJD rose significantly during the research period. While in the mid-70s the whole department consisted of two lawyers, by the mid-90s the number had risen to 15, and currently 25 lawyers serve in this department.

44 Much like their American counterparts in the Office of the Solicitor General, *see, e.g.*, Rebecca M. Salokar, The Solicitor General: The Politics of Law (1992).

45 *See* Dotan, *supra* note 36.

46 *Id.* About 50 percent of all Supreme Court justices during the 1990s came from the bureaucracy of the Ministry of Justice and the OAG. Some Supreme Court justices (such as Haim Cohen, Meir Shamgar, Ahron Barak, Yitzhak Zamir, and Elyakim Rubinstein) served as Attorney General before being appointed. Others (such as Gabriel Bach and Dorit Beinisch) served as General Prosecutors. At least four HCJ justices during the

1990s served, at a certain stage of their career, in the HCJD (Mishael Cheshin, Miriam Naor, and Dorit Beinisch) and another member of the HCJD was appointed during the 2000s (Uzi Fogelman).

47 The categorization of the parties (both petitioners and respondents) was based on the first party that was listed as petitioner or respondent. In a small number of cases in our sample the first respondent was a private party against whom the petition was issued along with other public authorities listed as second or third respondent, etc.

48 The procedure regarding petitions to the HCJ can be roughly divided into two main stages. The first stage is preliminary. The main object of the petitioner at this stage is to convince the court to issue a conditional order (order *nisi*) that would open the door for a full hearing at the second stage. The procedure at the preliminary stage is brief. The respondent is only required to answer the petition by way a short document called a "respondent notice" that need not be supported by affidavits: the hearing before the court is very brief and does not involve a thorough examination of the facts of the case. Only after the court issues a conditional order does the main stage of the litigation ensue. This stage includes a more comprehensive inquiry on behalf of the court into the facts and legal questions, and it is based on affidavits and full arguments (both oral and written) by the parties. Therefore, the decision to issue a conditional order has substantial importance for the procedural settings of the litigation and, presumably, on its outcome. I discuss this issue elsewhere, *see* Yoav Dotan, Lawyering for the Rule of Law: Government Lawyers and the Rise of Judicial Power in Israel (2013).

49 Success and failure were defined in relation to the petitioner's claim: thus, success was when the case ended in favor of the petitioner, and failure was when it ended in favor of the respondent. The original variable included five categories: success in the decision held in court (when the petition was either fully or partially accepted); failure in the decision held in court (the petition was turned down either after a conditional order was issued or without a conditional order); success in the settlement (when a settlement was achieved or when the respondent backed down); failure in the settlement (when the petitioner backed down from his petition); and other outcomes. Success in court and settlement were united into one category, and failure in both court and settlement were united into another category. All other cases were omitted from the analysis. When looking at the ability of the independent variables to predict the outcome of the petition, we see that while for the null model the overall percentage of prediction was 64.2 percent; the overall percent of cases that are correctly predicted by the full model rose to 80.3 percent, thus, the variables improved the prediction by 16.1 percent.

50 When looking at the ability of the independent variables to predict the type of proceeding conducted, we see that while for the null model the overall percentage of prediction was 50 percent, the overall percent of cases that are correctly predicted by the full model rose to 67.2 percent, thus, the variables improved the prediction by 17.2 percent.

References

Arend, Anthony Clark and Catherine B. Lotrionte, 2001. Congress Goes to Court: The Past, Present, and Future of Legislator Standing. *Harvard Journal of Law and Public Policy* 25: 210–18.

Barak, Aharon. 1993. A Constitutional Revolution: Israel's Basic Laws. *Constitutional Forum* 4: 83–84.

Barak-Erez, Daphne. 1995. From an Unwritten Constitution to a Written Constitution: The Israeli Challenge in American Perspective. *Columbia Human Rights Law Review* 26: 309–355.

Canon, Bradley C. 1983. Defining the Dimensions of Judicial Activism. *Judicature* 66: 236–247.

Cohn, Margit, and Mordechai Kremnitzer. 2005. Judicial Activism: A Multidimensional Model. *Canadian Journal of Law and Jurisprudence* 18: 333–356.

Cooter, Robert, Stephen Marks, and Robert Mnookin. 1982. Bargaining in the Shadow of the Law: A Testable Model of Strategic Behavior. *The Journal of Legal Studies* 11: 225–251.

Cross, Frank B., and Stefanie A. Lindquist. 2006. The Scientific Study of Judicial Activism. *Minnesota Law Review* 91: 1752–1784.

Dotan, Yoav. 1998. Judicial Review and Political Accountability: The Case of the High Court of Justice in Israel. *Israel Law Review* 32: 448–474.

——1999. Judicial Rhetoric, Government Lawyers, and Human Rights: The Case of the Israeli High Court of Justice during the *Intifada*. *Law and Society Review* 33: 319–363.

——2005. The Spillover Effect of Bills of Rights: A Comparative Assessment of the Impact of Bills of Rights on Courts in Canada and Israel. *The American Journal of Comparative Law* 53: 293–341.

——2011. Judicial Activism and Government Practices in Litigation in the Israeli High Court of Justice 1970–2000. Unpublished manuscript. San Francisco, Law and Society Association Annual Meeting, June.

——2013. *Lawyering for the Rule of Law: Government Lawyers and the Rise of Judicial Power in Israel*. Cambridge: Cambridge University Press.

Dotan, Yoav, and Menachem Hofnung. 2001. Interest Groups in the Israeli High Court of Justice: Measuring Success in Litigation and in Out-of-Court Settlements. *Law and Policy* 23: 1–27.

——2005. Legal Defeats – Political Wins: Why Do Elected Representatives Go to Court? *Comparative Political Studies* 38: 75–103.

Easterbrook, Frank H. 2002. Do Liberals and Conservatives Differ in Judicial Activism. *University of Colorado Law Review* 73: 1401–1416.

Gavison, Ruth, Mordechai Kremnitzer, and Yoav Dotan. 2000. *Judicial Activism at the High Court of Justice: For and Against*. Jerusalem: Magnes.

Hirschl, Ran. 1998. Israel's"Constitutional Revolution': The Legal Interpretation of Entrenched Civil Liberties in an Emerging Neo-Liberal Order. *The American Journal of Comparative Law* 46: 427–452.

Kmiec, Keenan D. 2004. The Origin and Current Meanings of "Judicial Activism". *California Law Review* 92: 1441–1478.

Kretzmer, David. 1992. The New Basic Laws on Human Rights: A Mini-Revolution in Israeli Constitutional Law. *Israel Law Review* 26: 238–246.

Marshall, William P. 2002. Conservatives and the Seven Sins of Judicial Activism. *University of Colorado Law Review* 73: 1217–1256.

Priest, George L., and Benjamin Klein. 1984. The Selection of Disputes for Litigation. *The Journal of Legal Studies* 13: 1–55.

Rubinstein, Amnon, and Barak Medina. 2005. *The Constitutional Law of Israel*. Tel Aviv: Shoken.

Salokar, Rebecca M. 1994. *The Solicitor General: The Politics of Law*. Philadelphia: Temple University Press.

Sunstein, Cass R. 2005. *Radicals in Robes*. New York: Basic Books.

Weinshall Margel, Keren. 2011. Attitudinal and Neo-Institutional Models of Supreme Court Decision Making: An Empirical and Comparative Perspective from Israel. *Journal of Empirical Legal Studies* 8: 556–586.

Young, Ernest A. 2002. Judicial Activism and Conservative Politics. *University of Colorado Law Review* 73: 1139–1216.

Zamir, Itzhak. 1996. Unreasonableness, Balance of Interests and Proportionality. Pp. 327–333 in *Public Law in Israel*, edited by Itzhak Zamir and Allen Zysblat. Oxford: Clarendon Press.

Zysblat, Allen. 1996. Introduction: The System of Government. Pp. 1–17 in *Public Law in Israel*, edited by Itzhak Zamir and Allen Zysblat. Oxford: Clarendon Press.

8 Case selection and dissent in courts of last resort

An empirical study of the Israel Supreme Court

Theodore Eisenberg, Talia Fisher, and Issi Rosen-Zvi[1]

Introduction

The jurisdictional basis of appellate court cases can be divided into mandatory and discretionary components. Whether jurisdiction is mandatory or discretionary is significantly associated with courts' patterns of affirmance and reversal. For example, the US Supreme Court, with almost wholly discretionary jurisdiction, reverses about 70 percent of the cases it agrees to hear, whereas US federal Courts of Appeal, with largely mandatory jurisdiction, reverse about 20 to 30 percent of the cases they review.[2] Even within the same court, jurisdictional source is significantly associated with reversal patterns. US state supreme courts and the Israel Supreme Court (ISC) hear both discretionary and mandatory appeals, and show higher reversal rates in discretionary appeals than in mandatory appeals.[3] The higher discretionary case reversal rate is likely associated with judges' authority to select their docket and a tendency to select for review cases with which they disagree. The associations among jurisdictional source, case selection, and case outcome can confound basic findings about judicial behavior. It is increasingly recognized that models of judicial behavior may be unreliable if they do not account for discretionary case selection.[4]

Despite its obvious importance, the case selection process is largely unstudied and, at the individual justice level, has never to our knowledge been the object of a large-scale study. In the US Supreme Court, perhaps the most studied court in the world, justices' votes on whether to review cases have not been publicly available so it has not been possible to evaluate justices' patterns of review-granting behavior or to study associations between votes to review and votes on the merits.[5] Information about review decisions in the ISC, although less readily available than information about ISC opinions in cases it decides on the merits, is available and offers a rare opportunity to study a high court's, and its justices', process of selecting cases for appeal.

The ISC is the highest judicial tribunal in Israel with final authority over all lawsuits. It issues thousands of judgments per year and plays a vital role in the shaping of public policy, both as a High Court of Justice with original jurisdiction and as an appellate court. In its capacity as a High Court of Justice the ISC adjudicates all cases brought against a public agency exercising its legal powers.[6] In its function as an appellate court, the ISC sits atop a high-quality common law legal system and exercises substantial appellate discretionary and mandatory jurisdiction. In some cases, the ISC has mandatory jurisdiction as the sole appellate court available to litigants.[7] In other cases, the ISC functions as a third instance of cassation, providing a second level of appellate review. In these second-level appellate review cases the ISC's jurisdiction is discretionary.[8]

The decision-making process underlying the ISC's appellate function has both open and hidden dimensions.[9] The exposed dimensions relate to case outcome and to central lines of reasoning,[10] including public statements of dissent.[11] The hidden segments, the impact of which on the shaping of legal doctrine and public policy are no less profound, relate, among other factors, to the case selection process and to the assignment of cases to particular justices for purposes of screening.

This chapter builds on our earlier study of the ISC in which we reported an association between jurisdictional source and appellate outcomes and associations between the government as litigant and outcomes.[12] It attempts to unravel the hidden dimensions of judicial decision-making processes in the ISC's capacity as an appellate court. It focuses on individual justices' patterns of behavior in selecting cases and investigates the association between jurisdictional source and patterns of dissent and concurrence in the Court.

While our findings concerning the case selection process and the association between jurisdiction source and dissent rates may initially seem mundane, these factors play a profoundly important role in the formation of the legal doctrine. Case selection is a large part of the work ISC justices perform, similarly to many of their peers in other courts of last resort. Despite its importance, the case selection process in the ISC and most other courts has gone unstudied. Part of the reason could be that even in legal circles in Israel, the screening of discretionary appeal cases is considered a very "technical" task of the justices, often assigned to new or temporary justices. Our study aims to correct this situation. In light of the great volume of cases that the ISC handles as instances of cassation, and in light of the power of the screening justice to deny discretionary appeals singlehandedly, the justices' gatekeeping patterns should not be overlooked.

Patterns of dissent and concurrence are also of special importance in the context of the ISC. Even within the same court, views about the legitimacy and desirability of individual dissents can vary across justices and over time.[13] The practice of dissent—of justices publishing their disagreements with the judgment or with the reasoning of their fellow justices—is closely associated by some with political legitimacy.[14] The ISC's legitimacy has been the object of recent debate, with some of its most vocal criticizers challenging the justices' homogeneity of background and opinion.[15] Therefore, findings regarding the ISC justices' patterns of dissent and concurrence should be of special interest to policymakers and to the public at large.

To summarize our results, we find substantial evidence that, in courts with discretionary jurisdiction, analyses of judicial activity, and of individual justices' behavior, are incomplete unless they account for the court's case selection process. The ISC process for assigning cases for preliminary screening by individual justices has a substantial nonrandom component, with justices specializing based on subject area and seniority. Over 95 percent of the discretionary jurisdiction criminal cases were screened by two justices, who significantly differed in the rate at which they referred cases to three-judge screening panels. Screening behavior also varied significantly in discretionary civil cases. The rate of granting review was highest in tort cases. The rate of granting review in criminal cases was substantially higher in cases involving female defendants than in cases involving male defendants, a pattern that persisted across justices. With respect to outcomes in cases granted full review, the high rate of reversal in discretionary jurisdiction cases was not a consequence of one or two justices' behavior. For every justice who screened a reasonable number of cases, the reversal rate in discretionary cases, civil or criminal, was well above the 24 percent to 32 percent reversal rate in mandatory jurisdiction cases. Dissent rates were low, less than 2 percent overall and only 3 percent in discretionary jurisdiction cases. Rates of concurrence with an opinion by an individual justice were substantially higher.

The next section of this chapter reviews the most relevant literature on the ISC, case selection, and dissent. The section thereafter provides more detailed institutional information about the Israeli judiciary. The fourth section, Hypotheses and empirical results, discusses our hypotheses, describes the data, and reports the results, which are discussed in the next section. The final section concludes.

Literature review

Studies of the ISC

In light of its importance in shaping public policy, scholars have studied various features of ISC decision-making.[16] Of particular importance for purposes of our study is the Shachar, Gross, and Harris 1996–97 paper, which dealt with dissent patterns in the ISC by conducting a study of 7,147 Israel Supreme Court cases, representing 40 percent of all cases published in the years 1948–94. Unlike our study, the Shachar, Gross, and Harris article relates to dissent practices both in the ISC's capacity as High Court of Justice and in its role as a court of appeal. The three scholars report a relatively low dissent rate in the ISC.[17] Dissent was reported in 368 cases out of 6,329 judgments, only 5.8 percent of the cases, issued by judicial panels.[18] Since the Shachar, Gross, and Harris study was restricted to published cases, our findings of dissent rates of less than 2 percent overall (for both published and unpublished cases) align with their findings. It is quite plausible that the dissent rate in published cases is higher than in the general class of cases in light of a possible correlation between the existence of a dissenting opinion and the decision to publish the judgment.[19]

The Shachar, Gross, and Harris study further examined the question of dissent from the perspective of case outcome. It reports a dissent rate of 9.8 percent for cases in which the outcome was reversal of the lower court ruling. This is slightly higher than the dissent rate for cases resulting in affirmation of the lower court ruling.[20] Another subdivision made in the Shachar, Gross, and Harris study relates to subject matter. The study reports a higher dissent rate when the ISC functions as the High Court of Justice than when it functions in its appellate capacity. Thus, while the dissent rate for High Court of Justice cases is 10.8 percent, the dissent rate in the category of civil appeals is 9.9 percent and the dissent rate in criminal appeals is 9.1 percent.[21] The Shachar, Gross, and Harris study also examines the tendency of individual justices to write dissenting opinions.[22]

The Shachar, Gross, and Harris study is very impressive in the coverage it offers for the issue of dissent in the ISC. However, it does not explore a fundamental feature of the dissent phenomenon—the possible distinction between mandatory jurisdiction cases and discretionary jurisdiction cases. As the Eisenberg and Miller study shows, jurisdiction source is closely associated with patterns of concurrence and dissent.[23] According to our findings below, while dissent rates in the ISC are less than 2 percent overall, they are higher in discretionary cases granted full review.

Another important distinction between our study and the Shachar, Gross, and Harris paper is the difference in the samples studied. Our dataset includes all of the appealed civil and criminal cases for which the Israeli Judicial Authority (IJA) database supplies information—namely, both published and nonpublished cases. The Shachar, Gross, and Harris study refers to 40 percent of published cases.[24] In light of the possible connection between a dissenting opinion and the decision to publish the case, our study is less prone to selection bias.

Studies of case selection and dissent

Studies of case selection

Studies of the exercise of discretion to review cases at the individual justice level are virtually non-existent. Studies at the case or court level suggest that justices respond to caseload pressures by exercising greater control over their docket, whether or not they are formally authorized to do so. US federal legislation in 1891 and 1925, which gave the US Supreme Court some control over its docket, was inadequate to control docket pressure. The Court responded by dismissing most purportedly mandatory review cases "for want of a substantial federal question,"[25] and Congress recognized the reality of the Court's control of its docket in legislation enacted in 1988.[26] Evidence exists that the Taiwan Supreme Court's docket practices were resistant to efforts to shift its role away from error correction and toward the development of legal doctrine.[27] Given the ISC's substantial mandatory docket and its role as High Court of Justice, one expects the Court's workload and docket pressure to contribute to a low rate of granting review. [28]

Studies of dissent

One can organize studies of dissent in high courts into three categories. Some studies search for structural breaks in the rate of dissent over time at the case level. The search for statistically supportable break points in dissent rates has led social science scholars to employ times series statistical methods. Most studies of the US Supreme Court conclude that the 1930s or early 1940s is the period during which a consensual norm on that Court declined.[29] These statistical approaches are consistent with M. Todd Henderson's less technical summary of the dissent data over time. He traces the variation in dissent rates in the US Supreme Court and reports that dissent rates were low for about 150 years after the Court was established. For the 35 years of John Marshall's service, 4 percent of opinions had dissents. For the next seven chief justices, through Chief Justice Hughes' tenure and ending in 1940, the dissent rate remained less than 10 percent. It increased to 27 percent during Chief Justice Vinson's tenure, peaked at 59 percent during Chief Justice Burger's service and was at 47 percent for the period 2005 to 2007 under Chief Justice Roberts.[30]

Russell Smyth and Paresh Kumar Narayan employed times series econometric methods to assess shifts in the norm of consensus. Although they acknowledge the common belief that there was one regime shift on the US Supreme Court, traceable to the 1930s or 1940s, they find three breaks in consensus. Two of the three breaks in dissenting opinions correspond closely to the beginning of Taney's and Stone's terms as Chief Justice, with the third occurring in the middle of Chase's term. These findings are consistent with a more than doubling of the percent of opinions with a dissent from the Marshall to the Taney and Chase courts, from 4 percent to 9 percent.

A second group of dissent studies seeks to explain the causes of observed changes in dissent rates. Here both less formal analyses of dissent rates and methods similar to those used in the descriptive studies have been published. Henderson attributes variation in dissent rates to differing views of the roles of opinions and of courts. Many regard certainty and consensus in the law as a critical value.[31] Some value the importance of a settled rule of law over the importance of a correct decision. Under this view, since dissent is associated with an unsettled view of the law, it can undermine confidence in courts as institutions. John Marshall is said to have "squelched virtually all dissent during his thirty-five years as Chief Justice."[32] Others regard dissent as a positive contribution to the law. Dissents can advance different legal theories to the community, can appeal to future justices, and are evidence of a truly deliberative body in which justices voice their independent views.[33]

Study of dissent over time in the Australian High Court takes a more formal econometric approach to consider factors in addition to subjective views of leadership style and a court's effort to shape its institutional role in government. Paresh Kumar Narayan and Russell Smyth examine the factors influencing dissent rates on the High Court of Australia from 1904 through 2001.[34] They hypothesized that institutional factors (the court's caseload, whether it had discretion to select the cases it hears, and whether it was a final court of appeal), socioeconomic complexity (proxied for by using the divorce rate, urbanization rate, and real GDP per capita), and leadership style would explain dissent rates over time. Their main finding is that caseload and real income most influenced dissent.

Since our study is a cross-sectional slice of ISC cases for a limited time period, and not a study extending over several years, we cannot identify dissent patterns that change over time. But the factors believed to influence dissent in prior studies can contribute to understanding the patterns we observe during the period studied.

A third class of dissent studies, including part of the Shachar, Gross, and Harris ISC study described above, also looks beyond time patterns and external explanatory variables and focuses on additional institutional factors influencing dissent rates. The authors reported what they regarded as a low rate of dissent. The explanation offered in the Shachar, Gross, and Harris study for the low rate is that in the internal workings of the ISC there exists "a mechanism that diminishes discrepancies of opinion and that pacifies debate throughout the decision-making process."[35] In the authors' opinion the negligible rate of dissent is not rooted in "complex negotiations and reciprocal influence" taking place among the justices. Rather it stems from the internal work procedures of the ISC "which ascribe a dominant opening position in the hands of one of the three justices, while disincentivizing his fellow justices to formulate a dissenting opinion, especially in the most complex of cases."[36] The disincentive, claim the authors, results from the fact that justices who choose to write dissenting opinions enhance their workload. The dissenting opinion is added on to the numerous cases in which they are responsible for the writing of the initial opinion (to which the other justices can either concur or dissent). Moreover, the authors claim that in order for the dissenting opinion to be effective, its quality must surpass that of the leading opinion in a substantial manner and on numerous dimensions. In light of the high workload costs associated with the writing of a dissenting opinion and the relatively low benefits involved (as a result of the a priori ineffectuality of such opinions), the internal culture that evolved in the ISC discourages open debate.[37]

The Israeli judiciary

Israel is a unitary state with a single system of traditional courts of general jurisdiction, as well as other tribunals or authorities with judicial power. The institutions other than the traditional courts have jurisdiction limited by subject matter or persons covered. Of the regular law courts, the judiciary law establishes three levels of courts: the ISC, district courts, and magistrates' courts.[38] District courts and magistrates' courts are trial courts; the Supreme Court functions as both an appellate court and, as noted above, as High Court of Justice (HCJ). Because the ISC HCJ function is not an appellate function, this study excludes cases in which the ISC acts as the HCJ. The judiciary portion of the Basic Law strives to assure judicial independence through methods of selecting judges, terms of office, and independence of other branches of government. There are no juries.

The 29 magistrates' courts are the basic trial courts. Magistrates' courts serve the locality and district in which they sit. They generally have criminal jurisdiction over offenses with a potential punishment of a fine or up to seven years imprisonment. They have civil jurisdiction in matters involving up to a specified monetary amount—which currently is 2.5 million shekels (approximately US$690,000)—as well as over the use, possession, and division of real property. Magistrates' courts also serve as traffic courts, municipal courts, family courts, and small claims courts. Generally, a single judge presides in each case unless the President of the magistrates' court directs that a panel of three judges hear the case.[39]

District courts have residual jurisdiction in any matter that is not within the sole jurisdiction of another court. The six district courts sit in Jerusalem, Tel Aviv, Haifa, Beersheva, Nazareth, and Petah-Tikva. The Petah-Tikva court was added in 2007.[40] As courts of first instance, district courts hear criminal cases in which the accused faces punishment of more than seven years imprisonment. District courts' civil jurisdiction extends to matters in which more than 2.5 million shekels are in dispute. District courts also hear cases dealing with, inter alia, companies and partnership, arbitration, prisoners' petitions, and appeals on tax matters, and serve as administrative courts. These courts also hear appeals of judgments of the magistrates' courts. Generally, a panel is composed of a single district court judge. A panel of three judges hears appeals of magistrates' courts' case judgments and hears cases in the first instance when the accused is charged with an offense punishable by imprisonment of ten or more years. A three-judge panel also sits when the President or Deputy President of the District Court so directs.[41]

The Supreme Court has jurisdiction to hear criminal and civil appeals from judgments of the district courts. Cases that begin in a district court are appealable, as of right, to the Supreme Court. Other matters, particularly the mass of cases that begin in the magistrates' courts, may be appealed only with the Supreme Court's permission. The Supreme Court's decisions are binding on lower courts and Israel adheres to the principle of stare decisis.[42]

The Supreme Court generally sits in panels comprised of three justices. The President or the Deputy President of the Court may expand the size of the panel to any uneven number of justices. Each panel also has the power to decide to expand its size. The Court can also decide to initiate a "further hearing" in which a panel of five or more justices will rehear a case decided by a smaller panel of the Supreme Court. A single justice may hear petitions for injunctions, temporary restraining orders, and other interim rulings, as well as for an order *nisi*, but a single justice may not refuse to grant an order *nisi* or make it contingent on only some of its assertions. A single justice may hear appeals against interim rulings of district courts or against the verdict of a single district court judge hearing an appeal from a case in a magistrate's court.[43]

Courts sitting on appeal, whether district courts or the ISC, are formally authorized to adjudicate both fact and law, but seldom intervene in factual matters and tend to limit their judgment to questions of law. The underlying rationale is that on appeal cases judges usually are not directly exposed to witnesses and other types of evidence. This does not negate the ability of the appellate court to examine whether the factual basis upon which the decision of the lower court is premised is anchored on sound evidentiary foundations, but the de facto appeal practice is not one of a de novo review. Our study refers both to civil and criminal appeals, which are regulated in a slightly differential manner under Israeli law. Therefore, we will address each of the categories separately.[44]

Civil cases

In civil cases, any party harmed by the final decision of the court of first instance can appeal as of right to a court of higher instance. Thus, cases initiated in the magistrates' courts entail a right of appeal to the district courts, while cases commencing in the district courts are appealed as of right to the ISC.

In addition to the appeal as of right, litigants can petition the court for discretionary appeal in two types of situations: First, when they wish to challenge an interim decision on a pending case in the court of first instance (either an interim decision of the district court sitting as a court of first instance or a decision of the district court sitting as a court of appeal on an interim decision of the magistrates' court).[45] This category of cases was excluded from the study.[46] Second, when they wish to challenge the final decision of a district court sitting as an appellate court. Thus, when a case is initiated in a magistrate's court and appealed as of right to a district court, litigants can petition the ISC for a second level of appellate review.[47]

The requirements of discretionary appeal were laid down in the landmark case of *Chenion Haifa v. Matzat Or*,[48] the most cited precedent in Israeli case law.[49] According to the ISC's ruling in *Chenion Haifa*, it should grant discretionary appeal only when there are significant legal or public issues at stake that exceed the interests of the litigating parties. Such legal or public issues may include, for example, conflicting rulings by lower courts that were not settled by the ISC and matters of constitutional significance. The ISC stresses that the outcome reached by the lower court—whether correct or erroneous, desirable or undesirable—is immaterial to the decision on the matter of granting a discretionary appeal.[50] In other words, at least in theory, the ISC should not take into consideration the merit of the lower-court ruling when deciding whether to grant a discretionary appeal.

When a request for discretionary appeal is filed, the ISC should proceed in two phases: First, examine whether the *Chenion Haifa* requirements are satisfied.[51] The general requirement is for a single justice to decide this phase. The justice can decide to deny review and thus dismiss the case, or to grant review, leading to the second phase—a panel of three justices who then hear the appeal and decide on the merits. In practice, as will be shown below, the boundaries between the two phases are blurred: The single justice often decides to deny review, grounding its decision not only on the *Chenion Haifa* requirements but also on the merits of the case. Similarly, the three-justice panel sitting on appeal sometimes rejects the case based on the procedural requirements laid out in *Chenion Haifa*.

Criminal cases

In criminal cases, a verdict issued by the district court sitting in the first instance can be appealed as of right to the ISC.[52] A verdict issued by the magistrates' court in the first instance can be appealed as of right to the district court. In Israel, both prosecution and defense have symmetric rights of appeal because the prosecution is authorized to appeal a defendant's acquittal.[53] Courts of appeals usually preside in panels of three judges.

When a case is initiated in the magistrates' court and appealed as of right to the district court, both the prosecution and the defense can petition the ISC for a second appellate review. Unlike the situation in civil cases, interim trial court decisions in criminal cases cannot be appealed,[54] with only limited exceptions such as judicial disqualification.[55]

The requirements of discretionary appeal laid down in *Chenion Haifa* apply to the criminal realm as well.[56] Namely, the result reached by the lower court should not play a role in the decision whether to grant or deny a discretionary appeal. Therefore, according to the current law, an argument made by the defendant concerning the stigmatizing effect of conviction,[57] or even the severity of punishment, is not a ground for a second appellate review.[58]

A request for discretionary appeal is usually reviewed by a single justice, but it can also be reviewed by a panel of three justices.[59] When the request for appeal is reviewed by a three-justice panel the panel is authorized to treat the request for appeal as an appeal and decide on the merits.[60]

Case selection

As discussed above, discretionary appeals are based, in most cases, on a preliminary screening by a single justice. Who are the screening justices? And how are cases assigned to them? The answer to these questions is not found in the law, which leaves these issues to be decided internally by the ISC's administration. During the time of our study (2006–07), two justices were screening criminal discretionary appeals (Justices A and B) and six justices were screening civil discretionary appeals (Justices B, C, D, E, F, and G), with one justice (Justice B) screening both civil and criminal discretionary appeals. Thus, in total, seven justices were screening cases concurrently.

Criminal discretionary appeals were assigned to the two screening justices randomly and the cases were divided between them fairly evenly, with Justice A screening 456 cases and Justice B screening 454 cases.

Civil discretionary appeals were assigned based on the subject matter of the case. The cases are divided into five categories: tort, arbitration, execution office, compensation officer, and other cases. Tort cases, the bulk of which are automobile accident cases, were assigned to Justice C. Arbitration includes all the cases that are initiated by arbitration. According to the Arbitration Law,[61] decisions made by the arbitrator can be appealed to the district court and the arbitration award can be either certified or cancelled by the district court. Either of the parties to the arbitration can petition the ISC for appellate review of the district court's decisions. Arbitration cases were assigned to Justice D. Execution office cases are cases initiated in the execution office, which is responsible for enforcing judgments. The district court has jurisdiction to review decisions made by the execution office registrar. Litigants can petition the ISC for appellate review of such district court decisions. Execution office cases were assigned to Justice B. Compensation officer's cases initiate at the Supreme Medical Committee, sitting under the auspices of the Ministry of Defense, which decides whether and how much compensation should be paid to people injured during their military service. According to the Disabled (Compensation and Rehabilitation) Law,[62] a compensation officer's decision can be appealed to the district court. Litigants can petition the ISC for appellate review of such district court decisions. Compensation officer's cases were assigned to either Justice B or Justice D. All other cases, which are the bulk of the cases, were divided randomly between Justice E and Justice F, with Justice E screening 113 civil cases and Justice F screening 135 civil cases. In April 2007, Justice G joined the ISC as an Acting Justice and joined Justices E and F in screening general civil discretionary appeals. It should be noted that the distribution of cases among the screening justices is not perfect and in some instances they receive cases from different categories. Yet, for the most part, the cases are distributed according to the categories discussed above.

Hypotheses and empirical results

Hypotheses

Prior studies show different appellate outcome patterns between discretionary and mandatory cases. Building on this result, our principal hypothesis is that understanding a high court's appellate process, and the behavior of its individual justices, requires accounting for the complete appellate process. One cannot limit study to just the usually visible portion of that process manifested in full dispositions on the merits with accompanying opinions.

We had little in the way of ex ante beliefs about the individual and panel-screening processes because so little detailed information about the ISC screening process was available. Indeed, prior to this study, the subject-based screening assignments within the ISC, described in the Case selection section above, had been largely unknown. Hypotheses that draw on other studies are difficult to formulate because data limitations have precluded systematic study of high court screening processes in other countries as well as in Israel.

Thus, a substantial part of the results we report are descriptive to enable assessment of our principal hypothesis. These results include the outcome of the initial screening process by individual justices, the treatment by three-judge panels of cases referred to the panels, and the treatment on the merits of cases that the panels allow to receive full review. When feasible, we report separately the results of panel outcomes and full review for the individual screening justice, along with tests of statistical significance in observed differences.

A plausible hypothesis with respect to screening behavior is that a justice that observes more cases of a particular type may be expected to apply a higher threshold to granting full review to cases of that type. A critical mass of cases is often needed in order to construct general guidelines that would allow cases to be distinguished. Until one reaches a certain threshold volume of cases, individual cases may be more likely to be viewed as posing novel or important issues.

Specific plausible hypotheses relate to the association among individual screening behavior, three-judge panel rates of granting full review, and case outcomes, and between workload and screening behavior. The more prone a justice is to referring cases to a three-judge panel, the less likely we think the probability of the panel reviewing the case on the merits. Justices with more generous standards of review should have the review rate in cases they screen pushed toward the ISC's institutional norm for review by the behavior of three-judge panels. In theory, justices with less generous standards of review should be subject to a similar effect (in this case, an increased likelihood of review), but such justices' refusal decisions are rarely, if ever, reviewed.

To the extent cases referred to a three-judge panel by a justice with a generous review standard survive three-judge panel review, we expect higher reversal rates in cases screened by that justice. Lower courts presumably correctly adjudicate most cases and a higher review rate should be associated with a lower reversal rate in the cases granted review.

According to *Chenion Haifa*, the decision to grant review should not turn on mere disagreement with the ruling below, so ISC reversal rates in discretionary cases might be expected to be close to reversal rates in mandatory cases or to at least not drift far from 50 percent. As our prior work suggests that *Chenion Haifa* is not routinely followed,[63] we do not emphasize this hypothesis in this study.

With respect to the dissenting and concurring opinion aspects of this study, a larger body of work was available. Based on the literature discussed above, we expect a low rate of dissent in the ISC because of its substantial workload. Nonetheless, cases in which the district court decision is reversed can be thought of as a priori "hard cases" and in those cases one might expect a more significant dissent rate. We had no ex ante view about the expected rate of concurrence other than that the same workload forces might reduce justices' inclinations to write concurring opinions as well as dissenting opinions.

Data and methodology

This study uses a data set initially constructed for our earlier study of appellate outcomes in the ISC, which includes a discussion of the data's limitations.[64] We describe here relevant aspects of the original data set and report additional coding activity with respect to the data.

The cases included in this study are: (1) for discretionary and mandatory jurisdiction criminal cases, all cases decided in the years 2006 and 2007; and (2) for discretionary and mandatory civil cases, all cases decided in 2007 and all cases decided in the months of August through December 2006. The study includes every ISC substantive opinion available online via the official IJA website for all cases decided in these time periods. Since the IJA website contains all of the cases decided by the ISC,[65] the resulting database provides a complete picture of ISC doctrinal decisional activity in the periods covered. We tested the comprehensiveness and accuracy of the database by comparing it with data obtained from the ISC's secretariat. This comparison suggested that the data obtained from the IJA website is indeed comprehensive, covering the full gamut of criminal and civil cases.

The cases identified by the methods described above were coded by student research assistants. Prior to the student coding, the authors designed a data form to structure the coding. After review of the performance of the form and the students in an initial set of cases, the form was revised and a final form constructed. The students used that revised form to code the cases, under the supervision of the authors.

Preliminary results indicated that the coding of case categories in our original data differed from the case categories that the ISC uses internally to assign discretionary jurisdiction cases to individual screening justices. Those categories are described above in the section entitled Case selection. We therefore reviewed every discretionary case in the original data to construct the case categories more relevant to this study, with its emphasis on screening by individual justices. In the course of reviewing the data, we corrected some errors in the coding of case outcomes, eliminated interlocutory appeal cases, and removed a few duplicate observations. The resulting useable sample contains 3,344 cases consisting of 941 discretionary criminal appeals, 1,410 mandatory criminal appeals, 396 discretionary civil appeals, and 597 mandatory civil appeals. Fewer cases may be reported in our results due to missing data for a variable included in a table. In reporting results we refer to individual justices by letter rather than by name to emphasize our interest in the institutional issues and not in the decisions of any particular justice.

Results

Rate of referring to three-judge panels

As explained above, a main focus of this chapter is the screening behavior of individual justices. Table 8.1 reports, for each individual justice with a reasonable number of cases, the outcome of the initial case-screening process by that justice. Panel A reports on discretionary jurisdiction criminal cases and Panel B reports on discretionary jurisdiction criminal cases. Both panels show that only two of the four screening outcomes reported occurred in a substantial number of cases. In criminal cases, the Total row shows that 91 percent of the cases were denied review and 8.2 percent of the cases were referred to a three-judge panel. The "Review granted" outcome was so rare as to preclude more detailed analysis. In civil cases, Panel B's Total row shows that 83.9 percent of cases were denied review and 14.9 percent were referred to a three-judge panel. So the vast majority of non-denial screening outcomes were references of cases to a three-judge panel for consideration of whether to grant review or take other action.

Panel A shows that the two principal screeners of criminal cases in our sample were Justices A and B. Together they screened 903 of the 933 (96.8 percent) cases for which we have data. They agreed that the overwhelming majority of criminal cases in which review was sought should not be referred to a three-judge panel. Justice A denied review in 96 percent of cases and Justice B denied review in 90.4 percent of cases.

Panel A also shows two interesting differences in screening behavior in criminal cases. As between the two principal justices, Justice B referred cases

Table 8.1 Rates of granting review and of referring to three-judge panels in discretionary criminal and civil cases

Justice	*Review denied*	*Referred to 3-judge panel*	*Review granted*	*Total*
A. Criminal cases				
Justice A	436	17	1	454
	96.0%	3.7%	0.2%	100%
Justice B	406	41	2	449
	90.4%	9.1%	0.5%	100%
Other	10	19	1	30
	33.3%	63.3%	3.3%	100%
Total	852	77	4	933
	91.3%	8.3%	0.4%	100%
B. Civil cases				
Justice B	17	6	0	23
	73.9%	26.1%	0.0%	100%
Justice C	41	23	3	67
	61.2%	34.3%	4.5%	100%
Justice D	16	6	1	23
	69.6%	26.1%	4.4%	100%
Justice E	102	10	1	113
	90.3%	8.9%	0.9%	100%
Justice F	128	5	0	133
	96.2%	3.8%	0.0%	100%
Justice G	22	0	0	22
	100%	0.0%	0.0%	100%
Other	1	8	0	9
	11.1%	88.9%	0.0%	100%
Total	327	58	5	390
	83.9%	14.9%	1.3%	100%

Note: For each justice, the first row is the number of cases with review denied or granted and the second row is the percentage of cases denying or granting review. In Panel A, justices who screened fewer than 100 criminal cases are combined as "Other." In Panel B, justices who screened fewer than ten cases are combined as "Other." The table excludes three criminal cases and six civil cases that screening justices dismissed. The sum of row percentages may exceed 100 percent due to rounding.

to three-judge panels at a noticeably higher rate, more than double, than did Justice A. Their difference in denial of review versus referring of cases to three-judge panels is highly statistically significant ($p < 0.001$).[66] Second, the rate (over 60 percent) at which justices other than Justices A and B referred cases to three-judge panels and the rate at which these two principal justices referred cases is also highly statistically significant.

Panel B shows substantial screening behavior variation in civil cases across justices. Limiting the sample to cases in which justices either denied review or referred a case to a three-judge panel, Justice C referred more than one-third of the cases to a three-judge panel and Justice G referred none of the cases to a panel.

One can reject the hypothesis of a no statistically significant difference among the justices in referral rates. For all justices in the table, the significance level is less than 0.001. This highly statistically significant result persists if one excludes the justices with the highest and lowest referral rates, Justices C and G, and also persists if one additionally excludes the residual category of "Other" justices.

Table 8.1 also shows that individual justices rarely take it upon themselves to grant review of a case. This practice was not anticipated by the rules of procedure that authorize a single judge to grant review. The effective ISC practice under which a single judge very rarely grants review imposes an additional hurdle in the way of appealing parties, and may lead to a higher instance of false negatives in this respect (namely of decisions not to grant review in cases when review should have been granted).

Three-judge panel action in referred cases

The variation in individual justices' rates of panel referral is one of the main outcomes of interest. A second important output, conditional on referral to a panel, is the panel outcomes in cases referred to them. In particular, are panel outcomes noticeably different across referring justices? Table 8.2 explores this topic. Panel A reports on criminal cases and Panel B reports on civil cases.

For Panel A, the rates at which panels granted review do not differ dramatically across referring justices. The higher rate of granting review is the 76.5 percent rate in cases referred by Justice A and the lower rate of granting review is the 58.5 percent rate in cases referred by Justice B. One cannot reject the hypothesis of no statistically significant difference in the rates at which three-judge panels grant review in cases referred by the justices in Panel A ($p = 0.402$).

This inability to reject a difference suggests substantial agreement by panels with the decisions of individual justices to allow cases to proceed to the panel stage of review. Overall, the panels agreed to review on the merits 62.3 percent of the criminal cases referred to them by individual justices. Whether this is due to deference by the panel to the referring justice's decision to refer a case, or the panel's independent assessment of the importance of full review of a case, or a combination of the two, is not ascertainable from our data.

Variation across screening justices is a bit higher in civil cases. Panel B shows that panels granted review in at least 50 percent of all cases referred to them by individual justices. Due to the increased variability, in civil cases one can reject the hypothesis of no difference in the rate at which three-judge panels grant review (in Panel B at $p = 0.052$). The significance or near significance of the result is largely attributable to the high rate of panel agreement with Justice C. This justice referred the largest number of civil cases (22) to full panels and had nearly complete panel agreement to full review (95.5 percent), with only one case being denied full review by the panel. Excluding Justice C, there is no statistically significant difference

Table 8.2 Rate of granting review in cases referred to three-judge panel in discretionary criminal and civil cases

Justice referring case to three-judge panel	*Review denied*	*Review granted*	*Total*
A. Criminal cases			
Justice A	4	13	17
	23.5%	76.5%	100%
Justice B	17	24	41
	41.5%	58.5%	100%
Other	8	11	19
	42.1%	57.9%	100%
Total	29	48	77
	37.7%	62.3%	100%
B. Civil cases			
Justice B	3	3	6
	50%	50%	100%
Justice C	1	21	22
	4.6%	95.5%	100%
Justice D	2	4	6
	33.3%	66.7%	100%
Justice E	2	8	10
	20%	80%	100%
Justice F	0	5	5
	0.0%	100%	100%
Other	2	6	8
	25%	75%	100%
Total	10	47	57
	17.5%	82.5%	100%

Note: For each justice, the first row is the number of cases with review denied or granted and the second row is the percentage of cases denying or granting review. In Panel A, justices who screened fewer than 100 criminal cases are combined as "Other." In Panel B, justices who initially screened fewer than ten cases are combined as "Other." The table treats cases in which the panel denied review and stated that it would have affirmed if review had not been denied as cases in which review was denied. The sum of row percentages may exceed 100 percent due to rounding.

in Panel B's pattern of outcomes ($p = 0.485$). As in criminal cases, panels show substantial agreement with individual justice's decisions that cases are important. In civil cases, the panels agreed to review on the merits 82.5 percent of the cases referred to them by individual screening justices. This rate is statistically significantly higher than the 62.3 percent rate at which full review was granted in criminal cases ($p = 0.013$). If we add to this the substantially lower rate at which screening justices tend to grant review or refer a case to a panel of three justices (8.6 percent in criminal cases and 16 percent in civil cases) it is clear that the probability of obtaining a full review on the merits in criminal cases is significantly lower than in civil cases.

Appellate outcomes in cases granted full review

An additional question is whether the outcome on the merits of fully reviewed cases is associated with the identity of the initial screening justice. The reversal rate of fully reviewed cases can supply useful implicit information about the factors that influence individual justices to refer cases to panel review. Table 8.3 reports, for individual justices, the outcomes on the merits of cases fully reviewed by a panel. As above, Panel A reports on criminal cases and Panel B reports on civil cases.

With respect to both criminal and civil cases, the table offers evidence that disagreement with the ruling in the district court is an important criterion in referring cases for all justices. Full reversal occurs in over 65 percent of both criminal and civil cases reviewed on the merits, as shown in the two totals rows in the table. The lowest full reversal rate is 53.9 percent in criminal cases screened by Justice B.[67]

Table 8.3 Rate of reversal in discretionary civil and criminal cases granted review

Justice	*Affirmed*	*Reversed*	*Affirmed in part, reversed in part*	*Total*
A. Criminal cases				
Justice A	1	13	0	14
	7.1%	92.9%	0.0%	100%
Justice B	4	14	8	26
	15.4%	53.9%	30.1%	100%
Other	1	8	4	13
	7.7%	61.5%	30.8%	100%
Total	6	35	12	53
	11.3%	66%	22.6%	100%
B. Civil cases				
Justice B	0	2	1	3
	0.0%	66.7%	33.3%	100%
Justice C	8	15	1	24
	33.3%	62.5%	4.2%	100%
Justice D	2	3	0	5
	40%	60%	0.0%	100%
Justice E	1	7	1	9
	11.1%	77.8%	11.1%	100%
Justice F	1	3	1	5
	20%	60%	20%	100%
Other	0	5	1	6
	0.0%	83.3%	16.7%	100%
Total	12	35	5	52
	23.1%	67.3%	9.6%	100%

Note: For each justice, the first row is the number of cases and the second row is the percentage of cases affirmed or reversed. In Panel A, justices who screened fewer than 100 criminal cases are combined as "Other." In Panel B, justices who screened fewer than ten cases are combined as "Other." The cases reported in Table 8.3 are limited to those in which we observed a screening result of "granted" by a single judge or by a three-judge panel.

If one combines full reversals with partial reversals (the second and third numerical columns in Table 8.3), however, the difference in affirmance and reversal across the three categories of criminal cases justices is not close to being statistically significant ($p = 0.742$). In civil cases, one cannot reject the hypothesis of no difference across screening justices ($p = 0.431$), a result that persists if one combines full reversals with partial reversals ($p = 0.413$). Of course, part of the reason for insignificance may be the sparse cells for some of the entries in the table.

Patterns of dissent and concurrence

Whatever the theoretical importance of dissent in appellate courts, very little expressed dissent exists in the ISC in its function as an appellate court. Table 8.4 shows the pattern of overall dissent for four groups of cases. Panel A shows the pattern in mandatory jurisdiction cases. In both civil and criminal cases, less than 2 percent of cases have dissenting opinions. Panel B shows that the dissent rate in mandatory jurisdiction cases increases, to over 3 percent combined, if one limits the mandatory jurisdiction cases to those with a reversal in whole or in part. Panel C shows the dissent rate in discretionary jurisdiction cases. Since little dissent is likely with respect to screening decisions, the rate of dissent in discretionary jurisdiction cases is low, less than 0.5 percent for both civil and criminal cases. Panel D shows that, given a grant of review on the merits, dissent in discretionary cases increases, but is still low with only three cases out of a hundred containing a dissent.

The ISC rates of concurrence are higher than its dissent rates. Table 8.5 shows the rates of concurrence for the same categories of cases as Table 8.4. We count a case as having a concurrence if a justice writes a separate statement or opinion and the ISC opinion does not merely state that a justice concurs. Panel A shows that, in mandatory jurisdiction criminal cases, justices concurred in 6.4 percent of 1,410 cases compared to a 9.1 percent concurrence rate in 597 mandatory civil cases. This difference is statistically significant at $p = 0.038$. Panel B shows that the increased rate of concurrence in civil cases persists if one limits the sample to mandatory jurisdiction cases that were reversed in whole or in part. In discretionary jurisdiction cases reported in Panel C, rates of concurrence are much lower because, as noted above, most discretionary jurisdiction cases do not receive full review by three-judge panels. Panel D shows that, in those discretionary jurisdiction cases reviewed on the merits by ISC panels, concurrence rates are 19.2 percent in criminal cases and 20.8 percent in civil cases. Both rates are more than double the rates in mandatory jurisdiction cases and are also higher than concurrence rates in mandatory jurisdiction cases with reversals in whole or in part.[68]

Discussion of results

Our effort to explain the pattern of descriptive results reported in the above section, Hypotheses and empirical results, is subject to the important limitation that we do not have objective evidence about the "review-worthiness" of the cases or of the

Table 8.4 Dissent rate in mandatory and discretionary cases

Case type	*Cases with dissent*	*Cases without dissent*	*Total*
A. Mandatory jurisdiction cases			
Criminal	26	1,384	1,410
	1.8%	98.2%	100%
Civil	8	589	597
	1.3%	98.7%	100%
Total	34	1,973	2,007
	1.7%	98.3%	100%
B. Mandatory jurisdiction cases reversed in whole or in part			
Criminal	13	343	356
	3.7%	96.4%	100%
Civil	4	143	147
	2.7%	97.3%	100%
Total	17	486	503
	3.4%	96.6%	100%
C. Discretionary jurisdiction cases			
Criminal	2	937	939
	0.2%	99.8%	100%
Civil	1	389	390
	0.3%	99.7%	100%
Total	3	1,336	1,339
	0.2%	99.8%	100%
D. Discretionary jurisdiction cases granted review with affirmance, reversal, or affirmance in part and reversal in part			
Criminal	2	50	52
	3.9%	96.2%	100%
Civil	1	47	48
	2%	98%	100%
Total	3	97	100
	3%	97%	100%

Note: For each case category, the first row is the number of cases with and without dissent and the second row is the percentage of cases with and without dissent. The cases reported in Panel C are limited to those in which we observed a screening result of "granted" by a single judge or by a three-judge panel.

correctness of the district court ruling in cases that panels reviewed on the merits. Nevertheless, some of our results show the importance of accounting for the full appellate process, both screening and merits stages, rather than studying them, as is almost always done, in isolation. We also explore some important possible associations between case characteristics and appellate screening outcomes and appellate merits outcomes, as well as offer thoughts about our data's implications for the source of low dissent rates on the ISC.

The importance of accounting for the screening and merits stages of the appellate process

Perhaps our study's purest illustration of the importance of considering the entire appellate process emerges from comparing the results for Justices A and B in discretionary criminal cases, each of whom screened over 400 criminal cases. Table 8.1 shows that Justice A referred 3.7 percent of screened cases for panel review compared

Table 8.5 Concurrence rate in mandatory and discretionary cases

Case type	*Cases with written concurrence*	*Cases without written concurrence*	*Total*
A. Mandatory jurisdiction cases			
Criminal	90	1,320	1,410
	6.4%	93.6%	100%
Civil	54	543	597
	9.1%	91%	100%
Total	144	1,863	2,007
	7.2%	92.8%	100%
B. Mandatory jurisdiction cases reversed in whole or in part			
Criminal	35	321	356
	9.8%	90.2%	100%
Civil	26	121	147
	17.7%	82.3%	100%
	61	442	503
Total	12.1%	87.9%	100%
C. Discretionary jurisdiction cases			
Criminal	13	926	939
	1.4%	98.6%	100%
Civil	12	378	390
	3.1%	96.9%	100%
Total	25	1,304	1,339
	1.9%	98.1%	100%
D. Discretionary jurisdiction cases granted review with affirmance, reversal, or affirmance in part and reversal in part			
Criminal	10	42	52
	19.2%	80.8%	100%
Civil	10	38	48
	20.8%	79.2%	100%
Total	20	80	100
	20%	80%	100%

Note: For each case category, the first row is the number of cases with and without a written concurrence and the second row is the percentage of cases with and without a written concurrence. The cases reported in Panel C are limited to those in which we observed a screening result of "granted" by a single judge or by a three-judge panel.

to Justice B's referral rate of 9.1 percent. This significant difference, standing alone, establishes the importance of the screening process in evaluating judicial appellate behavior.

Suppose, for example, that the two justices showed the exact same voting pattern with respect to the merits of the pool of screened cases that proceeded to full review. A study limited to cases reviewed on the merits—the dominant kind of study of appellate outcomes—would fail to detect a vital difference between these two justices' judicial activity. Justice B, left on his own, would allow full merits review of more than twice as many cases as Justice A. If the two justices share common reversal rates for merits cases, Justice B would reverse convictions twice as often as Justice A. Evaluating the behavior of the justices requires knowledge of the screening process.

The inner workings of the screening process studied here provide another result relevant to evaluating judicial behavior. Table 8.2's Panel A shows that the three-judge panels reacted differently to cases screened by Justices A and B. The panels granted full review to 58.5 percent of the cases screened by Justice B and 76.5 percent of the cases screened by Justice A. This difference is not statistically significant (p = 0.241) and we therefore hesitate to regard it as strong evidence of different panel reactions to the cases screened by the two justices. The difference is nevertheless substantial and the significance level may be limited by the relatively small sample. The difference constitutes some evidence of a tendency by reviewing panels to deny full review to cases screened by Justice B compared to cases screened by Justice A. The more liberal rate of granting review by Justice B is offset by panel decisions that are more restrictive of granting review to Justice B's cases. This suggests that the usual ISC practice of screening by an individual justice, followed by screening by a full panel, can diminish the differences in review rates that would exist if screening were only by single justices.

We should add that we offer no opinion on whether Justice A or Justice B has the more appropriate rate of granting full review. Such an opinion would require individual evaluation of each screening decision based on the record available in the case and, even then, reasonable experts might differ in their views of the propriety of full review for many cases. Our point is not one about who is acting more correctly. It is that knowledge of justices' screening behavior is essential to understanding and assessing justices' behavior.

Gender

Accounting for defendants' gender provides a second illustration of the importance of full knowledge of the appellate process. Studies of criminal justice often show gender effects, with male defendants faring significantly worse than female defendants. It is reported that in the US there is little debate that greater leniency is shown to female defendants charged with homicide.[69] Given equal crimes, women in the US tend to receive shorter sentences than men.[70] And women on death row are more likely than men on death row to have sentences commuted[71] or to otherwise get off death row.[72] In Israel there is one study that disputes this argument suggesting that female defendants charged with homicide and other violent crimes fare worse than male defendants charged with the same crimes, both in terms of the probability of acquittal and in terms of the sentences they receive.[73] We therefore explored case outcomes as a function of gender, with gender in criminal cases coded based on the defendants' names. Table 8.6 reports the results.

Table 8.6 shows, for example, that the rate of granting review was substantially higher in cases involving female defendants than in cases involving male defendants. For example, in cases screened by Justice A, 7.7 percent of cases involving female defendants were granted review compared to 3.9 percent of cases granted review in male defendant cases. A similar difference persists for Justice B and for the residual category of "Other" justices. The total difference in the rate of granting review (the last row in Panel A) between the two genders is significant at $p = 0.056$. In cases appealed by defendants only (thus excluding government appeals), the pattern was slightly more extreme, with 17 percent of female appeals

Table 8.6 Rate of granting review (or referring to three-judge panel) and rate of reversal in discretionary criminal cases, by gender and screening judge

	Female defendant	*Male defendant*	*Total*
A. Rate of granting review or referring to three-judge panel			
Justice A	26	406	432
	7.7%	3.9%	4.2%
Justice B	18	416	434
	16.7%	9.1%	9.4%
Other	3	26	29
	100%	61.5%	65.5%
Total	47	848	895
	17%	8.3%	8.7%
B. Rate of reversal in cases granted review			
Justice A	1	13	14
	100%	92.3%	92.9%
Justice B	2	15	17
	100%	73.3%	76.5%
Other	1	6	7
	100%	83.3%	85.7%
Total	4	34	38
	100%	82.4%	84.2%

Note: Cases shown in table are limited to those in which the gender of the defendant could be reasonably identified from case names. For each justice, the first row is the number of cases with defendants of the column's gender and the second row is the percentage of cases reversed for that column. In Panel A, justices who screened fewer than 100 criminal cases are combined as "Other." In Panel B, justices who screened fewer than six cases are combined as "Other." Table excludes cases in which the result was affirmed in part and reversed in part.

obtaining review compared to 7.5 percent of male appeals, a difference significant at $p = 0.046$.[74] The pattern of higher review rates for female than for male defendants is not close to statistically significantly different across individual justices.

Panel B of Table 8.6 reports, by gender, the appellate outcome for the discretionary criminal cases granted review. It shows, for example, that the ISC reversed the district court in 100 percent of the female defendant cases; but note that the sample consists of only four cases. For males, the reversal rate was 82.6 percent. The result is not close to statistically significant.

Nevertheless, the relation between the two panels in Table 8.6 has important implications for studies of appellate courts with discretionary jurisdiction. If we ignore for purposes of illustration the small number of female defendant cases, once one accounts for case-screening activity, the lower male reversal rate may provide interesting information. This is because, as noted above, Table 8.6 also shows that the ISC agreed to review female defendant convictions at about twice the rate of male defendant convictions. The higher female review rate is independently interesting. We are interested here, however, in the light it may shed on the lower male reversal rate. Taking the screening and the reversal rates together, the ISC was more lenient in accepting female defendant cases for review, and was more likely to reverse the female defendant cases it agreed to review. Combining the screening and reversal rates indicates that male and female defendants had different rates of obtaining review, and those different rates were, if anything, enhanced by the gender-specific probabilities of reversal in cases granted review. Observers who reported gender effects based on either stage in isolation likely would want to rethink their results once information is available about the complete appellate process. We do not intend to downplay the interesting, near-significant, pro-female screening effect, and that itself is perhaps worthy of additional study. Our point for present purposes is that the reversal rates may take on a different character when viewed in light of the female screening rate.

Explaining variation in grants of review and appellate outcomes

The results described above already explore the relation between two factors and outcome—the overall category of case (criminal or civil) and the identity of the screening justice. As noted above, the rate (over 60 percent) at which justices other than A and B referred criminal cases to three-judge panels significantly differed from the rate at which these two principal justices referred cases. A similar pattern emerged in civil cases as between justices who regularly screened categories of civil cases and the residual category of other justices who individually screened few civil cases.

Volume of screened cases

We hypothesize, but cannot conclusively prove, that the greater referral rates in the residual justices category of criminal and civil justices is attributable to what might be termed a "jaded" effect. Justices A and B, who screened hundreds of criminal cases, may become more skeptical about the need for reviewing any particular case. With their daily duties including the individual screening of masses of cases, they may develop a higher threshold for regarding a case as sufficiently important to refer to a three-judge panel. This could be because they see so many cases that it is more difficult for individual cases to stand out as important and because their criminal case screening volume forces them to be more selective simply as a mechanism of docket control. The workload of the ISC does not permit these justices to allow a high percentage of criminal cases to be referred to three-judge panels. Justices who screen fewer cases may develop less of their own sense for what cases are important enough to warrant further review and may feel less docket pressure with respect to the criminal cases they screen.

Similar factors may explain part of the pattern of civil case screening outcomes. The two justices with the highest volume of civil cases to screen, Justices E and F, referred cases to three-judge panels at rates noticeably lower than the overall rate of 14.9 percent. Table 8.1 shows that Justice E referred 8.9 percent of the screened cases to three-judge panels and Justice F referred only 3.8 percent of the screened cases to three-judge panels. Justice C combined a relatively high volume of cases (67) with a high referral rate (34.3 percent). This may be attributable to his subject matter specific class of cases—the vast majority of cases he reviewed were tort cases. We cannot determine from the available data whether Justice C's high rate of referral to panels is a justice effect or a case category effect.

Government as litigant

Our individual justice results can also serve to eliminate some possible explanation for the pattern of ISC appellate outcomes. We use our justice-level results to explore prior findings about the government as litigant and about the role of ethnicity in the Israeli criminal justice system.

We have previously detected patterns of case outcomes that differ between the government and other litigants.[75] Although relatively few appeals involved a governmental entity as appellant, our focus on individual justices can shed light on this effect. Specifically, the higher rate of governmental entities obtaining review is not attributable to a particular justice. Table 8.7 reports the rate of granting review or referring to a three-judge panel for each justice, subdivided by cases with and without government appellants.

In discretionary criminal cases, we have screening judge and screening result information on nine government appeals. Both Justice A and Justice B granted review in 100 percent of the government appeals they screened, and the residual group of justices granted review in 80 percent of the government appeals. In eight of nine discretionary criminal government appeals referred to three-judge panels, the panels granted full review. In discretionary civil cases, we have individual justice screening data in ten cases, and the higher rate of granted review in governmental cases cannot be attributed to one justice. Justices who did not refer any government appeals to three-judge panels denied referral in only one case each.

Table 8.7 Rate of granting review (or referring to three-judge panel) in discretionary cases, by government appellant status

	Nongovernment appellant	*Government appellants*
A. Criminal cases		
Justice A	451	3
	3.3%	100%
Justice B	448	1
	8.9%	100%
Other	25	5
	64.0%	80.0%
Total	924	9
	7.9%	88.9%
B.Civil cases		
Justice B	22	1
	27.3%	0.0%
Justice C	63	3
	36.6%	66.7%
Justice D	22	1
	31.8%	0.0%
Justice E	108	4
	8.3%	50.0%
Justice F	132	1
	3.8%	0.0%
Justice G	22	0
	0.0%	—
Total	369	10
	15.3%	40.0%

Note: For each justice, the first row is the number of cases with nongovernment or government appellants and the second row is the percent of that justice's cases granted review or referred to a three-judge panel.

The three-judge panels granted full review in 75 percent of the discretionary civil cases referred to them.

Ethnicity

Evidence exists that pretrial release decisions in Israeli criminal cases are associated with the ethnicity of the defendant and the judge. Israeli Jewish judges in magistrates' courts in Haifa, Nazareth, and Acre tended to grant more favorable outcomes to Jewish defendants than to Arab defendants. And Israeli Arab judges tended to grant more favorable outcomes to Arab defendants than to Jewish defendants.[76] We therefore explored the relation among individual justices, defendant ethnicity, and case outcomes. We determined ethnicity based on the names of defendants in criminal cases and report case outcomes in Table 8.8.

Panel A of Table 8.8 reports, for our three categories of discretionary case screening justices, the ethnicity of defendants and case outcomes. For example, the first entry in the first numerical column shows that Justice A screened 137 discretionary criminal cases with Arab defendants and granted review or referred to a three-judge panel 5.1 percent of those cases. Table 8.8 shows that all three adjudicators were a bit more likely to grant review or refer to a three-judge panel cases involving Arab defendants than cases involving Jewish defendants. The difference in the grant rate across all justices combined, however, is not statistically significant ($p = 0.507$). In addition, for each individual justice, the grant rate is far from statistically significant. Our data thus provide no evidence of a difference in granting review by ethnicity or by the combination of ethnicity and individual justices. It should be noted that Justice B is the only justice of Arab origin presiding on the Supreme Court.

This absence of effect is not conclusive as the ISC decisions come at the end of a process of case selection for prosecution and appeal involving decisions of both prosecutors and defense attorneys. Ethnic effects early in the process may exist but be unobservable at the tail end of the criminal justice process, which is the part

Table 8.8 Rate of granting review (or referring to three-judge panel) and rate of reversal in discretionary criminal cases, by ethnicity and screening judge

Screening justice	*Arab defendant*	*Jewish defendant*	*Total*
A. Rate of granting review or referring to three-judge panel			
Justice A	137	269	406
	5.1%	4.1%	4.4%
Justice B	118	289	407
	11.9%	8.0%	9.1%
Other	6	20	26
	66.7%	65.0%	65.4%
Total	261	578	839
	9.6%	8.1%	8.6%
B. Rate of reversal in cases granted review			
Justice A	6	8	14
	100%	87.5%	92.9%
Justice B	4	11	15
	75.0%	81.8%	80.0%
Other	2	4	6
	50%	100%	83.3%
Total	12	23	35
	83.3%	87%	85.7%

Note: Cases shown in the table are limited to those with an Arab or Jewish defendant. For each justice, the first row is the number of cases with the defendant having the column's ethnicity and the second row is the percentage of cases granting review or reversed for that column. In Panel A, justices who screened fewer than 100 criminal cases are combined as "Other." In Panel B, justices who screened fewer than six cases are combined as "Other." Table excludes cases in which the result was affirmed in part and reversed in part.

that we can observe using our data. Another qualification in this regard relates to the high percentage of Arabs among the (appealing) defendant population, which significantly exceeds the percentage of Arabs in the Israeli population at large.

Panel B of Table 8.8 reports the appellate outcome for the relatively small subset of discretionary criminal cases granted review. It shows, for example, that the district court decision was reversed in all of the Arab defendant cases that Justice A screened for review and that were reviewed on the merits by a three-judge panel. Differences in reversal rates by ethnicity are minor except for the 50 percent reversal rate in Arab defendant cases screened by the residual category of "Other" screening justices. But that rate is based on only two cases. The ethnicity category reversal rates are not statistically significantly different.[77]

Implications of results for pattern of mandatory and discretionary reversal rates

Our earlier study of ISC appeals showed a significant difference in reversal rates between mandatory jurisdiction and discretionary jurisdiction cases. Table 8.3 above shows reversal rates in discretionary criminal and civil cases that exceed 65 percent and that exceed 75 percent if one includes partial reversals in coding reversals. The mandatory case reversal rate is significantly lower.[78] Table 8.3 suggests that the higher discretionary case reversal rate is not a consequence of one or two justices who happened to screen cases using different criteria than the mass of other justices. Table 8.3 shows that for every justice with a reasonable number of cases, the reversal rate in discretionary cases, civil or criminal, screened by that justice, was well above the 24 percent to 32 percent reversal rate in mandatory cases.[79] Thus, the pattern of higher reversals in discretionary cases that we previously reported is an ISC pattern, not a pattern reflecting individual justices' behavior. The tendency to grant review of cases with which one disagrees runs deep, transcends individual justices' screening behavior, and calls into question every justice's implementation of the principle announced in *Chenion Haifa*.

Our coding of defendant ethnicity and gender for purposes of this study allows us to address some other possible explanations for the difference in mandatory and discretionary jurisdiction reversal rates. Tables 8.9 and 8.10 report the rates of reversal, separately for mandatory and discretionary jurisdiction cases. The tables do so separately for Arab and Jewish defendant cases and for female and male defendant cases.

The tables show stability in reversal rates across ethnic status and gender, regardless of the jurisdictional source. Whatever the effect of the screening process in discretionary jurisdiction cases, it does not produce reversal rates significantly different by ethnicity or gender.[80]

Dissent and concurrence rates

Tables 8.4 and 8.5 above show much higher concurrence rates than dissent rates in the ISC. At an absolute level, the dissent rates are trivial and the concurrence

Table 8.9 Rate of reversal in mandatory and discretionary criminal cases by ethnicity

	Arab defendant	*Jewish defendant*	*Total*
Mandatory cases	461 22.6%	572 23.8%	1,033 23.2%
Discretionary cases	13 76.9%	24 83.3%	37 81.1%

Note: Cases shown in the table are limited to those with an Arab or Jewish defendant, with ethnicity identified based on the defendant's name. For each type of jurisdiction, the first row is the total number of cases with defendants of the column's ethnicity and the second row is the percentage of cases reversed. For discretionary cases, the table excludes cases in which the result was affirmed in part and reversed in part.

rates are not. This suggests that, in its appellate role, the ISC does not have a norm against justices expressing their individual views. There thus does not appear to be a fear that the Court will be regarded as less legitimate if justices often speak for themselves to qualify their agreement with the Court's disposition of a case or provide an additional rationale for the final decision in which they concur.

The low dissent rate has more than one possible explanation. First, it may reflect a view that individual expression via concurrence is qualitatively different than individual expression via dissent. The former does not call into question the ISC's disposition of the case whereas the latter does. In this sense, dissent may threaten the Court's perceived legitimacy more than concurrence.

Second, dissenting may impose more work on a justice than concurring. A concurring opinion can emphasize a single point and be highly selective in the issues it addresses because it need not support a different disposition of the case. A dissenting opinion should supply all the reasoning necessary to support a different outcome. On average, a dissent imposes more work on a justice than does a concurrence. Part of the reason for the low dissent rate may be a function of a substantial workload. The ISC justices, sitting as the High Court of Justice, have substantial work in addition to their appellate case workload. Sufficient time

Table 8.10 Rate of reversal in mandatory and discretionary criminal cases by gender

	Female defendant	*Male defendant*	*Total*
Mandatory cases	27 29.6%	1,314 23.8%	1,341 23.9%
Discretionary cases	4 100%	37 75.7%	41 78.0%

Note: Cases shown in the table are limited to those in which the gender of the defendant could be reasonably identified from case names. For each type of jurisdiction, the first row is the total number of cases with defendants of the column's gender and the second row is the percent of cases reversed for that column. Table excludes cases in which the result was affirmed in part and reversed in part.

to author well-reasoned dissents may be infrequently available. An explanation based on workload is consistent with Shachar, Gross, and Harris's explanation for what they regarded as low dissent rates, as reported above.

Conclusion

Studying individual justices and their screening behavior yields insight into the pattern of ISC case outcomes as well as insight into individual behavior. Assignment of preliminary case screening is at least in part nonrandom with a strong association between individual justices and particular case categories. Analysis of screening also informs about performance in areas of substantive interest. The Court granted review in a higher percentage female defendant cases and also reversed convictions at a higher, albeit statistically insignificant, rate for female defendants. The high rate of reversal in discretionary jurisdiction cases, previously shown to call into question the Court's adherence to the principles announced in *Chenion Haifa*, is not a consequence of one or two justices' behavior. The reversal rate in discretionary cases, civil or criminal, was far above the 24 percent to 32 percent reversal rate in mandatory jurisdiction cases regardless of the initial screening justice. Dissenting opinions were rare in ISC appellate cases, with dissent rates of less than 2 percent overall and 3 percent in discretionary jurisdiction cases. Rates of concurrence with an opinion by an individual justice were much higher, especially in discretionary jurisdiction cases. Our results indicate that analyses of judicial activity, and of individual justices' behavior, in courts with discretionary jurisdiction should account for the court's case selection process.

Notes

1 We thank Na'ama Schlam and Noam Guttman for invaluable research assistance, for their insightful comments, and for coordinating the work with the students in a superb manner. We are also grateful to Efrat Zilberbush, Na'ama Daniel, Nitzan Ilani, and Gadi Ezra for their assistance in collecting the data. This study was supported in part by a research grant from Cegla Center for Interdisciplinary Research of the Law at Tel Aviv University. It was prepared for the Second International Conference on Empirical Studies of Judicial Systems, hosted by the Institutum Iurisprudentiae, Academia Sinica.

2 Theodore Eisenberg, Talia Fisher & Issi Rosen-Zvi, *Israel's Supreme Court Appellate Jurisdiction: An Empirical Study*, 96 Cornell L. Rev. 693, 696–97 (2011).

3 *See* Theodore Eisenberg & Geoffrey P. Miller, *Reversal, Dissent, and Variability in State Supreme Courts: The Centrality of Jurisdictional Source*, 89 B.U. L. Rev. 1451 (2009); Eisenberg, Fisher & Rosen-Zvi, *supra* note 2.

4 Anna Harvey & Barry Friedman, *Ducking Trouble: Congressionally Induced Selection Bias in the Supreme Court's Agenda*, 71 J. Pol. 574, 574–76 (2009). "[T]he Court's selection process raises the potential for selection bias in the inferences we draw from its cases." Jonathan P. Kastellec & Jeffrey R. Lax, *Case Selection and the Study of Judicial Politics*, 5 J. Empirical Legal Stud. 407, 408 (2008).

5 US Supreme Court Justice Harry Blackmun's papers, available at the Library of Congress, contain the certiorari votes of each justice and enable study of these matters for the period of his service on the Court. *See* Library of Congress, Harry A.

Blackmun Papers, 1913–2001. Access to docket sheets is available at Lee Epstein, Jeffrey A. Segal & Harold J. Spaeth, *The Digital Archive of the Papers of Harry A. Blackmun* (2007), *available at* http://epstein.law.northwestern.edu/research/BlackmunArchive.html.

6 Yoav Dotan, *Do the "Haves" Still Come Out Ahead? Resource Inequalities in Ideological Courts: The Case of the Israeli High Court of Justice*, 33 Law & Soc'y Rev. 1059, 1061 (1999).

7 *See* Courts Act, 5744–1984, SH No. 1123 p. 198 (Isr.), Art. 41(a).

8 *See id.* Art. 41(b).

9 Yoram Shachar, Miron Gross & Ron Harris, *Anatomy of Discourse and Dissent in the Supreme Court – Quantitative Analyses*, 20 Tel Aviv U. L. Rev. 749, 750 (1996–1997).

10 *Id.*

11 The exposure of dissent in the highest tribunal is not a universal phenomenon. *See* Kevin M. Stack, *The Practice of Dissent in the Supreme Court*, 105 Yale L.J. 2235 (1996).

12 *See* Eisenberg, Fisher & Rosen-Zvi, *supra* note 2.

13 *See* M. Todd Henderson, *From Seriatim to Consensus and Back again: A Theory of Dissent*, 2007 Sup. Ct. Rev. 283 (2007).

14 *E.g.*, Stack, *supra* note 11.

15 *See, e.g.*, http://www.haaretz.co.il/hasite/spages/973324.html (last visited May 4, 2012). Until the early 1990s the ISC enjoyed a high level of legitimacy among the Israeli public and was one of the most popular state institutions. In a 1994 study, over two-thirds of respondents viewed the ISC as representative of the common citizen. *See* Gad Barzilai, Ephraim Yuchtman-Yaar & Ze'ev Segal, The Israeli Supreme Court and the Israeli Public 211 (1994). Over the course of the last decade, we have been witness to a decrease in public trust of the ISC. In a 2008 study conducted by Arye Rattner and Meir Ya'ish, only 48 percent of Jewish respondents and 53 percent of Arab respondents expressed trust in the ISC. (A parallel study, conducted by Rattner in 2000, showed that 80 percent of Jewish respondents and 66 percent of Arab respondents expressed trust in the ISC). *See* http://www.haaretz.co.il/hasite/spages/ 972853.html (last visited May 4, 2012). Due to the decrease in public legitimacy, the role and status of the ISC became much more controversial, and moved, in recent years, to the center stage of the political debate. Questions regarding the nomination of justices, the ISC jurisdiction, its power of judicial review, and, more generally, the question of judicial activism, are currently hotly debated among Israeli politicians, and raise great public and media interest. For an elaborate discussion, *see* Menachem Mautner, Law & Culture in Israel in The Beginning of the 21st Century (2008) (Heb.).

16 Previous empirical studies conducted with respect to the ISC include the following: Shachar, Gross & Harris, *supra* note 9; Miron Gross & Yoram Shachar, *How Are Supreme Court Panels Selected – A Quantitative Analysis*, 29 Hebrew U. L. Rev. 567 (1999); Yoram Shachar, Ron Harris & Miron Gross, *Reference Patterns of the Supreme Court – A Quantitative Analysis*, 27 Hebrew U. L. Rev. 119 (1996); Yoram Shacher, Miron Gross & Chanan Goldshmidt, *100 Leading Precedents – A Quantitative Analysis*, 7 Haifa U. L. Rev. 243 (2003); Yoav Dotan & Menachem Hofnung, *Interest Groups in the High Court of Justice: Measuring Success in Litigation and in Out-of-Court Settlements*, 23 L. & Pol'y 1 (2001); Dotan, *supra* note 7; Eli Salzberger, *Acting Justices in the Supreme Court and Judicial Independence – Theoretical Analysis and Empirical Findings*, 19 Bar Ilan L. Rev. 541 (2003); Barzilai, Segal & Yaar, *supra* note 15; Menachem Hofnung & Keren Weinshall-Margel, *Judicial Setbacks, Material Gains: Terror Litigation at the Israeli High Court of Justice*, 7 J. Empirical Legal Stud. 664 (2010); Keren Weinshall-Margel, *Attitudinal and Neo-Institutional Models of Supreme Court Decision Making: An Empirical and Comparative Perspective from*

Israel, J. EMPIRICAL LEGAL STUD. 556 (2011); Bryna Bogoch & Rachelle Don-Yechiya, THE GENDER OF JUSTICE: BIAS AGAINST WOMEN IN ISRAELI COURTS (1999).

17 Shachar, Gross & Harris, *supra* note 9, at 752.

18 *Id.* at 755.

19 Shachar, Gross & Harris made a similar claim. *See id.* at 756. As anecdotal evidence supporting this assessment, the authors report that they sampled 1,000 nonpublished cases and did not detect a single case of dissent among them.

20 *Id.* at 758.

21 *Id.*

22 *Id.* at 771–76.

23 Eisenberg & Miller, *supra* note 3, at 1454–55 (2009) (reporting that 26.7 percent of the discretionary cases generated at least one dissenting opinion, as compared with 18.8 percent of the mandatory cases).

24 The cases included in our study are: (1) for discretionary and mandatory jurisdiction criminal cases, all cases decided in the years 2006 and 2007, (2) for discretionary and mandatory civil cases, all cases decided in 2007, and all cases decided in the months of August through December 2006. While our study includes all ISC cases, both published and unpublished, the Shachar, Gross, and Harris study referred to 40 percent of published cases for the years 1948–94.

25 *E.g.*, Zucht v. King, 260 US 174 (1922). *See generally* Theodore Eisenberg, *Congressional Authority to Restrict Lower Federal Court Jurisdiction,* 83 YALE L.J. 498, 522 (1974).

26 Pub. L. No. 100–352, 102 Stat. 662 (codified at 28 U.S.C. § 1257 (2006)).

27 *See* Theodore Eisenberg & Kuo-Chang Huang, *The Effects of Rules Shifting Supreme Court Jurisdiction from Mandatory to Discretionary – An Empirical Lesson from Taiwan*, 32 INT'L REV. L. & ECON. 3 (2012).

28 Studies of the US Supreme Court have suggested the importance of the views and participation of the government, acting through the Solicitor General. *See* David C. Thompson & Melanie F. Wachtell, *An Empirical Analysis of Supreme Court Certiorari Petition Procedures: The Call for Response and the Call for the Views of the Solicitor General*, 16 GEO. MASON L. REV. 237 (2009). The category of case and the type of party were associated with Solicitor General/court interactions. *Id.* at 278–82.

29 *See* Russell Smyth & Paresh Kumar Narayan, *Multiple Regime Shifts in Concurring and Dissenting Opinions on the US Supreme Court*, 3 J. EMPIRICAL LEGAL STUD. 79 (2006).

30 Henderson, *supra* note 13, at 323. For a study of the phrasing used by dissenting US Supreme Court justices, *see* Note, *From Consensus to Collegiality: The Origins of the "Respectful" Dissent*, 124 HARV. L. REV. 1305 (2011).

31 Henderson, *supra* note 13, at 283–84.

32 *Id.* at 283.

33 *E.g.*, William J. Brennan, Jr., *In Defense of Dissents*, 37 HASTINGS L.J. 427 (1986); Ruth Bader Ginsburg, *Speaking in a Judicial Voice*, 67 N.Y.U. L. REV. 1185 (1992).

34 *See* Paresh Kumar Narayan & Russell Smyth, *What Explains Dissent on the High Court of Australia? An Empirical Assessment Using a Cointegration and Error Correction Approach*, 4 J. EMPIRICAL LEGAL STUD. 401 (2007).

35 *See* Shachar, Gross & Harris, *supra* note 9.

36 *Id.*

37 The description of the Israeli judiciary in the first two subsections of the Israeli judiciary section is based on the description in Eisenberg, Fisher & Rosen-Zvi, *supra* note 2.

38 *See generally* Courts Law (Consolidated Version), 5744–1984, 38 LSI 271 (1983–1984) (Isr.).

39 Courts Law (Consolidated Version) Ch. 2, Art. 3.

40 Ordinances of Courts (Establishment of The Central District Court), 2007, KT 6585, 824 (Isr.). In results not reported below, we assessed whether screening outcomes in

the ISC differed based on the district court being reviewed. We found no significant differences.

41 Courts Law (Consolidated Version) ch. 2, Art. 2.

42 Basic Law: Judicature § 20.

43 Courts Law (Consolidated Version) §§ 26, 30.

44 *See, e.g.*, CrimA 125/50 David Ya'akobovich v. State of Israel 5(1) PD 519 [1950] (Isr.).

45 This was the legal situation at the time period relevant for this study. *See* Courts Law (Consolidated Version) §§ 41, 52 (effective prior to the amendment described below). As of 2009, litigants in civil cases can no longer petition the court for discretionary appeal of all interim decisions. In 2008 the Courts Law was amended to include a restriction according to which the Minister of Justice is authorized to issue a decree stating types of decisions that are immune from interlocutory appeal. The Minister issued such a decree on March 7, 2009, stating such types of decisions, including postponement of court hearings, size of judicial documents, and the like. *See* Courts Decree (Types of Decisions on Which no Interlocutory Appeal Would Be Granted), 2009.

46 Our earlier study also sought to exclude interim appeals. Eisenberg, Fisher & Rosen-Zvi, *supra* note 2, at 702. In preparing the instant study, we discovered that some interim appeals unintentionally had been included in the prior study. One of the authors then reviewed every discretionary case in our data and eliminated those cases judged to be interim appeals. This accounts in part for differences in the number of observations in this study compared to our prior study.

47 Courts Law (Consolidated Version) § 41(b).

48 CA 103/82 Chenion Haifa v. Matzat Or 36(3) PD 123 [1982] (Isr.).

49 According to Dinim Veod, an Israeli online legal database, the case has been cited in 1,187 cases—more than any other Israeli court ruling. *See* Dinim Veod, *Search Results*, http://www.dinimveod.co.il (last updated Feb. 27, 2011) (search "case No. 103/82") (Hebrew).

50 *See* CA 103/82 Chenion Haifa v. Matzat Or 36(3) PD 123, 127–28 [1982] (Isr.).

51 *See id.*

52 *See* Courts Law (Consolidated Version) § 41(a).

53 Israeli law, which does not differentiate between appeals of acquittals and convictions, grants the prosecution the authority to appeal a defendant's acquittal. For discussion of this authority, *see* Eisenberg, Fisher & Rosen-Zvi, *supra* note 2, at 783 n.52.

54 For a comment on effort to bypass the prohibition on interlocutory appeals, *see id.* at 704 n.53.

55 Criminal Procedure Law (Consolidated Version), 5742–1982, 36 LSI 35, §§ 146–147 (1981–1982) (Isr.).

56 *See* DC 4927/92 State of Israel v. Ben Yehuda (unpublished opinion) (Isr.).

57 CrimA 1245/93 Shtarkman v. State of Israel 47(2) PD 177 [1993] (Isr.).

58 DC 3251/91 Yishai v. State of Israel 45(5) PD 441 [1991) (Isr.).

59 Criminal Procedure Rules, 5734–1974, § 44(7).

60 Criminal Procedure Law (Consolidated Version), 5742–1982, 36 LSI 35, § 205 (1981–1982) (Isr.).

61 *See* Arbitration Law, 1968.

62 *See* Disabled (Compensation and Rehabilitation) Law, 1959 (consolidated version).

63 *See* Eisenberg, Fisher & Rosen-Zvi, *supra* note 2.

64 *Id.*

65 The website does not include cases decided in camera, but since those cases are but a fraction of the cases decided by the Court, the omission does not materially affect the analysis here. *See* Courts Law (Consolidated Version), § 70(a).

66 Significance levels are reported based on Fisher's exact test.

67 The degree to which merits outcomes differ across screening justices depends in part on how one accounts for cases affirmed in part and reversed in part. In Panel A's criminal

cases, one can reject the hypothesis of no difference for the 3-by-3 table at the level of $p = 0.079$. This result is driven by the absence of partial affirmance/reversal in cases screened by Justice A. Panels overwhelmingly tend to reverse in full criminal cases screened by this justice.

68 The difference in the two Panel A concurrence rates is statistically significant at $p = 0.013$. The difference in the two Panel B concurrence rates is statistically significant at $p = 0.017$. The difference in the two Panel D concurrence rates is not statistically significant ($p = 0.999$). The difference in the Panel A and Panel D concurrence rates in criminal cases is statistically significant at $p = 0.002$ and the difference in the Panel A and Panel D concurrence rates in civil cases is statistically significant at $p = 0.019$. The difference in the Panel B and Panel D concurrence rates in criminal cases is significant at $p = 0.056$. The difference in the Panel B and Panel D concurrence rates in civil cases is not statistically significant ($p = 0.670$).

69 John Wooldredge, Timothy Griffin, Amy Thistlethwaite & Fritz Rauschenberg, *Victim-Based Effects on Racially Disparate Sentencing in Ohio*, 8 J. Empirical Legal Stud. 85, 89 (2011). For evidence of little difference between male and female defendants with respect to motions to reduce sentences, *see* Laura Braslow & Ross E. Cheit, *Judicial Discretion and (Un)equal Access: A Systematic Study of Motions to Reduce Criminal Sentences in Rhode Island Superior Court (1998–2003)*, 8 J. Empirical Legal Stud. 24, 40 (2011).

70 John Blume & Theodore Eisenberg, *Judicial Politics, Death Penalty Appeals, and Case Selection: An Empirical Study*, 72 S. Cal. L. Rev. 465, 498 (1999).

71 *See* John Kraemer, *An Empirical Examination of the Factors Associated with the Commutation of State Death Row Prisoners' Sentences Between 1986 and 2005*, 45 Am. Crim. L. Rev. 1389 (2008).

72 Blume & Eisenberg, *supra* note 70, at 497.

73 Bogoch & Don-Yechiya, *supra* note17, at 121–22. The study's dataset consisted of 426 criminal mandatory appeals to the ISC (violent crimes and homicide cases) between the years 1988 and 1993. The sample included 545 male defendants and 19 female defendants as either the appellant or the appellee. Thus, the authors admit that it is impossible to obtain statistically significant results with such a small sample of female defendants. Yet, they maintain that a pattern of bias against women can be inferred from the data: When the state appealed either an acquittal of female defendants (one case) or the leniency of their sentence (five cases) the ISC reversed the district court's decision in 100 percent of the cases, while in the case of male defendants the percentages were 69 percent for acquittals and 74 percent for leniency of the sentence. When female defendants appealed either a conviction or a harsh sentence, the ISC reversed 12 percent of the cases (convictions) and 17 percent of the cases (length of sentence) for female defendants, while the percentages for male defendants were 17 percent and 21 percent respectively. Thus, the authors conclude that the few female defendants are disadvantaged at the ISC level.

74 Government appeals in criminal cases only occurred in cases involving male defendants.

75 *See* Eisenberg, Fisher & Rosen-Zvi, *supra* note 2.

76 *See* Oren Gazal-Ayal & Raanan Sulitzeanu-Kenan, *Let My People Go: Ethnic In-Group Bias in Judicial Decisions – Evidence from a Randomized Natural Experiment*, 7 J. Empirical Legal Stud. 403 (2010).

77 Our results can shed light not only on issues relating to the study of individual justices and explanations of case outcomes. The large volume of criminal cases referred to Justices A and B provides an opportunity for quantifying the degree of legal expert agreement. If we can assume random assignment of criminal cases as between Justices A and B, then the difference in their rates of referring cases to three-judge panels is attributable to these two justices and not to other factors about the cases. *E.g.*, Orley

Ashenfelter, Theodore Eisenberg & Stewart J. Schwab, *Politics and the Judiciary: The Influence of Judicial Background on Case Outcomes*, 24 J. LEGAL STUD. 257, 259–60 (1995). Although Justices A and B agreed that the great majority of cases should be denied further review, they significantly differed in the rate at which further review was warranted.

This rate of disagreement may help calibrate rates of agreement in other contexts in the legal system. For example, juries and judges observed the same evidence agree on conviction or acquittal about 80 percent of the time. Theodore Eisenberg *et al.*, *Judge–Jury Agreement in Criminal Cases: A Partial Replication of Kalven and Zeisel's The American Jury*, 2 J. EMPIRICAL LEGAL STUD. 171, 173 (2005); Harry Kalven, Jr. & Hans Zeisel, THE AMERICAN JURY 58 (1966). The legal question faced by Justices A and B—whether to refer a case to a panel—differs from the acquittal/conviction decision faced at trial. The trial question is based on assessing the facts, usually uncertain in trials, whereas Justices A and B addressed a purely legal question. One might expect two highly qualified experts to agree more about a question of law than even they would agree about questions of inherently uncertain facts. That two experts substantially disagree about a question of law across many cases helps put in perspective the rate of agreement observed between judges and juries in other studies.

78 Eisenberg, Fisher & Rosen-Zvi, *supra* note 2, at 714.

79 *Id.*

80 Our findings with regard to the noneffect of the defendant's ethnicity on the probability of reversal at the ISC level aligns with the findings of the Bogoch & Don-Yechiya study. *See* Bogoch & Don-Yechiya, *supra* note 16, at 126–27. When one accounts for different parties appealing in mandatory criminal cases, the outcome of male defendant and female defendant cases does significantly differ. *See* Theodore Eisenberg, Talia Fisher & Issi Rosen-Zvi, *Does the Judge Make a Difference? Exploiting Random Assignment on a Court of Last Resort to Assess Judge and Case Selection Effects*, 9 J. EMPIRICAL LEGAL STUD. 246 (2012). In the analysis showing such a gender effect the outcome of interest is not reversal but rather whether a justice voted for the defendant or the state. A vote favors the state if it is to affirm an appeal brought by a defendant or to reverse an appeal brought by the state. A vote favors the defendant if it is to affirm an appeal brought by the state or to reverse an appeal brought by the defendant.

References

Ashenfelter, Orley, Theodore Eisenberg, and Stewart J. Schwab. 1995. Politics and the Judiciary: The Influence of Judicial Background on Case Outcomes. *Journal of Legal Studies* 24: 257–281.

Barzilai, Gad, Ephraim Yuchtman-Yaar, and Ze'ev Segal. 1994. *The Israeli Supreme Court and the Israeli Public*. Tel Aviv: Papirus.

Blume, John, and Theodore Eisenberg. 1999. Judicial Politics, Death Penalty Appeals, and Case Selection: An Empirical Study. *South Califonia Law Review* 72: 465–503.

Bogoch, Bryna, and Rachelle Don-Yechiya. 1999. *The Gender of Justice: Bias Against Women in Israeli Courts*. Jerusalem: Jerusalem Institute for Israel Research (Heb.).

Braslow, Laura, and Ross E. Cheit. 2011. Judicial Discretion and (Un)equal Access: A Systematic Study of Motions to Reduce Criminal Sentences in Rhode Island Superior Court (1998–2003). *Journal of Empirical Legal Studies* 8: 24–47.

Brennan, William J., Jr. 1986. In Defense of Dissents. *Hastings Law Journal* 37: 427–438.

Dotan, Yoav. 1999. Do the "Haves" Still Come Out Ahead? Resource Inequalities in Ideological Courts: The Case of the Israeli High Court of Justice. *Law and Society Review* 33: 1059–1080.

Dotan, Yoav, and Menachem Hofnung. 2001. Interest Groups in the High Court of Justice: Measuring Success in Litigation and in Out-of-Court Settlements. *Law and Policy* 23: 1–27.

Eisenberg, Theodore. 1974. Congressional Authority to Restrict Lower Federal Court Jurisdiction. *Yale Law Journal* 83: 498–533.

Eisenberg, Theodore, and Geoffrey P. Miller. 2009. Reversal, Dissent, and Variability in State Supreme Courts: The Centrality of Jurisdictional Source. *Boston University Law Review* 89: 1451–1504.

Eisenberg, Theodore, and Kuo-Chang Huang. 2012. The Effects of Rules Shifting Supreme Court Jurisdiction from Mandatory to Discretionary – An Empirical Lesson from Taiwan. *International Review of Law & Economics* 32: 3–18.

Eisenberg, Theodore, Paula L. Hannaford-Agor, Valerie P. Hans, Nicole L. Waters, G. Thomas Munsterman, Stewart J. Schwab, and Martin T. Wells. 2005. Judge–Jury Agreement in Criminal Cases: A Partial Replication of Kalven and Zeisel's The American Jury. *Journal of Empirical Legal Studies* 2: 171–207.

Eisenberg, Theodore, Talia Fisher, and Issi Rosen-Zvi. 2011. Israel's Supreme Court Appellate Jurisdiction: An Empirical Study. *Cornell Law Review* 96: 693–725.

——2012. Does the Judge Matter? Exploiting Random Assignment on a Court of Last Resort to Assess Judge and Case Selection Effects. *Journal of Empirical Legal Studies* 9: 246–290.

Epstein, Lee, Jeffrey A. Segal, and Harold J. Spaeth. 2007. Digital Archive of the Papers of Harry A. Blackmun. Available at: http://epstein.law.northwestern.edu/blackmun.php.

Gazal-Ayal, Oren, and Raanan Sulitzeanu-Kenan. 2010. Let My People Go: Ethnic In-Group Bias in Judicial Decisions – Evidence from a Randomized Natural Experiment. *Journal of Empirical Legal Studies* 7: 403–428.

Ginsburg, Ruth Bader. 1992. Speaking in a Judicial Voice. *New York University Law Review* 67: 1185–1209.

Gross, Miron, and Yoram Shachar. 1999. How Are Supreme Court Panels Selected – A Quantitative Analysis. *Hebrew University Law Review* 29: 567–585.

Harvard Law Review. 2011. Note, From Consensus to Collegiality: The Origins of the "Respectful" Dissent. *Harvard Law Review* 124: 1305–1326.

Harvey, Anna, and Barry Friedman, 2009. Ducking Trouble: Congressionally Induced Selection Bias in the Supreme Court's Agenda. *The Journal of Politics* 71: 574–592.

Henderson, M. Todd. 2007. From Seriatim to Consensus and Back Again: A Theory of Dissent. *Supreme Court Review* 2007: 283–344.

Hofnung, Menachem, and Keren Weinshall-Margel. 2010. Judicial Setbacks, Material Gains: Terror Litigation at the Israeli High Court of Justice. *Journal of Empirical Legal Studies* 7: 664–692.

Kalven, Harry, Jr., and Hans Zeisel. 1966. *The American Jury*. New York, NY: Little, Brown.

Kastellec, Jonathan P., and Jeffrey R. Lax. 2008. Case Selection and the Study of Judicial Politics. *Journal of Empirical Legal Studies* 5: 407–446.

Kraemer, John. 2008. An Empirical Examination of the Factors Associated with the Commutation of State Death Row Prisoners' Sentences Between 1986 and 2005. *American Criminal Law Review* 45: 1389–1418.

Library of Congress. Harry A. Blackmun Papers, 1913–2001. Catalog entry. Available at http://lccn.loc.gov/mm99084430.

Mautner, Menachem. 2008. *Law & Culture in Israel in the Beginning of the 21st Century*. Tel Aviv: Tel Aviv University Press (Heb.).

Narayan, Paresh Kumar, and Russell Smyth. 2007. What Explains Dissent on the High Court of Australia? An Empirical Assessment Using a Cointegration and Error Correction Approach. *Journal of Empirical Legal Studies* 4: 401–425.

Salzberger, Eli. 2003. Acting Justices in the Supreme Court and Judicial Independence – Theoretical Analysis and Empirical Findings. *Bar Ilan Law Review* 19: 541–568.

Shachar, Yoram, Miron Gross, and Ron Harris. 1996–1997. Anatomy of Discourse and Dissent in the Supreme Court – Quantitative Analyses. *Tel Aviv University Law Review* 20: 749–795.

Shachar, Yoram, Ron Harris, and Miron Gross. 1996. Reference Patterns of the Supreme Court – A Quantitative Analysis. *Hebrew University Law Review* 27: 119–217.

Shacher, Yoram, Miron Gross, and Chanan Goldshmidt. 2003. 100 Leading Precedents – A Quantitative Analysis. *Haifa University Law Review* 7: 243–303.

Smyth, Russell, and Paresh Kumar Narayan. 2006. Multiple Regime Shifts in Concurring and Dissenting Opinions on the US Supreme Court. *Journal of Empirical Legal Studies* 3: 79–98.

Stack, Kevin M. 1996. The Practice of Dissent in the Supreme Court. *Yale Law Journal* 105: 2235–2259.

Thompson, David C., and Melanie F. Wachtell. 2009. An Empirical Analysis of Supreme Court Certiorari Petition Procedures: The Call for Response and the Call for the Views of the Solicitor General. *George Mason Law Review* 16: 237–302.

Weinshall-Margel, Keren. 2011. Attitudinal and Neo-Institutional Models of Supreme Court Decision Making: An Empirical and Comparative Perspective from Israel. *Journal of Empirical Legal Studies* 8: 556–586.

Wooldredge, John, Timothy Griffin, Amy Thistlethwaite, and Fritz Rauschenberg. 2011. Victim-Based Effects on Racially Disparate Sentencing in Ohio. *Journal of Empirical Legal Studies* 8: 85–117.

9 Determinants of constitutionally safeguarded judicial review

Insights based on a new indicator[1]

Jerg Gutmann, Bernd Hayo, and Stefan Voigt

Introduction

The judicialization of politics is a frequently acclaimed phenomenon. Judicial review (JR)—the power of the judiciary to review the compatibility of legislation with the constitution—is perhaps the most important aspect of that phenomenon.[2] In this chapter, we describe the evolution of constitutional review around the world since 1950. Our contribution is thus primarily empirical rather than theoretical.

In their introduction to "The Global Expansion of Judicial Power," Tate and Vallinder propose a large number of factors that could be driving this expansion.[3] If constitutional review (CR) is a central aspect of judicial power, then these same factors might also be underlying the expansion of constitutional review. They mention the breakdown of socialist countries; the democratization in Latin America, Asia, and Africa; the mounting influence of American jurisprudence and political science; the jurisprudence of the European Court of Human Rights; the distrust of members of both the executive and the legislature; the weakness of political parties; and belonging to the common law family.

In this chapter, we test some of these conjectures—and many more—empirically. It is part of a larger project on constitutionally safeguarded aspects of the judiciary. All in all, we have documented the ways in which 23 aspects of judicial independence (JI) broadly conceived are safeguarded in constitutional documents of up to 100 countries.[4] To see whether important changes have occurred over time, we have coded constitutions on an annual basis between 1950 (or the first year of a country's independence) and 2005. Our dataset makes constitutional review comparable across countries by drawing on four variables. It thus allows us to empirically test the various hypotheses regarding the diffusion of constitutional review.

Here, the data are used as dependent variables. We are, hence, interested in identifying the determinants of both the original choice of constitutional review and its change over time.[5] This implies that very stable variables such as geography and history are analyzed, as well as more contemporaneous ones like the constitutional choices made simultaneously with the choice of implementing constitutional review. In this systematic exploration of our comprehensive and novel set of data, we concentrate on the analysis of bivariate patterns. Given our focus on description rather than inference, there is the risk of omitted variable bias, which would need to be taken into account in further work. However, we believe it is important to systematically document important characteristics of judicial review across the world before using the dataset for testing specific research questions.

The rest of this chapter is organized as follows: The next section summarizes a number of conjectures regarding the choice of constitutional review. The section thereafter, Measuring constitutional review, describes in detail our variables used to proxy for JR. The penultimate section, Analysis of the data, contains our analysis of the data, and the final section concludes.

Some conjectures on the choice of constitutional review

Defining constitutional review

Before we present a number of conjectures regarding the choice of constitutional review, we need to define our central concepts. Stone-Sweet writes: "Constitutional review is the authority of an institution to invalidate the acts of government—such as legislation, administrative decisions, and judicial rulings—on the grounds that these acts have violated constitutional rules, including rights."[6]

The delineation chosen by Stone-Sweet is extremely broad. It includes the review of acts of all three branches of government. Furthermore, the actor doing the review does not need to be part of the judiciary. Our preferred definition of constitutional review is narrower. We propose to define judicial review as the authority of (only) the judiciary to invalidate legislation on the grounds that it violates the constitution. One could argue that the differences in definition reflect the differences between—the broader—constitutional review and—the narrower—judicial review. However, we prefer to use the two terms interchangeably here.

The details of judicial review are reflected in the answers to the following questions:

- Who has the power to initiate judicial review?
- When can judicial review be initiated (it could be only before newly passed legislation enters into force, only after it has entered into force, or both)?
- Which body is responsible for the interpretation of the constitution?
- What are the consequences of a review that finds legislation to be incompatible with the constitution?

These are the four variables that we have coded and that are being used as proxies in this study.

The central function of constitutional review

We are now ready to introduce our central conjecture regarding the function of constitutional review. It has been pointed out that the scarcest resource of governments is their own credibility.[7] If governments command vast powers, their promise to use them only in specific ways is often not credible if a different use of these powers can make the governing better off. The constitution can already be considered as an attempt to make specific promises (like the rights enumerated in the document) more credible by their being entrenched. It constrains the possible scope of future legislation since this legislation will need to be within the limits delineated in the constitution. But if newly passed legislation simply does not conform to the constraints laid out in the constitution, then the promises made in that document are unlikely to increase government credibility. An entrenched constitution that is combined with the authority of a "neutral" actor to review the compatibility of legislation with the more basic rules set down in the constitution might consequently help to reduce the commitment problem of governments. Given that constitutional review functions like this, governments are constrained by a neutral actor, namely the judiciary.

This argument shows the intricate connection between constitutional review and judicial independence. We argue that judicial independence is a necessary condition for constitutional review. Constitutional review will only help a government to mitigate its problem of credibly committing to some basic rules if the would-be arbiter, i.e. the relevant judicial actor, is sufficiently independent from government.[8] As long as it remains under the tutelage of government, no gains in credibility can be expected. To sum up: Constitutional review—in combination with judicial independence and entrenched constitutional rules—could thus increase the credibility of the state and the promises of its representatives.[9]

IF actors determining constitutional review

In this chapter, we are interested in the first time choice of constitutionally safeguarded judicial review, as well as in changes thereof over time. It has become sort of a standard to ask whether a number of "very" exogenous factors, such as the geographic location of a country, have any impact on its institutional setting. Factors regularly controlled for include the respective continent and the distance of a country (more specifically, its centroid) from the equator. By themselves, these factors are unlikely to contain much explanatory power. Most likely, some more specific explanations hide behind them.

Exogenous factors

Historical factors are almost as exogenous as the just-mentioned geographic ones. Historical factors that are often analyzed when the quality of institutions is at stake include settler mortality, whether a country has been a colony and if so who was the colonizer, the legal family, the degree of ethno-linguistic fractionalization, and so on. Shapiro[10] has been interpreted as conjecturing that cultures where judges are associated with the liberal ideal of limited government are more likely to introduce CR.[11] The British common law tradition would support this idea, which is why CR would also be more likely in former British colonies.

Frequently, the text of a new constitution is the outcome of complicated negotiations between various groups with partially contradictory interests. The constitution can then be interpreted as a contract that has important distributive consequences.[12] Those who command a majority in the post-constitutional period might, however, be tempted to change the constitution or reinterpret it in their own favor. Constitutional review might be a means to prevent the latter from happening. This implies that it can be interpreted as insurance for those groups who might be in a minority position in the post-constitutional period. JR is thus a constraint on a potential tyranny of the majority in democratic societies.[13]

Indicators of ethno-linguistic fractionalization measure how likely it is that two randomly selected individuals from the same country belong to different ethnic groups, speak different languages, or practice different religions. Given that any of these often reflect serious cleavages within societies, it seems likely that the insurance function of judicial review plays a more prominent role in highly fractionalized societies. An alternative indicator has been christened "polarization." It is based on the assumption that it is not the sheer number of different groups, but their size, that matters. The most difficult situation would be one where there are two groups of approximately equal size. But the insurance argument also applies to this measure. We hence expect more constitutionally safeguarded JR in societies with a high degree of polarization.

This ends our very short discussion of exogenous factors. We now move on to develop a number of conjectures that focus on possible interrelationships between CR and other constitutional features, such as electoral formula, the form of government, and so on.

Constitutional factors

It is well known that electoral systems have wide-ranging effects on a country's political landscape. Duverger's law posits that first-past-the-post or majoritarian systems are likely to generate two-party systems.[14] In two-party systems, one major party will always be in a minority. Assuming that rational actors anticipate this during the constitutional convention, insurance against majority decisions seems to be more important under majority systems than under proportional ones. We hence expect to see a higher degree of CR under them.

The form of government could also be relevant for the chosen degree of CR. Conventionally, the presidential form of government is distinguished from the parliamentary one. The survival of the head of the executive in parliamentary systems depends on her capacity to secure a majority in the legislature. Presidents, in turn, cannot be kicked out of office by legislative majorities. Thus, many observers conclude that the degree of the separation of powers is higher under presidential systems.[15] But there is a high probability that the president as the head of the executive does not belong to the party that commands a majority in the legislature.[16] This means that a president would have to enforce legislation produced by legislators who have preferences different from his. At times, he might doubt the constitutionality of newly produced legislation and, therefore, refuse to sign a bill passed by the legislature. To prevent the entire political system from destabilizing, CR might be a way out. We thus conjecture that presidential systems are likely to provide for a higher degree of CR than parliamentary ones.[17]

Tate and Vallinder put forward a list of factors that might be driving what they call "judicialization."[18] Among these factors, they list weak political parties. By "weak," they mean parties whose representatives vote according to their individual preferences and do not follow an official party line. This would make it easier for the opposition to draw on the judiciary. Connecting their argument with the observation that weak parties are more likely to come about in presidential rather than parliamentary systems leads again to the conjecture that presidential systems should be experiencing a relatively faster movement toward judicialization.

The choice of a federal structure is often the result of negotiations between different regions with different preferences. Again, it makes sense to interpret the constitution as a compromise. To ensure implementation of the compromise reached at the constitutional convention and to prevent the passing of fresh legislation not in accordance with it, CR is expected to reach higher levels in federal than in unitary states.

Countries with direct democracy can be interpreted as having an additional political actor, namely the electorate in its entirety. If legislation can be passed by direct democratic means, it is possible that a minority suffers from decisions made by the majority. A court guaranteeing basic constitutional rights might thus be in higher demand in countries relying on some aspects of direct democracy.

This brings us to an aspect that reflects the actual implementation of constitutional principles rather than the principles themselves. It has been argued that the judicialization of politics is more likely in democratic polities.[19] Ginsburg was one of the first to view both judicial independence and constitutional review from an insurance perspective: losers of an election are assured that the basic tenets of the polity will remain unchanged due to JI and CR.[20] Moreover, Fox and Stephenson refer to potential adverse effects of democratic elections on political decision-making and their mitigation through CR. Politicians that are up for reelection could against their better knowledge promote policies that are popular in the short run, but which are actually non-optimal for a majority of voters. They could also take dramatic actions with unforeseeable consequences so as to appear competent to voters by solving even large problems, although a more modest reaction or no action at all would be preferable.[21] Judicial review by independent courts might provide an answer to these problems by delegating the interpretation of commitments in the constitution to judges who are not under similar electoral pressure. This encourages a stronger consideration of the long-term effects of political decisions in democratic systems.[22] A straightforward argument is that autocrats do not like to experience restrictions to their decisions-making power, which includes courts with the right to review the constitutionality of their legislation. This would, hence, be an additional argument to see higher levels of CR under democratic regimes. Yet, this argument might be premature: all governments, including autocrats, can make themselves better off if they are able to credibly commit themselves.[23] Acemoglu *et al.* even argue that voters in weakly institutionalized democracies, which are vulnerable to lobbying and bribes by the elites, might decide to dismantle checks and balances on the government themselves to insulate politicians from nonelectoral influences by increasing their rents.[24] Seen like this, it is unclear whether democracies really display higher levels of CR.

A related argument deals with CR in socialist states: If the party has assembled all necessary wisdom to make good decisions, there is no systematic place for the review of constitutionality of legislation by courts. It has often been argued that there was no place for CR in socialist states.[25] Our database allows us to check that claim.[26]

Finally, the process by which the constitution is brought about might have an impact on the degree of constitutionally safeguarded JR: Suppose the constitution is penned by a small, homogenous elite that is confident it will remain in power for the foreseeable future. Confront this with a constitutional assembly whose members come from all walks of life and whose deliberations are widely publicized. If CR is indeed a potential constraint on future politicians, then it seems more likely that CR will be observed in the second than in the first scenario.

Preferences

A high degree of inequality combined with a high level of democracy could make those whose wealth is above the median nervous.[27] They might only agree to a constitutional bargain if private property is not only guaranteed in the constitution, but also if CR is established in order to increase the likelihood of the enforcement of private property over time. Higher levels of inequality are, hence, predicted to be correlated with higher levels of CR.

Do political parties take a different stance on CR depending on their position in the ideological spectrum? Stone-Sweet conjectures that this is indeed the case because "left-wing parties, especially, fiercely opposed judicial review, seeing in it the spectre of the dreaded 'government of judges'."[28] CR can also be interpreted as an instrument to make the constitutional bargain endure over time as it is one way to bind current legislators to the decisions made by their constitutional predecessors. In a sense, CR thus introduces an element of conservatism. Following Stone-Sweet, we conjecture that left-wing parties are less likely to introduce CR than parties that are not left wing.

Models of constitutional review

There are various possibilities to design constitutional review: (i) It can be allocated to each and every court of a country, as in the US; there is thus no specialized court. This implies that constitutional review is a posteriori, and the uniformity of jurisdiction is secured by the highest court of the country (in the US the Supreme Court). (ii) In the Austrian model as proposed by Hans Kelsen, a specialized constitutional court deals with constitutional matters. It can entail both abstract and concrete review, as well as ex ante and ex post review.[29] (iii) In the French model, constitutional matters are dealt with by a special body (e.g. the *Conseil Constitutionnel* in France until very recently) that is constrained to ex ante review.[30]

There is no clear-cut hypothesis concerning the effects of the various systems. It could, however, be argued that judicial influence is broadest where the judiciary has the competence to check upon the constitutionality of laws both ex ante and ex post and where constitutional review can be both abstract and concrete. In the US model, constitutional review is restricted to ex post and concrete review. Formal competencies of judiciaries organized along the lines of the Austrian model are often broader since they can also encompass ex ante and abstract constitutional review. The French model is more restricted from the other side of the spectrum: There, constitutional review is only possible before a law has come into force. If laws are only recognized to be incompatible with the constitution after they have been in force for a while there is nothing much that the *Conseil Constitutionnel* can do. On the basis of the formal capacity of the judiciary to keep the other two branches within the limits spelled out in the constitution, we would thus expect the Austrian model to have some advantages over the US model as well as over the French system. Between these two, the French seems to be the one conferring least competence to the judiciary.[31]

Measuring constitutional review

In the last section we have repeatedly referred to the degree of CR to be observed in different countries, thus presupposing that some indicator existed to measure—and compare—various degrees of CR across countries. In this section, we present a number of variables proxying for various aspects of CR and propose a way to aggregate them into a CR indicator that can, indeed, be used to compare the levels of CR across countries. We are, hence, not only interested in knowing whether JR exists at all, but also to what degree it exists. This means that we need to be more precise in explaining what we mean by the degree of JR. What we have in mind is simply the degree to which the other branches of government are constrained by the possibility of having the conformity of legislation checked by the judiciary.

The indicator to be developed in this section is constrained in at least two ways: First, it only takes into consideration CR that is explicitly laid down in the constitution. Second, it takes into consideration the de jure situation only; this might be misleading as the actual relevance of CR might be very imperfectly reflected in the respective de jure information. This does not necessarily mean that the actual situation is worse than the one stipulated in the constitution: The US Constitution, for example, nowhere stipulates JR—but ever since Marbury vs. Madison (1803) nobody would doubt that the US Supreme Court does have that power.

Legal systems can allocate the competence of constitutional review to different actors. As the definition by Stone-Sweet cited above makes clear, it is not necessarily confined to the judiciary. Our first variable thus asks to whom the constitution assigns the responsibility to interpret the constitution (INTERP). A first categorical distinction is between representatives of the judiciary on the one hand and representatives of the other branches on the other. Among the representatives of the judicial branch, this variable distinguishes between four different cases, namely:

1 any ordinary court has the competence,
2 only a specific constitutional court has the competence,
3 only the supreme court has the competence, and
4 only a special chamber of the supreme court has the competence.

The distinction between these three (four) possibilities reflects the various models of constitutional review briefly described in the last section. Ex ante, it is unclear whether any of these is unequivocally better than its competitors. Therefore, we propose a very simple coding of this variable: all countries whose constitutions preview any of the three (four) possibilities just mentioned are coded 1, all others 0. In 2005, 80 of our 100 countries are coded 1 and the remaining 20 are coded 0.[32]

A second important aspect of CR is who has the power to initiate it? Again, a straightforward distinction seems to make sense, namely that between representatives of the executive, the legislature, and the judiciary broadly conceived. The variable CHALLEG provides this information in an even more fine-grained way: it takes into account three representatives of the executive who might possibly have standing, namely: (1) the head of state, (2) the head of government, and (3) the government/cabinet. Regarding representatives of the legislature, it distinguishes between: (4) the first (or only) chamber, (5) the second chamber, and (6) both chambers in conjunction. Finally, with reference to the judiciary very broadly conceived, it covers: (7) lawyers, (8) the public (by complaint), and (9) the courts. Since we cannot exclude that there are even more possibilities to give more actors standing, an additional option is that there are other possibilities.

Judicial review is potentially more constraining the easier it is to initiate it. We therefore propose a very simple and straightforward coding rule: We sum up all of the options just mentioned and divide them by 9. This variable can therefore take on values between 0 and 1.[33]

In 2005, 47 of our 100 constitutions assign the power to initiate constitutional review to members of the executive (17 of them assign it to members of the executive only). In 18 cases, members of the legislature themselves have the competence to challenge the constitutionality of legislation. There is only a single constitution in which only the legislature has that power. In 42 countries, the respective competence rests with the judiciary or the public, and in 19 of them it is even restricted to the judiciary or the public only. Finally, ten countries belong to all three groups, meaning that the competence to initiate constitutional review is given to all three branches.

Of our 100 countries, 22 explicitly allow the public to challenge the constitutionality of law by complaint. At the same time the constitutions of 29 countries provide for lawyers initiating constitutional review.[34]

A third dimension of JR is at what stage of the legislative process bills can be reviewed for their conformity with the constitution (CHALSTAG). In some countries, it can only be initiated before the promulgation of a law, in other countries it is the exact opposite. Our conjecture is that JR is most constraining on the other branches if it can take place both before and after the promulgation of legislation. We further conjecture that between the pre- or the post-promulgation options, the latter is more constraining than the former. This is so for various reasons: first, there is only a small window to initiate CR if it can only be initiated before a law has been promulgated. Second, the inconformity of legislation with the constitution might only become apparent as it is implemented in various contexts. Constraining it to ex ante review implies that the relevant actors are able to foresee all possible contingencies that might overstretch their rationality. We therefore propose the following coding: 1 if cr can be initiated both before and after the promulgation of a law, ½ if it can be initiated after its promulgation only, and 0 if it can be initiated before its promulgation only. It is difficult to foresee the consequences if none of these options is explicitly mentioned in the constitution. The degree of uncertainty with respect to the judiciary's competence to perform JR will definitely increase, but it is unclear at what stages of the legislative process JR will be observable. Since nothing prevents the executive from passing a legal act restricting JR to pre-promulgation, we again code 0.

Finally, there are different ways to deal with laws that have been deemed unconstitutional: (1) the law is void, (2) the law is void only for the specific case under consideration, and (3) the law is returned to the legislature for revision/reconsideration. This issue is covered by the variable CHALUNCN. Arguably, the constraining effect of CR is particularly high if a decision by the judiciary makes the law void in its entirety. This is coded 1. Between the other two options, it is hard to construct an unequivocal ranking: on the one hand, option (2) has an immediate effect but it is constrained to the case at hand. On the other hand, option (3) could have a broader effect but presupposes the cooperation of the legislature. We therefore decided to code both options with ½ and all others (like the effect being explicitly left to non-constitutional law) with 0.[35]

These are the four variables used to describe the central dimensions of JR as described in various constitutions. Their determinants—but also their effects—can be estimated separately. On top of that, we propose an aggregate indicator of JR based on all four variables. Since we do not have strong theoretical priors indicating different weights of the different dimensions, we attach equal weight to variables (2) through (4). We argue that we need to deal differently with the first variable: Talk of JR only makes sense if the judiciary is attributed the power to review the constitution. Hence, variables (2) through (4) are only taken into consideration given that (1) was coded respectively. This indicator reflects the average quality of the different features of CR as they are safeguarded in the constitution and takes values from zero to one.[36]

Analysis of the data

This section serves multiple purposes. It contains the bivariate correlations between the four aspects of JR described in the last section. This is interesting for a number of reasons: It allows us to identify tradeoffs between the different

Table 9.1 Selection of countries

Country	*First year of constitution*	*Country*	*First year of constitution*	*Country*	*First year of constitution*
Albania	1950	El Salvador	1950	Niger	1960
Andorra	1993	Equ. Guinea	1968	Nigeria	1960
Angola	1975	Eritrea	1997	Norway	1950
Antigua and Barbuda	1981	Estonia	1992	Pakistan	1956
Argentina	1950	Ethiopia	1950	Panama	1950
Armenia	1995	France	1950	Paraguay	1950
Australia	1950	Gambia	1970	Peru	1950
Austria	1950	Georgia	1995	Poland	1950
Azerbaijan	1995	Germany	1950	Portugal	1950
Bahamas	1973	Ghana	1957	Romania	1991
Bangladesh	1972	Greece	1952	Singapore	1965
Barbados	1966	Grenada	1974	Slovakia	1992
Belarus	1994	Guatemala	1950	Slovenia	1991
Belgium	1950	Guinea	1958	Spain	1950
Belize	1981	Haiti	1950	Sri Lanka	1950
Bolivia	1950	Honduras	1950	St. Kitts and Nevis	1983
Botswana	1966	Hungary	1989	St. Vincent and the Grenadines	1979
Brazil	1950	Iceland	1950	Sweden	1950
Bulgaria	1950	India	1950	Syria	1950
Cameroon	1961	Indonesia	1950	Taiwan	1950
Canada	1950	Ireland	1950	Tajikistan	1994
Chile	1950	Italy	1950	Thailand	1950
China	1950	Jamaica	1962	Togo	1961
Colombia	1950	Japan	1950	Trinidad and Tobago	1962
Congo	1961	Kenya	1963	Turkmenistan	1992
Congo, Democratic Rep.	1964	Kyrgyzstan	1993	Ukraine	1996
Cuba	1950	Latvia	1991	United States	1950
Cyprus	1960	Lebanon	1950	Uruguay	1950
Czech Republic	1992	Lithuania	1992	Uzbekistan	1992
Denmark	1950	Luxembourg	1950	Venezuela	1950
Dominica	1978	Macedonia	1991	Yemen	1962
Dominican Rep.	1950	Mexico	1950	Zimbabwe	1965
Ecuador	1950	Netherlands	1950		
Egypt	1950	Nicaragua	1950		

Note: Yemen comprises the Republic of North Yemen and the Arab Republic of Yemen (first year of constitution: 1990).

categories empirically. It could, for example, be that many actors have standing to challenge the constitutionality of a law (high value of CHALLEG) but that this can only be done ex ante (low value of CHALSTAG). The coding of the four variables will also allow us to assess the dispersal of the three main models of JR named in the literature, namely the US, the Austrian, and the French models. This section further contains a short discussion of the synthetic indicator described in the previous section.

But this section is also interested in documenting the chronological as well as the geographical diffusion of JR in the period from 1950 to 2005. Finally, it asks whether there are systematic correlations between the dimensions of JR and other constitutional traits such as the form of government, electoral system, and so on. However, a test of the different theories on the determinants of JR against each other is beyond the scope of this explorative study.

Our dataset

Our analysis is based on a sample of 100 countries coded from 1950 to 2005. Alternatively, if the country became independent after 1950, we start coding with the first year after independence for which it had an own constitution. The data cover a diverse group of countries with regard to geographic location, size, age, religious background, and state of economic development.

In 2005, 80 countries (80 percent) provided for judicial review in their constitution, even under our rather narrow definition. Given that in 1950 CR was only implemented in 24 out of 50 constitutions (48 percent) and another 34 of the 50 countries (68 percent) that became independent later provided for CR in their first constitution, a substantial increase in the appreciation of constitutional review conducted by the judiciary seems obvious.

As illustrated in Table 9.2, for the 50 countries with a constitution in place by 1950 constitutional change is omnipresent. However, change in the constitutional base of JR was relatively scarce in the 1950s, it intensified in the 1960s and 70s, and reached a peak in the 1990s. The largest number of changes occurred in the 1990s regarding who has the power to initiate CR.

During the time period 1950 to 2005, many new states were formed and new constitutions were drafted. A number of new states in the less-developed countries were created during the 1960s and 1970s, and the fall of the Iron Curtain resulted in a surge of constitutional activity by transformation countries in the

Table 9.2 Number of changes in countries' constitutional base of judicial review

	1950s	*1960s*	*1970s*	*1980s*	*1990s*	*2000s*
INTERP	1	10	13	3	12	1
CHALLEG	2	11	14	8	20	7
CHALSTAG	0	8	10	5	10	3
CHALUNCN	3	13	9	6	17	1
SYNTHETIC	3	14	16	12	25	9

Table 9.3 Age of constitutions, constitutional change and judicial review

Age of constitution	*CR in original constitution*		*CR not in original constitution*	
	in 2005 const.	*not in 2005 const.*	*in 2005 const.*	*not in 2005 const.*
1950/earlier	22 (44%)	2 (4%)	16 (32%)	10 (20%)
1951–1960	4 (57%)	1 (14%)	2 (29%)	0
1961–1970	7 (50%)	0	5 (36%)	2 (14%)
1971–1980	2 (33%)	0	1 (17%)	3 (50%)
1981–1990	3 (75%)	0	0	1 (25%)
1991–2000	17 (89%)	0	1 (5%)	1 (5%)
2001–2005	0	0	0	0
Total number	55	3	25	17

1990s, particularly in Eastern Europe. Nevertheless, 50 of the 100 countries in our sample had their constitution in place by 1950.

Table 9.3 reports the prevalence of constitutional review in countries' original or 1950 constitution and its potential introduction or abolition until 2005. Of the 24 countries that have included CR in their constitution as of 1950, 22 countries maintained this provision until 2005. Only one country, that is Nigeria, became independent after 1950 and had a provision for CR in its original, but not in its 2005, constitution. Of the 26 countries that had not included CR in their constitution as of 1950, over 60 percent introduced CR by 2005. Interestingly, the 1970s is the period in which by far the highest share of new countries (50 percent) introduced a constitution without CR and kept this state until 2005.

In 17 of the 19 countries (89 percent) that became independent in the 1990s, CR was and has remained part of their first constitution. This was also the case for only 52 percent of the countries that became independent in the preceding four decades. Overall, 89 percent of permanent changes in the consideration of JR in the constitution concern its introduction. Comparing Table 9.2 and Table 9.3, it becomes clear that changes in CR can be rather unstable. While 18 countries have introduced or abolished CR permanently as of 2005, it has been temporarily abolished or implemented in another 11 cases.

The age of a constitution can be an important explanatory variable for the probability of explicitly providing for CR. The drafters of more recent constitutions can draw on a greater pool of knowledge and experience, especially from other countries. Consequently, these constitutions are based on updated prior probabilities with respect to the potential consequences of a constitutional rule.[37] When we correlate the age of the constitution with the permanent existence of JR, we find a negative but marginally insignificant correlation coefficient of –0.19. Thus, the "age hypothesis," indicating that a country's original or 1950 constitution is less likely to allow CR, is not supported in our data. Although the age of the constitution is not relevant for the existence of a constitutional provision for CR, there might still be an effect on the likelihood of changes in the constitution. We

Table 9.4 Bivariate correlations between CR indicators

	CHALLEG	*CHALSTAG*	*CHALUNCN*
CHALLEG	1		
CHALSTAG	0.502 (0.000)	1	
CHALUNCN	0.411 (0.000)	0.268 (0.007)	1

Note: Pearson correlation coefficients; t-probabilities in parentheses.

find a highly significant positive correlation coefficient of 0.30 for changes in the constitution. This result implies that older constitutions are more likely to be replaced or amended by a document that implements (or abolishes) CR permanently. Calculating the same correlation only for the 81 constitutions from the non-Western states yields an even higher coefficient of 0.38. Thus, it is primarily older constitutions from the non-Western world that are subject to permanent changes in the constitutional base of JR.

Bivariate correlations

In this section, we show the bivariate correlations among the different indicators of CR and their correlations with other constitutional or very exogenous variables. Furthermore, we investigate the same relationships for changes in our CR indicators to find out whether they are associated with the geographic location, history, or the constitutional context.

As shown in Table 9.4, our individual CR indicators are positively correlated with each other at a high level of significance. The weakest correlation coefficient (0.27) is between the consequences of the court finding a legal act to be unconstitutional and the stage of the legislative process at which CR is performed. These results indicate that the different aspects of CR are used as complements rather than substitutes. Our composite indicator of JR should therefore provide a fair impression of the quality of constitutionally safeguarded JR regarding its single dimensions.

Likewise, the cases in which the constitutional base of JR faces an enduring change in one of its dimensions are strongly correlated with each other (see Table 9.5). The correlation coefficients are statistically significant at all plausible levels of significance.

In Figure 9.1, we show the distribution of court models in our sample of countries, i.e. the US model, the Austrian/continental European model, the French model, and the mixed model. It shows that, first, our sample covers almost all countries of North and South America as well as Europe, whereas we are missing a substantial number of countries in Africa and Asia.

The section entitled Models of constitutional review has described different ways of designing the court system for constitutional review. We start by analyzing correlations based on those "original" constitutions that are not subject to

Table 9.5 Bivariate correlations for changes in CR indicators

	CHALLEG	*CHALSTAG*	*CHALUNCN*
CHALLEG	1		
CHALSTAG	0.516 (0.000)	1	
CHALUNCN	0.491 (0.000)	0.453 (0.000)	1

Note: Pearson correlation coefficients; t-probabilities in parentheses.

permanent constitutional change until 2005. In a second step, we study the occurrence of enduring changes between the original constitution and the constitution valid in 2005. The first analysis is based on 63 countries, and the second on 26. The cross-tabulation between the implementation of CR in the original constitution and the court model in Table 9.6 shows a statistically significant association. The Austrian/continental European type of court model is positively related to CR, whereas the opposite holds for the US type court model. Both correlation coefficients of 0.35 and –0.41 are highly statistically significant.

However, this finding does not hold when we investigate the association between court model and constitutional amendments regarding CR. In Table 9.7, we report the cross-tabulation between these two variables. There is no statistically significant association between them.

We also find a statistically significant association between the average quality of JR features safeguarded in the constitution and a country's court model. The Austrian/continental European type of court model is positively correlated with the average quality of JR, whereas the opposite holds for the US type of court model (correlation coefficients: 0.43 and –0.31, significant at a 1 percent and 5 percent level). Regarding change in the aggregate indicator, only the US type court model shows a negative correlation coefficient of –0.25 that is significant at a 5 percent level. Countries with a US type court model are thus less likely to implement changes to the constitution that modify the average quality of CR.

Table 9.6 Court model and declarations of CR in constitution

	US (24)	*Austrian/continental European (31)*	*Mixed (7)*	*French (1)*
CR in original constitution	14 (58%) exp. 19	29 (94%) exp. 25	6 (86%) exp. 6	1 (100%) exp. 1
CR not in original constitution	10 (42%) exp. 5	2 (6%) exp. 6	1 (14%) exp. 1	0 exp. 0

Note: Testing actual vs. expected frequencies: Pearson $Chi^2(3) = 10.7$ (marginal level of significance: 0.013). Inclusion/exclusion of constitutionally safeguarded JR is coded solely on the basis of the INTERP variable described above.

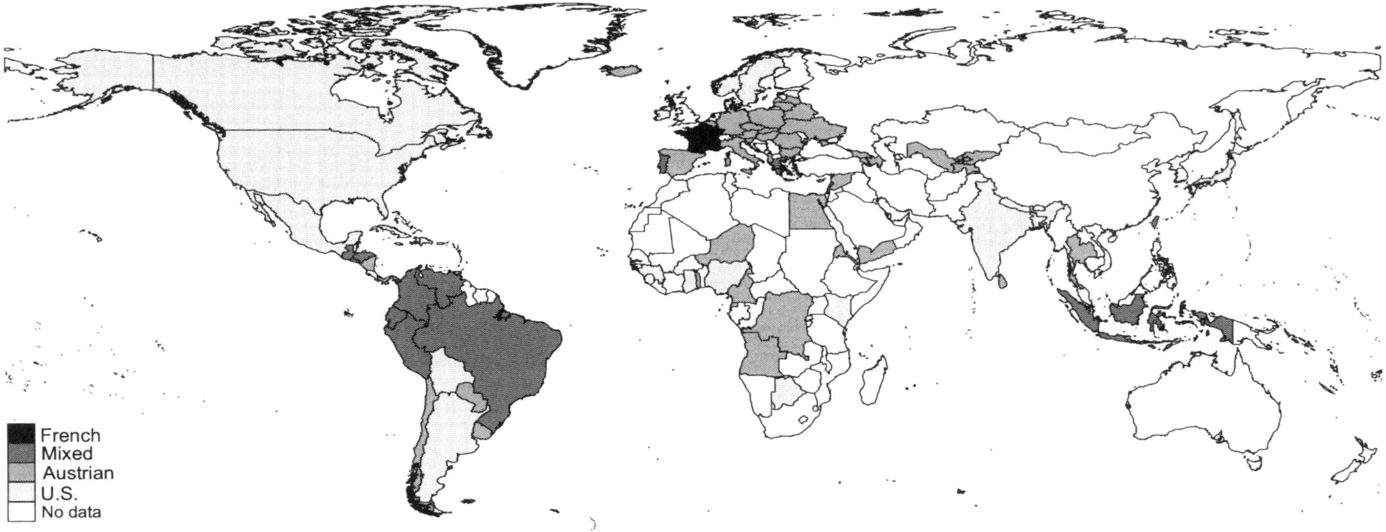

Figure 9.1 The distribution of court models in 89 countries around the world

Geography

The various dimensions of geography are obviously exogenous to the choice of constitutional rules. It has been noted that distance from the equator is a good predictor of the quality of a country's institutions, as well as is its per capita income.[38] It is also interesting to see whether regional influences affect the likelihood of including CR in the constitution.

Drawing on the absolute distance from the equator (i.e. latitude), we find that the correlation coefficient between this geographical indicator and CR as originally implemented in the constitution is –0.02, which is not significant. Thus, there is no statistically reliable association between absolute distance from the equator and a constitutional declaration of CR. However, the correlation coefficient of latitude with our aggregate indicator is 0.26 and statistically significant at the 10 percent level. Thus, the average quality of JR is increasing with the distance from the equator.

Instead of relying exclusively on a geographical definition of regions, it may be more informative to take into account cultural, social, economic, and political closeness. Therefore, Table 9.8 divides our sample countries into seven regional groups and assesses their relationship with constitutionally safeguarded JR.

In most regions, a majority of original constitutions contain a reference to CR and all states in our sample from the Middle East and North Africa (MENA) and Asia do. Also Eastern Europe and Sub-Saharan Africa are dominated by states that have laid down JR in their constitution. The sole exception is the group of Caribbean states, the constitutions of which address CR only in one-third of the cases explicitly. Testing statistically, we can easily reject the hypothesis of a random allocation of numbers to the cells. Noteworthy is the negative relation with Caribbean countries (Pearson correlation coefficient: –0.38), which is significant at the 1 percent level, as well as the positive association of CR with Eastern European countries (Pearson correlation coefficient: 0.23, significant at the 5 percent level). The correlation coefficient of the Western states is –0.20 and marginally significant at the 10 percent level. Analyzing the association between our composite indicator of CR and regional location we find only one significant and positive relationship, that is for Eastern Europe (correlation coefficient: 0.55, significant at the 1 percent level).

Table 9.7 Court model and changes in the declaration of CR in the constitution

	US (30)	*Austrian/continental European (46)*	*Mixed (12)*	*French (1)*
Change in constitution	6 (20%) exp. 9	15 (33%) exp. 13	5 (42%) exp. 4	0 exp. 0
No change in constitution	24 (80%) exp. 21	31 (67%) exp. 33	7 (58%) exp. 9	1 (100%) exp. 1

Note: Testing actual vs. expected frequencies: Pearson $Chi^2(3) = 2.8$ (marginal level of significance: 0.423).

Table 9.8 Regions and declaration of CR in the constitution

	Eastern Europe (17)	*Latin America (13)*	*MENA (2)*	*Sub-Saharan Africa (11)*	*Western States (15)*	*Asia (5)*	*Carib-bean (9)*
CR in constitution	16 (94%) exp. 13	10 (77%) exp. 10	2 (100%) exp. 2	10 (91%) exp. 8	9 (60%) exp. 12	5 (100%) exp. 4	3 (33%) exp. 7
CR not in constitution	1 (6%) exp. 4	3 (23%) exp. 3	0 exp. 1	1 (9%) exp. 3	6 (40%) exp. 4	0 exp. 1	6 (67%) exp. 2

Note: Testing actual vs. expected frequencies: Pearson $Chi^2(6) = 17.9$ (marginal level of significance: 0.006).

Next, we study how these regional dimensions relate to constitutional change in JR. There is a correlation coefficient of –0.16 between absolute latitude and constitutional change, which is marginally insignificant at the 10 percent level. Hence, the likelihood of a country implementing or abolishing CR in its constitution does not decrease with the distance from the equator. However, the likelihood of changes in the aggregate indicator for CR decreases with the distance from the equator (correlation coefficient: –0.20, significant at the 5 percent level). Table 9.9 reports the relevant frequencies of constitutional change after dividing the countries into the regions outlined above.

Constitutional change occurs relatively frequently in the MENA countries, whereas there is almost no change in the original constitutions of Eastern European, Western, and Caribbean countries. Yet, there is no statistically significant association between countries' location and changes in their constitution regarding the provision of JR. When correlating changes in the composite indicator of CR with a country's regional location, we find a positive coefficient of 0.24 (significant at a 5 percent level) for Sub-Saharan African countries and a negative coefficient of –0.25 (significant at a 5 percent level) for Caribbean countries.

Whereas a country's regional location can be associated to the anchoring of CR in that country's constitution, there is no such relationship between any of the tested geographical attributes and a country's likelihood of implementing or abolishing CR permanently. With respect to the quality of CR features, we find that

Table 9.9 Regions and changes in the declaration of CR in the constitution

	Eastern Europe (21)	*Latin America (19)*	*MENA (5)*	*Sub-Saharan Africa (16)*	*Western States (19)*	*Asia (10)*	*Caribbean (10)*
Change in constitution	4 (19%) exp. 6	6 (32%) exp. 5	3 (60%) exp. 1	5 (31%) exp. 5	4 (21%) exp. 5	5 (50%) exp. 3	1 (10%) exp. 3
No change in constitution	17 (81%) exp. 15	13 (68%) exp. 14	2 (40%) exp. 4	11 (69%) exp. 12	15 (79%) exp. 14	5 (50%) exp. 7	9 (90%) exp. 7

Note: Testing actual vs. expected frequencies: Pearson $Chi^2(6) = 8.0$ (marginal level of significance: 0.235).

it increases with distance from the equator, while the likelihood of changes in the composite indicator decreases. Eastern European countries have a significantly higher quality of CR, whereas South-Saharan African countries are more likely, and Caribbean countries are less likely, to face changes in the composite indicator.

History

A country's colonial history can have long-lasting consequences for its choice of institutions and thereby for its development. Quite often, current political, economic, and legal institutions are heavily influenced by those prevalent when the country was a colony. Therefore, Table 9.10 cross-tabulates the explicit inclusion of CR in the constitution and countries' colonial history. In our sample, about 49 percent of the countries were never a colony. Of those that have a colonial history, most were governed either by Great Britain (26 percent) or Spain (17 percent); there are only few cases of former French, Belgian, and Portuguese colonies.

All former French, Belgian, and Portuguese colonies provide for CR in their constitution and so do over two-thirds of the other countries. There is no statistically significant evidence that colonial history and constitutionally safeguarded JR are related, which is also true for the aggregate indicator of CR.

In Table 9.11, we analyze whether colonial history affects the likelihood of constitutional change as to CR.

Again, we find no statistically significant evidence that constitutional change and colonial history are related. Changes in our composite indicator are negatively correlated with not having a colonial history and with having a British colonial history, but positively correlated with having a Spanish colonial history (correlation coefficients: –0.17, –0.17, and 0.18, all significant at a 10 percent level). Having a French colonial history is even more strongly related to changes in the aggregate indicator with a coefficient of 0.24 that is significant at a 5 percent level. We therefore conclude that constitutionally provided CR and constitutional change regarding the existence of CR are not notably influenced by colonial history. But the likelihood of changes in the average quality of the features of CR is related to having no colonial history or a British, a Spanish, or a French colonial history.

Table 9.10 Colonial history and declaration of CR in the constitution

	Never colony (35)	*Former Spanish colony (12)*	*Former British colony (19)*	*Former French colony (4)*	*Former Belgian, Dutch, or Portuguese colony (2)*
CR in constitution	27 (77%) exp. 27	9 (75%) exp. 9	13 (68%) exp. 15	4 (100%) exp. 3	2 (100%) exp. 2
CR not in constitution	8 (23%) exp. 8	3 (25%) exp. 3	6 (32%) exp. 5	0 exp. 1	0 exp. 1

Note: Testing actual vs. expected frequencies: Pearson $Chi^2(4) = 2.5$ (marginal level of significance: 0.636).

Table 9.11 Colonial history and changes in the declaration of CR in the constitution

	Never colony (45)	*Former Spanish colony (18)*	*Former British colony (25)*	*Former French colony (8)*	*Former Belgian, Dutch, or Portuguese colony (4)*
Change in constitution	10 (22%) exp. 13	6 (33%) exp. 5	6 (24%) exp. 7	4 (50%) exp. 2	2 (50%) exp. 1
No change in constitution	35 (78%) exp. 32	12 (67%) exp. 13	19 (76%) exp. 18	4 (50%) exp. 6	2 (50%) exp. 3

Note: Testing actual vs. expected frequencies: Pearson $Chi^2(4) = 4.1$ (marginal level of significance: 0.395).

Legal origin is often considered a forceful determinant of a country's legal environment. La Porta *et al.* distinguish between common law and civil law.[39] Within civil law, they further distinguish between French, Scandinavian, German, and socialist law, and find that the legal origin of commercial law is also a good predictor for the quality of institutions. It is somewhat open to question whether the origin of a country's commercial law will have any bearing on its de jure degree of CR, which is an element of public law, but the papers by La Porta *et al.* are very influential and we thus explicitly take into account the possible effects of legal origin. Table 9.12 cross-tabulates legal origin with the declaration of CR in the constitution, as well as with change of an existing constitution.

In our sample, most constitutions have a French legal origin (42), followed by those based in the common law (32), socialist (18), and German/Scandinavian (8) traditions. All constitutions of German legal origin provide for JR. None of the Scandinavian legal origin constitutions are changed with respect to JR. We can reject the hypothesis that the anchoring of CR in the constitution and respective changes to the constitution are the result of a random process with respect to the countries' legal origin at any reasonable level of significance. Two results are particularly noteworthy: Scandinavian countries are significantly less likely to mention CR explicitly in their constitutions (Pearson correlation coefficient: –0.29). Conversely, French

Table 9.12 Legal origin, declarations of CR in constitution, and constitutional change

	Common law (32)	*Socialist (18)*	*French (42)*	*German (4)*	*Scandinavian (4)*
CR in original constitution	17 (53%) exp. 18	12 (67%) exp. 10	21 (50%) exp. 23	4 (100%) exp. 2	1 (25%) exp. 2
CR not in original constitution	9 (28%) exp. 5	1 (6%) exp. 3	4 (10%) exp. 7	0 exp. 1	3 (75%) exp. 1
Original constitution changed with respect to CR	6 (19%) exp. 9	5 (28%) exp. 5	17 (40%) exp. 12	0 exp. 1	0 exp. 1

Note: Testing actual vs. expected frequencies: Pearson $Chi^2(8) = 22.0$ (marginal level of significance: 0.005).

constitutions are more likely to be changed with respect to CR (Pearson correlation coefficient: 0.24). Having a socialist legal origin is correlated with our composite indicator (correlation coefficient: 0.39, significant at the 1 percent level), which is not surprising since this group consists also of many Eastern European countries. Changes in our indicator are positively correlated with having a French legal origin and negatively with having a common law or Scandinavian legal origin (correlation coefficients: 0.34, –0.22, and –0.19, significant at the 1 percent, 5 percent, and 10 percent level, respectively).

Ethno-linguistic fractionalization has been a standard control for economic growth models ever since Easterly and Levine showed that this variable explains much of the variation in African countries' growth rates.[40] It is also frequently used to explain the quality of institutions. A population highly fractionalized on ethnic or religious grounds and possibly also language-diverse might have lower levels of trust and be more prone to internal conflict. In such a situation, the conflict-resolving capacities of the judiciary could be particularly important. JR could provide an independent control that the various groups of society follow the rules of the constitution when they are in power.

Most studies using ethno-linguistic fractionalization rely on data provided by a Soviet institute in the 1960s or on data averaged from several studies. Alesina *et al.* recalculate three fractionalization indices in which they distinguish very carefully between three dimensions of fractionalization that previously tended to be mixed together, namely, ethnic, linguistic, and religious fractionalization. Because their fractionalization data are widely recognized and computed for a far larger number of countries than is the case in previous studies, we rely on their data.[41]

We study the impact of ethnic diversity on CR as it appears in the original constitution. The correlation coefficient is 0.11, which is not statistically significant. Further, the correlation between implemented CR and diversity of languages within a society is 0.16, which is also not significant at any reasonable level of significance. Finally, regarding religious diversity, we find a correlation coefficient of –0.02, which is again not significant. Hence, we find no significant evidence that diversity in language, ethnicity, or religion affect the likelihood of constitutionally safeguarded JR.[42] The same holds for our aggregate indicator of CR quality.

Analyzing constitutional amendments with regard to CR, the correlation between ethnic diversity and change is 0.18 and significant at a 10 percent level. Those countries more fractured along ethnic lines are more likely to implement constitutional change. More language diversity and religious diversity again have no effect on constitutional change regarding JR; the correlation coefficients are 0.05 and –0.10, but both are statistically insignificant.[43] Countries with higher levels of ethnic fractionalization are more likely to face changes in the composite indicator. Thus, the only important dimension of fractionalization for safeguarding CR in the constitution is linked to ethnic diversity. Societies with more ethnic diversity are more likely to change their constitution with regard to adjusting formal CR and its average quality. And although religious fractionalization does not affect the implementation of or changes regarding CR in the constitution, religious polarization has a positive effect on the likelihood that an original constitution safeguards JR and a positive effect on changes in the composite indicator.

Putnam claims that Italian regions characterized by a large number of voluntary associations having a horizontal organization structure are successful in the production of high-quality local public goods. He further argues that the Catholic Church has a vertical organization structure.[44] La Porta *et al.* asked whether this result could be generalized and, additionally, classified Islam and the various Orthodox churches as having hierarchical structures. They find that holding per capita income constant, "countries with more dominant hierarchical religions have less efficient judiciaries, greater corruption, lower-quality bureaucracies, higher rates of tax evasion, lower rates of participation in civic activities and professional associations, a lower level of importance of large firms in the economy, inferior infrastructures, and higher inflation."[45]

Thus, if adherence to a particular religion provides information regarding a propensity to accept vertical structures of authority, such might be reflected in a country's constitutional structure. We would expect countries in which religions that are deemed to have a vertical hierarchy have a high share of adherents to implement constitutions with fewer safeguards for CR, interpreting judicial review as a type of horizontal control, in other words, a type of control somewhat antithetical to members of vertical hierarchy religions.

This hypothesis is different from the one on religious fractionalization discussed above because it focuses on the beliefs and the structures of specific religions rather than on the number of competing beliefs in a country. We differentiate our sample countries on the basis of their share of Catholics, Muslims, Protestants, and other religions. The correlation coefficients with CR as appearing in the original constitution are 0.05, 0.14, –0.44, and 0.14, respectively. Thus, societies with a large share of Catholics, Muslims, and/or other religions exhibit a greater probability of implementing CR in their constitutions, whereas those containing a relatively large share of Protestants are characterized by a lower probability of doing so. Statistically, only the negative association between CR and Protestants is statistically significant at the 1 percent level. At the same time, the share of Protestants is positively associated to the average quality of CR features in the constitution (correlation coefficient: 0.26, significant at a 10 percent level).

With respect to the probability of constitutional amendments involving CR, we find correlation coefficients of 0.03, 0.03, –0.22, and 0.09 for the respective shares of Catholics, Muslims, Protestants, and other religions. Again, only the share of Protestants in the population has a noteworthy negative effect on constitutional change regarding CR that is significant at a 5 percent level. Regarding changes in the aggregate indicator, a high share of Protestants and a low share of Catholics have a negative effect (correlation coefficients: –0.26 and 0.23, significant at the 1 percent and 5 percent level, respectively).

Constitutional context

A constitution will most likely be the result of compromise. The choice of variables underlying our indicator for CR is therefore part of a larger legal context that includes other vital aspects of the constitution. It is beyond the scope of this chapter to thoroughly analyze the bargaining dynamics that led to the observed constitution. However, to generate at least some preliminary insights, we study whether there are significant correlations between CR and other features of the constitution. We discuss five such features, namely:

1. the electoral formula,
2. the form of government,
3. the vertical structure of the state (unitary vs. federal),
4. the opportunity for citizens to intervene directly, and
5. the length of the entire constitution.

Electoral formula

We use data collected by Golder to study the relationship between electoral rules and the degree of constitutional safeguards for CR.[46] In Table 9.13, we provide absolute and relative frequencies for the cross-tabulation of electoral rules and constitutionally safeguarded JR.

We find that a majoritarian voting system is the most preferred type of electoral rule in our sample. However, fewer than expected countries characterized by this rule have CR implemented in their constitutions. In contrast, countries that have adopted a multitier or mixed system are more likely than expected to have a constitutional reference to JR. The statistical test shows that we cannot reject a random distribution of these variables at any reasonable level of significance. If we combine multitier and mixed systems into one category, we find again a statistically insignificant correlation coefficient of 0.21. Thus, countries' electoral rules are not associated with a different probability of implementing constitutionally safeguarded JR. However, countries with multitier electoral systems are associated with significantly higher average CR quality (correlation coefficient: 0.41, significant at a 1 percent level).

Table 9.13 Electoral rule and declarations of CR in constitution

	Majoritarian (21)	*Proportional (14)*	*Multitier (10)*	*Mixed (10)*
CR in original constitution	13 (62%) exp. 15	10 (71%) exp. 10	8 (80%) exp. 7	9 (90%) exp. 7
CR not in original constitution	8 (38%) exp. 6	4 (29%) exp. 4	2 (20%) exp. 3	1 (10%) exp. 3

Note: Testing actual vs. expected frequencies: Pearson $Chi^2(3) = 3.0$ (marginal level of significance: 0.388).

Table 9.14 Electoral rules and changes in the declaration of CR in the constitution

	Majoritarian (28)	*Proportional (21)*	*Multitier (12)*	*Mixed (11)*
Change in constitution	7 (25%) exp. 7	7 (33%) exp. 5	2 (17%) exp. 3	1 (9%) exp. 3
No change in constitution	21 (75%) exp. 21	14 (67%) exp. 16	10 (83%) exp. 9	10 (91%) exp. 8

Note: Testing actual vs. expected frequencies: Pearson $Chi^2(3) = 2.7$ (marginal level of significance: 0.434).

In Table 9.14, we record the cross-tabulation with respect to those countries that made enduring constitutional changes in CR. We find that almost none of the countries with a multitier or mixed electoral rule changed their constitutions with respect to CR. There are no significant correlations between any electoral rule and the probability of a change in the constitution regarding CR or a change in the aggregate indicator.

Form of government

Again, we distinguish between only two types of government: parliamentary and presidential systems. It is argued that presidential systems systematically achieve a higher degree of separation of powers than parliamentary systems because the executive is more independent from parliament in presidential systems.[47] However, such systems could give rise to serious conflicts between parliament and president and thus a judiciary that checks the compliance with the rules of the constitution could be instrumental in securing stability of the political system. Provided that presidential systems really have a higher degree of separation of powers, the judiciary might be assigned the task of arbitrator, should the other branches find themselves in conflict about the interpretation of the constitution.

To analyze the relationship between the form of government and constitutionally safeguarded JR, we rely on data measuring the degree of parliamentary responsibility collected by Banks.[48] He refers to the degree to which a premier must depend on the support of a majority in the lower house of a legislature in order to remain in office and distinguishes four forms of government:

1. an office of premier does not exist (irrelevant),
2. an office exists, but there is no parliamentary responsibility,
3. the premier is to a certain extent constitutionally and effectively dependent on a legislative majority, and
4. the premier is constitutionally and effectively dependent on a legislative majority.

Table 9.15 contains the result of cross-tabulating form of government with our primary variable of interest; the results are insignificant.

Table 9.15 Form of government and declarations of CR in the constitution

	Irrelevant (23)	*No parliamentary responsibility (11)*	*Limited parliamentary responsibility (8)*	*Full parliamentary responsibility (30)*
CR in original constitution	20 (87%) exp. 18	8 (73%) exp. 8	7 (88%) exp. 6	20 (67%) exp. 23
CR not in original constitution	3 (13%) exp. 5	3 (27%) exp. 3	1 (13%) exp. 2	10 (33%) exp. 7

Note: Testing actual vs. expected frequencies: Pearson $Chi^2(3) = 3.6$ (marginal level of significance: 0.305).

In countries where the office of the premier does not exist or where there is limited parliamentary responsibility we typically find explicit constitutional declarations of CR. The correlation between declarations of CR and full parliamentary responsibility is –0.19, but marginally insignificant at the 10 percent level. Thus, we find, at most, weak evidence that parliamentary democracies tend to have less constitutional safeguarding of CR. In Table 9.16, we investigate whether constitutional change with regard to CR is associated with any form of government.

As Table 9.16 reveals, CR-related constitutional change occurs most often in those countries where there is no parliamentary responsibility. Their correlation coefficient of 0.23, which is statistically significant at a 5 percent level, indicates that these countries are indeed more likely to change their constitution in relation to a concrete reference to CR. We find only quite few constitutional changes in countries with full parliamentary responsibility. A correlation coefficient of –0.19, which is significant at a 10 percent level, underpins the fact that there is a meaningful statistical relationship. Given that constitutional change regarding JR is almost synonymous to its implementation, one could conjecture that although countries with presidential systems have not been more likely to provide for CR in their original constitution, these countries have subsequently felt the need to introduce constitutionally safeguarded JR. For our aggregate indicator we find that countries where the relationship between government and parliament is irrelevant are more likely to be subject to changes, whereas countries with full parliamentary responsibility are

Table 9.16 Form of government and changes in the declaration of CR in the constitution

	Irrelevant (33)	*No parliamentary responsibility (21)*	*Limited parliamentary responsibility (10)*	*Full parliamentary responsibility (36)*
Change in constitution	10 (30%) exp. 9	10 (48%) exp. 6	2 (20%) exp. 3	6 (17%) exp. 10
No change in constitution	23 (70%) exp. 24	11 (52%) exp. 15	8 (80%) exp. 7	30 (83%) exp. 26

Note: Testing actual vs. expected frequencies: Pearson $Chi^2(3) = 6.7$ (marginal level of significance: 0.082).

negatively correlated with changes in the extend of CR (correlation coefficients: 0.23 and –0.25, both significant at a 5 percent level).

Vertical structure of the state

We distinguish between federal and unitary states. It can be argued that one important function of an independent judiciary is to reduce disagreement between the various branches of government about the kind of legislation that is reconcilable with the constitution. In the absence of an impartial arbiter, conflicts between government branches are more likely to develop into power games, with adverse effects on the country's political stability. We conjecture that the potential for conflict between political actors is higher in federally organized states because there are more constitutional actors. Thus, members of the constitutional convention in federal states would prefer a higher level of de jure CR than would those in unitary states. However, our data show that neither the original constitutional choice nor the changes over time are correlated with a dummy variable for federalism. This holds for both, the constitutional safeguarding of CR *per se* and its quality in terms of our aggregate indicator.

Possibility of citizens intervening directly

We distinguish between two direct democratic instruments here, namely initiatives that can be initiated by the citizens and referenda that can be initiated by government. One can think of them as direct democracy "from below" vs. "from above." Initiatives can be interpreted as one way the principal (the citizens at large) can directly control its agent (the government). One can also interpret direct democratic institutions as a broader separation of powers, as one more veto player becomes relevant. At least two conjectures regarding the relationship between CR and initiatives come to mind: First, if direct democratic institutions exist, CR becomes all the more important as more conflicts are likely due to the existence of an additional player. But it could, second, also be the case that the citizens at large function as the highest court of the country—and formally granted CR becomes not only less needed but also less likely to be included in the constitution. The latter argument applies to cases where the state might want to overstep its constitutionally granted competences. However, initiatives in contrast to CR will increase rather than decrease the likelihood of a tyranny of the majority. Referenda are initiated from above. Conjectures regarding their relationship with CR are even muddier: If they can be initiated from above they would not seem to constitute an additional constraint and their relationship with CR remains to be empirically ascertained.

Our data regarding direct democratic institutions are from Elkins *et al.*[49] We only consider countries that have not experienced any changes in these variables during our observation period. It is interesting to note that initiatives and referenda are highly significantly correlated but that the correlation coefficient still is only 0.36 (which is significant at the 1 percent level). Constitutionally safeguarded JR and initiatives are not significantly correlated. However, there is a positive correlation

(correlation coefficient: 0.27, significant at a 10 percent level) between initiatives and our composite indicator. This can be interpreted as evidence in favor of a complementary, rather than a substitutive, relationship of these two institutions. We find a similar relationship between CR and referenda: The partial correlation for the implementation of CR is 0.20 and not statistically significant, whereas the correlation coefficient of 0.27 with our aggregate indicator is again statistically significant at a 10 percent level. As a result, initiatives and referenda are not associated with a higher likelihood of constitutionally safeguarded JR, but with a higher quality of the safeguarded features of CR. Constitutional changes are not significant with regard to either initiatives or referenda.

Length of entire constitution

Constitutions are by necessity incomplete contracts. Short constitutions leave many questions open, leading to an increased demand for legal interpretation by the judiciary.[50] Lengthy constitutions may be the result of attempts to be as comprehensive as possible on as many issues as possible. Such constitutions can be interpreted as a device for reducing uncertainty as detailed regulations in the constitution are assumed to decrease uncertainty more than giving courts decision-making and interpretation powers. Explicitly outlining many rules in the constitution only makes sense if laws are actually checked for their conformity with these specific regulations. Also, a highly comprehensive constitutional text might reduce the costs of CR as it can be interpreted straightforwardly. Therefore, we expect longer constitutions to be correlated with higher degrees of CR. We find, however, that the original inclusion of CR in the constitution is not significantly correlated with the length of the document (correlation coefficient: 0.19). There is also no correlation between constitutional changes in CR and the length of a constitution (correlation coefficient: –0.01). For our composite indicator we find no statistically significant relationships.

Organizational structure of the judiciary

Above, we have dealt with the correlation between the court structure and CR. Here, we confine ourselves to the analysis between CR and judicial independence. We argue that JI is a necessary condition for CR; La Porta *et al.* argue that JI and CR are two different concepts that cannot only be kept apart theoretically, but also empirically.[51] First, we analyze the association between the different indicators for CR in the original constitution and a country's choice to safeguard JI explicitly in its original constitution. We find a positive and highly significant correlation coefficient of 0.60 for the implementation of CR in the constitution (INTERP). For the indicators reflecting the number of parties who are able to initiate CR (CHALLEG), the legislative stage at which CR takes place (CHALSTAG) and the potential consequences of CR (CHALUNCN) we find correlation coefficients of 0.25, 0.25, and 0.37 that are significant at the 10 percent, 5 percent, and 1 percent level, respectively. Also, our composite indicator of CR is positively correlated with JI (correlation coefficient: 0.41, significant at a 1 percent level). When analyzing the association between changes in CR and a country's choice to safeguard JI explicitly in its original constitution, we find no significant correlation for the abolition or introduction of CR. Nevertheless, the number of parties with the competence to challenge the constitutionality of a law and our composite indicator are positively correlated with coefficients of 0.27 and 0.25 (significant at a 5 percent level). The stage at which CR is initiated has a correlation coefficient of 0.21 that is significant at the 10 percent level. Changes in the potential consequences of CR are not significantly correlated to constitutionally safeguarded JI. Finally, we analyze the relationship between changes in the constitutional base of JI and CR. An amendment of constitutional safeguards of JI in the constitution is positively correlated with constitutional change regarding the existence of CR (correlation coefficient: 0.25, significant at a 5 percent level). Among the features of CR, only changes to the consequences of finding a law unconstitutional are positively correlated to an amendment of constitutionally safeguarded JI (correlation coefficient: 0.18, significant at a 10 percent level).

A country's choice to safeguard judicial independence explicitly in its original constitution is thus associated with a higher likelihood of also providing for CR in the original constitution and a higher quality of the CR features stipulated in the constitution. However, with respect to constitutional change regarding CR, there are only significant relationships with the quality of CR. While changes in the potential consequences of CR are the only changes in a feature of CR that are not correlated to the existence of JI in the constitution, they are at the same time the only ones positively correlated to the amendment of explicit JI to the constitution.

Inequality

Fractionalization (and polarization) is not confined to ethnic, linguistic, or religious dimensions. Keefer and Knack study inequality in income, as well as in land ownership, and find that high degrees of inequality are inimical to secure property rights.[52] In a country with a general franchise and a high degree of inequality, elections can be won by promising redistribution to the poor. Under such circumstances, rich citizens could make consent to the constitution conditional on a high degree of CR if doing so promises to make their earnings more secure.

Vanhanen presents a number of proxy variables for the distribution of resources within societies.[53] In our analysis, we draw on several indicators. For democratic competition and participation, competition is operationalized by the percentage of votes that are not cast for the largest party and participation is measured by the percentage of the population that actually voted in the last election.[54] The correlation between CR-related declarations in the constitution and this indicator is –0.30, which is significant at the 10 percent level. The correlation coefficient of –0.38 with constitutional change is significant at the 1 percent level. Thus, countries characterized by more democratization are less likely to include explicit provisions on CR in their constitutions. The correlation with our composite indicator is insignificant. However, changes in the composite indicator are negatively correlated with the democratic competition and participation indicator, particularly in the Western states (correlation coefficients: –0.24 and –0.45, both significant at the 10 percent level).

Share of family farms counts the area of family farms as a percentage of total farmland. Although perhaps less relevant for industrial countries, it is an appropriate indicator for the distribution of resources in many less-developed countries. The correlation coefficient with CR is –0.22, which is not statistically significant.[55] However, when differentiating the sample between Western and non-Western countries, we obtain correlations of –0.64 and 0.42 (significant at the 5 percent and 10 percent level), respectively. Hence, it is those Western countries where the area of family farms as a percentage of total cultivated area is particularly high that are less likely to implement constitutional safeguards for CR. The correlation coefficients for constitutional change are –0.21, –0.27, and –0.02 for all, the Western, and the non-Western countries, but none of them is significant at any reasonable level. For the quality of CR, we find that the association with the share of family farms is negative in Western and positive in non-Western countries (correlation coefficients: –0.68 and 0.59, both significant at a 5 percent level). Changes in the aggregate indicator are negatively correlated with the share of family farms (correlation coefficient: –0.32, significant at the 5 percent level).

Knowledge distribution measures how available knowledge resources are to members of the society. It is based on the arithmetic mean of the percentage of students and the percentage of literate in a country. Countries with a wider distribution of education are less likely to feature declarations on CR in their constitutions (correlation coefficient: –0.29, which is marginally insignificant at a 10 percent level).[56] However, the likelihood of constitutional change is reduced with a wider distribution of education (correlation coefficient: –0.28, significant at a 5 percent level). A country's knowledge distribution cannot be associated with the quality of constitutionally safeguarded features of CR. But again, there is a negative relation to the likelihood of changes in our composite indicator (correlation coefficient: –0.25, significant at a 10 percent level).

Finally, urban influence is the arithmetic mean of the percentage share of urban dwellers to total population and the percentage of nonagricultural population. It proxies for the relative importance of city versus rural dwellers in a country. The correlation with CR is –0.37, which is statistically significant at the 5 percent level.[57] Also, the correlation coefficient with constitutional change of –0.32 is significant at the 5 percent level. Thus, when many citizens live in urban areas and are engaged in nonagricultural work, it is less likely that CR will be explicitly mentioned in the constitution. And although there is no statistically significant association with the average quality of CR, these countries are also less likely to change the average quality (correlation coefficient: –0.30, significant at a 5 percent level).

Overall, the distribution of resources is significantly associated with the implementation of CR in the original constitution and, most of the time, also with constitutional change regarding CR. Conversely, the results on the composite indicator provide a rather unclear picture, whereas changes in the indicator can clearly be associated to the distribution of resources in society.

Conclusion and outlook

Over the last ten years, not only research into effects and causes of judicial independence has made important progress, substantial new insights have also been gained regarding economic effects of constitutions. These two branches are combined in this chapter. We have created a panel dataset containing 23 variables of various aspects of constitutionally safeguarded JI.

In this chapter, we confine ourselves to the description and analysis of four variables describing the existence and quality of constitutionally safeguarded JR. Our key findings are: First, a country's court model is significantly correlated with the explicit safeguarding of CR and the quality of its features in the constitution. Austrian/continental European type court models can be associated positively with the implementation and quality of CR, whereas the US type of court model shows a negative association. Second, the regional location of a country is significantly related to its implementation of JR in the constitution. Caribbean and Western countries are less likely to provide for JR, while the opposite holds for Eastern European countries. The latter also exhibit a higher average quality of JR features. Third, countries with a Scandinavian legal origin are significantly less likely to mention CR in their constitution, and constitutions of French legal origin are more likely to be changed in this respect. Countries with a Socialist legal origin have a higher average quality of JR. Fourth, countries with a higher share of Protestants in the population are less likely to safeguard CR in their constitution, but at the same time their quality of CR features is higher. Fifth, countries with a multitier electoral system are associated with significantly higher average CR quality. Sixth, presidential systems exhibit a lower quality of CR features safeguarded in the constitution and are more likely to change their constitution regarding a concrete reference to CR. Seventh, countries with constitutionally prescribed initiatives and referenda are not associated with a higher likelihood of constitutionally safeguarded JR, but with a higher quality of the safeguarded features of CR. Eighth, we find a positive relationship between the explicit safeguarding of JI in the constitution and the implementation of CR, as well as the quality of its different features. Finally, the distribution of resources in society has a strong effect on the implementation of JR.

A natural follow-up to this study is to inquire into the various consequences that different degrees of CR have on a number of outcome variables, such as predictability of legislation or the rule of law. Moreover, conducting a test of the different competing theories for explaining the constitutional status of JR would be desirable.

Appendix 1

Definition of variables

AL_ETHNIC:
Reflects probability that two randomly selected people from a given country will not belong to the same ethno-linguistic group. The higher the number, the more fractionalized society. The definition of ethnicity involves a combination of racial and linguistic characteristics. The result is a higher degree of fractionalization than the commonly used ELF-index (see el_elf60) in, for example, Latin America, where people of many races speak the same language; source: Alesina *et al.* (2003).

AL_LANGUAGE:
Reflects probability that two randomly selected people from a given country will not belong to the same linguistic group. The higher the number, the more fractionalized society; source: Alesina *et al.* (2003).

AL_RELIGION:
Reflects probability that two randomly selected people from a given country will not belong to the same religious group. The higher the number, the more fractionalized society; source: Alesina *et al.* (2003).

BANKS_S21F7
Refers to the degree to which a premier must depend on the support of a majority in the lower house of a legislature in order to remain in office. 0: Irrelevant. Office of premier does not exist, 1: Absent. Office exists, but there is no parliamentary responsibility. 2: Incomplete. The premier is, at least to some extent, constitutionally responsible to the legislature. Effective responsibility is, however, limited, 3: Complete. The premier is constitutionally and effectively dependent upon a legislative majority for continuance in office; source: Banks (2004).

CHALLEG:
Who has standing to initiate challenge to the constitutionality of legislation? 1: head of state (use this choice for single executive systems), 2: head of government, 3: first (or only) chamber of the legislature, 4: second chamber of the legislature, 5: both chambers of the legislature are required, 6: lawyers, 7: public (by complaint), 8: the courts, 9: left explicitly to nonconstitutional law, 25: the government/cabinet; source: Elkins *et al.* (2009).

CHALSTAG:
At what stage of the legislative process can bills be reviewed for constitutionality? 1: pre-promulgation, 2: post-promulgation, 3: either, 4: left explicitly to nonconstitutional law; source: Elkins *et al.* (2009).

CHALUNCN:
What is the effect of a determination of unconstitutionality? 1: law is void, 2: void for specific case, but law still exists, 3: returned to legislature for revision/reconsideration, 4: left explicitly to nonconstitutional law; source: Elkins *et al.* (2009).

CONLENGTH: The length of the current constitution of a state in words; schedules and other complementary documents are not counted; source: Voigt (2009).
COURTMODEL: Organizational structure of the court system: 0: US, 1: Austrian, 2: mixed, 3: French; source: Harutyunyan and Mavčič (1999).
FEDERALISM: Dummy variable equal to 1 if a country has a federal political structure, 0 otherwise; source: Elazar (1995).
GOL_EST: Variable indicating the type of electoral system used: 1: majoritarian (employs plurality, absolute majority, qualified majority, limited vote, alternative vote, single nontransferable vote or modified Borda count in a single electoral tier), 2: proportional (employs party list or single transferable vote in a single electoral tier), 3: multitier (employs a single electoral formula, majoritarian or proportional, across multiple tiers), 4: mixed (employs a mixture of majoritarian and proportional electoral rules in one or more electoral tiers); source: Golder (2005).
HT_COLONIAL: This is a tenfold classification of the former colonial ruler of the country. Following Australia, Israel and New Zealand), and exclusively focused on "Western overseas" colonialism. This implies that only Western colonizers (e.g. excluding Japanese colonialism), and only countries located in the non-Western hemisphere "overseas" (e.g. excluding Ireland and Malta), have been coded. Each country that has been colonized since 1700 is coded. In cases of several colonial powers, the last one is counted, if it lasted for ten years or longer. The categories are the following: 0: never colonized by a Western overseas colonial power, 1: Dutch, 2: Spanish, 3: Italian, 4: US, 5: British, 6: French, 7: Portuguese, 8: Belgian, 9: British-French, 10: Australian; source: Teorell and Hadenius (2007).
HT_REGION: This is a tenfold politico-geographic classification of world regions, based on a mixture of two considerations: geographical proximity (with the partial exception of category 5 below) and demarcation by area specialists having contributed to a regional understanding of democratization. The categories are as follow: 1: Eastern Europe and post Soviet Union (including Central Asia), 2: Latin America (including Cuba, Haiti, and the Dominican Republic), 3: North Africa and the Middle East (including Israel, Turkey, and Cyprus), 4: Sub-Saharan Africa, 5: Western Europe and North America (including Australia and New Zealand), 6: East Asia (including Japan and Mongolia), 7: South-East Asia, 8: South Asia, 9: the Pacific (excluding Australia and New Zealand), 10: the Caribbean (including Belize, Guyana, and Suriname, but excluding Cuba, Haiti, and the Dominican Republic); source: Teorell and Hadenius (2007).

INITIAT:	Does the constitution provide for the ability of individuals to propose legislative initiatives (referenda from below)? 1: yes, 2: no; source: Elkins *et al.* (2009).
INTERP:	To whom does the constitution assign the responsibility for the interpretation of the constitution? 1: any ordinary court, 2: constitutional court/council, 3: supreme court only, 4: special chamber of the supreme court, 5: first (or only) chamber of the legislature, 6: second chamber of the legislature, 7: both chambers of the legislature are required, 8: left explicitly to nonconstitutional law; source: Elkins *et al.* (2009).
JUDIND:	Does the constitution contain an explicit declaration regarding the independence of the central judicial organ(s)? 1: yes, 2: no; source: Elkins *et al.* (2009).
LP_CATHO80:	Catholics as percentage of population in 1980; source: La Porta *et al.* (1999).
LP_LAT_ABST:	The latitude of the centroid of a country divided by 90 (to take values between 0 and 1); source: La Porta *et al.* (1999).
LP_LEGOR:	Identifies the legal origin of the company law or commercial code of each country. There are five possible origins: 1: English common law, 2: French commercial code, 3: socialist/communist laws, 4: German commercial code, 5: Scandinavian commercial code; source: La Porta *et al.* (1999).
LP_MUSLIM80:	Muslims as percentage of population in 1980; source: La Porta *et al.* (1999).
LP_PROTMG80:	Protestants as percentage of population in 1980; source: La Porta *et al.* (1999).
REFEREN:	Does the constitution provide for the ability to propose a referendum (or plebiscite)? 1: yes, 2: no; source: Elkins *et al.* (2009).
REY_ETHPOL:	Index of ethno-linguistic polarization calculated using the data of the World Christian Encyclopedia; source: Montalvo and Reynal-Querol (2005).
REY_RELPOL:	Index of religious polarization calculated using *L'Etat des Religions dans le Monde* and *The Statesmen Yearbook*; source: Montalvo and Reynal-Querol (2005).

VAN_COMP:	The competition variable portrays the electoral success of smaller parties, that is, the percentage of votes gained by the smaller parties in parliamentary and/or presidential elections. The variable is calculated by subtracting from 100 the percentage of votes won by the largest party (the party that wins most votes) in parliamentary elections or by the party of the successful candidate in presidential elections. The variable thus theoretically ranges from 0 (only one party received 100 percent of votes) to 100 (each voter cast a vote for a distinct party); source: Vanhanen (2003).
VAN_FAMILYF:	The area of family farms as a percentage of total cultivated area or total area of holdings. Family farms refer to holdings that are mainly cultivated by the holder family and that are owned by the cultivator family or held in owner-like possession. The upper hectare limit and other criteria of family farms vary from country to country and over time. Moreover, the data for the 1980s is based on information from 1960–80, and for the 1990s mostly from 1980, but also from the 1970s and the 1960s. In other words, comparisons across time and space must be interpreted with great caution; source: Vanhanen (2003).
VAN_INDEX:	This index combines two basic dimensions of democracy—competition and participation—measured as the percentage of votes not cast for the largest party (competition) times the percentage of the population who actually voted in the election (participation). This product is divided by 100 to form an index that in principle could vary from 0 (no democracy) to 100 (full democracy). (Empirically, however, the largest value is 49); source: Vanhanen (2003).
VAN_KNOWDIST:	The arithmetic mean of students percent (van_studentsp) and literates percent (van_literates); source: Vanhanen (2003).
VAN_OCCUP:	The arithmetic mean of urban population percent (van_urban) and nonagricultural population percent (van_nagric); source: Vanhanen (2003).
VAN_PART:	The percentage of the total population who actually voted in the election; source: Vanhanen (2003).
VAN_URBAN:	Urban population as a percentage of total population. Note that comparisons across time and space must be interpreted with caution as the concept of urbanity has changed over time and to some extent varies from country to country; source: Vanhanen (2003).

Notes

1 The results presented in this chapter are the outcome of a substantial effort in coding constitutions. An encompassing project was originally started by Zachary Elkins *et al.*, *Comparative Constitutions Project*. Regarding the coding of the variables presented here, most of the coding was done by a team of research assistants composed of Marc Berendsen, Dante Castillo, Nora El Bialy, Nora Heil, Jens Merte, and Max Thesing. The team was coordinated by Jerg Gutmann. Their help is gratefully acknowledged.

2 For a recent survey, *see* Tom Ginsburg, *The Global Spread of Constitutional Review*, *in* The Oxford Handbook of Law and Politics 81 (Gregory A. Caldeira *et al.*, eds., 2008).

3 *See* C. Neal Tate & Torbjörn Vallinder, *The Global Expansion of Judicial Power: The Judicialization of Politics*, *in* The Global Expansion of Judicial Power 1 (C. Neal Tate & Torbjörn Vallinder eds., 1995).

4 Our coding effort started on the basis of the preliminary data provided by Zachary Elkins *et al.*, in their *Comparative Constitutions Project* (2009), *available at* www.comparativeconstitutionsproject.org. We checked and sometimes corrected all of their codings and added many missing observations.

5 We are, however, not interested in the history of the emergence of judicial review. Excellent accounts are Edward S. Corwin, *The Establishment of Judicial Review I.*, 9 Mich. L. Rev. 102 (1910); David Deener, *Judicial Review in Modern Constitutional Systems*, 46 Am. Polit. Sci. Rev. 1079 (1952); and Herman Schwartz, *A Brief History of Judicial Review*, *in* The Self-Restraining State – Power and Accountability in New Democracies 145 (Andreas Schedler *et al.*, eds., 1999).

6 Alec Stone-Sweet, Governing with Judges: Constitutional Politics in Europe 21 (2000).

7 *See* Giandomenico Majone, *Temporal Consistency and Policy Credibility: Why Democracies Need Non-Majoritarian Institutions*, EUI-RSCAS Working Papers (1996), *available at* hdl.handle.net/1814/1472.

8 However, even though de facto independence of the judiciary is a necessary condition for the ability to credibly commit, it is not always sufficient. In the end, governments have to implement court decisions and powerful informal institutions might discourage courts from exercising judicial review.

9 In essence, we argue that judicial independence and constitutional review are complementary. Note that this view is not uncontested. Drawing on Friedrich A. Hayek, The Constitution of Liberty (1960), Rafael La Porta *et al.*, *Judicial Checks and Balances*, 112 J. Pol. Econ. 445 (2004) argue that judicial independence is an aspect of the separation of powers in which the legislature produces legislation whereas the judiciary would enforce it without the interference of either of the other two branches. Constitutional review, in turn, could rather be seen as an aspect of checks and balances because it makes the production of legislation itself subject to review by courts.

10 *See* Martin Shapiro, *The Success of Judicial Review*, *in* Constitutional Dialogues in Comparative Perspective 193 (Sally J. Kenney *et al.*, eds., 1999).

11 *E.g.*, Ginsburg, *supra* note 2.

12 *See* Stefan Voigt, Explaining Constitutional Change: A Positive Economics Approach (1999), Chapter 5 develops the argument of the constitution in contract-theoretic terms in more detail.

13 *See* Robert K. Fleck & F. Andrew Hanssen, *Judicial Review as a Constraint on Tyranny of the Majority*, Hamburg Lectures on Law & Economics (2011), *available at* www.ile-hamburg.de/_data/Hamburg_Lectures_Hanssen_Paper_Paper.pdf.

14 *See* Maurice Duverger, Political Parties, Their Organization and Activity in the Modern State (1954).

15 For a competing view, *see* Bernd Hayo & Stefan Voigt, *Determinants of Constitutional Change: Why do Countries Change their Form of Government?* 38 J. COMP. ECON. 283 (2010).
16 Various names are being used to describe the phenomenon: "Gridlock" in the US, "cohabitation" in France, and so on.
17 Stone-Sweet, *supra* note 6, at 37 (conjecturing that the European model of CR is so popular because it can be more easily combined with the parliamentary form of government).
18 *See* Tate & Vallinder, *supra* note 3.
19 C. Neal Tate, *Why the Expansion of Judicial Power? in* THE GLOBAL EXPANSION OF JUDICIAL POWER 27, 28 (C. Neal Tate & Torbjorn Vallinder eds., 1995).
20 *See* Tom Ginsburg, *Economic Analysis and the Design of Constitutional Courts*, 3 THEORETICAL INQUIRIES L. 49 (2002); *see also* George Tridimas, *Constitutional Judicial Review and Political Insurance*, 29 EUR. J.L. ECON. 81 (2010).
21 *See* Justin Fox & Matthew C. Stephenson, *Judicial Review as a Response to Political Posturing*, 105 Am. Pol. Sci. Rev. 397 (2011).
22 *See* Christopher L. Eisgruber, CONSTITUTIONAL SELF-GOVERNMENT (2001).
23 *See* RULE BY LAW: THE POLITICS OF COURTS IN AUTHORITARIAN REGIMES (Tom Ginsburg & Tamir Moustafa eds., 2008).
24 *See* Daron Acemoglu *et al.*, *Why Do Voters Dismantle Checks and Balances?* (17293 NBER Working Paper Series, 2011), *available at* www.nber.org/papers/w17293.
25 *E.g.*, Robert F. Utter & David C. Lundsgaard, *Comparative Aspects of Judicial Review: Issues Facing the New European States*, 77 JUDICATURE 240, 242 (1994); Erik S. Herron & Kirk A. Randazzo, *The Relationship between Independence and Judicial Review in Post-Communist Courts*, 65 J. POL. 422, 427 (2003).
26 Schwartz, *supra* note 5, at 149 points out that some formerly socialist states did introduce constitutional courts. Yugoslavia was the first in 1963. Poland and the Soviet Union followed suit in 1982 and 1988, respectively.
27 *See* Allan H. Meltzer & Scott F. Richard, *A Rational Theory of the Size of Government*, 89 J. POL. ECON. 914 (1981).
28 Stone-Sweet, *supra* note 6, at 40.
29 *See* Hans Kelsen, *La Garantie Juridictionnelle de la Constitution*, 45 Revue du Droit Public et de la Science Politique en France et à l'Etranger 197 (1928); Hans Kelsen, *Judicial Review of Legislation: A Comparative Study of the Austrian and the American Constitution*, 4 J. POL. 183 (1942).
30 *See* Gagik Harutyunyan & Arne Mavčič, CONSTITUTIONAL REVIEW AND ITS DEVELOPMENT IN THE MODERN WORLD: A COMPARATIVE CONSTITUTIONAL ANALYSIS (1999). Most, but not all, constitutional systems can be grouped into one of the three models presented. Additionally, Harutyunyan & Mavčič name a "new (British) commonwealth model" implemented by Mauritius, and a "mixed (American continental) model" which can be found in a number of states, inter alia in Portugal, Columbia, Ecuador, Guatemala, and Peru.
31 Stone-Sweet, *supra* note 6, at 33 claims that a French law of August 16, 1790 would remain in force today—and has never been violated: "Courts cannot interfere with the exercising of legislative powers or suspend the application of the laws."
32 Interestingly, there are three states in our sample that allocate the power to interpret the constitution not to the judiciary but to the legislature. These are China, Cuba, and Ecuador.
33 It might appear awkward to consider option (6) in exactly the same way as the other ones because it requires the consent of two—and not just one—actor. One possibility is to correct for this by only giving it half the weight of all other options. Additionally, one might also correct for the number of chambers in existence. It would seem unfair to attribute a lower coding regarding JR to a country simply because it has only one chamber and not two.

34 Other actors who are regularly accorded standing include the general prosecutor, representatives of lower government levels, certain councils and independent agencies, the president of the national assembly, and many more.
35 In concreto, there are a great many institutional solutions. In some countries, the respective legislation is returned to the executive (and not the legislature). At times, only specific passages of a law and not the law in its entirety are declared unconstitutional.
36 To prevent positive values of our indicator, although aspect (1) has been coded 0, the sum of variables (2) to (4) is multiplied with variable (1) and divided by three.
37 *E.g.*, Martin Shapiro & Alec Stone-Sweet, *The New Constitutional Politics of Europe*, 26 COMP. POL. STUD. 397 (1994) explain that "no one expected [the European constitutional courts established after 1945] to develop into powerful institutional actors or policymakers. ... Constitutional review, however, developed in unexpected ways."
38 *See* Robert E. Hall & Charles I. Jones, *Why Do Some Countries Produce So Much More Output Per Worker than Others?* 114 Q. J. ECON. 83 (1999).
39 *See* Rafael La Porta *et al.*, *Law and Finance*, 106 J. POL. ECON. 1113 (1998); Rafael La Porta *et al.*, *The Quality of Government*, 15 J.L. ECON. ORG. 222 (1999).
40 *See* William Easterly & Ross Levine, *Africa's Growth Tragedy: Policies and Ethnic Divisions*, 112 Q. J. ECON. 1203 (1997).
41 *See* Alberto Alesina *et al.*, *Fractionalization*, 8 J. ECON. GROWTH 155 (2003). Of late, there has been a discussion whether "fractionalization" or "polarization" is the more adequate variable: fractionalization reaches its maximum if each member of society makes up his or her own group, whereas polarization reaches its maximum if there are two groups of identical size. Those who argue in favor of using polarization (*e.g.*, Joan-María Esteban & Debraj Ray, *On the Measurement of Polarization*, 62 ECONOMETRICA 819 (1994); José G. Montalvo & Marta Reynal-Querol, *Ethnic Polarization, Potential Conflict, and Civil Wars*, 95 AM. ECON. REV. 796 (2005)) argue that chances of impasse and instability are higher under the latter condition and point to estimates showing that the likelihood of civil war can be better predicted with the polarization measure. Alesina *et al.*, *supra* point out that the two measures are highly correlated and that in explaining both growth and the quality of institutions, the fractionalization measure works slightly better than the polarization index. Our results do, however, not support that statement.
42 However, based on religious polarization, the correlation is 0.32, which is significant at the 5 percent level.
43 Based on the polarization data by Montalvo & Reynal-Querol, *supra* note 41 the correlation coefficients are 0.10 and 0.18, respectively, and both are insignificant at any reasonable level of significance.
44 *See* Robert D. Putnam, MAKING DEMOCRACY WORK: CIVIC TRADITIONS IN MODERN ITALY (1993).
45 *See* Rafael La Porta *et al.*, *Trust in Large Organizations*, 87 AM. ECON. REV. 333 (1997).
46 *See* Matt Golder, *Democratic Electoral Systems around the World, 1946–2000*, 24 ELECT. STUD. 103 (2005).
47 *E.g.*, Torsten Persson & Guido E. Tabellini, THE ECONOMIC EFFECTS OF CONSTITUTIONS (2003). For a critique of that view, *see* Hayo & Voigt, *supra* note 15.
48 *See* Arthur S. Banks, *Cross-National Time-Series Data Archive*, *available at* www.databanksinternational.com.
49 *See* Elkins *et al.*, *supra* note 4.
50 *See*, for an analysis of the determinants of constitutional length, Stefan Voigt, *Explaining Constitutional Garrulity*, 29 INT. REV. L. ECON. 290 (2009).
51 *See* La Porta *et al.*, *supra* note 9.
52 *See* Philip Keefer & Stephen Knack, *Polarization, Politics and Property Rights: Links between Inequality and Growth*, 111 PUB. CHOICE 127 (2002).

53 *See* Tatu Vanhanen, Democratization: A Comparative Analysis of 170 Countries (2003).
54 The correlation coefficient is based on 33 observations.
55 The correlation coefficient is based on 32 observations.
56 The correlation coefficient is based on 32 observations.
57 The correlation coefficient is based on 32 observations.

References

Acemoglu, Daron *et al.*, 2011. *Why Do Voters Dismantle Checks and Balances?* (17293 NBER Working Paper Series). Available at www.nber.org/papers/w17293.

Acemoglu, Daron, James A. Robinson, and Ragnar Torvik. 2011. Why Do Voters Dismantle Checks and Balances? Forthcoming, Review of Economic Studies. Available at http://www.restud.com/paper/why-do-voters-dismantle-checks-and-balances/.

Alesina, Alberto, Arnaud Devleeschauwer, William Easterly, Sergio Kurlat, and Romain Wacziarg. 2003. Fractionalization. *Journal of Economic Growth* 8(2): 155–194.

Banks, Arthur S. 2004. Banks' Cross-National Time-Series Data Archive, distributed by Databanks International. Jerusalem: Israel. Available at www.databanksinternational.com.

Corwin, Edward S. 1910. The Establishment of Judicial Review. I. *Michigan Law Review* 9:102–125.

Deener, David. 1952. Judicial Review in Modern Constitutional Systems. *American Political Science Review* 46: 1079–1099.

Duverger, Maurice. 1954. *Political Parties: Their Organization and Activity in the Modern State*. London: Methuen.

Easterly, William, and Ross Levine. 1997. Africa's Growth Tragedy: Policies and Ethnic Divisions. *Quarterly Journal of Economics* 112: 1203–1250.

Eisgruber, Christopher L. 2001. *Constitutional Self-Government*. Cambridge, MA: Harvard University Press.

Elazar, Daniel J. 1995. From Statism to Federalism: A Paradigm Shift. *Publius: The Journal of Federalism* 25(2): 5–18.

Elkins, Zachary, Tom Ginsburg, and James Melton. 2009. The Comparative Constitutions Project. Available at www.comparativeconstitutionsproject.org.

Esteban, Joan-María, and Debraj Ray. 1994. On the Measurement of Polarization. *Econometrica* 62: 819–851.

Fleck, Robert K., and F. Andrew Hanssen. 2011. *Judicial Review as a Constraint on Tyranny of the Majority*. Hamburg Lectures on Law & Economics. Available at www.ile-hamburg.de/_data/Hamburg_Lectures_Hanssen_Paper_Paper.pdf.

——2013. Judicial Review as a Constraint on Tyranny of the Majority. *Journal of Law, Economics and Organization* 29(2): 303–331.

Fox, Justin, and Matthew C. Stephenson. 2011. Judicial Review as a Response to Political Posturing. *American Political Science Review* 105: 397–414.

Ginsburg, Tom. 2002. Economic Analysis and the Design of Constitutional Courts. *Theoretical Inquiries in Law* 3: 49–85.

——2008. The Global Spread of Constitutional Review. In *Oxford Handbook of Law and Politics*, pp. 81–108, edited by Keith E. Whittington, R. Daniel Kelemen, and Gregory A. Caldeira. Oxford: Oxford University Press.

Ginsburg, Tom, and Tamir Moustafa eds. 2008. *Rule by Law: The Politics of Courts in Authoritarian Regimes*. Cambridge: Cambridge University Press.

Golder, Matt. 2005. Democratic Electoral Systems around the World, 1946–2000. *Electoral Studies* 24: 103–121.
Hall, Robert E., and Charles I. Jones. 1999. Why Do Some Countries Produce So Much More Output Per Worker than Others? *Quarterly Journal of Economics* 114(1): 83–116.
Harutyunyan, Gagik, and Arne Mavčič. 1999. *Constitutional Review and Its Development in the Modern World (A Comparative Constitutional Analysis)*. Yerevan & Ljubljana: Hayagitak.
Hayek, Friedrich A. 1960. *The Constitution of Liberty*. Chicago, IL: University of Chicago Press.
Hayo, Bernd, and Stefan Voigt. 2010. Determinants of Constitutional Change: Why Do Countries Change Their Form of Government? *Journal of Comparative Economics* 38: 283–305.
Herron, Erik S., and Kirk A. Randazzo. 2003. The Relationship between Independence and Judicial Review in Post-Communist Courts. *The Journal of Politics* 65: 422–438.
Keefer, Philip, and Stephen Knack. 2002. Polarization, Politics and Property Rights: Links between Inequality and Growth. *Public Choice* 111: 127–154.
Kelsen, Hans. 1928. La Garantie Juridictionnelle de la Constitution. *Revue du Droit Public et de la Science Politique en France et à l'Etranger* 45: 197–257.
——1942. Judicial Review of Legislation: A Comparative Study of the Austrian and the American Constitution. *The Journal of Politics* 4: 183–200.
La Porta, Rafael, Florencio Lopez-de-Silanes, Andrei Shleifer, and Robert W. Vishny. 1997. Trust in Large Organizations. *American Economic Review* 87: 333–338.
——1998. Law and Finance. *Journal of Political Economy* 106: 1113–1155.
——1999. The Quality of Government. *The Journal of Law, Economics, and Organization* 15(1): 222–279.
La Porta, Rafael, Florencio Lopez-de-Silanes, Christian Pop-Eleches, and Andrei Shleifer. 2004. Judicial Checks and Balances. *Journal of Political Economy* 112: 445–470.
Majone, Giandomenico. 1996. Temporal Consistency and Policy Credibility: Why Democracies Need Non-Majoritarian Institutions, European University Institute Working Paper RSC No. 96/57. Available at hdl.handle.net/1814/1472.
Meltzer, Allan H., and Scott F. Richard. 1981. A Rational Theory of the Size of Government. *Journal of Political Economy* 89: 914–927.
Montalvo, José G., and Marta Reynal-Querol. 2005. Ethnic Polarization, Potential Conflict, and Civil Wars. *American Economic Review* 95(3): 796–816.
Persson, Torsten, and Guido Tabellini. 2003. *The Economic Effects of Constitutions*. Cambridge, MA: MIT Press.
Putnam, Robert D. 1993. *Making Democracy Work: Civic Traditions in Modern Italy*. Princeton, NJ: Princeton University Press.
Schwartz, Herman. 1999. A Brief History of Judicial Review. In *The Self-Restraining State – Power and Accountability in New Democracies*, pp. 145–150, edited by Andreas Schedler, Larry J. Diamond, and Marc F. Plattner. London: Lynne Rienner Publishers.
Shapiro, Martin. 1999. The Success of Judicial Review. In *Constitutional Dialogues in Comparative Perspective*, pp. 193–219, edited by Sally J. Kenney, William M. Reisinger and John C. Reitz. London: Macmillan.
Shapiro, Martin, and Alec Stone-Sweet. 1994. The New Constitutional Politics of Europe. *Comparative Political Studies* 26: 397–420.
Stone-Sweet, Alec. 2000. *Governing with Judges: Constitutional Politics in Europe*. Oxford: Oxford University Press.

Tate, C. Neal. 1995. Why the Expansion of Judicial Power? In *The Global Expansion of Judicial Power*, pp. 27–37, edited by C. Neal Tate and Torbjörn Vallinder. New York, NY: New York University Press.

Tate, C. Neal, and Torbjörn Vallinder. 1995. The Global Expansion of Judicial Power: The Judicialization of Politics. In *The Global Expansion of Judicial Power*, pp. 1–10, edited by C. Neal Tate and Torbjörn Vallinder. New York, NY: New York University Press.

Teorell, Jan, and Axel Hadenius. 2007. Determinants of Democratization: Taking Stock of the Large-N Evidence. In *Democratization: The State of the Art*, 2d ed., pp. 69–95, edited by Dirk Berg-Schlosser. Leverkusen: Barbara Budrich.

Tridimas, George. 2010. Constitutional Judicial Review and Political Insurance. *European Journal of Law and Economics* 29: 81–101.

Utter, Robert F., and David C. Lundsgaard. 1994. Comparative Aspects of Judicial Review: Issues Facing the New European States. *Judicature* 77: 240–247.

Vanhanen, Tatu. 2003. *Democratization: A Comparative Analysis of 170 Countries*. London: Routledge.

Voigt, Stefan. 1999. *Explaining Constitutional Change: A Positive Economics Approach*. Cheltenham: Edward Elgar.

——2009. Explaining Constitutional Garrulity. *International Review of Law and Economics* 29(4): 290–303.

Index